# SAINT BASIL

## EXEGETIC HOMILIES

*Translated by*
SISTER AGNES CLARE WAY, C.D.P.

*Our Lady of the Lake College*
*San Antonio, Texas*

Originally published in 1963
by the Catholic University of America Press
in the series *The Fathers of the Church*, no. 46.

*Nihil Obstat*: Rev. Harry A Echle, Censor Librorum

*Imprimatur*: +Patrick A. O'Boyle, Archbishop of Washington

Jan. 7, 1963

*Visit us*

COPYRIGHT © 2015 EX FONTIBUS CO.
DATE OF THIS PUBLICATION: 2015-02-20
ALL RIGHTS RESERVED.
NO PART OF THIS PUBLICATION MAY BE REPRODUCED, STORED IN A RE-TRIEVAL SYSTEM, OR TRANSMITTED, IN ANY FORM OR BY ANY MEANS, ELECTRONIC, MECHANICAL, PHOTOCOPYING, RECORDING OR OTHER-WISE, WITHOUT PRIOR PERMISSION OF EX FONTIBUS CO.

CONTACT@EXFONTIBUS.COM
EXFONTIBUSCOMPANY@GMAIL.COM
HTTP://WWW.EXFONTIBUS.COM
HTTP://WWW.FACEBOOK.COM/EXFONT

## CONTENTS

INTRODUCTION ............................. vii
HOMILIES
    1  On the Hexaemeron........................ 3
    2  On the Hexaemeron........................ 21
    3  On the Hexaemeron........................ 37
    4  On the Hexaemeron........................ 55
    5  On the Hexaemeron........................ 67
    6  On the Hexaemeron........................ 83
    7  On the Hexaemeron........................ 105
    8  On the Hexaemeron........................ 117
    9  On the Hexaemeron........................ 135
  10  On Psalm 1............................... 151
  11  On Psalm 7............................... 165
  12  On Psalm 14.............................. 181
  13  On Psalm 28.............................. 193
  14  On Psalm 29.............................. 213
  15  On Psalm 32.............................. 227
  16  On Psalm 33.............................. 247
  17  On Psalm 44.............................. 275
  18  On Psalm 45.............................. 297
  19  On Psalm 48.............................. 311
  20  On Psalm 59.............................. 333
  21  On Psalm 61.............................. 341
  22  On Psalm 114............................. 351
INDICES ..................................... 361

# INTRODUCTION

THE EXEGETIC WRITINGS usually attributed to St. Basil include the nine homilies on the *Hexaemeron*, seventeen on the *Psalms*, and the *Commentary on Isaia* in sixteen chapters. These are all found in the 'Opera Sancti Basilii' of the *Patrologia Graeca*, Vols. 29-32. Four of the homilies on the psalms, the first, *On Psalm 14*, a second one *On Psalm 28*, one *On Psalm 37*, and that *On Psalm 115*, as well as the *Commentary on Isaia*, are placed by the Benedictine editors in the Appendix of Volume 1 of St. Basil's works, *Patrologia Graeca*, Vol. 30, as doubtful or clearly spurious works of St. Basil. Two other exegetic homilies, *On the Form of Man*, are included by the Benedictine editors among St. Basil's doubtful works and are also found in the works of St. Gregory of Nyssa,[1] who says that at the request of his brother, Peter, he had finished the *Hexaemeron* of St. Basil. Since these two homilies are contained also in St. Gregory's works and since we do not find the works which St. Basil had promised at the end of homily nine on the *Hexaemeron* on 'Man as the Image of God,' it is quite possible that St. Gregory added these two homilies to his brother's commentary in place of the two which St. Basil had promised. They are usually attributed to St. Gregory. In my translation I am including only those exegetic homilies generally acknowledged to be genuine.

The high esteem with which the ancients regarded the homilies of St. Basil, especially those on the *Hexaemeron*, is well known. St. Gregory of Nazianzus says: 'When I take his *Hexaemeron* in my hand and read it aloud, I am with my

---

1 Cf. Migne, PG 44 cols. 61 and 124.

Creator, I understand the reasons for creation, and I admire my Creator more than I formerly did when I used sight alone as my teacher. . . . When I read his other explanations of Scripture, which he unfolds for those who understand but little, writing in a threefold manner on the solid tablets of my heart, I am prevailed upon not to stop at the letter, nor to view only the higher things, but to pass beyond and to advance from depth to depth, calling upon abyss through abyss, finding light through light, until I reach the loftiest heights.'[2] St. Gregory of Nyssa, an ardent admirer of his brother, St. Basil, says: 'All who have read that divinely inspired exposition of our Father on the same subject [the creation of the world as handed down by Moses] admire it no less than the writings of Moses, and, in my opinion, they do well and reasonably.'[3]

The high esteem in which St. Ambrose held this work is evident from the fact that he not only imitated and borrowed from the *Hexaemeron* of St. Basil, but even inserted passages directly translated from the Greek of St. Basil in his own treatise on the *Hexaemeron*. Not so well known is the fact that he did the same in his expositions of several psalms.[4] St. Jerome and Socrates also praise in their writings the *Hexaemeron* of St. Basil.[5] Eustathius Afer translated the *Hexaemeron* of St. Basil into Latin about the year 440.[6] This translation is preserved among the works of St. Basil in the *Patrologia Graeca*, vol. 30. Rufinus of Aquileia, a few years after St. Basil's death, translated seven of his homilies, among which are the homilies *On Psalm 1* and *On Psalm 49*, one letter,[7] and extracts from the two monastic *Rules*.[8] According

---

2 Gregory Nazianzen, *Homily 43*, p.l.
3 Cf. Migne, PG 44 col. 61.
4 Cf. *Ibid.* 29 cols. 209-210.
5 Cf. *Ibid.* cols. 1-2.
6 Cf. Bardenhewer, *Patrology* 285.
7 Cf. Migne, PG 31 cols. 1723-1794.
8 Cf. Bardenhewer, *ibidem*.

to his testimony, St. Basil spoke these homilies extemporaneously, as was his custom to speak.⁹ This declaration of Rufinus seems to be confirmed by St. Basil's own statement in the homily *On Psalm 114*. St. Basil says: 'That we may not distress you by detaining you longer, after lecturing briefly on the psalm which we found you singing on our arrival and providing your souls, as far as we are able, with the word of consolation, we shall dismiss all of you for the care of your bodies.' Again, in homily eight on the *Hexaemeron*, St. Basil suddenly interrupts his thought to say: 'Perhaps, many wonder why, when my sermon was hurrying along without a break, I was silent for a long time. It is not, however, the more studious of my audience who are ignorant of the cause of my speechlessness. Why should they be, who by their glances and nods to each other had turned my attention toward them and had led me on to the thought of things omitted? For, I had forgotten an entire class of creatures, and this by no means the least; moreover, my discourse was nearly finished, leaving that class almost entirely uninvestigated.'

The time at which these homilies on the *Hexaemeron* were delivered is not definitely known. Maran[10] believes that the nine homilies on the *Hexaemeron* were delivered before the episcopate. Fialon[11] thinks that they date from the very time of his episcopate. Both agree that the homilies on the psalms should be assigned to the time of his priesthood. Fialon bases the reason for his decision on St. Gregory of Nazianzus' statement of St. Basil's threefold method of presenting his explanations. He sees in the homilies on the psalms a moral and allegorical presentation with some sacrifice of the literal meaning, while in the homilies on the *Hexaemeron*, he notes that St. Basil, without neglecting the moral and allegorical meaning, gives an exact literal explanation. Origen, who had sacri-

---

9 Cf. Rufinus of Aquileia, *Liber* 2 c.9.
10 Cf. Pr. Maran, *Vita S. Basilii* in Migne, PG 29. clxii.
11 Cf. E. Fialon, *Étude historique et littéraire sur S. Basile* 292.

ficed the literal meaning entirely for the mystic, and Eusebius, who had accepted the literal meaning equally with the historic, were St. Basil's masters and models. St. Basil, following them in his earlier years, used the allegorical method of interpretation, but found under it a strong moral meaning and, at the same time, did not sacrifice completely the literal sense. In the homilies on the *Hexaemeron,* St. Basil became more independent, and held scrupulously to an exact literal interpretation, while still showing the allegorical meaning in which, however, with the maturity of age and of talent he tended to avoid the earlier exaggerations.[12]

St. Basil's audience was composed not only of the elite of Caesarea, but also of the artisans, the workers 'who with difficulty provide a livelihood for themselves from their daily toil.'[13] In homily eight on the *Hexaemeron,* he mentions among those present the silk spinners. It was to such as these that he explained the theories of science as it was understood in his day and that he spoke the language of the schools; and these men and women of the people, for whose sake he abridged his lecture 'lest they be drawn away too long from their work,'[14] understood and applauded his words.

St. Basil had received the best education of the time in Caesarea, Constantinople, and Athens, and his works reflect the knowledge of the period in the various branches of learning. In one respect, namely, in geography, he may not have given the true picture of his time. The geography of Europe, perhaps because he did not feel that Europe merited much attention in comparison with Asia Minor, was presented almost entirely from Aristotle's point of view, although certainly in that period more exact knowledge of the countries, rivers, and mountains was available.

St. Basil describes most vividly and with the greatest exact-

---

12 Cf. *Ibid.* 287-294.
13 *Homily 3,* cf. *infra* p. 37.
14 *Ibid.*

ness of detail all the different aspects of nature. Nothing is too immense, nothing too insignificant to merit his attention. Yet, he is not a mere lover of nature. He is the Christian teacher who uses every creature of God to raise the minds and hearts of his hearers to an understanding and love of the God who created them. He knew thoroughly the works of the learned men of Greece and he used the discoveries of their great minds to impress the truths of the power of God on his hearers. For his exposition of the universe and its plant and animal life, he drew upon the teachings of Plato, Plotinus, Aratus, Theophrastus, Herodotus, Aristotle, and others. In his accounts of animals, insects, birds, and fish, drawn especially from Herodotus and Aristotle, he made fables, in which he described the habits, tendencies, and dispositions of the various creatures, then he drew a moral lesson which he applied to his hearers. It was in this way that he attacked the vices of the people or showed the beauty of virtue.

No class of persons and almost no vice was left without its fable, and the people listened and understood, for he was speaking of things with which they were familiar in their daily life. 'The majority of fish,' he says, 'eat one another, and the smaller among them are food for the larger. If it ever happens that the victor over a smaller becomes the prey of another, they are both carried into the one stomach of the last. Now, what else do we men do in the oppression of our inferiors? How does he differ from that last fish, who with a greedy love of riches swallows up the weak in the folds of his insatiable avarice? That man held the possessions of the poor man; you, seizing him, made him a part of your abundance. You have clearly shown yourself more unjust than the unjust man and more grasping than the greedy man. Beware, lest the same end as that of the fish awaits you—somewhere a fishhook, or a snare, or a net. Surely, if we have committed many unjust deeds, we shall not escape the final retribution.'[15]

---
15 *Homily 7*, cf. *infra* p. 109.

Again he says: 'If at some time a camel has been struck, he saves up his wrath for a long time, but, when he finds a suitable opportunity, he repays the evil. Hear, you sullen men who pursue vengeance as though it were a virtue, who it is that you resemble when you harbor for so long a time your resentment against your neighbor like a spark hidden in ashes, until, finding material, you kindle your wrath like a flame.'[16] In his comments on the actions of the bees, St. Basil says: 'Some of the irrational creatures are like members of a state, if, indeed, it is characteristic of citizenship that the activities of the individuals tend to one common end. This may be seen in the case of bees. Their dwelling is common, their flight is shared by all, and the activity of all is the same; but, the most significant point is that they engage in their work subject to a king and to a sort of commander, not taking it upon themselves to go to the meadows until they see that the king is leading the flight. In their case the king is not elected; in fact, the lack of judgment on the part of the people has frequently placed the worst man in office. Their king does not hold a power acquired by lot; the chances of lot, which frequently confer the power on the basest of all, are absurd. Nor is he placed on the throne through hereditary succession; for the most part, even such men through softness and flattery become rude and ignorant of all virtue. But, he holds the first place among all by nature, differing in size and appearance and in the gentleness of his disposition. The king has a sting, but he does not use it for vengeance. There is this positive unwritten law of nature, that they who are placed in the highest positions of power should be lenient in punishing. Those bees, however, which do not follow the example of the king, quickly repent of the indiscretion, because they die after giving a prick with their sting. Let the Christians heed, who have received the command to "render to no man evil for

---

16 *Homily 8,* cf. *infra* p. 119.

evil," but to "overcome evil with good." '[17] Again, he says: 'They say that the turtledove, when once separated from her mate, no longer accepts union with another, but, in memory of her former spouse remains widowed, refusing marriage with another. Let the women hear how the chastity of widowhood, even among irrational creatures, is preferred to the unseemly multiplicity of marriages.'[18]

The infinite wisdom and goodness of God are impressed upon the people with remarkable clarity in his descriptions and observations on the various animals. He urges them to observe carefully and to see that in the almost infinite variety of plants and animals God has made nothing superfluous and yet has omitted nothing that is necessary. 'Carnivorous animals,' he says, 'He has fitted with sharp teeth; there was need of such for the nature of their food. Those which are only half equipped with teeth, He provided with many varied receptacles for the food. Because the food is not ground sufficiently the first time, He has given them the power to chew again what has already been swallowed. . . . The camel's neck is long in order that it may be brought down to the level of his feet and he may reach the grass on which he lives. The bear's neck and also that of the lion, tiger, and the other animals of this family, is short and is buried in the shoulders, because their food does not come from the grass and they do not have to bend down to the ground. They are carnivorous and secure their food by preying upon animals. . . . Not only among the large animals is it possible to see His inscrutable wisdom, but even among the smallest it is possible to find no less marvels. . . . I do not admire the huge elephant more than the mouse, which is formidable to the elephant, or than the very fine sting of the scorpion, which the Craftsman hollowed out like a tube so that through it the poison is injected into those stung.'[19]

---
17 *Ibid.*, cf. *infra* p. 123f.
18 *Ibid.*, cf. *infra* p. 127.
19 *Homily 9*, cf. *infra* p. 144-146.

From nature, too, St. Basil draws examples to show the mighty power of God. He quotes the words of Jeremia, 'Will you not then fear me, saith the Lord? I have set the sand a bound for the sea.' Then he adds: 'With the weakest of all things, sand, the sea irresistible in its violence is bridled. And yet, what would have hindered the Red Sea from invading the whole of Egypt, which was lower than it, and joining with the other sea adjacent to Egypt, had it not been fettered by the command of the Creator?'[20] Elsewhere he says: ' "Let the earth bring forth." This brief command became immediately mighty nature and an elaborate system which brought to perfection more swiftly than our thought the countless properties of plants. That command, which even yet is inherent in the earth, impels it in the course of each year to exert all the power it has for the generation of herbs, seeds, and trees. For, just as tops, from the first impulse given to them, produce successive whirls when they are spun, so also the order of nature, having received its beginning from that first command, continues to all time thereafter, until it shall reach the common consummation of all things.'[21]

Not only in these commentaries did St. Basil manifest his intense devotion to the Holy Scriptures but throughout his writings, in all of which he supported his statements by quotations from the Bible. That he attempted to awaken in his people a similar reverence for it may be seen from his declaration in homily six on the *Hexaemeron*, 'I have mentioned these things as a demonstration of the great size of the luminaries and as a proof that none of the divinely inspired words, even as much as a syllable, is an idle word.'

The present translation was based on the Garnier and Maran edition of the *Opera Omnia Basilii*, Paris, 1839. There is an earlier English translation of the *Hexaemeron*, that of B. Jackson in Volume 8 of the *Nicene and Post-Nicene Fathers*,

---

20 *Homily 4*, cf. *infra* p. 58.
21 *Homily 5*, cf. *infra* p. 82.

1895, but no previous translation of the homilies on the psalms. The Scriptural quotations are taken from the Confraternity of Christian Doctrine editions of the Book of Genesis and the New Testament, and from the Douay-Rheims edition of the Old Testament. In numerous places the wording of the English text had to be changed somewhat to a more literal translation of the Greek so as to agree with St. Basil's interpretations. Often, too, his quotations, being directly from the Septuagint, varied slightly from the Vulgate and English translations.

I wish to take this opportunity to express my indebtedness for many valuable suggestions to Mother Mary Angelique, through whom this work was made possible for me and who graciously read the manuscript, and to Sister James Aloysius of the Department of French and Sister Mary Clare of the Department of Biology, who also read the manuscript.

### SELECT BIBLIOGRAPHY

*Texts and Translations:*

Garnier, and Maran, *Basilii Caesareae Gappadociae Archiepiscopi Opera Omnia* (Paris 1839).

B Jackson, *The Nine Homilies of the Hexaemeron of St Basil the Great* (in *Select Library of Nicene and Post-Nicene Fathers* 8, New York 1895).

J. P. Migne, *S P.N. Basilii Opera Omnia* (*Patrologia Graeca* 29, Paris 1886).

*Secondary Sources:*

Aratus, *Phaenomena* translated by G. G. Mair (in *Loeb Classical Library*, New York 1921).

Aristotle, *Works* (in *Great Books of the Western World*, Vols. 8 and 9, Chicago, 1955).

Otto Bardenhewer, *Geschichte der altkirchlen Literatur.* Freiburg im Breisgau, 1913-1932 (5 vols., vol. 1 and 2 in 2nd edit, reprint of vol. 3 with additions).

_____, *Patrology* translated by Thomas Shahan, (St. Louis 1908).

Herodotus, *History* translated by A. D. Godley (in *Loeb Classical Library*, New York 1928).

Hesiod, *Works and Days* translated by Hugh G. Evelyn-White (in *Loeb Classical Library*, New York 1920).

Hippocrates, *Hippocratic Writings* translated by Francis Adams (in *Great Books of the Western World*, vol. 6, Chicago 1955).

Livy, *History* translated by B. O. Foster (in *Loeb Classical Library*, New York 1924).

Lucian, *Timon* translated by A. M. Harmon (in *Loeb Classical Library*, New York 1915).

Plato, *Dialogues of Plato* (in *Great Books of the Western World*, vol. 7, Chicago 1955).

———, *Timaeus* translated by R. G. Bury (*in Loeb Classical Library*, New York 1929).

Pliny, *Natural History*, Bk. 10, translated by H. Rackham (in *Loeb Classical Library*, New York, 1940).

Plotinus, *The Six Enneads* translated by Stephen McKenna and B. S. Page (in *Great Books of the Western World*, vol. 17, Chicago 1955).

William Smith, *Dictionary of Greek and Roman Geography*, (London 1870).

Strabo, *Geography of Strabo* translated by H. L. Jones (in *Loeb Classical Library*, New York 1917).

Theophrastus, *Enquiry into Plants* translated by A. Hort (in *Loeb Classical Library*, New York 1916).

Vergil, *Poems* translated by James Rhoades (in *Great Books of the Western World*, vol. 13, Chicago 1955).

Xenophon, *Symposium* translated by O. J. Todd (in *Loeb Classical Library*, New York 1922).

# SAINT BASIL
## EXEGETIC HOMILIES

# HOMILY 1

*Creation of the Heavens and the Earth*

(ON THE HEXAEMERON)

IN THE BEGINNING God created the heavens and the earth.[1]

An appropriate beginning for one who intends to speak about the formation of the world is to place first in the narration the source of the orderly arrangement of visible things. For, the creation of the heavens and earth must be handed down, not as having happened spontaneously, as some have imagined, but as having its origin from God. What ear is worthy of the sublimity of this narrative? How well prepared should that soul be for the hearing of such stupendous wonders? Cleansed from the passions of the flesh, undarkened by the cares of life, devoted to labor, given to investigation, watchful on all sides to see if from some place or other it may receive a worthy concept of God.

Before weighing the accuracy of these expressions, however, and examining how much meaning there is in these few words, let us consider who is speaking to us. For, even if we do not attain to the profound thoughts of the writer because of the weakness of our intellect, nevertheless, having regard for the authority of the speaker we shall be led spontaneously to agree with his utterances. Now, Moses is the author of this narrative, that Moses who while still a child at the breast was

---

1 Gen. 1.1.

acknowledged to be 'acceptable to God'; he, whom the daughter of Pharaoh adopted and royally reared,[2] appointing as masters for his instruction the wise men of Egypt. He, who, hating the pomp of royalty, returned to the lowly state of his own race and preferred to suffer affliction with the people of God rather than to have the ephemeral enjoyment of sin. He, who, possessing naturally a love for justice, on one occasion, even before the government of the people was entrusted to him, was seen inflicting on the wicked, punishment to the extent of death because of his natural hatred of villainy.[3] He, who, banished by those to whom he had been a benefactor, gladly left the uproar of the Egyptians and went to Ethiopia[4] and, spending there all his time apart from others, devoted himself for forty entire years to the contemplation of creation. He, who, having already reached the age of eighty years, saw God as far as it is possible for man to see Him, or rather, as it has not been granted to anyone else according to the very testimony of God: 'If there be among you a prophet of the Lord, I will appear to him in a vision, or I will speak to him in a dream. But it is not so with my servant Moses, who is the most faithful in all my house: For I speak to him mouth to mouth: and plainly, and not by riddles.'[5] So then, this man, who is made equal to the angels, being considered worthy of the sight of God face to face, reports to us those things which he heard from God. Let us hear, therefore, the words of truth expressed not in the persuasive language of human wisdom,[6]

---

2 Cf. Acts 7.20-22: 'At this time Moses was born, and he was acceptable to God; he was nourished three months in his father's house, and when he was exposed, Pharaoh's daughter adopted him and brought him up as her own son. And Moses was instructed in all the wisdom of the Egyptians.'
3 Cf. Ex. 2.12: 'And when he had looked about this way and that way, and saw no one there, he slew the Egyptian.'
4 Cf. Ex. 2.15: 'But he fled from his sight, and abode in the land of Madian.'
5 Num. 12.6-8.
6 Cf. 1 Cor. 2.4: 'And my speech and my preaching were not in the persuasive words of wisdom, but in the demonstration of the Spirit.'

but in the teachings of the Spirit, whose end is not praise from those hearing, but the salvation of those taught.

(2) 'In the beginning God created the heavens and the earth.'[7] Astonishment at the thought checks my utterance. What shall I say first? Whence shall I begin my narration? Shall I refute the vanity of the heathens? Or shall I proclaim our truth? The wise men of the Greeks wrote many works about nature, but not one account among them remained unaltered and firmly established, for the later account always overthrew the preceding one. As a consequence, there is no need for us to refute their words; they avail mutually for their own undoing. Those, in fact, who could not recognize God, did not concede that a rational cause was the author of the creation of the universe, but they drew their successive conclusions in a manner in keeping with their initial ignorance. For this reason some had recourse to material origins,[8] referring the beginning of the universe to the elements of the world; and others imagined that the nature of visible things consisted of atoms[9] and indivisible particles, of molecules and interstices; indeed, that, as the indivisible particles now united with each other and now separated, there were produced generations and deteriorations; and that the stronger union of the atoms of the more durable bodies was the cause of their permanence. Truly, it is a spider's web that these writers weave, who suggest such weak and unsubstantial beginnings of the heavens and earth and sea. It is because they did not know how to say: 'In the beginning God created the heavens and the earth.' They were deceived by the godlessness present within them into thinking that the universe was without guide

---

7 Gen. 1.1.
8 Cf. Aristotle, *Metaphysics* 1.3.983b: 'Of the first philosophers, then, most thought the principles which were of the nature of matter were the only principles of all things.'
9 The founders of the Atomist philosophy are Leucippus and Democritus who lived in the 5th century B.C. Their views are presented by Aristotle, *On the Soul* 1.2.403b, and by Cicero, *On the Nature of the Gods* 1.24-26. (The translation of *On the Nature of the Gods* is always that of C. D. Yonge.)

and without rule, as if borne around by chance. In order that we might not suffer this error, he who described the creation of the world immediately, in the very first words, enlightened our mind with the name of God, saying: 'In the beginning God created.' How beautiful an arrangement! He placed first 'the beginning,' that no one might believe that it was without a beginning. Then he added the word, 'created,' that it might be shown that what was made required a very small part of the power of the Creator. In fact, as the potter, although he has formed innumerable vessels by the same art, has exhausted neither his art nor his power, so also the Creator of the universe, possessing creative power not commensurate with one world, but infinitely greater, by the weight of His will alone brought the mighty creations of the visible world into existence. If, then, the world has a beginning and was created, inquire: 'Who is He that gave it the beginning, and who is the Creator?' Rather, lest in seeking through human reasoning you might perhaps turn aside from the truth, Moses has taught us beforehand, imprinting upon our hearts as a seal and a security, the highly honored name of God, saying: 'In the beginning God created.' The blessed Nature, the bounteous Goodness, the Beloved of all who are endowed with reason, the much desired Beauty, the Origin of things created, the Fount of life, the spiritual Light, the inaccessible Wisdom, He is the One who 'in the beginning created the heavens and the earth.'

(3) Do not, then, imagine, O man, that the things which you see are without a beginning, and do not think, because the bodies moving in the heavens travel around in a circle and because the beginning of the circle is not easily discerned by our ordinary means of perception, that the nature of bodies moving in a circle is without a beginning. Indeed, this circle, I mean the plane figure circumscribed by one line, just because it escapes our perception and we are not able to find out whence it began or where it stops, we ought not, forthwith, to

assume is without a beginning. But, even if it does escape our observation, assuredly, He who drew it with a center and a certain radius truly began from some point. Thus, indeed, because objects, moving in a circle close in upon themselves, and the evenness of their motion is interrupted by no intervening break, do not maintain the illusion of the existence of a world without beginning and without end. 'For this world as we see it is passing away.'[10] 'Heaven and earth will pass away.'[11] That which is now given in brief in the first statement of the divinely inspired teachings is the preliminary proclamation of the doctrine concerning the end and the changing of the world.

'In the beginning God created.' It is absolutely necessary that things begun in time be also brought to an end in time. If they have a beginning in time, have no doubt about the end. Really, to what end are geometry and arithmetical investigations, the diligent study of solids and the much-discussed astronomy—all very laborious vanity—directed, if those who pursue them have believed that this visible world is co-eternal with God, the Creator of all things; if they attribute to a circumscribed world which possesses a material body the same glory as to the limitless and invisible Nature; and if they are not able to understand even this much, that the whole of anything whatsoever, whose parts are subject to corruption and change, must also at some time submit to the same changes as its parts? But, to such an extent 'they have become vain in their reasonings, and their senseless minds have been darkened, and while professing to be wise, they have become fools,'[12] that some have declared that heaven is co-existent with God from eternity;[13] others, that it is God Himself without

---
10 1 Cor. 7.31.
11 Matt. 24.35.
12 Rom. 1.21,22.
13 Cf. Aristotle, *On the Heavens* 2.1.283b: 'That the heaven as a whole neither came into being nor admits of destruction, as some assert, but is one and eternal, with no end or beginning . . . we may convince ourselves.'

beginning and without end, and that it is responsible for the arrangement of every individual thing.[14]

(4) Doubtless, their superfluous worldly wisdom will one day make their condemnation more grave because, while they are so keenly aware of vain matters, they have been blinded to the comprehension of the truth. They who measure the distances of the stars and register both those in the north, which are always shining above the horizon, and those which lie about the south pole visible to the eye of man there, but unknown to us; who also divide the northern zone and the zodiac into numberless spaces; who carefully observe the rising of the stars, their fixed positions, their descent, their recurrence, and the length of time in which each of the wandering stars completes its orbit; these men have not found one means from all this either to understand that God is the Creator of everything and the just Judge who gives the deserved reward for the actions of our life, or to acknowledge the idea of a consummation of all things consequent upon the doctrine of judgment, namely that it is necessary for the world to be changed if truly the state of the souls is to change to another form of life. As the present life has a nature akin to this world, so also the future existence of our souls will receive a lot consistent with its state. They, however, are so far from holding to these truths that they laugh broadly at us when we explain about the end of this world and the regeneration of life. Now, since the beginning naturally stands before that which proceeds from it, necessarily in talking about that which has its existence in time he placed this word before all others, saying: 'In the beginning he created.'

(5) In fact, there did exist something, as it seems, even

---

[14] Cf. Cicero, *On the Nature of the Gods* 1.14: 'Cleanthes, ... a disciple of Zeno at the same time with Aristo, in one place says that the world is God.' Cf. also Origen, *Contra Celsum* 5.581: 'The Greeks say plainly that the whole world is God: the Stoics, that it is the first god; the followers of Plato, that it is the second; but some of them, that it is the third.'

before this world, which our mind can attain by contemplation, but which has been left uninvestigated because it is not adapted to those who are beginners and as yet infants in understanding. This was a certain condition older than the birth of the world and proper to the supramundane powers, one beyond time, everlasting, without beginning or end. In it the Creator and Producer of all things perfected the works of His art, a spiritual light befitting the blessedness of those who love the Lord, rational and invisible natures, and the whole orderly arrangement of spiritual creatures which surpass our understanding and of which it is impossible even to discover the names. These fill completely the essence of the invisible world, as Paul teaches us when he says: 'For in him were created all things,' whether visible or invisible, 'whether Thrones, or Dominations, or Principalities, or Powers,'[15] or Forces, or hosts of Angels, or sovereign Archangels. When at length it was necessary for this world also to be added to what already existed, primarily as a place of training and a school for the souls of men, then was created a fit dwelling place for all things in general which are subject to birth and destruction.

Adapted by nature to the world and to the animals and plants in it, the passage of time began, always pressing on and flowing past, and nowhere checking its course. In truth, is this not the nature of time, whose past has vanished, whose future is not yet at hand, and whose present escapes perception before it is known? Such also is the nature of all that has been made, either clearly growing or decaying, but possessing no evident settled state nor stability. Therefore, it was proper for the bodies of animals and plants, bound, as it were, by force to a sort of current, and maintained in a motion which leads to birth and corruption, to be possessed of the nature of time, which has the peculiar character natural to things which change. Here he who wisely taught us about the generation of the world fittingly added to the account con-

---
[15] Col. 1.16.

cerning it, these words: 'In the beginning he created'; that is, in this beginning according to time. Not because he is testifying that according to seniority it was first of all that exists, does he say that in the beginning it was created, but he is describing the beginning of the existence of these visible and sensible creatures after that of the invisible and spiritual.

A first movement also is called the beginning, as 'The beginning of a good way is to do justice.'[16] For, by just actions we first advance toward the blessed life. Again, that is also called the beginning from which something is produced but still remains inherent in it, as the foundation in a house and the keel in a ship, according to the saying: 'The fear of the Lord is the beginning of wisdom.'[17] In fact, piety is, as it were, the groundwork and basis for perfection. Art is also the beginning of works of art; thus, the skill of Beseleel was the beginning of the adornment of the tabernacle.[18] Frequently too, the useful aim of the activity is the beginning of actions, for example, approval from God is the beginning of charity, and the end contained in the promises is the beginning of every virtuous action.

(6) Although 'beginning' is so varied in sense, see if the word in this place is not in agreement with all its meanings. In fact, it is even possible for you to learn when the formation of this world began, if only going back from the present to the past you would strive to discover the first day of the generation of the world. You will in this way find from what moment the first movement in time came; then, too, that the heavens and the earth were laid down, first, like foundation

---

16 Prov. 16.5 (Septuagint version Prov. 16.7).
17 *Ibid.* 1.7, 9.10.
18 St. Basil here follows closely the explanation of Aristotle, *Metaphysics* 5.1.1012b and 1013a: 'Beginning means (1) that part of a thing from which one would start first, . . . (2) That from which each thing would best be originated, . . . (3) That from which, as an immanent part, a thing first comes to be, e.g. as the keel of a ship and the foundation of a house, . . . (4) That . . . from which the movement or the change naturally first begins . . . (5) . . . and so are the arts, and of these especially the archetectonic arts [called beginnings].'

stones and groundwork; and next, that there was some systematic reason directing the orderly arrangement of visible things, as the word 'the beginning' shows you. Moreover, you will find that the world was not devised at random or to no purpose, but to contribute to some useful end and to the great advantage of all beings, if it is truly a training place for rational souls and a school for attaining the knowledge of God, because through visible and perceptible objects it provides guidance to the mind for the contemplation of the invisible, as the Apostle says: 'Since the creation of the world his invisible attributes are clearly seen . . . being understood through the things that are made.'[19] Or, perhaps, the words 'In the beginning he created,' were used because of the instantaneous and timeless act of creation, since the beginning is something immeasurable and indivisible. As the beginning of the road is not yet the road, and the beginning of the house, not yet the house, so also, the beginning of time is not yet time, on the contrary, not even the least part of it. And, if anyone should say contentiously that the beginning is time, let him know that he will be dividing it into parts of time. And these parts are beginning and middle and end. But, it is entirely ridiculous to think of the beginning of a beginning. Moreover, he who divides the beginning will make two instead of one, or rather, many and unlimited beginnings, since the part which is divided is always cut into other parts. In order, therefore, that we may be taught that the world came into existence instantaneously at the will of God, it is said: 'In the beginning he created.' Other interpreters of this, giving the meaning more clearly, have said: 'God made summarily,' that is, immediately and in a moment. Such, then, to mention a few from the many points, is the explanation concerning the beginning.

(7) Yet, of the arts some are said to be creative, others prac-

---

[19] Rom. 1.20.

tical, and others theoretical.[20] The aim of the theoretical skills is the action of the mind; but that of the practical, the motion itself of the body, and, if that should cease, nothing would subsist or remain for those beholding it. In fact, there is no aim in dancing and flute playing; on the contrary, the very action ends with itself. However, in the case of the creative skills, even though the action ceases, the work remains, as that of architecture, carpentry, metal work, weaving, and of as many such arts as, even if the craftsman is not present, ably manifest in themselves the artistic processes of thoughts, and make possible for you to admire the architect from his work, as well as the metal worker and the weaver. That it might be shown, then, that the world is a work of art, set before all for contemplation, so that through it the wisdom of Him who created it should be known, the wise Moses used no other word concerning it, but he said: 'In the beginning he created.' He did not say: 'He produced,' nor 'He fashioned,' but 'he created.' Inasmuch as many of those who have imagined that the world from eternity co-existed with God[21] did not concede that it was made by Him, but that, being, as it were, a shadow of His power, it existed of itself coordinately with Him, and inasmuch as they admit that God is the cause of it, but involuntarily a cause, as the body is the cause of the shadow and the flashing light the cause of the brilliance, therefore, the prophet in correcting such an error used exactness in his words, saying: 'In the beginning God created.' The thing itself did not provide the cause of its existence, but He created, as One good, something useful; as One wise, something beautiful; as One powerful, something mighty. Indeed, Moses showed you a Craftsman all but pervading the substance of

---

20 Cf. Aristotle, *Metaphysics* 6 1.1025b: 'Therefore, if all thought is either practical or productive or theoretical, physics must be a theoretical science.'
21 Cf. Plotinus *Ennead* 2.1.1: 'We hold that the ordered universe, in its material mass, has existed for ever and will for ever endure: but simply to refer this perdurance to the Will of God, however true an explanation, is utterly inadequate.'

the universe, harmonizing the individual parts with each other, and bringing to perfection a whole, consistent with itself, consonant, and harmonious.

'In the beginning God created the heavens and the earth.' From two extremes Moses implied the existence of the whole, giving to the heavens precedence of generation and asserting that the earth was second in existence. Assuredly, whatever intervenes between these was made at the same time as the extremities. Therefore, even though he says nothing about the elements, fire, water, and air, nevertheless, by the judgment of your own intelligence, reflect, in the first place, that all things are compounded with all others, and that you will find water and air and fire in the earth, if really fire is struck from stones, and if from iron, which itself has its source from the earth, a plentiful fire is wont to shine forth when there is friction. This also is deserving of wonder, that the fire which exists in the bodies lies harmlessly hidden, but on being called forth to the outside consumes that which hitherto preserved it. That water exists in the earth is proved by the diggers of wells; and that air does is shown by the vapors which are sent up from the moistened earth when it is heated by the sun. Moreover, since the heavens naturally occupy the place above, and the earth is lowest, because light objects are borne to the heavens but the heavy objects are wont to fall down to the earth, and since height and depth are the very opposite of each other, he who made mention of those things which stand farthest apart according to nature also indicated by way of synecdoche those which fill up the intervening space. Therefore, do not look for a detailed account of each, but understand those passed over in silence through those which were set forth.

(8) 'In the beginning God created the heavens and the earth.' An inquiry into the substance of each of the things which exist, whether they fall under our contemplation or lie open to our perception, brings into the explanation a long and

disconnected account, so that in the examination of this problem more words would be used than in everything else that can be said about each of the objects investigated. Besides, a concern about these things is not at all useful for the edification of the Church. Concerning the substance of the heavens we are satisfied with the sayings of Isaia, who in simple words gave us a sufficient knowledge of its nature when he said: 'He established the heaven as if smoke,'[22] that is, He gave the substance for the formation of the heavens a delicate nature and not a solid and dense one. And, as to their form, sufficient for us are the words which he spoke in the glorification of God: 'He that stretcheth out the heavens as a vaulted ceiling.'[23] These same thoughts, let us also recommend to ourselves concerning the earth, not to be curious about what its substance is; nor to wear ourselves out by reasoning, seeking its very foundation; nor to search for some nature destitute of qualities, existing without quality of itself; but to realize well that all that is seen around it is related to the reason of its existence, forming an essential part of its substance. You will end with nothing if you attempt to eliminate by reason each of the qualities that exist in it. In fact, if you remove the black, the cold, the weight, the density, the qualities pertaining to taste, or any others which are perceptible, there will be no basic substance.

Therefore, I urge you to abandon these questions and not to inquire upon what foundation it stands. If you do that, the mind will become dizzy, with the reasoning going on to no definite end. If you say that air is spread under the surface of the earth,[24] you will be at a loss as to how its soft and porous nature, pressed down under such a weight, endures and does

---

22 Cf. Isa. 51.6 (Septuagint version).
23 Isa. 40.22 (Septuagint version).
24 Cf. Aristotle, *On the Heavens* 2.13.294b: 'Anaximenes and Anaxagoras and Democritus give the flatness of the earth as the cause of its staying still. Thus, they say, it does not cut, but covers like a lid, the air beneath it.'

not slip through in all directions in order to escape from under the sinking weight and flow continuously over that which compresses it. Again, if you suppose that water is the substance placed under the earth,[25] even so you will inquire how it is that the heavy and dense body does not pass through the water, but instead, although excelling in weight, is supported by the weaker nature. In regard to seeking the foundation for the water itself, you are again at a loss as to what watertight and firmly standing support its uppermost depth rests upon.

(9) If you suggest that there is another body heavier than the earth to prevent the earth from going downward you will notice that, that too, needs some like support to keep it from falling down. And, if we are able to fashion some support and place it underneath, our mind will seek again the support for that, and thus we shall go on endlessly, always inventing other bases in turn for the bases found.[26] Moreover, the farther we advance in our reasoning, the greater is the supporting force we are compelled to bring in, that will be able to withstand the whole superimposed mass. Set a limit, then, to your thoughts, lest the words of Job should ever censure your curiosity as you scrutinize things incomprehensible, and you also should be asked by him: 'Upon what are its bases grounded?'[27] But, even if at some time in the Psalms you hear: 'I have established the

---

25 Cf. *Ibid.* 294a: 'Others say the earth rests upon water. This, indeed, is the oldest theory that has been preserved, and is attributed to Thales of Miletus. It was supposed to stay still because it floated like wood and other similar substances, which are so constituted as to rest upon water but not upon air. As if the same account had not to be given of the water which carries the earth as of the earth itself! . . . Again, as air is lighter than water, so is water than earth: how then can they think that the naturally lighter substance lies below the heavier?'

26 Cf. *Ibid.*: 'Some have been led to assert that the earth below us is infinite, saying, with Xenophanes of Colophon, that it has "pushed its roots to infinity,"—in order to save the trouble of seeking for the cause. Hence the sharp rebuke of Empedocles in the words "if the deeps of the earth are endless and endless the ample ether—such is the vain tale told by many a tongue, poured from the mouths of those who have seen but little of the whole." '

27 Job 38.6.

pillars thereof,'[28] believe that the sustaining force is called the pillars. As for the saying: 'He hath founded it upon the seas,'[29] what else does it signify than that the water is spread around the earth on all sides? Now, how does water, which exists as a fluid and naturally tends to flow downward, remain hanging without support and never flow away? Yet, you do not consider that the earth, suspended by its own power, provides the same or even a greater need for a reason, since it has a heavier nature. Moreover, we must, even if we grant that the earth stands by its own power and if we say that it rides at anchor on the water, depart in no way from the thought of true religion, but admit that all things are kept under control by the power of the Creator. Therefore, we must say this to ourselves and to those asking us on what this immense and insupportable weight of the earth is propped up: 'In the hand of God are all the ends of the earth.'[30] This is safest for our own understanding and is most profitable for our hearers.

(10) Already some of the inquirers into nature say with a great display of words that the earth remains immovable for the following reasons: that, because of its holding the middle place of the universe and because of the equal distance on all sides to the edge, not having place to incline farther on any side, necessarily then, it rests upon itself, since the equal space encircling it on all sides makes an inclination toward any one side entirely impossible for it.[31] And they add that the earth did not obtain the middle place by chance, nor of itself, but that this is the natural and necessary situation for the

---

28 Ps. 74.4.
29 *Ibid.* 23.2.
30 *Ibid.* 94.4.
31 Cf. Aristotle, *Ibid.* 2.13.295b: 'But there are some, Anaximander, for instance, among the ancients, who say that the earth keeps its place because of its indifference. Motion upward and downward and sideways were all, they thought, equally inappropriate to that which is set at the centre and indifferently related to every extreme point; and to move in contrary directions at the same time was impossible: so it must needs remain still.' Cf. also Plato, *Phaedo* 108 and 109.

earth.³² For, since the heavenly body occupies the highest position, whatever heavy weights, they assert, we might assume to fall from above, will be brought together to the center from all sides. To whatever point the parts are borne, there the whole mass, of course, will be pressed together. If stones and wood and all earthy material are carried downward, this would be the proper and suitable situation for the whole earth; but, if one of the lighter objects is carried away from the center, clearly it will move toward the higher regions. Therefore, the proper motion for the very heavy objects is downward; but reason has shown that downward is the center. Do not, then, wonder that the earth never falls, since it holds naturally the middle place. It is positively obliged to remain in that place, or being moved, contrary to nature to be displaced from its proper location. And, should any of these things which have been said seem to you to be plausible, transfer your admiration to the wisdom of God which has ordered them so. In fact, our amazement at the greatest phenomena is not lessened because we have discovered the manner in which a certain one of the marvels occurred. But, if this is not so, still let the simplicity of faith be stronger than the deductions of reason.

(11) We might say this same thing also concerning the heavens, namely, that most verbose treatises have been written by the wise of the world on the nature of the heavens. Some have said that it is composed of the four elements, as though it were tangible and visible, and that it shares in the nature of earth because of its solid surface, of fire because it is seen,

---

32 Cf. *Ibid.* 295b, 296a: 'The place to which any fragment of earth moves must necessarily be the place to which the whole moves; and in the place to which a thing naturally moves, it will naturally rest. The reason then is not in the fact that the earth is indifferently related to every extreme point: for this would apply to any body, whereas movement to the centre is peculiar to earth. . . . Thus for all the indifference theory shows to the contrary, earth also would have moved in this manner away from the centre, unless the centre had been its natural place.'

and of the other elements because of their mingling together.[33] Others have rejected this reasoning as unlikely, and, acting at random and according to their own minds, have introduced a certain fifth elemental substance for the formation of the heavens. Now, in their opinion there is a certain ethereal body which, they say, is neither fire, nor air, nor earth, nor water, nor any at all of the simple elements, because motion in a straight line is proper to simple objects, light objects being borne upward and heavy objects downward. But, upward and downward motion is not the same as circular motion; on the whole, straight motion differs very much from circular motion. And of those objects of which the natural motions happen to differ, the substances also, they say, necessarily must differ. It is not even possible, however, for us to assume that the heavens are formed of primary bodies which we call elements, because bodies which are compounded from unlike bodies cannot have an even and unforced motion, since each of the simple bodies inherent in the composite ones has a different impulse from nature. In the first place, then, it is with effort that the composite bodies are kept in continual motion, because one motion cannot be in harmony and agreement with all the contrary motions; but the motion peculiar to the light object is opposed to that of the heavy one. Indeed, whenever we are borne downward, we use violence against the fiery part of our being, dragging it down contrary to its nature. This pulling of the elements in contrary directions is an occasion of their dissolution. For, that which is under compulsion and in opposition to nature, although it resists for a little while, violently and utterly, is quickly dissolved into the elements from which it was composed, since each of those which had come together returns to its own place. Because of these

---

[33] Cf. Plato, *Timaeus* 31b: 'Thus it was that in the midst between fire and earth God set water and air, and having bestowed upon them so far as possible a like ratio one towards another—air being to water as fire to air, and water being to earth as air to water—he joined together and constructed a Heaven visible and tangible.'

logical necessities, as they say, those who assume a fifth element for the generation of the heavens and the stars in it, having rejected the opinions of their predecessors, needed an hypothesis of their own. But, another, strong in persuasive argumentation, rising in his turn against them, refuted and dissolved these theories and introduced his own personal opinion.

If we undertake now to talk about these theories, we shall fall into the same idle chatter as they. But, let us allow them to refute each other, and let us stop talking about the substance, since we have been persuaded by Moses that 'God created the heavens and the earth.' Let us glorify the Master Craftsman for all that has been done wisely and skillfully; and from the beauty of the visible things let us form an idea of Him who is more than beautiful; and from the greatness of these perceptible and circumscribed bodies let us conceive of Him who is infinite and immense and who surpasses all understanding in the plenitude of His power. For, even if we are ignorant of things made, yet, at least, that which in general comes under our observation is so wonderful that even the most acute mind is shown to be at a loss as regards the least of the things in the world, either in the ability to explain it worthily or to render due praise to the Creator, to whom be all glory, honor, and power forever. Amen.

# HOMILY 2

*Invisible and Unfinished State of the Earth*

(ON THE HEXAEMERON)

THIS MORNING when we dwelt upon a few words, we found such hidden depth of thought that we despair completely of what follows. If the court of the sanctuary is so beautiful, and the vestibule of the temple is so august and magnificent, dazzling the eyes of our soul with its surpassing beauty, what must be the holy of holies? And who is fit to venture within the innermost shrine? Or who can look into its secrets? Indeed, even a glimpse of them is unattainable, and to explain what the mind conceives of them is exceedingly difficult. Since, however, rewards by no means contemptible are assigned by the just Judge even for merely undertaking needful tasks, let us not hesitate to investigate. In fact, even if we err in our opinion, nevertheless, if by the assistance of the Spirit we do not depart from the meaning of the Scripture, we ourselves shall not be judged entirely deserving of rejection, and with the help of grace we shall furnish some edification to the Church of God.

'But the earth was invisible and unfinished,' Moses says.[1] How is it, if both the heavens and the earth were of equal honor, that the heavens were brought to perfection and the earth is still imperfect and unfinished? Or, in short, what was the lack of preparation of the earth? And for what reason was

---

1 Gen. 1.2 (Septuagint version).

it invisible? Surely, the perfect condition of the earth consists in its state of abundance: the budding of all sorts of plants, the putting forth of the lofty trees both fruitful and barren, the freshness and fragrance of flowers, and whatever things appeared on earth a little later by the command of God to adorn their mother. Since as yet there was nothing of this, the Scripture reasonably spoke of it as incomplete. We might say the same also about the heavens; that they were not yet brought to perfection themselves, nor had they received their proper adornment, since they were not yet lighted around by the moon nor the sun, nor crowned by the choirs of the stars. For, these things had not yet been made. Therefore, you will not err from the truth if you say that the heavens also were incomplete.

Scripture called the earth invisible for two reasons: because man, the spectator of it, did not yet exist, or because, being submerged under the water which overflowed its surface, it could not be seen. For, not yet had the waters, which later God gathered together and called seas, been collected into their own places. Now, what is invisible? On the one hand, what cannot be seen by the eyes of the body, as our mind; and on the other, that which, really visible by nature, is hidden because of the interposition of a body lying upon it, like iron in the depths of the earth. In accordance with this interpretation we believe that 'invisible' means that the earth was concealed by the water. Then, of course, since light had not yet been made, it is not to be wondered at that the earth, lying in darkness, because the air above it was not illumined, was for this reason also called by Scripture 'invisible.'

(2) But, the counterfeiters of truth, who do not teach their minds to follow the Scripture, but distort the meaning of Scripture according to their own will, say that matter is implied by these words. This, they say, is naturally invisible and unfinished, being without qualities because of its condition, and dissociated from all form and shape. Having taken

## HOMILY 2

it over, the Craftsman formed it by His own intelligence, reduced it to order, and thus through it gave visible things existence.

If matter itself is uncreated, it is, in the first place, of equal rank with God, worthy of the same honors. What could be more impious than this, that the most extreme unsightliness, without qualities, without form, unshapen ugliness (I have used, indeed, their own expressions) be considered worthy of the same superior ranking as the wise and powerful and all-good Craftsman and Creator of all things? In the next place, if matter is so great as to take in entirely the intelligence of God, on this supposition also, in a way, they compare its substance with the inscrutable power of God, since it would be capable of measuring by itself all the intelligence of God. But, if matter is inferior to the activity of God, then also their explanation will be turned into a more absurd blasphemy, since His own works would be keeping God unsuccessful and inefficacious because of the deficiency in matter. In truth, the poverty of their human nature deceived them. Since among us each art is definitely occupied with a certain material, as the art of metalworking with iron, and of carpentry with wood; and in them the substance is one thing; the form, another; and that made from the form, another; furthermore, since the material is received from the outside, but the form is adapted to it by art, and the finished product is the combination of both, that is, of the form and the material; so they think also that in the divine creative activity the plan of the world was produced by the wisdom of the Maker of all things, but matter was appropriated to the Creator from the outside and a composite world came into existence, having its fundamental matter and substance from the outside, but receiving its plan and form from God.[2] From this fact it is possible for them

---

[2] Cf. Plato, *Timaeus* 30 A: 'When He [God] took over all that was visible, seeing that it was not in a state of rest but in a state of discordant and disorderly motion, He brought it into order out of disorder, deeming that the former state is in all ways better than the latter.'

to say that the great God is not the author of the formation of all beings, but, somewhat as a member of a partnership, He has Himself contributed a small portion for the generation of all that exists.

They are unable because of the shallowness of their reasoning to perceive the sublimity of truth, since in this world the arts come into being later than the materials, introduced because of the need of employing them in living. Wool existed first and the art of weaving came afterwards to fulfill of itself the deficiency of nature. Again, there was wood, and the art of carpentry, taking up and shaping the material according to the required need on each occasion, showed us the usefulness of wood, providing the oar for sailors, the winnowing fan for farmers, and the shield for soldiers. God, however, before any of the objects now seen existed, having cast about in His mind and resolved to bring into being things that did not exist, at one and the same time devised what sort of a world it should be and created the appropriate matter together with its form. For the heavens He assigned a nature suitable for the heavens; and for the plan of the earth He produced a substance peculiar and destined for it. And fire and water and air He moulded variously as He wished, and He formed them into substance when the reason for the existence of each demanded. The whole world, which consists of diverse parts, He bound together by an unbroken bond of attraction into one fellowship and harmony, so that objects which are farthest apart from each other in position seem to have been made one through affinity. Let those cease, therefore, from their mythical fictions, who attempt in the weakness of their own reasonings to measure power incomprehensible to their understanding and wholly inexpressible in human speech.

(3) 'God created the heavens and the earth,'[3] not each one by halves, but the entire heavens and the whole earth, includ-

---

3 Gen. 1.1.

## HOMILY 2

ing the substance itself with the form. He is not the Inventor of the shapes, but the Creator of the very nature of all that exists. Otherwise, let them answer us as to how the active power of God and the passive nature of matter came in contact with each other, the one providing substance without form, and the other possessing an understanding of shapes but without matter, so that what was lacking to each might come from the other—to the Creator, the possession of an opportunity to display His art; to matter, the ability to lay aside its unsightliness and absence of form. But so far concerning these matters.

Let us return to the original statement: 'The earth was invisible and unfinished.' When Moses said: 'In the beginning God created the heavens and the earth,' he left unmentioned many things—water, air, fire, the conditions produced from these—all of which, as forming an essential part of the world, He assuredly called into existence at the same time as the universe. But, the narrative made omissions to accustom our mind to a ready understanding and to permit the rest to be deduced from slight resources. Now, although mention has not been made concerning the fact that God created water, but it was stated that the earth was invisible, consider for yourself by what it was covered that it was not plainly seen. Certainly, fire was not able to hide it. In fact, fire would provide illumination and clearness rather than obscurity for those things to which it would attach itself. Nor again, was air at that time the cloak of the earth. For, the nature of air is rare and transparent, admitting all the forms of visible objects and transmitting them to the eyes of spectators. Accordingly, it remains for us to believe that water abounded on the surface of the earth because the liquid substance had not yet been separated and spread in its allotted place. For this reason, not only was the earth invisible but it was also unfinished. Excess of moisture, indeed, is even now a hindrance to productiveness for the earth. There is, therefore, the same cause both for its being unseen and for its being unfinished, if, indeed, the finishing of the earth is the adornment proper to it and according to its nature—corn fields waving in the hollows, meadows verdant and abounding with varied flowers, woodland vales in bloom, and mountain peaks shaded over with forest trees. It had none of these as yet, being in travail with the birth of all things through the power stored up in it by the Creator, and waiting for the proper times that it might bring forth its offspring into the open at the divine command.

(4) 'And darkness,' Moses said, 'was on the face of the deep.'[4] Here, again, are other opportunities for myths and sources for more impious fabrications, since men pervert the words according to their own notions. They explain the darkness, not as some unlighted air, as is natural, or a place overshadowed by the interposition of a body, or, in short, a place deprived of light through any cause whatsoever, but, they explain the darkness as an evil power, or rather, as evil itself, having its beginning from itself, resisting and opposing the goodness of God. If 'God is light,'[5] they say, assuredly in conformity with the meaning, the power warring against Him would be darkness, a darkness not having its being from another, but a self-begotten evil. Darkness, enemy of souls, producer of death, adversary of virtue. They falsely think that the very words of the Prophet indicate that it subsisted and had not been made by God. From this beginning, then, what wicked or godless dogmas have not been invented! What fierce wolves, beginning with these insignificant words, have not preyed upon souls, scattering God's flock![6] Have not the

---

4 *Ibid.* 1.2.
5 1 John 1.5.
6 Cf. Acts 20.29: 'I know that after my departure fierce wolves will get in among you, and will not spare the flock.'

HOMILY 2

Marcionites?[7] And have not the Valentinians[8] come from the same source? Has not the abominable heresy of the Manichaeans?[9] And, if anyone calls that the putrefaction of the churches, he will not deviate from the truth. Why do you flee far from the truth, O man, planning opportunities of destruction for yourself? The expression is simple and easily understood by all. He says: 'The earth was invisible.' What is the cause? Because it had the 'deep' covering it. And what is the meaning of the 'deep?' Fathomless water, with downward limits hard to reach. But, we know that many bodies frequently are seen through rather shallow and translucent water. How, then, did no part at all of the earth show through the waters? Because the air flowing above it was still unlighted and in darkness. A ray of the sun penetrating through the waters does often reveal pebbles on the bottom, but, in the depth of night, in no way may anyone perceive objects under the water. Thus, the statement that 'the deep overspread it and was itself in darkness' is capable of establishing the fact that the earth was invisible. The deep, then, is not a mass of opposing powers, as some have imagined, nor is darkness some sovereign and wicked force let loose against good. For, two equal powers in opposition to each other will be entirely and mutually destructive of their own nature, and they will continuously have and unceasingly provide troubles for each other

---

7 The Marcionites were an heretical sect founded in Rome in 144. They rejected the writings of the Old Testament and taught that Christ was not the Son of the God of the Jews but of the good God. They anticipated the Dualism of Manichaeism by which they were later absorbed. They existed about 300 years in the West, but longer in the East.
8 The Valentinians were an heretical sect founded in the middle of the second century. They attempted to amalgamate the most fantastic Greek and Oriental speculations with Christian ideas. Valentinus used freely some books of the New Testament but interpreted them to correspond with his views. He was dominated by dualistic ideas.
9 The Manichaeans practiced a form of religious Dualism, holding the theory of two eternal principles, good and evil. It professes to be a true synthesis of all religious systems known in the latter half of the third century. It spread throughout the East and West, but especially in the land of its origin, Mesopotamia, Babylonia, and Turkestan.

when engaged in war. But, if one of the opponents excels the other in power, he altogether annihilates the conquered one. So, if they say that the opposition of evil against good is equally balanced, they introduce a ceaseless war and a continuous destruction, since in turn they conquer and are conquered. But, if the good exceeds in power, what reason is there that the nature of evil is not completely destroyed? If it is otherwise, however, which it is impious to say, I wonder how those falling into such unlawful blasphemy do not endeavor to flee from themselves.

Again, it is impious to say that evil has its origin from God, because naught contrary is produced by the contrary. Life does not generate death, nor is darkness the beginning of light, nor is disease the maker of health, but in the changes of conditions there are transitions from one condition to the contrary. In genesis, however, each being comes forth not from its contrary, but from those of the same type. Accordingly, they say, if it is not uncreated nor created by God, whence does it have its nature? No one who is in this world will deny that evils exist. What, then, do we say? That evil is not a living and animated substance, but a condition of the soul which is opposed to virtue and which springs up in the slothful because of their falling away from good.

(5) Do not, therefore, contemplate evil from without; and do not imagine some original nature of wickedness, but let each one recognize himself as the first author of the vice that is in him. Always in the course of events, some things happen to us naturally, such as old age and infirmities, and others accidentally, as the unanticipated experiences of extraneous origin, of which some frequently are sad and others more cheerful, as the discovery of a treasure when digging a well or the meeting with a mad dog when hastening to the market. Others, however, are in our own power, as mastering our desires or neglecting to bridle our pleasures, as controlling our anger or laying our hands upon one who has provoked us, telling the

## HOMILY 2

truth or lying, being of a good and temperate disposition or swollen and exalted with false pretenses. So, you yourself are master of these actions; do not seek elsewhere their beginnings, but recognize that evil in its proper sense has taken its origin from our voluntary falls. If, indeed, it were involuntary and not in our own power, such great fear of the laws would not hang over the wrongdoers, and the penalties of the courts measuring out to the malefactors according to their deserts would not be so unmerciful. But, let this suffice concerning evil in its proper sense. Now, as regards disease and poverty and ignominy and death and whatever else causes men sorrow, it is not right for them to be reckoned among evils, because we do not count among our greatest blessings what is opposed to them. And some of them are according to nature and others seem to be for the advantage of many. Passing over in silence all figurative and allegorical explanation at the present time, let us accept the concept of darkness simply and without curiosity, following the meaning of Scripture.

Reason asks whether darkness was made at the same time as was the world and whether it is anterior to light and why the older is inferior? Therefore, we answer that this darkness did not subsist in substance but is a condition incident to the air because of the deprivation of light. Of what light, then, was the region of the world suddenly found bereft, so that darkness was on the face of the water? We infer that, if there had been anything before the formation of this perceptible and destructible world, certainly it would have existed in light. For, neither the ranks of angels nor all the heavenly armies, nor, in short, any other of the rational natures, whether named or unnamed, or of the ministering spirits,[10] lived in darkness; but in light and in all spiritual gladness enjoyed a condition proper to them.

And no one will gainsay this, certainly not anyone who expects heavenly light among the promised blessings, concern-

---
10 Cf. Heb. 1.14: 'Are they not all ministering spirits, sent for service?'

ing which Solomon says: 'The just have light eternal';[11] and the Apostle says: 'Rendering thanks to God the Father, who has made us worthy to share the lot of the saints in light.'[12] If, indeed, the damned are sent 'into the darkness outside,'[13] certainly, those who have performed acts deserving of approbation have their rest in the supramundane light. When, then, the heavens were made by the command of God, surrounding completely the space enclosed by their own circumference with an unbroken body capable of separating the parts within from those outside, necessarily they made the regions within dark, since they had cut off the rays of light from the outside. It is necessary for three things to concur in the case of a shadow, namely, the light, the body, and an unlighted place. Accordingly, the earthly darkness existed in consequence of the shadow of the heavenly body. Now, understand my explanation from a clear example of setting around yourself at midday a tent of thick and impenetrable material and shutting yourself up in its improvised darkness. Suppose that darkness, then, to be such, not subsisting as the initial state but resulting from other causes. This darkness, indeed, is said to settle upon the face of the deep, since the limits of the air naturally make contact with the visible surfaces of bodies. At that time water was covering the surface of all things. Therefore, necessarily, darkness was said to be upon the surface of the deep.

(6) 'And the spirit of God,' he says, 'was stirring above the waters.'[14] If this spirit means the diffusion of the air, understand that the author is enumerating to you the parts of the world, saying that God created the heavens, the earth, water, and air; and this latter was spreading and flowing. Or, what is truer and approved by those before us, the Holy Spirit is called the Spirit of God, because it has been observed that It alone and specially was considered worthy by the Scripture of such

---

11 Prov. 13.9 (Septuagint version).
12 Col. 1.12.
13 Matt. 22.13.
14 Gen. 1.2.

## HOMILY 2

mention, and there is named no other Spirit of God than the Holy Spirit which forms an essential part of the divine and blessed Trinity. Admitting this meaning, you will find the advantage from it greater. How, then, was It stirring above the waters? I will tell you an explanation, not my own, but that of a Syrian who was as far removed from worldly wisdom as he was near the knowledge of truth. Now, he claimed that the language of the Syrians was more expressive and because of its resemblance to the Hebrew language approached somewhat more closely to the sense of Scripture; therefore, the meaning of the statement was as follows. As regards the verb 'was stirring above,' they interpret in preference to that, he says, 'warmed with fostering care,' and he endued the nature of the waters with life through his comparison with a bird brooding upon eggs and imparting some vital power to them as they are being warmed. Some such meaning, they say, was implied by this word, as if the Spirit were warming with fostering care, that is, was preparing the nature of water for the generation of living beings. Therefore, from this there is sufficient proof for the inquiries of certain men that the Holy Spirit is not wanting in the creative power.

'And God said, "Let there be light." '[15] The first word of God created the nature of light, did away with the darkness, put an end to the gloom, brightened up the world, and bestowed upon all things in general a beautiful and pleasant appearance. The heavens, so long buried in darkness, appeared, and their beauty was such as even yet our eyes bear witness to. The air was illumined, or rather, it held the whole light completely permeating it, sending out dazzling rays in every direction to its uttermost bounds. It reached upward even to the ether itself and the heavens, and in extent it illuminated in a swift moment of time all parts of the world, north and south and east and west. For, such is the nature of ether, so rare and transparent, that the light passing through

---
15 *Ibid.* 1.3.

it needs no interval of time. As it passes our glances along instantaneously to the objects at which we are looking, so also it receives the rays of light on all its boundaries in a moment of time, so that one could not conceive a shorter space of time. And the air is more pleasant after the light, and the waters brighter, since they not only admit but also return the brightness from themselves by the reflection of the light, the sparkling rays rebounding from all parts of the water. The divine word transformed all things into a most pleasing and excellent state. Just as men who throw oil in deep water create a clear space, so the Creator of all things, by His word instantly put the gracious gift of light in the world.

(7) 'Let there be light.' In truth, the command was itself the act, and a condition of nature was produced than which it is not possible for human reasonings to conceive anything more delightfully enjoyable. When we speak of a voice and a word and a command with reference to God, we mean the divine word, not a sound sent out through phonetic organs, nor air struck by the tongue, but we believe that the bent of His will is presented in the form of a command, because it is easily comprehended by those who are being instructed.

'And God saw that the light was good.'[16] What could we say that would be worthy praise of light which beforehand possesses from the Creator the testimony that it is good? Among us speech reports the judgment made by the eyes; even so, it is unable to say anything at all as great as our senses previously have borne witness to. But, if beauty in the body has its being from the symmetry of its parts with each other and from the appearance of beautiful color, how, in the case of light, which is simple in nature and similar in parts, is the idea of beauty preserved? Or, is it that the symmetry of light is not evinced in its individual parts but in the joy and pleasure at the visual impression? In this way even gold is beautiful, which holds an attraction and pleasure for the sight, not from

---

16 *Ibid.* 1.4.

the symmetry of its parts, but from the beauty of its color alone. And the evening star is the most beautiful of the stars, not because the parts of which it was formed are proportionate, but because from it there falls upon our eyes a certain joyous and delightful brightness. Then, too, the judgment of God concerning the goodness of light has been made, and He looks not wholly at the pleasure in the sight but also looks forward to the future advantage. For, there were not yet eyes able to discern the beauty in light.

'And God separated the light from the darkness.'[17] That is, God made their natures incapable of mixing and in opposition, one to the other. For, He divided and separated them with a very great distinction between them.

(8) 'And God called the light Day and the darkness Night.'[18] Now, henceforth, after the creation of the sun, it is day when the air is illuminated by the sun shining on the hemisphere above the earth, and night is the darkness of the earth when the sun is hidden. Yet, it was not at that time according to solar motion, but it was when that first created light was diffused and again drawn in according to the measure ordained by God, that day came and night succeeded.

'And there was evening and morning, one day.'[19] Evening, then, is a common boundary line of day and night; and similarly, morning is the part of night bordering on day. In order, therefore, to give the prerogative of prior generation to the day, Moses mentioned first the limit of the day and then that of the night, as night followed the day. The condition in the world before the creation of light was not night, but darkness; that which was opposed to the day was named night; wherefore it received its name later than the day did. So 'there was evening and morning.' This means the space of a day and a night. No longer did He call them day and night

---

17 *Ibid.*
18 Gen. 1.5.
19 *Ibid.* (Septuagint version).

but assigned as the whole name that belonging to the important one. You may find this practice everywhere in the Scripture, namely, that in the measuring of time days are counted and not nights with the days. 'The days of our years,' the psalmist says.[20] And again, Jacob says: 'The days of my life are few and evil.'[21] And again, 'All the days of my life.'[22] Therefore, the words now handed down in the form of history are the laws laid down for later usage.

'And there was evening and morning, one day.' Why did he say 'one' and not 'first'? And yet, it is more consistent for him who intends to introduce a second and a third and a fourth day, to call the one which begins the series 'first.' But, he said 'one' because he was defining the measure of day and night and combining the time of a night and day, since the twenty-four hours fill up the interval of one day, if, of course, night is understood with day. Therefore, even if at the time of the solstices of the sun it happens that one of them exceeds the other in length, still the durations of both are entirely included in the time defined. It is as if one would say that the measure of twenty-four hours is the length of one day, or that the return of the heavens from one point to the same point once more occurs in one day; so that, as often as through the revolution of the sun evening and morning traverse the world, the circle is completed, not in a longer period of time, but in the space of one day. Or, is the reason handed down in the mysteries more authoritative, that God, having prepared the nature of time, set as measures and limits for it the intervals of the days, and measuring it out for a week, He orders the week, in counting the change of time, always to return again in a circle to itself? Again, He orders that one day by recurring seven times complete a week; and this, beginning from itself and ending on itself, is the form of a circle. In fact, it

---

20 Ps. 89.10.
21 Gen. 47.9 (Septuagint version).
22 Ps. 22.6.

is also characteristic of eternity to turn back upon itself and never to be brought to an end. Therefore, He called the beginning of time not a 'first day,' but 'one day,' in order that from the name it might have kinship with eternity. For, the day which shows a character of uniqueness and nonparticipation with the rest is properly and naturally called 'one.' If, however, the Scripture presents to us many ages, saying in various places 'age of age,' and 'ages of ages,'[23] still in those places neither the first, nor the second, nor the third age is enumerated for us, so that, by this, differences of conditions and of various circumstances are shown to us but not limits and boundaries and successions of ages. 'The day of the Lord is great and very terrible,'[24] it is said. And again, 'To what end do you seek the day of the Lord? And this is darkness, and not light.'[25] But darkness, certainly, for those who are deserving of darkness. For, Scripture knows as a day without evening, without succession, and without end, that day which the psalmist called the eighth, because it lies outside this week of time. Therefore, whether you say 'day' or 'age' you will express the same idea. If, then, that condition should be called day, it is one and not many, or, if it should be named age, it would be unique and not manifold. In order, therefore, to lead our thoughts to a future life, he called that day 'one,' which is an image of eternity, the beginning of days, the contemporary of light, the holy Lord's day, the day honored by the Resurrection of the Lord. 'There was, then, evening and morning, one day,' he said.

But, in truth, my words concerning that evening, being overtaken by the present evening, mark the end of my speech. May the Father of the true light, however, who has decked the day with the heavenly light, who has brightened the night

---

23 *Ibid.* 148.6; Jude 25.
24 Joel 2.11.
25 Cf. Amos 5.18: 'To what end is it for you? the day of the Lord is darkness, and not light.'

with gleams of fire, who has made ready the peace of the future age with a spiritual and never ending light, illumine your hearts in a knowledge of the truth, and preserve your life without offense, allowing you 'to walk becomingly as in the day,'[26] in order that you may shine forth as the sun in the splendor of the saints for my exultation in the day of Christ, to whom be glory and power forever. Amen.

---

26 Cf. Rom. 13.13: 'Let us walk becomingly as in the day.'

# HOMILY 3

## *The Firmament*

### (ON THE HEXAEMERON)

We have spoken of the works of the first, or rather, of one day. Let us not, indeed, deprive it of its dignity, which it naturally possesses, since it was produced separately by the Creator and was not counted in the general arrangement with the others. But, since my discourse yesterday reviewed the occurrences of that day and divided the explanation for the hearers, providing their souls with both morning nourishment and evening joy, now we are passing on to the wonders of the second day. I say this, not referring to the power of the narrator, but to the grace of the written words, since it is naturally easy of acceptance and gentle and pleasant to the mind of all those who prefer truth to plausibility. Wherefore, the psalmist, showing the charm of truth most emphatically says: 'How sweet are thy words to my palate! more than honey to my mouth.'[1] Yesterday, therefore, having gladdened your souls, as much as I was able, with a discourse on the eloquent words of God, today, the second day, we have met again to contemplate the wonders of the works of the second day.

It has not escaped my notice, however, that many workers of handicrafts, who with difficulty provide a livelihood for themselves from their daily toil, are gathered around us. These compel us to cut short our discourse in order that they may not be drawn away too long from their work. And what do I say to them? That the portion of time lent to God is not

---
1 Ps. 118.103.

lost; He gives it back with a great increase. Whatever circumstances there are, in fact, that cause you trouble, these the Lord will remove, giving to those, who prefer the spiritual, strength of body, alacrity of spirit, skill in transactions, and prosperity for their whole life. Even if at present our efforts do not succeed according to our hopes, still the teaching of the Spirit is a goodly treasure for the future life. Therefore, free your heart of all solicitude for your livelihood and give yourself wholly to me. For, there is no advantage from the presence of the body if the heart is busy about earthly treasure.

(2) 'Then God said, "Let there be a firmament in the midst of the waters to divide the waters." '[2] Only yesterday we heard the words of God, 'Let there be light.'[3] And today, 'Let there be a firmament.' These words seem to involve something more because the utterance did not stop with a bare command but in addition it specified the reason which required the formation of the firmament. It says, 'To divide the waters.' Resuming, therefore, let us first inquire how God speaks. Is it in our manner? Or, is the image of the objects first formed in His intellect, then, after they have been pictured in His mind, does He make them known by selecting from substances the distinguishing marks characteristic of each? Finally, handing over the concepts to the vocal organs for their service, does He thus manifest His hidden thought by striking the air with the articulate movement of the voice? Surely, it is fantastic to say that God needs such a roundabout way for the manifestation of His thoughts. Or, is it not more in conformity with true religion to say that the divine will joined with the first impulse of His intelligence is the Word of God? The Scripture delineates Him in detail in order that it may show that God wished the creation not only to be accomplished, but also to be brought to this birth through some co-worker. It could have related everything fully as it began, 'In the beginning God created the heavens and the earth,' then, 'He created

---
2 Gen. 1.6.
3 *Ibid.* 1.3.

light,' next, 'He created the firmament.' But, now, introducing God as commanding and speaking, it indicates silently Him to whom He gives the command and to whom He speaks, not because it begrudges us the knowledge, but that it might inflame us to a desire by the very means by which it suggests some traces and indications of the mystery. That which has been acquired by labor is received with the greatest joy and guarded with the greatest diligence; however, the possession of those things whose attainment is easy is readily despised. By these means Scripture leads us on to the idea of the Only-begotten in a certain orderly way. And surely, for an incorporeal nature there was no need for vocal speech, since the thoughts themselves could be communicated to His Co-worker. So, what need was there of speech for those who are able by the thought itself to share their plans with others? In fact, voice was made for hearing, and hearing for voice. Where there is no air nor tongue nor ear nor winding passage carrying the sounds to the perceptive faculty in the head, there no need of words exists, but the communication of the will comes from the very thoughts in the mind, as one might say. As I was saying, therefore, this way of speaking has been wisely and skillfully employed so as to rouse our mind to an inquiry of the Person to whom these words are directed.

(3) Secondly, we must examine whether this firmament, which was also called the heavens, is different from the heavens created in the beginning, and whether, in short, there are two heavens. The philosophers who have been discussing the heavens would prefer to give up their tongues rather than to admit this as truth. They assume that there is one heaven[4]

---

4 Cf. Plato, *Timaeus* 31 A: 'Are we right, then, in describing the Heaven as one, or would it be more correct to speak of heavens as many or infinite in number? One it must be termed, if it is to be framed after its Pattern. For that which embraces all intelligible Living Creatures could never be second, with another beside it; . . . but there is and will continue to be this one generated Heaven, unique of its kind.' Plato ends the *Timaeus* with the statement: 'even this one Heaven sole of its kind.'

and that it does not possess such a nature that a second or a third or a greater number can be added to it, since all the substance of the heavenly body was consumed in the formation of the one, as they think. For, they say that the body which moves in a circle is one and finite. If, then, this body was commensurate with the first heavens, nothing is left for the production of a second or third. This, indeed, is what those who introduce an uncreated substance in addition to the Creator imagine, slipping from the first fabulous invention into the consequent fallacy. But, we ask the wise men of the Greeks not to scoff at us before they come to an agreement with each other. For, there are among them men who say that there are infinite heavens and worlds;[5] and, when those who employ more weighty proofs will have exposed their absurdity and will prove by the laws of geometry that nature does not support the fact that another heaven besides the one has been made, then we shall only laugh the more at their geometrical and artificial nonsense. For, although they see bubbles, not only one but many, produced by the same cause, they yet doubt as to whether the creative power is capable of bringing a greater number of heavens into existence. Whenever we look upon the transcending power of God, we consider that the strength and greatness of the heavens differ not at all from that of the curved spray which spurts up in the fountains. And so, their explanation of the impossibility is laughable. We, however, are so far from doubting the second heavens that we even seek for the third, of the sight of which the blessed Paul[6] was considered worthy. The psalm, too, speaking of the heavens of heavens,[7] gives us an idea of even more. Certainly, this is not more incredible than the seven circles

---

5 Cf. Cicero, *On the Nature of the Gods* 1.10.25: 'It was Anaximander's opinion that the Gods were born; that after a great length of time they died; and that they are innumerable worlds.'

6 Cf. 2 Cor. 12.2: 'I know a man in Christ who fourteen years ago—whether in the body I do not know, or out of the body I do not know, God knows—such a one was caught up to the third heaven.'

7 Cf. Ps. 148.4: 'Praise him ye heavens of heavens.'

through which nearly all philosophers with one consent agree that the seven planets are borne, and which they say are fitted one into the other like jars inserted into each other. And these, carried around in the opposite direction to everything else, when they cleave through the ether, give out such a melodious and harmonious sound that it surpasses the sweetest of singing.[8] Then, when those who say these things are asked for sensible proofs, what do they say? That, having become accustomed to this sound from our birth, we fail to notice the sound through our early familiarity with it and because of habitually hearing it, like men in smithies who have their ears incessantly dinned. To refute their subtleties and unsoundness, made so clearly evident to all from their first word, is not the practice of a man who either knows how to use time sparingly or has regard for the intelligence of his hearers.

But, leaving the accounts of outsiders to those outside, we are turning back to the explanation of the Church. Now, some of those before us have said that this is not the generation of a second heaven but a more detailed account of the first, because on the former occasion the creation of the heavens and the earth was presented to us in brief, but here the Scripture teaches us in greater detail the manner in which each was made. We, however, say that, since both a second name and a function peculiar to the second heaven was recorded, this is

---

[8] Cf. Plato, *Republic* 10.615: 'Now the whorl is in form like the whorl used on earth; and the description of it implied that there is one large hollow whorl which is quite scooped out, and into this is fitted another lesser one, and another, and another, and four others, making eight in all, like vessels which fit into one another; the whorls show their edges on the upper side, and on their lower side all together form one continuous whorl, . . . Now the whole spindle has the same motion; but, as the whole revolves in one direction, the seven inner circles move slowly in the other, . . . The spindle turns on the knees of Necessity; and on the upper surface of each circle is a siren, who goes round with them, hymning a single tone or note. The eight together form one harmony; and round about, at equal intervals, there is another band, three in number, each sitting upon her throne: these are the Fates, . . . who accompany with their voices the harmony of the sirens.' Cf. also *Timaeus* 36 D and 38 D; Aristotle, *On the Heavens* 2.9. 290b and 291a.

a different one from that created in the beginning, one of a more solid nature and furnishing a special service for the universe.

(4) 'Then God said, "Let there be a firmament in the midst of the waters to divide the waters." And God made the firmament, dividing the waters that were below the firmament from those that were above it.'[9] Before we touch upon the meaning of the writings, however, let us attempt to solve the arguments brought against it from other sources. They ask us how, if the body of the firmament is spherical, as sight shows it to be, and if water flows and slips off high spots, it would be possible for the water to lie on the convex circumference of the firmament. What, then, shall we say to this? First of all, that, if some body appears circular to us because of an inner concavity, it is not necessary for the outer surface to be made completely spherical, and the whole to be perfectly rounded and smoothly finished. Let us look, indeed, at the stone vaults of the baths and the structures of cavelike buildings which, rounded to a semicircular form according to their interior appearance, often have a flat surface on the upper sections of the roof. Therefore, let them cease making trouble for themselves or for us, alleging that water cannot be kept in the upper regions.

Next, we should tell what the nature of the firmament is and why it was ordered to lie between the waters. It is customary in the Scripture to assign the name of firmament to those things which excel in strength, as when it says: 'The Lord is my firmament and my refuge,'[10] and 'I have established the pillars thereof,'[11] and 'Praise ye him in the firmament of his power.'[12] The heathens call a body solid which is firm and full, and it is so called in distinction from the mathematical body. The mathematical body is the one which has

---
9 Gen. 1.6, 7.
10 Ps. 17.3.
11 *Ibid.* 74.4.
12 *Ibid.* 150.1.

its existence only in dimensions, in width, I mean, and depth, and height; and the solid body is one which possesses resistance in addition to its dimensions. It is customary for the Scripture to call the strong and unyielding substance a firmament, so that it frequently uses this word in the case of air that is condensed, as when it says, 'He who strengthens the thunder.'[13] In fact, Scripture called the force and resistance of the wind which is enclosed in the hollows of the massed clouds and produced the crashes of thunder by bursting out violently, the strength of thunder. Here, therefore, we believe that this word has been assigned for a certain firm nature which is capable of supporting the fluid and unstable water. And, surely, we need not believe, because it seems to have had its origin, according to the general understanding, from water, that it is like either frozen water or some such material which takes its origin from the percolation of moisture, such as is the crystalline rock which men say is remade by the excessive coagulation of the water, or as is the element of mica which is formed in mines. This is a translucent stone, possessing a peculiar and most clear transparency, and if one is found perfect in nature, neither enclosing any decay nor split interiorly by germinations, it is almost like the air in transparency. Now, we compare the firmament to none of these things. Truly, it is peculiar to a childish and simple intellect to hold such notions about the heavens. Not even if all elements are in all, fire in the earth, air in water, and likewise of the other elements, the one in the other; and not even if no one of the elements falling under our perception is pure and free from mixture, either with its medium element or with the contrary element, do we, on this account, dare to say that the firmament is made either from one of the simple elements or from a mixture of them, since we have been taught by the Scripture to permit our mind to invent no fantasy beyond the knowledge that has been granted it. But, let not

---

13 Amos 4.13 (Septuagint version).

this be forgotten, that, after God gave the command, 'Let there be a firmament,' Scripture did not say simply, 'and the firmament was made,' but, 'And God made the firmament'; and again, 'God divided.' Hear, ye deaf, and look up, ye blind. And who is deaf, except he who does not hear the Spirit when He calls so loudly? And who is blind? He who does not discern such clear arguments concerning the Only-begotten. 'Let there be a firmament.' This is the utterance of the first and principal Cause. 'God made the firmament.' This is the testimony of the efficient and creative Power.

(5) Let us, however, return to our subject in order to continue the explanation. 'Let it divide the waters,' He said. The flood of waters which were flowing over the earth in waves from all sides and were suspended over it, was infinite, as it seems, so that even the proportion of water compared to the other elements seemed to be beyond all measure. Therefore, the deep, it was said previously, surrounded the earth on all sides. We shall give the reason for the great amount subsequently. No one of you, assuredly, not even of those who have trained their mind extensively and are sharp-sighted in respect to this perishable and ever flowing nature will denounce our opinion, as if we were assuming theories impossible and imaginary according to reason, nor will he demand an account from us of what it is upon which the element of water has been established. By the same reasoning by which they draw the earth, which is heavier than water, away from the extremities and suspend it in the center, they will, I presume, agree that that boundless water, both because of its natural motion downward and because of its equilibrium on all sides, remains motionless around the earth. Therefore, the immense mass of water was poured around the earth, not in proportion to it, but exceeding it many times over, since the mighty Craftsman from the beginning was looking toward the future and arranging the first things according to the consequent need. What need was there for the water to

abound to such an ineffable degree? Because the substance of fire is necessary for the universe, not only for the plan of earthly things, but also for the completion of the universe; for, the whole would be incomplete if it fell short in the one greatest and most vital of all things. Now, these, fire and water, are antagonistic to each other, and the one is destructive of the other, fire of water when it prevails over it by its strength, and water of fire when it surpasses it in quantity. It was necessary, then, that there should not be strife between them nor that an opportunity should be afforded to the universe for dissolution by the complete cessation of one or the other. The Ruler of the universe ordained from the beginning such a nature for moisture that, although gradually consumed by the power of fire, it would hold out even to the limits prescribed for the existence of the world. He who disposes all things by weight and by measure (for, 'easily numbered by Him are even the drops of rain,' according to Job[14]) knew how long a time He had appointed to the world for its continuance, and how much had to be set aside from the first for consumption by the fire. This is the explanation for the superabundance of water in creation. But surely, no one is so absolutely unconcerned with the affairs of life that he requires to be taught by his reason the necessity of fire for the world, not only because the arts which support life all need labor with fire, the art of weaving, I mean, and of shoemaking, and architecture, and farming, but also because neither the sprouting of trees nor the ripening of fruits nor the generation of land or water animals, nor the rearing of these, would have taken place in the beginning or have endured through time, if heat were not present. Therefore, the creation of heat was necessary for the formation and continuance of things made; and the abundance of moisture is necessary because the consumption by fire is ceaseless and inevitable.

(6) Look around all creation and you will see the power

---

14 Job 36.27 (Septuagint version).

of heat exercising dominion over all things in their generation and destruction. Because of it much water was poured over the earth and was carried away beyond visible things and besides, was spread through the whole depth of the earth, whence are the copious fountains and the flowing wells and flooding rivers, both torrents and ever flowing streams, for maintaining the moisture in the many and varied reservoirs. From the east, from the winter solstices the Indus river flows, the largest of all rivers, as they who describe the courses of the earth record. From the central regions of the east are the Bactrus[15] and the Choaspes[16] and the Araxes,[17] from which the Tanais,[18] separating, pours out into the Palus Maiotis.[19] Besides these, there is the Phasis[20] flowing down from the Caucasian Mountains, while numberless others flow from the northern regions into the Euxine Sea.[21] From the western summer haunts of the sun at the foot of the Pyrenees Mountains are the Tartessus[22] and the Ister,[23] of which the one empties itself into the sea beyond the Pillars, but the Ister, flowing through Europe, pours out into the Euxine Sea. And what need is there to enumerate the others which the Rhipean Mountains[24] call into existence, those mountains beyond innermost Scythia? From them comes the Rhone with numberless other rivers, all of them navigable, which, flowing past the western Gauls and Celts and the neighboring barbarians, all pour out into the western sea. Others flow from the higher regions of the south through Ethiopia. Some enter the sea near us; others empty into the sea beyond the part traversed

---

15 Modern Balkh.
16 Modern Kerkhah.
17 Probably the Volga or Rha, according to the situation, although there are several rivers of that name.
18 Don.
19 Sea of Asov.
20 Rion.
21 Black Sea.
22 Guadalquivir.
23 Danube.
24 A fabled mountain range extending across northern Europe.

HOMILY 3    47

by ships, namely, the Aegon[25] and the Nyses and the one called Chremetes,[26] and also the Nile, which is not like rivers in its nature, when it floods Egypt like a sea.[27] Thus the part of the world which is inhabited is surrounded by water, being both bounded by immense seas and watered by countless ever flowing rivers, through the ineffable wisdom of Him who ordained that this rival power to fire should be hard to consume.

Yet, there will be a time when all things will be burnt up by fire, as Isaia says when he addresses the God of the universe: [You] 'who say to the deep: Be thou desolate, and I will dry up all thy rivers.'[28] Casting aside, therefore, the wisdom that has been turned to foolishness,[29] receive with us the teaching of truth, homely in speech, but infallible in doctrine.

(7) Therefore, 'Let there be a firmament in the midst of the waters to divide the waters.'[30] I have already said what the word 'firmament' in Scripture signifies. Not a firm and solid nature, which has weight and resistance, it is not this that the word 'firmament' means. In that case the earth would more legitimately be considered deserving of such a name. But, because the nature of superincumbent substances is light and rare and imperceptible, He called this firmament, in comparison with those very light substances which are incapable of perception by the senses. Now, imagine some place which tends to separate the moisture, and lets the rare and filtered part pass through into the higher regions, but lets the coarse and earthy part drop below, so that, by the gradual reduction

---

25 According to Aristotle the Aegon and Nyses rivers are in Libya, flowing from the Aethiopian Mountains into the sea. Cf. *Meteorology* 1.13.350b: 'So, too, in Libya there flow from the Aethiopian mountains the Aegon and the Nyses.'
26 Senegal.
27 St. Basil seems to have taken this whole enumeration of rivers directly from Aristotle, *Meteorology* 1.13.350a and b.
28 Isa. 44.27.
29 Cf. 1 Cor. 1.20: 'Has not God turned to foolishness the "wisdom" of this world?'
30 Gen. 1.6.

of the liquids, from the beginning to the end the same mild temperature may be preserved. You do not believe in the vast amount of water, but you do not consider the great quantity of the heat, which, even if it is insignificant in magnitude, is able, because of its power, to consume much moisture. It attracts the moisture lying near it, as the gourd clearly shows, and then consumes what it has attracted, like the flame of a lamp, which, drawing the available fuel through its wick, by a quick transition, burns it to ashes. Who doubts that the ether is firelike and exceedingly hot? And if it is not restrained within limits appointed by its Creator, what would prevent it from setting on fire and burning up everything near it and consuming at the same time all the moisture in what exists? For this reason there is aerial water, when the upper region is clouded over by the rising vapors, which the rivers and fountains and pools and marshes and all the seas send forth, to prevent the ether from seizing upon and burning up the universe. Indeed, we see this sun in the season of summer frequently leaving a wet and pool-covered land entirely dry and without moisture in a very brief moment of time. Where, then, is that water? Let the all-clever ones show us. Is it not evident to all that it was evaporated and consumed by the heat of the sun? And yet, they say that the sun is not hot; such is the result of speaking to them. Now, consider on what sort of proof they lean to resist the evidence. Since it is white in color, they say, and not reddish nor yellow, therefore, it is not fiery in nature; moreover, they also say that its heat results from its rapid whirling around.[31] What gain are they providing for themselves from that statement? That the sun seems to consume none of the moistures? But I, even though what is said is not true, nevertheless, do not reject it, because it assists me in establishing

---

[31] Cf. Aristotle, *op. cit.* 1.3.341a: 'Now the sun's motion alone is sufficent to account for the origin of terrestrial warmth and heat. . . . Besides, the sun, which most of all the stars is considered to be hot, is really white and not fiery in color.'

the explanation. The statement was made that, because of the loss due to the heat, the vast amount of waters was necessary. But, it makes no difference in producing the same condition in the same materials whether the heat is due to its nature or whether the heat results from its action. If, in fact, pieces of wood rubbed against each other enkindle a flaming fire, or if they are burnt up by a flame that has been enkindled, the result is exactly the same in both cases. And yet, we see the great wisdom of the universal Ruler, which changes the sun from one side to the other, in order that it may not ruin the orderly arrangement with its excessive heat by remaining always in the same place. Now He leads it to the southern part about the time of the winter solstice, now transfers it to the sign of the equinox, and from there brings it back to the northern parts during the summer solstice, so that by its gradual shifting a good temperature is preserved in the regions around the earth.

Let those consider whether they are not caught in their own snare, who say that the sea is not in flood from the rivers because the sun consumes the water, and besides, is left briny and bitter when the fine and drinkable part has been consumed by the heat, a thing which happens especially because of the sun's power of separating, which carries off what is light but leaves what is coarse and earthy, such as mud and sediment. And because of this there is present in the sea bitterness and brine and the power of drying up. They, who actually say this about the sea, again changing about, assert that there is no dimunition of moisture due to the sun.

(8) 'And God called the firmament Heaven.'[32] Although the name 'heavens' refers to the former, yet, in accordance with its likeness, this firmament also shares its name. We have observed in many places that the visible region is called the heavens due to the density and continuity of the air which

---

32 Gen. 1.8.

clearly comes within our vision and which has a claim to the name of heaven from the word 'seen,'[33] namely, where the Scripture says: 'The birds of the heavens,'[34] and again, 'the flying creatures below the firmament of the heavens.'[35] Such also is the following: 'They mount up to the heavens.'[36] And Moses, blessing the tribe of Joseph, bestows his benedictions 'from the fruits of the heavens and from the dew, from the solstices of the sun and the conjunctions of the moons, and from the tops of the mountains and of the everlasting hills,'[37] inasmuch as the region about the earth was flourishing because of the good condition in these. Even in the maledictions upon Israel he says: 'Be the heaven, that is over thee, of brass.'[38] What does this mean? Absolute dryness and lack of aerial waters through which the earth produces its fruits.

When, therefore, Scripture says that the dew and the rain are brought from the heavens, we understand that they are from the waters which are appointed to occupy the region above. For, after the vapors are gathered about the higher region and the air is condensed by the pressure of the winds, whenever the particles of moisture, for a time scattered mistily and tenuously in the cloud, approach each other, they become drops which are carried downward by the weight of the combined particles; and this is the origin of rain. But, when the moisture, beaten by the violence of the winds, is reduced to foam, and afterwards the whole mass, chilled excessively, is frozen together, the cloud is shattered and comes down as

---

33 A wrong etymology. Acc. to Arist. *Mu.* 400a.7, from oros and ano; acc. to Plato, *Cra.* 396c, from oran and ano; but true etymology is doubtful, cf. Liddell and Scott.
34 Ps. 8.9 (Septuagint version).
35 Gen 1.20 (Septuagint version).
36 Ps. 106.26.
37 Cf. Deut. 33.13-15 (Septuagint version).
38 Deut. 28.23.

HOMILY 3                                      51

snow.³⁹ In short, by the same reasoning you can see that every form of moisture exists in the air above our heads.

And let no one compare the simplicity and lack of artifice of spiritual discourse with the futile questioning of philosophers about the heavens. For, as the beauty in chaste women is far preferable to that of the prostitute, so is the excellence of our discourses above that of the heathens. They introduce in their explanations a forced persuasiveness; here the truth is set forth bare of artifices. But why trouble ourselves to refute their falsehood, since it suffices for us to set out their books in opposition to each other and sit in all silence as spectators of their war? Not less in number, nor inferior in dignity, but even far superior in variety of speech, they oppose the reasoning which is contrary to theirs, and they say that the universe is being utterly consumed and again comes to life from the seminal principles which remain in what has been completely burnt up. From this assertion, also, they introduce infinite destructions and regenerations of the world.⁴⁰ But, these men, severed from the truth on both sides, find for themselves, on this side and on that, bypaths toward error.

(9) We have also some argument concerning the division of the waters with those writers of the Church who, on a pretext of the spiritual sense and of more sublime concepts, have recourse to allegories, saying that spiritual and incorpo-

---

39 Cf. Aristotle, *op. cit.* 1.11.347a and b: 'So moisture is always raised by the heat and descends to the earth again when it gets cold. . . . There fall three bodies condensed by cold, namely rain, snow, hail. Rain is due to the cooling of a great amount of vapour, for the region from which and the time during which the vapour is collected are considerable. . . When cloud freezes there is snow, when vapour freezes there is hoar-frost. Hence snow is a sign of a cold season or country.'
40 Cf. Cicero, *op. cit.* 2.46: 'Hence we Stoics conclude—which Paenitius is said to have doubted of—that the whole world at last would be consumed by a general conflagration, when, all moisture being exhausted, neither the earth could have any nourishment, nor the air return again, since water, of which it is formed, would then be all consumed, so that only fire would subsist; and from this fire, which is an animating power and a Deity, a new world would arise and be re-established in the same beauty.'

real powers are signified figuratively by the waters, that the more excellent have remained up above the firmament, but the malignant remain below in the terrestrial and material regions. For this reason, they say, the waters above the heavens praise God; that is, the good powers, being worthy because of the purity of their reasoning, pay to the Creator becoming praise. But, the waters under the heavens are the spirits of malice, which have fallen down from their natural height to the depth of wickedness. Inasmuch as these are tumultuous and factious and agitated by the uproar of the passions, they are named 'sea' from the instability and inconstancy of their voluntary movements. Dismissing such explanations as dream interpretations and old women's tales, let us consider water as water, and let us receive the separation that was made beneath the firmament according to the reason given us.

And, even if the waters above the heavens are sometimes invited to praise the common Master of the universe, yet we do not for this reason consider them to be an intellectual nature. The heavens are not endowed with life because they 'show forth the glory of God,'[41] nor is the firmament a perceptive being because it 'declareth the work of his hands.' And, if someone says that the heavens are speculative powers, and the firmament, active powers productive of the good, we accept the expression as neatly said, but we will not concede that it is altogether true. For, in that case, dew, hoarfrost, cold, and heat, since they were ordered by Daniel[42] to praise in hymns the Creator of the universe, will be intelligent and invisible natures. The meaning in these words, however, accepted by speculative minds, is a fulfillment of the praise of the Creator. Not only the water which is above the heavens, as if holding the first place in honor because of the pre-eminence added to it from its excellence, fulfills the praise of God, but, 'Praise

---
41 Ps. 18.2.
42 Cf. Dan. 3.64-70.

him,' the psalmist says, 'from the earth, ye dragons, and all ye deeps.'[43] So that even the deep, which those who speak allegories relegated to the inferior portion, was not itself judged deserving of rejection by the psalmist, since it was admitted to the general chorus of creation; but even it harmoniously sings a hymn of praise to the Creator through the language assigned to it.

(10) 'And God saw that it was good.'[44] It is not to the eyes of God that things made by Him afford pleasure, nor is His approbation of beautiful objects such as it is with us; but, beauty is that which is brought to perfection according to the principle of art and which contributes to the usefulness of its end. He, therefore, who proposed to Himself a clear aim for His works, having recourse to His own artistic principles, approved them individually as fulfilling His aim. In fact, a hand by itself or an eye alone or any of the members of a statue, lying about separately, would not appear beautiful to one chancing upon them; but, set in their proper place, they exhibit beauty of relationship, scarcely evident formerly, but now easily recognized by the uncultured man. Yet, the artist, even before the combination of the parts knows the beauty of each and approves them individually, directing his judgment to the final aim. God is described on the present occasion as such an artistic Commender of each of His works, but He will render becoming praise also to the whole completed world.

Let our explanations concerning the second day, however, be brought to a close here, so as to afford time to our industrious hearers for a review of what they have heard. Thus, if there is anything useful in it, they may keep it in their memory, and by their diligent rehearsal, as if by a sort of ripening, they may expect an assimilation of the benefits. Thus also, it may give to those busy about their livelihood opportunity to dispose of their business in the intervening

---

43 Ps. 148.7.
44 Gen. 1.8 (Septuagint version).

time, so that they may present themselves for the evening banquet of words with a soul free from anxieties. May God, who created such mighty things and ordained that these petty words be spoken, grant to you an understanding of His truth in its entirety, in order that from visible objects you may comprehend the invisible Being, and from the greatness and beauty of creatures you may conceive the proper idea concerning our Creator. 'For since the creation of the world his invisible attributes are clearly seen—his everlasting power also and divinity.'[45] Therefore, in the earth, in the air, and in the heavens, in water, in night and in day, and in all things visible, clear reminders of the Benefactor grip us. We shall not give any opportunity for sins, nor shall we leave any place in our hearts for the enemy, if we have God as a dweller in us by our constant remembrance of Him, to whom be all glory and adoration, now and always, and for all ages of ages.

---

45 Rom. 1.20

# HOMILY 4

## The Gathering of the Waters

(ON THE HEXAEMERON)

THERE ARE SOME COMMUNITIES that feast their eyes on the manifold spectacles of conjurors from the dim morning twilight until evening itself. Nevertheless, they never have their fill of listening to soft and dissolute melodies, which undoubtedly engender in souls great impurity. Many even pronounce such people happy, because, leaving behind their business in the market or their plans for a livelihood from the arts, they pass the time of life allotted to them in all laziness and pleasure. They do not know that a theatre, flourishing with impure sights, is a common and public school of licentiousness for those who sit there, and that the elaborate melodies of the flutes and the lewd songs, sinking into the souls of the listeners, do nothing else than move them all to unseemly behavior, as they imitate the notes of the lyre or flute players. For instance, some of those who are mad with love of horses, wrangle over their horses in their sleep, unyoking the chariots and transferring the drivers, and they do not at all leave off their daytime folly even in their dreams. And we, whom the Lord, the great Wonder-worker and Craftsman, has called together for a manifestation of His works, shall we become weary in contemplating or reluctant to hear the eloquence of the Spirit? Rather, shall we not, standing around this vast and varied workshop of the divine creation, and going back in thought, each one, to the times past, contemplate the orderly arrangement of the whole? The heavens standing, according to the word of prophecy, like a vaulted chamber;[1] the earth, limitless in magnitude and weight, established upon itself; the diffused air, soft and fluid by nature, providing the proper and uninterrupted sustenance to all creatures that breathe, but yielding and parting around bodies in motion because of its softness, so that it presents no obstacle to moving bodies, since it always easily replaces itself, flowing around to the rear of the objects which cleave it, finally, the element of water, both that which sustains us and is provided for our other needs, and also that orderly gathering of it into the appointed places; all this you will clearly see from the words we have just read.

(2) 'Then God said, "Let the waters below the heavens be gathered into one place and let the dry land appear." And so it was, and the waters below the heavens were gathered into their places, and the dry land appeared. And God called the dry land Earth and the assembled waters Seas.'[2] How much trouble you caused me in my previous lectures, demanding the reason for the invisibility of the earth, since color is naturally present in every body, and every color is perceptible to the sense of sight! Perhaps, my words did not seem to you to be sufficient, namely that the word 'invisible' was used in reference not to its nature, but to us, because it was concealed by the water which at that time covered the entire earth. Behold! hear now the Scripture explaining itself. 'Let the waters be gathered and the dry land appear.' The covering was drawn aside in order that the hitherto invisible might become visible. Someone may, perhaps, ask this also. First, why does the Scripture reduce to a command of the Creator that tendency to flow downward which belongs naturally to water? Because, as long as the water happens to be lying on a level surface, it is stable, since it has no place to flow; but, when it finds some

---

1 Cf. Isa. 40.22 (Septuagint version).
2 Gen. 1.9, 10.

incline, immediately, as the forward part starts, that portion in contact with it, when it has moved, takes over its position and the water which follows takes over the latter's position. Thus, the front is always swiftly flowing onward and the oncoming mass pressing forward; the motion, too, becomes so much more rapid in proportion to the weight of the downward moving water and the depression of the place to which it is flowing. If, then, water has this tendency by nature, the command ordering the waters to be gathered together into one place would be superfluous. It was destined, at any rate, because of its natural downward tendency to spread itself over the most hollow part of the earth and not to be brought to a stop until its surface was level. Now, there is no place as flat as the surface of water. Then, how, someone says, were the waters ordered to gather together into one place, since there appear to be many seas, situated very far from each other? To the first of the inquiries we say this, that you recognized very well the movements of the water after the command of the Lord, both that it is unsteady and unstable and that it is borne naturally down slopes and into hollows; but, how it had any power previous to that, before the motion was engendered in it from this command, you yourself neither know nor have you heard it from one who knew. Reflect that the voice of God makes nature, and the command given at that time to creation provided the future course of action for the creatures. Day and night were created once for all, and from that time even to the present moment they have not ceased succeeding each other and dividing the time into equal parts.

(3) 'Let the waters be gathered.' The element of water was ordered to flow, and it never grows weary when urged on unceasingly by this command. This I say, having in view only the flowing property of the waters. For, some flow of their own accord, as the springs and the rivulets, but others are collected from diverse places and are stationary. At present, however, my discourse is about the moving waters. 'Let the

waters be gathered into one place.' Did the thought ever come to you as you stood beside a stream yielding plentiful water, who is He who causes this water to gush from the fissures of the earth? Who is forcing it onward? What kind of reservoirs are there from which it comes forth? To what place is it hastening? How is it that these waters are never lacking, and those do not fill up? All these things depend upon that first word. It was the signal for the waters to flow.

Through all the story of waters be mindful of that first word, 'Let the waters be gathered.' It was necessary for them to flow that they might reach their own place; then, being in the places appointed, to remain by themselves and not to advance further. For this reason, according to the saying of Ecclesiastes, 'All the rivers run into the sea, yet the sea doth not overflow.'[3] It is through the divine command that waters flow, and it is due to that first legislation, 'Let the waters be gathered into one place,' that the sea is enclosed within boundaries. Lest the flowing water, spreading beyond the beds which hold it, always passing on and filling up one place after another, should continuously flood all the lands, it was ordered to be gathered into one place. Therefore, the sea, frequently raging with the winds and rising up in waves to towering heights, whenever it merely touches the shores, breaks its onrush into foam and retires. 'Will you not then fear me, saith the Lord? I have set the sand a bound for the sea.'[4] With the weakest of all things, sand, the sea, irresistible in its violence, is bridled. And yet, what would have hindered the Red Sea from invading the whole of Egypt, which was lower than it, and joining with the other sea adjacent to Egypt, had it not been fettered by the command of the Creator? That Egypt lies lower than the Red Sea, those have persuaded us by their action, who have wished to join the seas to each other,

---

3 Eccles. 1.7.
4 Jer. 5.22.

## HOMILY 4

the Egyptian Sea[5] and the Indian Ocean, in which is the Red Sea. Therefore, they ceased their attempt, both he who first initiated it, Sesostris the Egyptian, and he who afterwards intended to accomplish it, Darius the Median.[6]

I have told these facts in order that we may understand the force of the command, 'Let the waters be gathered into one place.' That is, let there be no other gathering apart from this, but let those once collected remain in the first gathering place.

(4) He who commanded the waters to be gathered into one place showed you, then, that there had been many waters scattered throughout many regions. For, the valleys of the mountains, intersected by deep chasms, held accumulations of water, and besides, there were many smooth plains inferior in extent to none of the vast seas, and countless channels, and deep valleys, scooped out in varied shapes, all at that time filled with water, and all were drained by the command of God, when the water was drawn together from all sides into one place. And let no one say that, if water was upon the surface of the earth, absolutely all the hollows, which now have admitted the sea, had originally been full. Indeed, where were the gatherings of waters to be, if the hollows had been filled beforehand? To this we say that the reservoirs were prepared at the time when it was necessary for the water to be separated and placed into one gathering. In fact, there was no sea beyond Gadeira,[7] nor that vast ocean, intolerable to

---
5 The Mediterranean Sea.
6 Cf. Aristotle, *Meteorology* 1.14 352b: 'The whole land of the Egyptians, whom we take to be the most ancient of men, has evidently gradually come into existence and been produced by the river. This is clear from an observation of the country, and the facts about the Red Sea suffice to prove it too. One of their kings tried to make a canal to it (for it would have been of no little advantage to them for the whole region to have become navigable; Sesostris is said to have been the first of the ancient kings to try), but he found that the sea was higher than the land. So he first, and Darius afterwards, stopped making the canal, lest the sea should mix with the river water and spoil it. So it is clear that all this part was once unbroken sea.'
7 Modern Cadiz.

sailors, which surrounds the British Isle and western Spain, but, at that moment a vast open space was made by the command of God and the great quantities of waters were contributed to it.

To the statement that our explanation of the creation of the world is contrary to experience, for all the water does not seem to have run together into one place, many answers can be given, which are immediately obvious to all. Perhaps, it is even ridiculous to argue on such points. Surely, they ought not to cite for us the waters of the marshes and those collected from thunderstorms, should they, and think that because of these they are refuting our explanation? But, He called the greatest and most complete concourse of the waters a 'gathering into one place.' In fact, the wells are gatherings of waters made by hand, since the scattered moisture flows to hollowed out parts of the earth. Consequently, the name of gathering does not indicate any chance accumulation of waters, but the outstanding and greatest one, in which all the element was displayed in one mass. Just as fire is broken up into small parts for use here, and also spreads itself in a mass in the ether, and air is distributed in small pockets and also encompasses the region near the earth in a mass, so, too, in the case of water, even if some small accumulations have been separated, yet there is one gathering which sets the whole element apart from the rest. The marshy lakes, both those in the northern parts and those that are around the regions of the Greeks, spread over Macedonia and the country of the Bithynians and that of the Palestinians, are, of course, gatherings; but at present my discourse is about the greatest of all, which is even comparable with the earth in extent. No one will deny that the former hold a great amount of water, but really, one would not reasonably apply to them the name 'seas,' not even if some have brine and soil as nearly as possible like the great sea, as the Dead Sea in Judaea and the Serbonian which extends along the Arabian desert, between Egypt and

Palestine. These are lakes, but the sea, as those who have travelled around the earth record, is one. Even if some believe that the Hyrcanian and the Caspian are enclosed within their own limits, still, if any attention must be paid to the geographers' accounts, they are connected with each other by a passage, and they open, both together, into the great Sea.[8] In the same way also, they say, the Red Sea is joined to that beyond Gadeira. How, then, someone says, did God call the accumulations of waters 'seas'? Because the waters ran together into one place, and the accumulations of the waters, that is, the gulfs, which were cut off in their own peculiar shape by the surrounding land, the Lord named seas: North Sea, South Sea, East Sea, and West Sea, which is still another. And there are names peculiar to the seas: Euxine Sea, Propontis, Hellespont, Aegaean and Ionian, Sardinian Sea and Sicilian, and the other, Tyrrhenian. In truth, there are countless names of seas, and to give an exact enumeration of them would be at present a long and foolish task. For this reason, then, God named the collections of waters seas. Now, really, the chain of our reasoning carried us on to this, but, let us return to the beginning.

(5) 'Then God said, "Let the waters be gathered into one place and let the dry land appear." '[9] He did not say: 'and let the earth appear,' in order that He might not show it again incomplete, muddy and mixed with water, and not yet invested with its proper form and power. At the same time, lest we attribute to the sun the cause of the drying of the earth, the Creator contrived the drying of the earth before the generation of the sun. Give your attention to the meaning of the Scripture, that not only the excess water flowed away from the

---

[8] The western part of the present Caspian Sea was called the Caspian and the eastern part the Hyrcanian. Although Aristotle, *Meteorology* 2.1.354a, says that the Hyrcanian and Caspian seas are distinct from the ocean and people dwell all around them, both Pliny and Strabo believed that it was connected with the Northern Ocean. Cf. Smith, *Dict. of Greek and Roman Geography*.
[9] Gen. 1.9

earth, but also whatever was mixed with it throughout its depths, obedient to the inexorable command of the Lord, also withdrew.

'And so it was.'[10] This introduction is sufficient to show that the voice of the Creator passed into action. But, in many of the copies there is added, 'And the waters below the heavens were gathered into their places, and the dry land appeared,' words which, indeed, some of the rest of the interpreters have not given, and which the usage of the Hebrews does not appear to retain. Actually, after the testimony that 'So it was,' the additional statement of the same things again is superfluous. Therefore, the more accurate copies are marked with an obelus; and the obelus is a symbol of rejection.

'And God called the dry land Earth, and the assembled waters Seas.'[11] Why, also, in the previous words was the statement made, 'Let the waters be gathered into one place, and let the dry land appear,' and it was not written, 'and let the earth appear'? And then again, 'The dry land appeared, and God called the dry land Earth'? Because dryness is the specific property, the characteristic, as it were, of the nature of the substance, but earth is a mere name of the body. In fact, just as reason is characteristic of man, but the word 'man' is indicative of the creature to which the characteristic belongs, so also dryness is characteristic of the earth and is peculiar to it. Therefore, that to which dryness properly belongs is called earth, just as the animal to which the faculty of neighing naturally belongs is called a horse. Not only in the case of the earth is this so, but each of the other elements has an individualizing quality allotted to it through which it is distinguished from the others and through which the nature of each is recognized. Water has as its peculiar quality, coldness; air, humidity; and fire, heat.

These elements, however, in accordance with reason are

---
10 *Ibid.*
11 *Ibid.* 1.10.

considered, in the manner already mentioned, as the primitive elements of compound matter; but those already incorporated in a body and subject to perception have the qualities closely united, and none of the visible and perceptible objects is absolutely unique and simple and pure. The earth is dry and cold, the water is cold and moist, the air is moist and warm, and fire is warm and dry. Thus, through their combining qualities each receives the faculty of mixing with the other; and, in fact, each through a common quality mixes with its neighboring element, and through the union with that which is near, it combines with its opposite. For example, earth, which is both dry and cold, is united with air, since water, placed between the two, as if grasping with two hands, lays hold of the elements lying nearby with each of its qualities, to the coldness of earth and to the humidity of air. Again, air in the middle position becomes mediator between the contending natures of water and fire, being joined with water by humidity and with fire by heat. And fire, being warm and dry in nature, closely combines with air by its warmth and, again, by its dryness returns to fellowship with the earth. Thus it becomes a circle and a harmonious choir, since all are in unison and have mutually corresponding elements. Therefore, the name of elements is properly applicable to them. I have said these things in presenting the reason for which God called the dry land earth, yet did not call the earth dry land. It is because dryness is not of the qualities later accruing to the earth, but of those making up its complete substance from the beginning. The things which provide a cause of existence are earlier by nature than those added afterwards and are more excellent. Therefore, reasonably the characteristics from the previous and older qualities were noted for designating the earth.

(6) 'And God saw that it was good.'[12] The Scripture does not point out exactly this, that a certain delightful vision of the sea presented itself to God. For, the Creator of all creation

---
12 *Ibid.*

does not look at beauty with eyes, but He contemplates in His ineffable wisdom the things made. A pleasant sight, indeed, is a whitened sea, when settled calm possesses it; and pleasant also when, ruffled on the surface by gentle breezes, it reflects a purple or bluish color to the spectators, when it does not beat violently the neighboring land, but, as it were, kisses it with peaceful embraces. Surely, we must not think that the meaning of the Scripture is that the sea appeared good and pleasant to God in this way, but here the goodness is determined by the purpose of the creative activity.

In the first place, the water of the sea is the source of all the moisture of the earth. This water passing through unseen minute openings, as is proved by the spongy and cavernous parts of the mainland into which the swift sea flows in narrow channels, is received in the curved and sinuous paths and hurried on by the wind which sets it in motion. Then, it breaks through the surface and is carried outside; and, having eliminated its bitterness by percolation, it becomes drinkable. If it has already taken in a warmer quality from metals in its passage, because of its motion it generally begins to seethe and becomes fiery hot. This can be observed in many places on the islands and on the seashores. Even in places inland some regions neighboring on the river waters—to compare small things with great—experience very nearly the same things. Now, for what purpose have I said this? To show that all the earth is full of underground passages and through unseen openings the water sinks down from the sources of the sea.

Consequently, the sea is good in God's sight because of the permeation of its moisture into the depths of the earth; and it is good because, being the receptacle of rivers, it receives the streams from all sides into itself but remains within its own limits. It is good also because it is a certain origin and source for aerial waters. Warmed by the rays of the sun, it gives forth through vapors a refined form of water, which, drawn to the upper regions, then chilled because it is higher than the reflection of the sun's rays from the ground and also because the shadow from the cloud increases the cooling, becomes rain and enriches the earth. And no one, I am sure, mistrusts these statements, who has noticed kettles being heated by a fire, which, although full of liquid, are frequently left empty when all is boiled and changed into vapor. Moreover, it is possible to see the water of the sea boiled by sailors, who, catching the vapors in sponges, relieve their thirst fairly well in times of need.

And it is good before God, above all, because it encircles the islands, providing them with both ornamentation and safety. Then, too, it joins together through itself mainlands far distant from each other, affording unhindered intercourse to sailors, through whom it bestows also a knowledge of things unknown; it becomes a patron of wealth to merchants, and it easily supplies the needs of life, providing for the exportation of superfluous articles by the prosperous and granting to the needy the remedy for their wants.

And why is it possible for me to see with minuteness all the beauty of the sea as it appeared to the eye of the Creator? If the sea is good and an object of praise to God, surely, the gathering of such a Church as this is more beautiful, from which there is sent out in our prayers to God the mingled voice of men and women and children, as of some wave beating upon the shore. A deep calm preserves it unshaken, since the spirits of evil are not able to disturb it with heretical teachings. May you be worthy of the approval of the Lord, preserving this goodly condition most becomingly, in Christ Jesus our Lord, to whom be glory and power forever. Amen.

# HOMILY 5

## *The Germination of the Earth*

### (ON THE HEXAEMERON)

WHEN GOD SAID, 'Let the earth bring forth vegetation: the plant producing seed of its own kind, and the fruit tree that bears fruit containing seed of its own kind.'[1] Consequently, after the earth, rid of the weight of the water, had rested, the command had come to it to bring forth first the herb, then the trees. And this we see still happening even at the present time. For, the voice which was then heard and that first command became, as it were, a law of nature and remained in the earth, giving it the power to produce and bear fruit for all succeeding time. 'Let the earth bring forth.' First in the generation of growing plants is the germination; then, when the shoots have emerged a little, it becomes a seedling; after it has grown, it is a grass, while little by little the growing plants are articulated and continue even to maturity with seed. The characteristic of being green and producing stalks is practically the same in the case of all plants. 'Let the earth bring forth vegetation.'

Let the earth bud forth by itself, needing no assistance from the outside. Since some think that the sun, drawing the productive power from the center of the earth to the surface with its rays of heat, is the cause of the plants growing from the earth, it is for this reason that the adornment of the earth is older than the sun, that those who have been misled may cease worshiping the sun as the origin of life. If they are

---

[1] Gen. 1.11.

persuaded that before the sun's generation all the earth had been adorned, they will retract their unbounded admiration for it, realizing that the sun is later than the grass and plants in generation.

Was food, then, prepared for the cattle beforehand, while our race appeared deserving of no forethought? Well, most certainly, He who prepared pasturage for the cattle and horses provided wealth and pleasure for you. In fact, He who sustains your flocks increases your assets of life. And what else is the production of seeds except a preparation for your subsistence. Moreover, many of the plants which still exist among grasses and vegetables really are the food of men.

(2) 'Let the earth bring forth vegetation: the plant producing seed,' He says, 'of its own kind.' Therefore, even if some kind of plant is useful for the other living creatures, not only the profit they receive passes over to us, but the use of the seeds also is allotted us. Consequently, this is the meaning of the words: 'Let the earth bring forth vegetation and the plant producing seed of its own kind.' The order of the words can be restored in this way, since the arrangement now seems to be unsuitable; and the appointed order of the dispensations of nature will be preserved. For, in the first place there is germination, then a green shoot, then a growth of grass, and then, when the plants are full grown, perfection in seed.

How is it, then, they say, that Scripture declares that all plants produced from the earth are seed-bearing, whereas neither the reed, nor dog's-tooth grass, nor mint, nor crocus, nor garlic, nor sedge, nor countless other kinds of plants seem to produce seed? To this we answer that many of the plants growing from the earth have the productive power of seeds in their stem and in their root.[2] For example, the reed, after

---

2 Cf. Theophrastus, *Enquiry into Plants* 2.2.1: 'The ways in which trees and plants in general originate are these:—spontaneous growth, growth from seed, from a root, from a piece torn off, from a branch or twig, from the trunk itself; or again, from small pieces into which the wood is cut up.'

the yearly growth, sends out from its root a certain shoot which contains the principle of seed for the future plant. Countless other plants also do this. These, spread all over the earth, possess in their roots their potential successors. Therefore, there is nothing truer than this, that each plant either has seed or there exists in it some generative power. And this accounts for the expression 'of its own kind.' For, the shoot of the reed is not productive of an olive tree, but from the reed comes another reed; and from seeds spring plants related to the seeds sown. Thus, what was put forth by the earth in its first generation has been preserved until the present time, since the species persisted through constant reproduction.

'Let the earth bring forth.' Reflect, I beg you, that in consequence of this short word and a command so brief, the earth, chilled and barren, was incessantly in travail and stirred up to productiveness, as if it had thrown aside some dark and dismal covering, had put on a more brilliant one, and, glorying in its own adornment, was presenting an infinite variety of growing plants.

I want the marvel of creation to gain such complete acceptance from you that, wherever you may be found and whatever kind of plants you may chance upon, you may receive a clear reminder of the Creator. First, then, whenever you see a grassy plant or a flower, think of human nature, remembering the comparison of the wise Isaia, that 'All flesh is as grass, and all the glory of man as the flower of the grass.'[3] For, the short span of life and the briefly-enduring pleasure and joy of human happiness have found a most apt comparison in the words of the prophet. Today he is vigorous in body, grown fleshy from delicacies, with a flowerlike complexion, in the prime of life, fresh and eager, and irresistible in attack; tomorrow that same one is piteous or wasted with age, or weakened by disease. This one is admired by all for his excessive wealth, and around him is a multitude of flatterers; a bodyguard of

---

3 Isa. 40.6.

false friends seeking his favor; a great number of kinsmen, and these, kinsmen only by pretense; a countless swarm of attendants, not only to provide for his food, but also for his other needs. With these trailing after him whenever he goes out or returns, he becomes an object of envy to those whom he meets. Add to his wealth some political power also, or even honors from kings, or the government of people, or the command of armies, a herald crying out loudly before him, lictors on this side and on that throwing his subjects into the deepest consternation with blows, confiscations, exiles, imprisonments, by which means intolerable fear is increased among his subjects. And what after this? One night either a fever or pleurisy or pneumonia comes, snatches up the man from among men and leads him away, suddenly stripping bare all the stage about him; and his former glory is proved a mere dream. Therefore, the prophet compared human glory to the frailest flower.

(3) 'Let the earth bring forth vegetation: the plant producing seed of its own kind and likeness.'[4] Even to the present day, the order in plants testifies to the first orderly arrangement. For, germination is the beginning of every herb and every plant. If something is produced from the root, coming out of the protuberance below, like the crocus or dog's-tooth grass, it must germinate and emerge; or, if it is produced from seed, even so it is necessary that there be first germination, then a seedling, then green foliage, and finally the fruit swelling on the stalk, which up to this time was dry and thick. 'Let the earth bring forth vegetation.' Whenever the seed falls on ground which contains moisture and heat in moderation, becoming spongy and very porous, it grasps the surrounding soil and draws to itself all that is proper and suitable for it. The very light particles of earth falling in and slipping around it in the pores expand its bulk even more, so that it sends roots downward and also thrusts shoots upward, producing stalks

---

4 Gen. 1.11 (Septuagint version).

equal in number to the roots; and, since the shoot is always being warmed, moisture, drawn through the roots by the attraction of the heat, brings from the earth the proper amount of nourishment, and distributes this to the stalk and the bark, to the husks and the grain itself, as well as to the beards. Thus, as the gradual increase continues, each of the plants reaches its natural proportions, whether it happens to be one of the grains or legumes or vegetables or shrubs. One grass, even one blade of grass is sufficient to occupy all your intelligence completely in the consideration of the art which produced it—how it is that the stalk of wheat is encircled with nodes, so that they, like some bonds, may bear easily the weight of the ears, when, full of fruit, they bend down to the earth. For this very reason, the oat stalk is completely devoid of these, inasmuch as its head is not made heavy by any weight. But, nature has strengthened the wheat with these bonds, placing the grain in a sheath so as not to be easily snatched by grain-picking birds; and besides, it keeps off any harm from small insects by the projecting barrier of the needlelike beards.

(4) What shall I say? What shall I pass over in silence? In the rich treasure of creation the finding of what is most precious is difficult, yet, if it is omitted, the loss is very hard to bear. 'Let the earth bring forth vegetation.' And immediately with the nutritive are produced the poisonous; with the grain, the hemlock; with the other edible plants, the hellebore and leopard's bane and mandrake and poppy juice. What, then? Shall we neglect to acknowledge our gratitude for the useful plants and blame our Creator for those destructive of our life? Shall we not consider this, that not everything has been created for our stomach? But, the nourishing plants, especially assigned to us, are readily accessible and familiar to all; and each plant produced realizes a certain peculiar reason in its creation. Just because the blood of the bull is poison for you, should the animal, therefore, whose strength we need for so many things in life, not have been produced or, if pro-

duced, be bloodless? On the contrary, you have sufficient sense of your own to guard against destructive things. Is it possible, tell me, that the sheep and goats know how to escape what is hurtful to their existence, although they discern the harmful by sense perception alone, yet you, who possess reason as well as the medical art, to provide what is useful, and the experience of predecessors to warn you to shun injurious objects, find it hard to avoid the poisons? There is not one plant without worth, not one without use. Either it provides food for some animal, or it has been sought out for us by the medical profession for the relief of certain diseases. In fact, starlings eat hemlock, escaping harm from the poison because of the constitution of their bodies. Since they have very tiny passageways in the heart, they digest the poison swallowed before its chilling effect has seized upon the vital organs. Hellebore is food for quails, who escape harm because of their peculiar constitution. These same plants are sometimes useful to us also. For instance, with mandrake doctors induce sleep[5] and with opium they lull violent pains of the body. Some also have already dulled even their mad appetites with hemlock, and with hellebore have banished many of the long continued sufferings.[6] So, the charge which you thought you had against the Creator has proved to be for you an additional cause for thankfulness.

(5) 'Let the earth bring forth vegetation.'[7] How much spontaneous provision does He embrace in these words—in

---

5 Cf. Lucian, *Timon* 2. 'And why not, when you lie asleep as if you were drugged with mandrake?' Cf. also Xenophon, *Symposium* 2.24: 'Wine does of a truth moisten the soul and lull our griefs to sleep just as the mandrake does with men.'
6 Cf. Hippocrates, *Aphorisms* 4.13-16: 'Persons who are not easily purged upward by the hellebores, should have their bodies moistened by plenty of food and rest before taking the draught. When one takes a draught of hellebore, one should be made to move about, and indulge less in sleep and repose.... When you wish the hellebore to act more, move the body, and when to stop, let the patient get sleep and rest. Hellebore is dangerous to persons whose flesh is sound, for it induces convulsions.'
7 Gen. 1.11.

the roots, in the foliage, and in the fruits as well! And how much more is added by us through care and farming! God did not order the earth to yield immediately seed and fruit, but to germinate and to grow green, and then to reach maturity with seed, so that this first command might be nature's lesson for the order to be followed thereafter. How, then, they say, does the earth bring forth seeds of the particular kind, when, after sowing grain, we frequently gather this black wheat? This is not a change to another kind, but, as it were, some disease and defect of the seed. It has not ceased to be wheat, but has been made black by burning, as it is possible to learn from the name itself.[8] For, since it was burnt up by the extreme cold,[9] it has changed to another color and taste. Yet, again, it is also said that, whenever it obtains suitable ground and mild weather, it returns to its original form. Therefore, you would find that nothing contrary to the command takes place among growing plants. The so-called darnel and whatever other bastard seeds are mixed in with the nutritious, which it is customary for Scripture to call tares, are not produced from a change of the grain, but have existence from their own origin, being a distinct kind. These plants may be compared with those who pervert the teachings of the Lord and who, not being truly instructed in the Scripture but corrupted by the teaching of the evil one, join themselves to the sound body of the Church in order that they may secretly inflict their harm on the more guileless. Now, the Lord compares the perfection of those who have believed in Him to the increase of the seeds, when He says: 'As though a man should cast seed into the earth, then sleep and rise, night and day, and the seed should sprout and grow without his knowing it. For, of itself the earth bears the crop, first the blade, then the

---

8 A wrong etymology. Liddell and Scott compare it with the Lithuanian pūrai, 'wheat.'
9 Cf. Aristotle, *Meteorology* 4.5.382b: 'Cold is sometimes actually said to burn and to warm, but not in the same way as heat does, but by collecting and concentrating heat.' Cf. also Vergil, *Georgics* 1.93.

ear, then the full grain in the ear.'¹⁰ 'Let the earth bring forth herbs.' And in the briefest moment of time the earth, beginning with germination in order that it might keep the laws of the Creator, passing through every form of increase, immediately brought the shoots to perfection. The meadows were deep with the abundant grass; the fertile plains, rippling with standing crops, presented the picture of a swelling sea with its moving heads of grain. And every herb and every kind of vegetable and whatever shrubs and legumes there were, rose from the earth at that time in all profusion. There was no failure among the plants brought forth then, since neither the inexperience of farmers nor the inclemency of the weather nor any other circumstance caused damage to what was produced. Nor did the sentence of condemnation interfere with the fertility of the earth. In fact, these things were earlier than the sin for which we were condemned to eat our bread in the sweat of our brow.[11]

(6) 'And the fruit tree,' He said, 'that bears fruit containing seed of its own kind and of its own likeness on the earth.'[12] At this saying all the dense woods appeared; all the trees shot up, those which are wont to rise to the greatest height, the firs, cedars, cypresses, and pines; likewise, all the shrubs were immediately thick with leaf and bushy; and the so-called garland plants—the rose bushes, myrtles, and laurels—all came into existence in a moment of time, although they were not previously upon the earth, each one with its own peculiar nature, separated from other varieties by most evident differences, and each one known by its own character. Only at that time the rose bush was without thorns;[13] later, the thorn was added

---

10 Mark 4.26-28.
11 Cf. Gen. 3.19: 'In the sweat of your brow you shall eat bread.'
12 Gen. 1.11 (Septuagint version).
13 The Benedictine editors call attention to the fact that St. Ambrose in lib. 3 *in Hexaem.* cap. 11, and St. Augustine in lib. 1 *de Genesi contra Manichaeos* cap. 13 agree with St. Basil that the rose at first had no thorns. However, in lib. 3 *de Genesi ad litteram* cap. 18 St. Augustine has changed his opinion.

to the beauty of the flower so that we might keep pain closely associated with the enjoyment of pleasure and remind ourselves of the sin for which the earth was condemned to bring forth thorns and thistles for us.[14] But, some one may say, the earth was ordered to yield 'the fruit tree that bears fruit containing its own seed upon earth,' yet, we see that many of the trees have neither fruit nor seed. What, then, shall we say? That the more important trees in nature have obtained the first mention; then, if we consider the matter carefully, that all trees will be seen either to have seed or to possess qualities equivalent to seeds. For instance, black poplars, willows, elms, white poplars, and all such trees, seem at sight to bear no fruit, but one would find on examing them carefully that each one has seed. The protuberance which lies below the leaf and which some of those who devote themselves to the inventing of names call 'mischos' has the productive power of seed. For, from it trees which are wont to reproduce by their branches generally send forth their roots. Perhaps, also, the saplings growing from the roots, which the gardeners tear off to increase the species, contain the principle of seed.

First, however, as we have said, the trees more essential to our life deserved mention, trees such as were to provide plentiful food for man by offering him their particular fruits, the grapevine which produces wine to rejoice the heart of man, the olive tree which provides fruit that is able to brighten his face with its oil. How many things produced by nature are combined in one plant! The root of the grapevine, the large thriving branches which hang down from all sides above the earth, the bud, the tendrils, the sour grapes, the bunches of ripe grapes! The vine, intelligently observed by your eyes, is sufficient to remind you of nature. You remember, of course, the parable of the Lord, when He proclaims Himself the vine and His Father the vine-dresser, and calls each one of us,

---

14 Cf. Gen. 3.18· 'Thorns and thistles shall it bring forth to you.'

engrafted by faith on the Church, the branches.[15] Moreover, He invites us to produce much fruit lest, convicted of sterility, we be delivered up to the fire; and He constantly compares the souls of men to vines. 'My beloved had a vineyard' He says, 'on a hill in a fruitful place.'[16] And, 'I planted a vineyard, and put a hedge about it.'[17] Evidently, He calls the human souls the vineyard, about which He has put as a hedge the security arising from His commandments and the custody of His angels. 'The angel of the Lord shall encamp round about them that fear him.'[18] And then He drove in props, as it were, for us, 'placing in the Church, first apostles, secondly prophets, thirdly teachers.'[19] And leading our thoughts upward by the examples of the blessed men of old, He did not let them fall, tossing about on the ground to be trampled upon. He wishes us also to cling to our neighbors with embraces of charity like tendrils of a vine, and to rest upon them, so that, keeping our desires always heavenward, we may, like certain climbing vines, reach the upmost heights of the loftiest teachings. He asks us also to permit ourselves to be dug about.[20] Now, our soul is 'dug about' when we put aside the cares of the world, which are a burden to our hearts. Therefore, he who has laid aside carnal love and the desire of possessions, or who has considered the violent desire for this wretched little glory detestable and contemptible, has, so to say, been 'dug about' and, freed of the vain burden of the earthy spirit, has breathed again. We must not, according to the meaning of the proverb, run to wood, that is, live our lives ostentatiously, or eagerly seek praise from those outside, but we must be fruitful, preserving for the true Farmer the proof of our works.

15 Cf John 15.1-5.
16 Isa. 5.1.
17 Cf. Matt. 21.33.
18 Ps. 33.8.
19 1 Cor. 12.28.
20 Cf. Luke 13.8: 'But he answered him and said, "Sir, let it alone this year too, till I dig around it and manure it." '

But, you also, be 'as a fruitful olive tree in the house of God,'[21] never destitute of hope, but always having about you the rich assurance of safety through faith. Thus, indeed, you will imitate the eternal verdure of this plant and emulate its fruitfulness, bestowing bounteous alms on every occasion.

(7) Let us now return to our examination of the artistic arrangements of creation. How many kinds of trees grew up at that time, some fruit-producing, others furnishing material for roofing, some suitable for shipbuilding, others for burning! Among these, again, in each tree the arrangement of its various parts differs, and it is difficult both to discover the distinctive properties of each and to recognize the variations in each of the different kinds. How is it that some of them have deep roots and others roots near the surface, and some are straight-growing and have one stem, and others low-growing and divide even from the root into many shoots? How is it that those whose long branches extend far up in the air also have deep roots, set for the most part in a large circumference, as if nature were placing foundations beneath proportionate to the weight above? How great are the differences in the barks! Some of the plants have smooth bark, others rough bark; some of them have but one layer, others many layers. But, the marvel is that you may find in plants the characteristics closely resembling those of human youth and old age. Around the young and thriving plants the bark is stretched smooth, but around the old it is as if wrinkled and rough. Some plants, when cut, sprout again; others remain sterile, as if the stump were enduring a kind of death. Certain men have already observed that, if pines are cut down or burned, they are changed into oak forests.[22] We know also that some trees are

---

21 Ps. 51.10.
22 Not an extraordinary occurrence. It is due to the presence of an undergrowth of oak with huge roots and slender tops about one or two feet in height, whose further development upward is hindered by the pines. If the pine is removed by burning or cutting, the oak proceeds to grow rapidly and in ten or fifteen years produces a transfer from a pine to an oak forest. Cf. B. C. Tharp, *Structure of Texas Vegetation* p. 39.

cured of their natural defects through the care given them by the farmers, for example, the sour pomegranate and the more bitter almond. The trunk of these trees is bored close to the root, and a rich wedge of pine is inserted in the center of the pith. This causes the bitter flavor of the juice to change to one pleasant to the taste. Let no one, therefore, who is living in vice despair of himself, knowing that, as agriculture changes the properties of plants, so the diligence of the soul in the pursuit of virtue can triumph over all sorts of infirmities.

(8) The difference in the productiveness of fruit-bearing trees is so great that one could never express it in words. Not only are there varieties of fruits in the different families, but even in the very species of the tree the variety is great, where, for instance, one type has been distinguished by the gardeners as fruit of males and another as that of females. They divide even the palms into males and females. And at times, too, one may see the so-called female among them letting down its branches, as if with passionate desire, and longing for the embrace of the male, at which the caretakers of the plants throw upon the branches a certain kind of seeds of the males, called 'psenes.' Then, as if it is consciously perceptive of fruition, it again raises its branches erect and restores the foliage of the plant to its proper form. The same is also said of the fig tree. Therefore, some plant wild figs beside the cultivated ones, while others remedy the deficiency of the productive cultivated fig trees by binding on them the fruit of the wild figs, and so retaining with the psenes of the wild figs the fruit which was already dropping off and being strewn about.[23] What does this puzzling example from nature mean to you?

---

23 Cf. Aristotle, *History of Animals* 5.32.557b: 'The fruit of the wild fig contains the psen, or fig-wasp. This creature is a grub at first; but in due time the husk peels off and the psen leaves the husk behind it and flies away, and enters into the fruit of the fig-tree through its orifice, and causes the fruit not to drop off; and with a view to this phenomenon, country folk are in the habit of tying wild figs on to fig-trees, and of planting wild fig-trees near domesticated ones.'

## HOMILY 5

That we must frequently borrow, even from those foreign to our faith, a certain vitality for a demonstration of our good works. If, indeed, you see one who lives the life of a pagan or who is cut off from the Church by some perverse heresy cultivating a chaste manner of life and other moral behavior, intensify your zeal to a greater degree, in order that you may be like the productive fig tree, which gathers strength from the presence of the wild figs, checks its shedding, and nourishes its fruit more carefully.

These, then, are differences in the manner of the generation of plants, to mention but a few from the many. But, who could ever describe in detail the diversity of the fruits themselves, their shapes, their colors, their peculiar flavors, and the use of each? How is it that some with no outer covering are ripened by the sun, and others are brought to maturity even though covered with shells? And those whose fruit is tender, like the fig, have a thick covering of foliage? And those whose fruits are more closely sheathed, like the nut, have a light screen of leaves? Because the former on account of their frailness need more protection, but, for the latter a thicker covering would be harmful because of the shade from the leaves. How is it that the leaf of the vine is serrated? In order that the bunch of grapes may both withstand injuries from the air and may receive plentifully through the openings the rays of the sun. Nothing happens without cause; nothing by chance; all things involve a certain ineffable wisdom.

What discussion can extend to all things? How can the human mind review everything with accuracy, so as to discern the peculiar properties, to distinguish clearly the differences in each, and to present unerringly the hidden causes? The same water, sucked up through the root, nourishes in different ways the root itself, the bark of the trunk, the wood, and the pith. The same water also becomes a leaf, it is distributed into boughs and branches and produces the growth of fruits; and the gum of the plant, too, and the juice come from the same source. And, how much these differ from each other, no words could fully express. The gum of the mastic is of one kind and the juice of the balsam tree of another; while the giant fennels in Egypt and Libya exude still another kind of juice. Then, there is a saying that amber is the juice of plants crystallized into a stonelike substance. The fragments of wood and very delicate little insects which remain visible in it, having been left behind when the juice was soft, confirm this saying.[24] On the whole, he who has not learned by experience the differences of the qualities of the juices will find no word to describe the active forms of water. Again, how is wine made in the vine and olive oil in the olive tree from the same moisture? Furthermore, not only is there the astonishing fact that the liquid in the one case has been sweetened and in the other made oily, but also that in the sweet fruits the difference in quality is inexpressibly varied. The sweetness in the grapevine, for instance, is of one sort, but it is of another in the apple tree, and another in the fig tree, and yet another in the date palm. Besides, I want you to employ skill in making this investigation as to how the same water is now soft to the palate when in certain plants it has been sweetened, and now it is pungent in taste when it has been made sour by passing through other plants. Again, it irritates our sense of taste by changing to extreme bitterness when it is in wormwood or scammony. In the acorns, too, or in the fruit of the dogwood it adopts an astringent and bitter quality, but in the terebinth and nut-bearing trees it is converted to a soft and oleaginous substance.

(9) Why is it necessary to say more, since even in the same fig tree the water passes from one part to another with most opposite qualities? Exceedingly bitter in the sap, it is very

---

24 Pliny, *Natural History* 37.11: 'One great proof that amber must have been originally in a liquid state is the fact that, owing to its transparency, certain objects are to be seen within, ants for example, gnats and lizards. These, no doubt, must have first adhered to it while liquid and then, upon its hardening, have remained enclosed within.'

sweet in the fruit itself. And in the case of the grapevines, it is most astringent in the branches, but very sweet in the bunches of grapes. And, how great is the variety in the colors! You might see in a meadow the same water become red in this flower, and in another, purple; dark blue in this one, and in that, white; and again, exhibit a difference in their odors greater than the variety in color. But, I see that in my insatiable desire for speculation my words are accumulating to excess, and unless I fetter and lead them back to the natural laws of creation, the day will fail me as I present to you great wisdom from most trifling things.

'Let the earth bring forth the fruit tree, that bears fruit upon the earth.' Immediately the summits of the mountains were covered with foliage; gardens were artistically laid out; and banks of rivers were made beautiful with innumerable plants. Some plants were ready to adorn man's table, others furnished food for the cattle from the leaves and from the fruits. Other plants procured for us medical aids, giving their juices, their saps, their stalks, their barks, their fruit. And, in general, whatever long experience, by collecting useful information from individual incidents, has discovered for us, this was brought into being by the keen foresight of the Creator, which from the beginning provided for us. But, may you, whenever you see cultivated plants or wild ones, water plants or land plants, flowering or flowerless, recognize grandeur in the tiniest thing, continue always in your admiration, and increase, I pray you, your love for the Creator. Ponder how He made some trees evergreens and others deciduous, and of the evergreens, how He made some which lose their leaves and others which always keep them. Olive trees and pines shed their leaves, even though they make the change imperceptibly, so that they never seem to be stripped of their foliage. But, the date palm is persistent, remaining always, from its first sprouting until its death, with the same foliage. Then, consider this, how the tamarisk is, as it were, a plant of double life, counted among the water plants, and also prevalent throughout the deserts. Therefore, Jeremia justly likens evil and double-dealing characters to such a tree.[25]

(10) 'Let the earth bring forth.' This brief command was immediately mighty nature and an elaborate system which brought to perfection more swiftly than our thought the countless properties of plants. That command, which even yet is inherent in the earth, impels it in the course of each year to exert all the power it has for the generation of herbs, seeds, and trees. For, as tops, from the first impulse given to them, produce successive whirls when they are spun, so also the order of nature, having received its beginning from that first command continues to all time thereafter, until it shall reach the common consummation of all things. Let all of us hasten, full of fruit and good works to this, in order that, planted in the house of the Lord, we may flourish in the courts of our God,[26] in Christ Jesus our Lord, to whom be glory and power forever. Amen.

---

25 Cf. Jer. 17.5.6. 'Thus saith the Lord: Cursed be the man that trusteth in man, and maketh flesh his arm, and whose heart departeth from the Lord. For he shall be like tamaric in the desert, and he shall not see when good shall come.'
26 Cf. Ps 91.14: 'They that are planted in the house of the Lord shall flourish in the courts of the house of our God.'

# HOMILY 6

## Creation of the Lights of the Heavens

### (ON THE HEXAEMERON)

HE WHO WATCHES athletes ought to participate to some extent himself in the contest, a fact that may be realized from the laws for festivals, which prescribe that those who are present in the stadium shall sit with head uncovered. It seems to me that this is in order that he may not be a spectator only of the competitors but that each one may also, in a measure, be a competitor himself. In the same way, therefore, the reviewer of the great and marvelous spectacles and the listener to truly consummate and inexpressible wisdom, when present, should have from within himself certain incitements for the contemplation of the wonders proposed and should share with me in the struggle according to his power, standing beside me less as a judge than as a fellow combatant, lest at some time the discovery of the truth should escape us and my error should become the common loss of my audience. Now, why do I say this? Because, since we are proposing to examine the structure of the world and to contemplate the whole universe, beginning, not from the wisdom of the world, but from what God taught His servant when He spoke to him in person and without riddles, it is absolutely necessary that those who are fond of great shows and wonders should have a mind trained for the consideration of what we propose.

If, at any time in the clear cool air of the night, while gazing intently at the indescribable beauty of the stars, you conceived an idea of the Creator of the universe—who He is who has dotted the heavens with such flowers, and why the usefulness is greater than the pleasure in visible things—or again, if at times you observed with sober reflection the wonders of the day and through visible things you inferred the invisible Creator, you come as a prepared listener and one worthy to fill up this august and blessed assembly. Come, then; for just as those unaccustomed to the cities are taken by the hand and led around, so also I myself shall guide you, as strangers, to the hidden wonders of this great city. In this city in which is our ancient home, and from which the man-slaying demon drove us, selling mankind into slavery by his allurements, here, I say, you will see the first origin of man and death, which immediately seized upon us and which had been begotten by sin, the first-born offspring of the demon, source of evil. You will recognize yourself as coming from the earth by nature, but the work of the divine hands, falling far short of the animals in strength, but an appointed ruler of the creatures without reason, inferior in physical constitution, but able by the benefit of reason to be lifted up to the very heavens. If we understand this, we shall learn to know ourselves, we shall know God, we shall worship the Creator, we shall serve the Lord, we shall extol the Father, we shall love our Provider, we shall revere our Benefactor, we shall not cease adoring the Author[1] of our present and future life, who not only confirms His promises by the riches which He has already provided but also strengthens our expectations by the experience of present benefits. Indeed, if transient things are thus, what will be the eternal? And, if visible things are so beautiful, what will be the invisible? If the grandeur of the heavens transcends the measure of the human intellect, what mind will be able to

---

1 Cf. Acts 3.15: 'But the author of life you killed, whom God has raised up from the dead.'

explore the nature of the everlasting? If the sun, subject to destruction, is so beautiful, so great, so swift in its motion, presenting such orderly cycles, possessing a magnitude so commensurate with the universe that it does not exceed its due proportions to the universe; if by the beauty of its nature it is as conspicuous in creation as a radiant eye; if the contemplation of it is incapable of satisfying us, what will be the beauty of the Sun of justice?[2] If it is a loss to a blind man to be unable to look upon this, how great a loss is it to a sinner to be deprived of the true Light?

(2) 'And God said, "Let there be lights in the firmament of the heavens for the illumination of the earth, to separate day from night." '[3] The heavens and the earth had come first; after them, light had been created, day and night separated, and in turn, the firmament and dry land revealed. Water had been collected into a fixed and definite gathering. The earth had been filled with its proper fruits; for, it had brought forth countless kinds of herbs, and had been adorned with varied species of plants. However, the sun did not yet exist, nor the moon, lest men might call the sun the first cause and father of light, and lest they who are ignorant of God might deem it the producer of what grows from the earth. For this reason, there was a fourth day, and at that time 'God said, "Let there be light," . . . and God made the two lights.'[4] Who spoke and who made? Do you not notice in these words the double Person? Everywhere in history the teachings of theology are mystically interspersed.

The need for the creation of the lights is added. 'For the illumination,' He says, 'of the earth.'[5] If the creation of light had preceded, why, now, is the sun in turn said to have been made to give light? First, do not let the peculiar form of the

---

2 Cf. Mal. 4.2: 'But unto you that fear my name, the Sun of justice shall arise.'
3 Gen. 1.14, 15 (Septuagint version).
4 *Ibid.* 1.14, 16.
5 *Ibid.* 1.14 (Septuagint version).

diction cause you to laugh, if indeed we do not follow your choice of words nor pursue rhythm in the arrangement of them. Among us there are no embellishers of words, no melodiousness of sounds, but everywhere clarity of expression is more precious. See, therefore, whether He does not make sufficiently clear what He wished by the word 'illumination'; instead of 'light' (phōtismos) He said 'illumination' (phausis). This does not conflict with what has been said about 'light' (phos). In fact, at that time the actual nature of light was introduced, but now this solar body has been made ready to be a vehicle for that first-created light. Just as fire is different from a lamp, the one having the power to give light, and the other made to show that light to those who need it, so also in this case the lights have been prepared as a vehicle for that pure, clear, and immaterial light. And, just as the Apostle says that there are certain lights in the world,[6] but the true Light of the world is something else, and by participation in it holy men become the lights of the souls whom they have taught, drawing them out from the darkness of ignorance, so also now, having prepared this sun for that most bright light, the Creator of the universe has lighted it around the world.

(3) Do not let what has been said seem to anyone to be beyond belief, namely, that the brilliance of the light is one thing and the body subjected to the light another. In the first place, we divide all composite bodies into the recipient substance and the supervenient quality. Just as, therefore, whiteness by nature is one thing, but a whitened body something else, so also the things just mentioned, although different by nature, are made one by the power of the Creator. And do not tell me that it is impossible for these to be separated. I certainly do not say that the separation of light from the solar body is possible for you and me, but that that which we are able to separate in thought can also be separated in actuality by the Creator of its nature. It is also inconceivable

---

6 Cf. Phil. 2 15: 'For among these you shine like stars in the world.'

## HOMILY 6

for you to separate the burning property of fire from its brilliancy; yet God, wishing to turn His servant back by an incredible spectacle, placed a fire in a bush, which was active only by its brilliance and had its power of burning inactive.[7] This, too, the psalmist testifies when he says: 'The voice of the Lord dividing the flame of fire.'[8] Whence also in the requital for the actions of our lives a certain obscure saying teaches us that the nature of fire will be divided, and the light will be assigned for the pleasure of the just, but for the painful burning of those punished.

Then, of course, it is also possible for us to find proof of our claims from the changes in the moon. For, although it wanes and decreases, it is not consumed in its entire body, but, putting aside and again assuming the surrounding light, it gives us the impression of diminishing and increasing. What is seen is a clear proof that the body itself of the waning moon is not consumed. In fact, if you observe it when the air is clear and free from all mist, especially when the moon happens to be crescent-shaped in appearance, it is possible for you to see its dark and unlit part circumscribed by such a circle as the whole moon itself fills out when it is full. Consequently, a perfect circle is clearly perceived, if our vision adds the faint and misty segment to the illuminated part. And do not tell me that the light of the moon is brought in from the outside because it decreases when it approaches the sun but increases again when it moves away. That is not proposed to us for examination at the present time, but the fact that its body is something different from its light. Consider, I beg you, something similar in the case of the sun; except that it, having received the light once for all and having it mixed with itself, does not put it aside; while the moon, as if continually stripping off and again putting on the light, confirms in itself what has been said about the sun.

---

7 Ex. 3.25.
8 Ps. 28.7.

These luminaries were ordered also 'to separate day from night.'[9] God had previously separated light from darkness; then, He set their natures in opposition so that they were unable to mix with each other and there was no common quality in light and darkness. That which is shadow in daytime must be considered to be the nature of darkness at night. If, when some light shines, every shadow falls from bodies on the side opposite to the light, and in the morning the shadow is spread out toward the west, but in the evening it turns back toward the east, while at midday it tends toward the north, night also withdraws to the part opposite the bright rays, since it is nothing else by nature than the shadow of the earth. As in the day the shadow is produced by that which blocks the light, so night naturally comes when the air about the earth is overshadowed. This, therefore, is the meaning of 'God separated the light from the darkness,' since darkness fled the approach of light when in the first creative activity the antipathy natural to them was engendered against each other. But, now He has made the sun master of the length of the day; and the moon, whenever it runs its complete orbit, He has made mistress of the night. For, the lights are then almost diametrically opposed to each other. When the sun rises above the horizon, the full moon is borne down out of sight; and again, when the sun sets, the moon frequently rises up in its turn from the East. If in its other phases the moonlight does not correspond exactly with the night, that is of no importance as regards the preceding words. However, whenever it attains its own most perfect state, it rules the night, eclipsing the stars with its own superior light and splendor, and illuminating the earth; and it divides the intervals of time equally with the sun.

(4) 'Let them serve as signs and for the fixing of seasons, days and years.'[10] The signs given by the luminaries are neces-

---
9 Gen. 1.15.
10 *Ibid.*

sary for human life. If anyone will investigate with ordinary care their signs, he will find that the observations derived through long experience with them are useful. Much information can be obtained about the heavy rains, much about droughts and the blowing of the winds, either of particular winds or winds in general, of violent or gentle ones. The Lord has given us one of the signs indicated by the sun when He says, 'It will be stormy, for the sky is red and lowering.'[11] In fact, whenever the sun rises in a mist, the rays are dimmed, and it looks like a burning coal and is blood red in color, the density of the air causing this illusion to our eyes. If the air, compressed to begin with, and dense, is not scattered by the rays of the sun, it evidently cannot be absorbed because of the flow of vapors from the earth, and because of the excessive moisture will bring on a storm in those places around which it is gathered. Likewise, when the moon is surrounded with moisture and when the so-called haloes encircle the sun, these indicate either an abundance of rain or a violent windstorm;[12] or also, when those which are called mock suns travel around with the motion of the sun, they are signs of certain aerial phenomena. So, too, those straight streaks which appear in the clouds of the color of the rainbow, point to heavy rains or violent storms or, in short, to a very great change of the weather.[13]

---

11 Matt. 16 3.
12 Cf. Aristotle, *Meteorology* 3.3.372b: 'Sight is reflected in this way [as a halo around the sun or moon] when air and vapor are condensed into a cloud and the condensed matter is uniform and consists of small parts. Hence in itself it is a sign of rain. . . since it shows that a process of condensation is proceeding which must, when it is carried to an end, result in rain.'
13 Cf. *Ibid.* 3.6.377b: 'A mock sun is caused by the reflection of sight to the sun. . . . Rods are seen . . . when there are clouds near the sun and sight is reflected from some liquid surface to the cloud. . . . The mock sun is a surer sign of rain than the rods; it indicates, more than they do, that the air is ripe for the production of water. Further a mock sun to the south is a surer sign of rain than one to the north, for the air in the south is readier to turn into water than that in the north.'

They also who have devoted themselves to these studies have observed many significant facts about the waxing and waning moon, as if the air about the earth necessarily changes with the moon's different phases. Indeed, when about the third day after new moon it is fine and clear, there is a promise of calm, fair weather; but, if the horns appear thick and reddish, it threatens a furious rainstorm or a violent windstorm from the south.[14] And, as to the significance of these things, who does not know how useful it is for our livelihood? It is possible for the sailor to keep his ship inside the harbors if he has foreseen dangers from the winds. It is possible for the traveler from afar to avoid injuries by awaiting a change in the sullen sky. And farmers, busy with seeds and the care of plants, find from the indications in the sky all the opportune times for their labors. The Lord has already foretold that the signs of the dissolution of the universe will appear in the sun and moon and stars; 'The sun shall be turned into blood, and the moon will not give her light.'[15] These are the signs of the consummation of the world.

(5) But some who go beyond bounds interpret the divine utterance as a defense of astrology and say that our life depends on the movement of the heavenly bodies and that, for this reason, the Chaldeans[16] take the signs of what happens to us from the stars. And they understand the simple words

---

14 Cf. Aratus, *Phenomena* 778-787: 'Scan first the horns on either side the Moon. For with varying hue from time to time the evening paints her and of different shape are her horns at different times as the Moon is waxing—one form on the third day and other on the fourth. From them thou canst learn touching the month that is begun. If she is slender and clear about the third day, she heralds calm: if slender and very ruddy, wind: but if thick and with blunted horns she show but a feeble light on the third and fourth night, her beams are blunted by the South wind or imminent rain.'

15 Cf. Joel 2.31: 'The sun shall be turned into darkness, and the moon into blood,' and Matt. 24.29: 'the sun will be darkened, and the moon will not give her light.' St. Basil seems to have confused the two.

16 The Chaldeans were the Assyro-Babylonian priests, the professional astrologers of classic antiquity. The origin of astrology goes back to the worship of the stars.

of Scripture, 'Let them serve as signs,' not of the conditions of the air, nor of the changes in season, but, as it seems to them, in respect to our lot in life. Indeed, what do they say? That the intermingling of these moving stars, when they come together with those lying in the Zodiac in a certain form, forecasts certain fortunes, and another position of the same ones produces the opposite lot in life.

It will not be useless, perhaps, for the sake of clearness, to say a little about these things, resuming from the above. I shall use none of my own words, but I shall avail myself of theirs in the proof against them, offering to those already infected a remedy for the harm, but to the rest a safeguard against falling into the same errors. The inventors of astrology, perceiving that in a broad extent of time many of the signs escaped them, enclosed the measurements of time within the narrowest limits, as if within even the smallest and briefest interval, 'in a moment, in the twinkling of an eye,'[17] as the Apostle says, there is the greatest difference between birth and birth. The person born in this brief interval is an absolute monarch of cities and a ruler of peoples, very rich and powerful; but, he who was born at the next moment is a beggar and a vagabond, going from door to door for his daily sustenance. For this reason, after having divided the so-called Zodiac into twelve parts, since in thirty days the sun travels through a twelfth part of the fixed sphere, as it is called, they divided each of the twelfths into thirty sections. Then, dividing each of these into sixty, they cut each of the sixtieths sixty times. Now, then, in determining the births of the infants, let us see if they will be able to preserve this accurate division of time. A child is born, and at once the midwife ascertains whether it is male or female; then she awaits the wail which is a sign of life in the infant. How many minutes, do you think, passed in this time? She announces the birth to the Chaldean. How many minutes do you want us to suppose passed before the

---
17 1 Cor. 15.52.

announcement of the midwife, especially if he who sets down the hour happens to be standing outside the women's apartment? Surely, he who is to observe the horoscope must register the hour with accuracy whether these things happen in the day or at night. Again, what a swarm of seconds sped by at this time! For, the star which is in the ascendant must be found, and not only in which twelfth it is, but also in what portion of the twelfth, and in which sixtieth into which we have said the portion was divided, or, to secure absolute precision, in which sixtieth subdivided from the first sixtieths. Further, this minute and unfathomable investigation of time, they say, must be made in the case of each of the planets, so that it may be ascertained what relation they had to the fixed stars and what figure they formed with each other at the moment of the birth of the child. Consequently, if it is impossible to find the hour accurately, and the change of even the very briefest interval causes utter failure, both those who devote themselves to this imaginary art and those who are all agape at them as if they were able to know their destinies are ridiculous.

(6) But, what are the results obtained? That one, they say, will have curly hair and bright eyes, for he has the sign of the Ram, and that animal has in a certain way such an appearance; but he will also have noble feelings since the ram possesses leadership, and will be both bountiful in giving and capable in acquiring since this animal gives up its wool without pain and is again easily clothed by nature. But, he who is born under Taurus, he says, is wretched and servile, since the bull is under the yoke. He who is born under Scorpio is a striker because of his similarity to that poisonous creature. He who is born under the influence of Libra is just, because of the justness of our balances. Now, what could be more ridiculous than this? The Ram from which you estimate the birth of a man, is a twelfth part of the sky, and the sun, when it is in it, touches the signs of spring. Libra and Taurus, like-

wise, are each a twelfth of the circle called the Zodiac. How, then, can you say that the principal causes for the lives of human beings start from here, and how can you fashion the characters of men, when they are being born, from the animals about us? He who is born under the Ram is generous, not because that part of the heavens is productive of such a quality, but because such is the nature of sheep. Why do you constrain us to believe by the plausibility of the stars and attempt to persuade us by these bleatings? If, indeed, the heavens receive and possess such peculiarities of characteristics from animals, it is itself also subject to external powers, since its causes depend on the beasts of the field. But, if to say this is ridiculous, it is much more ridiculous to attempt to introduce persuasive arguments in our speech from those things which have nothing in common. These wise sayings of theirs are like spider webs, in which, if a gnat or a fly or any similar weak creature is entangled, it is bound fast and is held; but, whenever any of the stronger insects approaches, it easily breaks through, tearing and carrying away the feeble webs.

(7) They do not stop at these things only, but the causes of those acts which are subject to the will of each of us (I mean the practices of virtue and vice), they also attribute to the heavens. It would be ridiculous to refute these in some other case, but, since they are preoccupied with their error, it should, perhaps, not be passed by in silence. First, then, let us ask them this, whether the figures made by the stars do not change numberless times each day. The so-called planets, being in perpetual motion, since some overtake others more quickly, while others describe their circuit more slowly, both see and are hidden from each other many times in the same hour; and it is of the greatest importance in births, as they say, if one is seen by a beneficent star or by an evil one. Frequently, not discovering the moment at which the beneficent star bore its testimony because they did not perceive one of the tiniest

spaces, they register the child as lying under the influence of the evil spirit. I am constrained to borrow their own expression. In such words, certainly, the folly is great, but the impiety many times greater. For, the maleficent stars transfer the responsibility for their own wickedness to Him who made them. If their wickedness is from nature, the Creator will be the author of evil, but, if they are evil by their own choice, first, they will be creatures endowed with a will and possessed of free and sovereign desires, a thing which it is more than madness to allege so falsely of inanimate creatures. Next, how senseless it is not to assign good and evil to each star according to its worth, but, to take for granted that, because a star was in this particular place, it is beneficent, and that, because it is seen by another particular star, the same one becomes maleficent, again, that when it turns aside from that figure, it immediately forgets its evil. But, let this suffice for that matter.

Now, if in each brief interval of time the stars are shifted to one figure after another, and in these numberless changes the patterns of royal birth are produced frequently during the day, why are not kings born every day? Or, why are the successions of the kingly office hereditary among them? Surely, each of the kings does not carefully fit the birth of his own son to the royal figure of the stars, does he? What man, indeed, has such a power? How, then, did 'Ozias begat Joatham, Joatham begat Achaz, Achaz begat Ezechias,'[18] and none of them met with the hour of birth of a slave? Then, if truly the origin of our vices and virtues is not within us, but is the unavoidable consequence of our birth, the lawgivers, who define what we must do and what we must avoid, are useless, and the judges, too, who honor virtue and punish crime, are useless. In fact, the wrong done is not attributable to the thief, nor to the murderer, for whom it was an impossibility to restrain his hand, even if he wished to, because of

---
18 Matt. 1.9.

# HOMILY 6

the unavoidable compulsion which urged him to the acts. Persons who cultivate the arts are the most foolish of all. At least the farmer will thrive, although he has not scattered his seeds nor sharpened his sickle; and the merchant will be exceedingly rich, whether he wishes or not, since his destiny is gathering up wealth for him. But, the great hopes of us Christians will vanish completely since neither justice will be honored nor sin condemned because nothing is done by men through their free will. Where necessity and destiny prevail, merit, which is the special condition for just judgment, has no place. But, our arguments against them thus far are sufficient. You, being sound yourselves, do not need more words and time does not permit us to denounce them excessively.

(8) Let us return to the words which follow: 'Let them serve,' He says, 'as signs and for the fixing of seasons, days, and years.'[19] We have already given the explanation about the 'signs.' We think that 'seasons' means the changes of the periods of time—winter, spring, summer, and autumn—which, due to the regularity of the movement of the luminaries, are made to pass by us periodically. It is winter when the sun tarries in the southern parts and produces much night shadow in the region about us, so that the air above the earth is chilled and all the damp exhalations, gathering around us, provide a source for rains and frosts and indescribably great snows. Afterwards, returning again from the southern regions, it arrives in the center, so that it divides the time equally between night and day, and the longer it tarries in the places above the earth, so much milder a climate does it bring back in turn. Then comes spring, which causes all plants to bud, brings returning life to most trees, and preserves the species for all land and water animals by a series of births. And now, the sun, moving thence toward the summer solstice in a northerly direction, offers us the longest days. And, because

---
19 Gen. 1.14.

it travels through the air a very great distance, it parches the very air above our heads and dries up all the land, aiding in this way the seeds to mature and hurrying the fruits of the trees to ripeness. When the sun is most fiery hot, it causes very short shadows at midday because it shines upon our region directly from above. Those days are longest in which the shadows are shortest, and again, the shortest days are those which have the longest shadows. This is so for us who are called Heteroscians[20] (Shadowed-on-one-side), who inhabit the northern part of the earth. Yet, there are some who for two days of every year are entirely shadowless at midday, upon whom the sun, shining from the zenith, pours equal light from all sides, so that it even lights up the water in the depth of the wells through narrow apertures. Consequently, some call them Ascians (Shadowless). But, those beyond the spice-bearing land have shadows that change from one side to the other. They are the only inhabitants in this world who cast shadows to the south at midday; whence some call them Amphiscians[21] (Shadowed-on-both-sides). All these phenomena happen when the sun has already passed across to the northern regions. From them it is possible to conjecture the intensity of the burning heat which exists in the air from the solar beam, and what effects it produces. The season of autumn, welcoming us in turn from summer, breaks the excessive stifling heat and, gradually lessening it, by its moderate temperature leads us unharmed out of itself into winter, that is to say, while the sun again turns back from the northerly

---

20 Cf. Strabo, *Geography* 2.5.43. 'The people are thought of . . . as Heteroscians, all whose shadows either always fall toward the north, as is the case with us, or always toward the south, as is the case with the inhabitants of the other temperate zone.'
21 Cf. *Ibid.*: 'The people are thought of . . . as Amphisicians, all whose shadows at noon sometimes fall toward the north, namely, when the sun strikes from the south the index (which is perpendicular to the horizontal surface beneath), and, at other times, fall in the opposite direction, namely, when the sun revolves round to the opposite side (this is the result for only those who live between the tropics).'

regions to the southern. These changes of the seasons, which follow the movements of the sun, govern our lives.

'Let them serve,' He says, 'for the fixing of days,' not for making days, but for ruling the days. For, day and night are earlier than the generation of the luminaries. This the psalm declares to us when it says: 'He placed the sun to rule the day, the moon and stars to rule the night.'[22] How, then, does the sun rule the day? Because, whenever the sun, carrying the light around with it, rises above our horizon, it puts an end to the darkness and brings us the day. Therefore, one would not err if he would define the day as air, lighted by the sun, or as the measure of time in which the sun tarries in the hemisphere above the earth. But, the sun and the moon were appointed to be for the years. The moon, when it has completed its course twelve times, measures a year, except that it frequently needs an intercalary month for the accurate determination of the seasons, as the Hebrews and the most ancient of the Greeks formerly measured the year. The solar year is the return of the sun from a certain sign to that same sign in its regular revolution.

(9) 'And God made the two great lights.'[23] Since 'great' holds an absolute meaning, as for instance, the heavens are great and the earth is great and the sea is great, but, for the most part, it is generally used with a relative meaning, as a great horse and a great ox, which take on an aspect of greatness not indeed because of the enormous size of the body, but in comparison with their like, how, then, shall we understand the meaning of 'great'? Shall we call the ant or any other of the animals naturally small, great, testifying to its superiority because of the comparison with those of similar kind? Or, in the present case, is the greatness such that magnitude is indicated by the very structure of the lights? Personally, I think so. The sun and moon are great, not because they are

---

22 Ps. 135.8, 9.
23 Gen. 1.16.

greater than the smaller stars, but because they are so immense in circumference that the brightness poured forth from them suffices to light up the heavens and the air, and at the same time to extend to the earth and the sea. Although they are in every part of the heavens, rising and setting and occupying the center, they appear equal to men from all sides, a fact which affords clear proof of their immense size, because the whole extent of the earth contributes nothing to their appearing to be larger or smaller. We see things which are situated afar off somehow rather small, but, as we approach nearer to them, we find out their actual size more and more. Now, no one is nearer to the sun nor farther away, but it shines from an equal distance on those dwelling in every part of the earth. The proof is that the Indians and the Britons look upon a sun of equal size. Neither when it sets does it decrease in size for those who dwell in the east, nor when it rises does it appear smaller to those who live in the west, nor when it is in mid-heaven does it vary in its appearance on either side. Do not let the appearance deceive you and do not, because it seems to observers to be but a span in size, consider that it is such. The size of objects seen at great distances is naturally reduced, since the power of sight is not able to cover the space between but, as it were, is exhausted in the middle and only a little part at a time reaches the visible objects. Now, since our visual impression is small, by imposing its own quality on the visible objects, it causes that which is seen to be considered small. Therefore, if the visual impression is false, its judgment is untrustworthy. Remember your own experiences and you will have proof of yourself of these words. If ever from the ridge of a great mountain you saw a vast plain spread out below, how large did the yokes of oxen appear to you? And how large were the plowers themselves? Did they not give you an impression of being ants? And, if from a hilltop, turning toward the vast open sea, you let your eyes fall upon the sea, how great did the greatest of the islands seem to you? And how large did one of the immense trading vessels appear as it was borne with its white sails over the dark blue sea? Did it not look smaller to you than any dove? As I have said, therefore, our visual impression, being spent in the air, becomes faint and is not sufficient for the accurate perception of the objects viewed. And actually, our sight says that the greatest mountains, cut by deep chasms, are round and smooth, since it falls only upon the eminences and is unable through weakness to enter the hollows between. So, too, it does not preserve the shapes of the bodies such as they are, but thinks that the square towers are rounded. Consequently, it is evident from every point that at very great distances it receives, not a distinct, but a confused image of the bodies. The light, then, is great, according to the testimony of Scripture, and infinitely greater than it appears.

(10) Let this be for you a clear proof of its magnitude. Though the stars in the heavens are countless in number, the light contributed by them is not sufficient to dispel the gloom of night. The sun alone, appearing above the horizon, or rather, while still expected, even before it was completely above the earth, caused the darkness to disappear, eclipsed the stars with its light, and dissolved and scattered the thick and compact air about the earth. From this source also the morning breezes and the dews flow around the earth in clear weather. Since the earth is so immense, how would it be possible to illuminate the whole in one moment of time, unless it sent out its light from a huge circle? Observe, then, I beg you, the wisdom of the Artificer, how He has given it heat in proportion to this distance. For, the heat of the sun is of such a nature that it neither burns up the earth through excess nor leaves it cold and sterile from its deficiency.

Consider the facts concerning the moon as akin to what has already been said. Its body, too, is immense and is the brightest after that of the sun. Not always, however, does its full size remain visible; now it appears complete in a circle, and now, when lessened and diminished, it shows a deficiency on one side. As it increases, it is shadowed on one side. But, its other side is obscured at the time of waning. And there is a certain hidden reason of the wise Artificer for this varied interchange of shapes. In truth, it is so as to provide for us a clear example of our nature. For, nothing human is stable, but some things advance from non-being to perfection, and others, having attained to their proper strength and increased to their highest limit, again, through gradual deterioration, decline and perish, and, after having decreased, are completely destroyed. Therefore, from the spectacle of the moon we are taught our own vicissitudes and that, taking thought of the swift change of things human, we should not be proud in the successes of life, nor glory in power, nor be lifted up by the uncertainty of wealth, but despise the flesh in which there is constant change, and care for the soul whose good is unchangeable. And, if the moon causes you grief by exhausting its splendor in gradual diminutions, a soul should distress you more, which, having possessed virtue, through neglect destroys its beauty and never remains in the same disposition but turns and changes constantly through fickleness of mind. Truly, as Scripture says: 'A fool is changed as the moon.'[24]

I think that perfection in the constitution of animals and in the other things that grow from the earth depends not a little on the changes in the moon. In fact, their bodies are affected one way when it is waning and another when it is waxing. When it wanes, they become thin and exhausted, but then, when it waxes and approaches to fullness, they also fill themselves out again, because imperceptibly it imparts some moisture tempered by its heat, which reaches to their depths. Moreover, persons who sleep under the moon prove this, since the open passages in their heads are filled with excessive moisture; also the freshly slaughtered meats are quickly spoilt by the moonlight falling upon them, as well as the brains of

---
24 Ecclus. 27.12.

animals and the moistest parts of the sea animals and the piths of trees. All these things would not be able to change simultaneously with its transformation unless there was in it, in accordance with the testimony of Scripture, some remarkable and extraordinary power.

(11) The conditions of the air, too, are sympathetically affected by its variations, as is testified to us during the time of the new moon both by the sudden disturbances arising after a calm and tranquil stillness in the air when the clouds are driven tumultuously and meet violently together, and by the flux and reflux of the straits and the ebb and flow of the so-called Ocean, which the inhabitants close by have found out follows regularly the course of the moon. For, the water of the straits flows from one side to the other during the different phases of the moon, but, at the time of its birth they do not remain quiet for the briefest instant, but they are constantly tossing and swaying backwards and forwards until the moon, again appearing, furnishes a certain order for their reflux. The Western Sea,[25] too, is subject to the tides, now sinking, again flooding, as if drawn backward by the inhaling of the moon, and again pushed forward to its proper limits by its exhaling.

I have mentioned these things as a demonstration of the great size of the luminaries and as a proof that none of the divinely inspired words, even as much as a syllable, is an idle word. And yet, our sermon has touched upon almost none of the principal points, for it is possible for one, if he considers carefully their operations and powers, to find out through reason many things about the magnitudes and distances of the sun and moon. Therefore, reasonably, we must accuse ourselves of our weakness in order that the greatest of the works of the Creator may not be measured by our speech. Yet, from the few words which were said you should conjecture how many and how great are the marvels which were at my dis-

---
25 The Atlantic Ocean.

posal. Do not, then, measure the moon with your eye, but with your reason, which is much more accurate than the eyes for the discovery of truth.

Certain ridiculous tales, told in their delirium by drunken old women, have been spread abroad on all sides; for instance, that the moon, moved from its proper place by certain magic tricks, is being brought down to the earth. Now, how will an enchantment of magicians disturb what the most High Himself has firmly founded? And what sort of a place could receive it when it was hauled down?

Do you wish to receive a proof of its immensity from mere trivial evidence? All the cities in the world, settled at the greatest distances from each other receive the moonlight equally in the streets which are turned toward the East. If it were not facing all these cities, it would light up completely the narrow streets directly opposite it, but those which went beyond its width, it would strike with oblique and diverted rays. It is possible to see this effect also in the case of lamps in the homes. When several persons stand around a lamp, the shadow of the one who stands directly opposite extends straightforward, but the other shadows incline to each side. Therefore, unless the body of the moon was something immense, even stupendous in size, it would not spread out uniformly opposite to all. In fact, when it rises in the equinoctial regions, both those who dwell in the frigid zone and lie under the path of the Bear, as well as those down along the valleys of the south in the neighborhood of the torrid zone share equally in its light. Since it extends beyond all of these in width, it furnishes the clearest proof of its huge size. Who, then, will deny that its body is immense, since it is equal in measurement to so many and at the same time such great distances? So far, then, concerning the magnitudes of the sun and moon.

May He who has granted us intelligence to learn of the great wisdom of the Artificer from the most insignificant objects of creation permit us to receive loftier concepts of the Creator from the mighty objects of creation. And yet, in comparison with the Creator, the sun and moon possess the reason of a gnat or an ant. Truly, it is not possible to attain a worthy view of the God of the universe from these things, but to be led on by them, as also by each of the tiniest of plants and animals to some slight and faint impression of Him. Let us be satisfied with what has been said, I, indeed, returning thanks to Him who has bestowed on me this small ministry of the word, and you to Him who nourishes you with spiritual foods, who even now has sustained you with our weak words, as if with barley bread. And may He nourish you forever, bestowing upon you in proportion to your faith the manifestation of the Spirit,[26] in Christ Jesus our Lord, to whom be glory and power forever. Amen.

---

26 Cf. 1 Cor. 12.7: 'Now the manifestation of the Spirit is given to everyone for profit.'

# HOMILY 7

## Creation of Crawling Creatures

(ON THE HEXAEMERON)

THEN GOD SAID, 'Let the waters bring forth crawling creatures' of different kinds 'that have life, and winged creatures' of different kinds 'that fly below the firmament of the heavens.'[1] After the creation of the lights, then the waters were filled with living creatures, so that this portion of the world also was adorned. The earth had received its ornamentation from its own plants; the heavens had received the flowers of stars and had been adorned with two great lights as if with the radiance of twin eyes. It remained for the waters, too, to be given their proper ornament. The command came. Immediately rivers were productive and marshy lakes were fruitful of species proper and natural to each; the sea was in travail with all kinds of swimming creatures, and not even the water which remained in the slime and ponds was idle or without its contribution in creation. For, clearly, frogs and mosquitoes and gnats were generated from them. Things still seen, even at the present time, are a proof of what is past. Thus all water was in eager haste to fulfill the command of its Creator, and the great and ineffable power of God immediately produced an efficacious and active life in creatures of which one would not even be able to enumerate the species, as soon as the capacity for propagating living creatures came to the waters through His command. 'Let the waters bring forth crawling creatures that

---
1 Gen. 1.20.

have life.' Now, for the first time an animal was created which possessed life and sensation. Plants and trees, even if they are said to live because they share the power of nourishing themselves and of growing, yet are not animals nor are they animate. For this reason, 'Let the earth bring forth crawling creatures.'

Every creature able to swim, whether it swims at the surface of the water or cuts through its depths, is of the nature of crawling creatures, since it makes its way through a body of water. Even though some of the aquatic animals have feet and are able to walk (especially the amphibians, which are many, for instance, seals, crocodiles, hippopotamuses, frogs, and crabs), yet the ability to swim is antecedent. Therefore, 'Let the waters bring forth crawling creatures.' In these few words what species has been omitted? What has not been embraced by the command of the Creator? Have not the vivipara, such as seals and dolphins and rays and those like them that are called cartilaginous? Are not the ovipara included, which are, roughly speaking, all the different kinds of fishes? Are not those which are scaly and those which are horny scaled, those which have fins and those which do not? The words of the command were few, rather, there was no word, but only the force and impetus of the will; yet, the variety of meaning in the command is as great as the various species and families of fishes. To mention all these accurately is like counting the waves of the sea or trying to measure the water of the sea in the hollow of the hand.

'Let the waters bring forth crawling creatures.' Among them are animals of the open sea, those frequenting the shores, those of the deep sea, those which cling to rocks, those which travel in shoals, those which live solitary, the sea monsters, the enormous, and the tiniest fish. By the same power and by an equal command, in fact, both the large and the small were given existence. 'Let the waters bring forth.' He showed you the natural kinship of the swimming creatures with water, and therefore, when the fish are removed from the water for a short time, they perish. They do not even have organs for breathing, so as to draw in this air; but, water is for the swimming species what air is for land animals. And the cause is evident. We have lungs, internal organs of loose texture and many passages, which receive air by the dilation of the chest, fan away our inner heat, and refresh us; but, for them the dilation and folding of the gills, which receive the water and eject it, fulfill the purpose of breathing organs.[2] Fish have a peculiar state, a characteristic nature, a distinct nourishment, a specific mode of life. For this reason none of the water animals is able to be tamed, nor does it endure at all the touch of the human hand.

(2) 'Let the waters bring forth crawling creatures of different kinds that have life.'[3] God orders the firstlings of each kind to be brought forth, seeds, as it were, for nature; and their numbers are controlled by successive progeny, whenever they must increase and become numerous. Of one kind are those which are called testaceans, such as mussels, scallops, sea snails, conchs, and numberless varieties of bivalves. Again, another kind besides these are the fish named crustaceans: crayfish, crabs, and all similar to them. Still another kind are the so-called soft fish, whose flesh is tender and loose: polyps, cuttlefish, and those like them. And among these, again, there are innumerable varieties. In fact, there are weevers, and lampreys, and eels, which are produced in the muddy rivers and swamps, and which resemble in their nature venomous animals more than fish. Another class is that of ovipara, and another, that of vivipara. The sharks and the dogfish and, in general, the cartilaginous fish are vivipara. And of the cetaceans the majority are vivipara, as dolphins and seals; these are said to readmit and hide in their belly the cubs, while still young, whenever they have for some reason or other been

---

2 Cf. Aristotle, *On the Parts of Animals* 3.6.669a: 'The external cooling agent [of the body] must be either air or water. In fishes the agent is water. Fishes therefore never have a lung, but have gills in its place.'
3 Gen. 1.20.

startled.⁴ 'Let the waters bring forth the different kinds.' The cetacean is one kind, and the tiny fish is another. Again, among the fish numberless varieties are distinguished according to species. Since their peculiar names and different food and form and size and qualities of flesh, all differ with the greatest variations from each other, the fish are placed in various classes. Now, what men who watch for tunneys are able to enumerate for us the varieties of its species? And yet, they say that they report even the number of fish in the great schools. Who of those who have grown old around the shores and beaches is able to acquaint us accurately with the history of all fishes?

The fishermen in the Indian Ocean know some kinds; those in the Egyptian Gulf, others; islanders, others; and Mauretanians,⁵ still others. That first command and that ineffable power produced all things, both small and great alike. Many are the differences of their modes of life; many also are the varieties in the method of perpetuation of the species. The majority of the fishes do not hatch out the young as the birds do, nor do they fix nests or nourish the young with their own labors; but the water, taking up the egg when it has been laid, brings forth the living creature. And the method of perpetuation for each species is invariable and is without mixture with any other nature. There are not such unions as produce mules on land or such as of some birds which debase their species. None of the fishes is halfway equipped with teeth, as among us the ox and the sheep are; indeed, none of them ruminates, except only, as some historians write, the parrot-wrasse.⁶ But,

---

4 Aelian, *On the Nature of Animals* 1.16, tells this of the 'glaucus' a fish apparently unknown, according to B. Jackson, *Nicene and Post Nicene Fathers* 8.91, n.1.
5 Inhabitants of modern Morocco.
6 Cf. Aristotle, *History of Animals* 8.2.591b: 'Of all fishes the so-called scarus, or parrot-wrasse, is the only one known to chew the cud like a quadruped.' Cf. also Pliny, *op. cit.* 9.29.1-3: 'At the present day, the first place is given to the scarus, the only fish that is said to ruminate, and to feed on grass and not on other fish.'

all the species are furnished with serried and very sharp pointed teeth, in order that the food may not slip through in the long-continued chewing; for, unless it is quickly cut up and swallowed, it is likely to be carried away by the water in the process of being ground.

(3) Different foods are assigned for different fish according to their species. Some feed on slime, others on seaweeds, and others are content with the plants that grow in the water. The majority of fish eat one another, and the smaller among them are food for the larger. If it ever happens that the victor over a smaller becomes the prey of another, they are both carried into the one stomach of the last. Now, what else do we men do in the oppression of our inferiors? How does he differ from that last fish, who with a greedy love of riches swallows up the weak in the folds of his insatiable avarice? That man held the possessions of the poor man; you, seizing him, made him a part of your abundance. You have clearly shown yourself more unjust than the unjust man and more grasping than the greedy man. Beware, lest the same end as that of the fish awaits you—somewhere a fishhook, or a snare, or a net. Surely, if we have committed many unjust deeds, we shall not escape the final retribution.

Since you have already perceived much wickedness and plotting in weak animals, I want you to avoid imitating the evildoers. The crab longs for the flesh of the oyster; but, because of the shell of the oyster, it is a prey hard for him to conquer. Nature has fastened the tender flesh in an unbroken enclosure. Therefore, the oyster is called 'sherd-hide.' Since the two enveloping shells, fitted exactly to each other, enclose the oyster, the claws of the crab are necessarily of no avail. What does he do, then? When he sees it pleasantly warming itself in spots sheltered from the wind and opening its valves to the rays of the sun, then, stealthily inserting a small pebble, he prevents it from closing and is found to gain through inventiveness what he fell short of by strength. This is the wickedness of the creatures endowed with neither reason nor voice. Now, I want you, although emulating the crabs' acquisitiveness and their inventiveness, to abstain from injury to your neighbors. He who approaches his brother with deceit, who adds to the troubles of his neighbors, and who delights in others' misfortunes, is like the crab. Avoid the imitation of those who by their conduct convict themselves. Be satisfied with your own possessions. Poverty with an honest sufficiency is preferred by the wise to all pleasure.

Let me pass over the deceitfulness and trickery of the octopus, which assumes on every occasion the color of the rock to which it fastens itself. As a result, many of the fish swimming unwarily fall upon the octopus as upon a rock, I suppose, and become an easy prey for the cunning fellow.[7] Such in character are those men who always fawn upon the ruling powers and adapt themselves to the needs of every occasion, not continuing always in the same principles, but easily changing into different persons, who honor self-control with the chaste, but incontinence with the incontinent, and alter their opinions to please everyone. It is not easy to avoid nor to guard against harm from them because the evil they have fostered in themselves is hidden under a pretext of profound friendship. Such characters the Lord calls ravenous wolves which show themselves in sheep's clothing.[8] Avoid inconstancy and fickleness, pursue truth, sincerity, simplicity. The serpent is subtle, and for that reason has been condemned to crawl. The just man is without pretense, such as was Jacob.[9] Therefore, 'The Lord maketh men of one manner to dwell in a house.'[10] So in this great sea, which stretcheth wide its arms: 'there are creeping things without number: Creatures little and

---

[7] Cf. Aristotle, *Ibid.* 9.37.622a: 'It [the octopus] seeks its prey by so changing its colour as to render it like the colour of the stones adjacent to it; it does so also when alarmed.'
[8] Cf. Matt. 7.15: 'Beware of false prophets, who come to you in sheep's clothing, but inwardly are ravenous wolves.'
[9] Cf. Gen. 25.27: 'Jacob was a plain man who stayed among the tents.'
[10] Cf. Ps. 67.7.

great.'[11] Nevertheless, there is a certain wisdom among them and an orderly arrangement. Not only are we able to bring charges against the fish, but there is also something worthy of imitation in them. How is it that all of the different species of fishes, having been allotted a place suitable for them, do not intrude upon one another, but stay within their own bounds? No surveyor apportioned the dwellings among them; they were not surrounded with walls nor divided by boundaries; but what was useful for each was definitely and spontaneously settled. This bay gives sustenance to certain kinds of fish and that one, to other kinds; and those that teem here are scarce elsewhere. No mountain extending upward with sharp peaks separates them; no river cuts off the means of crossing; but there is a certain law of nature which allots the habitat to each kind equally and justly according to its need.

(4) We, however, are not such. Why? Because we pass beyond the ancient bounds which our fathers set.[12] We cut off a part of the land amiss; we join house to house and field to field, so that we may take something of our neighbor's. The cetaceans know the habitats assigned them by nature. They have taken the sea beyond the inhabited regions, that part free from islands, in which there is no continent confronting them on the opposite side, because, since neither desire of inquiry nor any necessity persuades the sailors to venture on it, it is not navigated. The cetaceans which occupy that sea, in size like the mightiest mountains, as they who have seen them say, remain within their own boundaries and do not injure the islands nor the seaboard cities. So then, each kind abides in the parts of the sea assigned to it, as if in certain cities or villages or ancient countries.

However, some of the fish also are migratory and, as if dispatched by a common council to foreign lands, set out all

---

11 Cf. *Ibid.* 103.25.
12 Cf. Prov. 22.28: 'Pass not beyond the ancient bounds which thy fathers have set.'

together at one preconcerted signal. When the appointed time for breeding arrives, being roused by the common law of nature, they migrate from the different bays, hastening toward the North Sea. And at the time of the journey up you may see the fish united and flowing like a stream through the Propontis into the Euxine Sea. Who is it who sets them in motion? What is the command of the King? What lists, set up in the market place, show the appointed time? Who are the guides? You see that the divine plan fulfills all things and extends even to the smallest. A fish does not oppose the law of God, but we men do not endure the precepts of salvation. Do not despise the fish because they are absolutely unable to speak or to reason, but fear lest you may be even more unreasonable than they by resisting the command of the Creator. Listen to the fish, who through their actions all but utter this word: 'We set out on this long journey for the perpetuation of our species.' They do not have reason of their own, but they have the law of nature strongly established and showing what must be done. Let us proceed to the North Sea, they say. That water is sweeter than that of the rest of the sea, because the sun, tarrying there only a short time, does not draw out all the freshness from it with its rays. And the sea animals rejoice in the sweet waters. For this reason they frequently swim up the rivers and go far from the sea. Therefore, they prefer the Euxine Sea to the rest of the bays as a suitable place for breeding and rearing the young. But, when their purpose has been satisfactorily accomplished, again, in a body they all turn back homeward.[13] Let us hear from these silent animals what the reason is. The North Sea, they say, is very shallow and, lying exposed to the violence of the winds,

---

13 Cf. Aristotle, *Ibid.* 8.13.598b: 'Furthermore, fish penetrate into this sea [Euxine] for the purpose of breeding; for there are recesses there favorable for spawning, and the fresh and exceptionally sweet water has an invigorating effect upon the spawn. After spawning, when the young fishes have attained some size, the parent fish swim out of the Euxine immediately after the rising of the Pleiads.'

has few beaches and shelters. The winds, therefore, easily upturn it from the bottom so as to stir even the deep sand with the waves. Moreover, it is also cold in the winter season since it is filled by many great rivers. For this reason, having taken advantage of it to a certain measure in the summer, in the winter they hasten again to the warmth in the depths and to the sunny regions and, fleeing the stormy arctic parts, they come for haven into less agitated bays.[14]

(5) I have seen these wonders myself and I have admired the wisdom of God in all things. If the unreasoning animals are able to contrive and look out for their own preservation, and if a fish knows what it should choose and what avoid, what shall we say who have been honored with reason, taught by the law, encouraged by the promises, made wise by the Spirit, and who have then handled our own affairs more unreasonably than the fish? Even though they know how to have some foresight for the future, yet we, through hopelessness for the future, waste our lives in brutish pleasure. A fish traverses so many seas to find some advantage; what do you say who pass your life in idleness? And idleness is the beginning of evil-doing. Let no one allege ignorance. Natural reason which teaches us an attraction for the good and an aversion for the harmful is implanted in us. I do not reject examples drawn from the sea, since these lie before us for examination. I have heard from one of the dwellers along the seacoast that the sea urchin, a quite small and contemptible creature, often forecasts calm or rough waters to the sailors. Whenever it foresees a disturbance from the winds, going under a strong pebble, it tosses about safely, clinging to this as to an anchor, prevented by the weight from being easily dragged away by the waves. When the sailors see this sign, they know that a violent windstorm is expected. No astrologer, no Chaldean,

---

14 *Ibid.* 8.12.597a: 'Fishes also in a similar manner shift their habitat now out of the Euxine and now into it. In winter they move from the outer sea in towards land in quest of heat; in summer they shift from shallow waters to the deep sea to escape the heat.'

estimating the disturbances of the air by the rising of the stars, taught these things to the sea urchin, but the Lord of the sea and of the winds placed in the small animal a clear sign of His own wisdom. There is nothing unpremeditated, nothing neglected by God. His unsleeping eye beholds all things.[15] He is present to all, providing means of preservation for each. If God has not put the sea urchin outside of His watchful care, does He not have regard for your affairs?

'Husbands, love your wives,'[16] even though external to each other, you came together into the union of marriage. May the bond of nature, may the yoke imposed by the blessing make as one those who were divided. A viper, the cruelest of reptiles, comes for marriage with the sea lamprey and, having announced its presence by hissing, summons it forth from the depths for the nuptial embrace. And the lamprey hearkens and is united with the venomous animal. What do my words mean? That, even if the husband is rough, even if he is fierce in his manners, the wife must endure and for no cause whatsoever permit herself to break the union. Is he a brawler? Nevertheless, he is your husband. Is he a drunkard? Nevertheless, he is united to you by Nature. Is he savage and ill-tempered? Nevertheless, he is your member and the most honored of your members.

(6) But, let the husband also listen to proper advice for himself. The viper, through respect for his marriage, disgorges his venom. Will you not put aside the roughness and cruelty of your soul through reverence for the union? Or, perhaps, the example of the viper will be useful for us in other ways also, because the union of the viper and the sea lamprey is an adulterous violation of nature. Therefore, let those who are plotting against other men's marriages learn what sort of reptile they resemble. The edification of the Church in every way is my one aim. Let the passions of the

---

15 Cf. Prov. 15.3: 'The eyes of the Lord in every place behold the good and the evil.'
16 Eph. 5.25.

incontinent be restrained and trained by these examples from the land and sea.

The weakness of my body and the lateness of the hour compel me to stop here, although I would be able to add much deserving of admiration about the things produced in the sea for my attentive audience. About the sea itself; how the water crystallizes into salt; how the very precious stone, the coral, is a plant in the sea but, when it is exposed to the air, it is changed into a hard stone; how it is that nature encloses the costly pearl in the most insignificant animal, the oyster. These stones, which the treasuries of kings covet, are scattered around the shores and beaches and sharp rocks, enclosed in the shells of the oysters. How do the sea pens produce their golden byssus, which no dyer up to this time has imitated? How is it that the shellfish bestow on kings the purple robes which surpass even the flowers of the meadow in beauty of color?

'Let the waters bring forth.' And what, that is necessary, has not been made? What precious object is there that has not been given for our life? Some things for the service of men; others for their contemplation of the marvel of creation; and some terrible things, taking to task our idleness. 'God created the great sea monsters.'[17] And not because they are larger than the shrimp and herring, are they called great, but, because with their immense bodies they are like huge mountains. Indeed, they frequently look like islands when they swim upon the surface of the water. These sea monsters, because they are so large, do not stay around the coasts and beaches, but inhabit the sea called the Atlantic. Such are the animals which have been created for our fear and consternation. And, if you hear that the very small fish, the remora, stops the greatest boat as it is being borne along by a fair wind with sails spread, so that it keeps the ship immovable for a very long time, as if firmly rooted in the sea itself,[18]

---
17 Gen. 1.21.
18 It receives its name, 'echenēís' or 'ship-holder,' from this supposed power.

would you not possess in this little fish also the same proof of the power of the Creator? Not only the swordfish, the sawfish, the dogfish, the whales, and the hammer-headed sharks are to be feared; but the spike of the sting ray, even when it is dead, and the sea hare, too, are not less fearful, since they bring swift and inevitable death. Thus, the Creator wants you to be kept awake by all things, in order that, through hope in God, you may escape the harm that comes from them.

But, let us come up from the depths and take refuge on the land. For, somehow, the wonders of creation, coming upon us one after another in continuous and quick succession like waves, have submerged our discourse. And yet, I would not be surprised if our spirit, though meeting up with greater wonders on land, would again, like Jona, slip away to the sea. It seems to me that my sermon, lighting upon the numberless marvels, has forgotten its proper measure and has had the same experience as sailors on the sea, who judging their progress from no fixed point, are ignorant frequently of the distance they have sailed. Truly, this seems to have happened in our case, that, as our discourse moved quickly through creation, we did not perceive the great multitude of creatures mentioned. But, even though this august assembly is pleased to listen and the narration of the wonders of the Master is sweet to the ears of His servants, let us bring our talk to anchor here and await the day for the explanation of the facts omitted. Let us rise and give thanks for what has been said; let us ask for the completion of the omissions.

While partaking of your food, may you discuss at table the stories which my words reviewed for you early in the morning and throughout the evening; and, falling asleep while engaged in thoughts of these things, may you enjoy the pleasure of the day, even while sleeping, so that it may be possible for you to say, 'I sleep and my heart watcheth,'[19] since it has meditated night and day on the law of the Lord, to whom be glory and power forever. Amen.

19 Cant. 5.2.

## HOMILY 8

*Creation of Winged Creatures and Those Living in the Waters*

(ON THE HEXAEMERON)

AND 'GOD SAID, "Let the earth bring forth all kinds of living creatures: cattle, crawling creatures, and wild animals." And so it was.'[1] The command came, proceeding step by step, and the earth received its proper adornment. Formerly He had said: 'Let the waters bring forth crawling creatures that have life';[2] here, 'Let the earth bring forth living creatures.' Is the earth, then, possessed of life? And do the mad-minded Manichaeans hold the vantage point, since they put a soul in the earth? No, when He said: 'Let it bring forth,' it did not produce what was stored up in it, but He who gave the command also bestowed upon it the power to bring forth. Neither did the earth, when it heard, 'Let it bring forth vegetation and the fruit trees,'[3] produce plants which it had hidden in it; nor did it send up to the surface the palm or the oak or the cypress which had been hidden somewhere down below in its womb. On the contrary, it is the divine Word that is the origin of things made. 'Let the earth bring forth'; not, let it put forth what it has, but, let it acquire what it does not have, since God is enduing it with the power of active force. And now, in the same way, 'Let the earth bring forth the living creature,' not that stored up in it, but that given to it by God through His command. On the contrary,

---
1 Gen. 1.24.
2 *Ibid.* 1.20.
3 *Ibid.* 1.11.

moreover, the teaching of the Manichaeans will refute itself. For, if the earth brought forth life, it left itself destitute of life. But, their loathesome opinion is well known of itself.

Why, indeed, were the waters ordered to bring forth crawling creatures that have life, but the earth living creatures? Well, we conclude that swimming animals seem to share in a life that is rather imperfect, because they live in the dense element of water. Their sense of hearing is slow and, since they look through the water, they see but dimly; moreover, they have no memory, no imagination, no recognition of the familiar. Therefore, Scripture points out, as it were, that the carnal life is the guide for the animal movements in aquatic creatures; in the case of land animals, however, as if their life were more perfect, the spirit refers all leadership to itself. In fact, in the majority of quadrupeds the apprehension of things present is sharper, and the memory of the past is accurate. For this reason, as it seems, in the case of aquatic animals, bodies possessed of life were created ('crawling creatures that have life' were produced from the waters), but in the case of land animals a soul governing the bodies was ordered to be produced, as if the animals which dwell upon the earth participate in the vital power somewhat more. Indeed, even land animals are irrational; nevertheless, each one through the voice of nature indicates many of the dispositions of its spirit. It manifests by a certain sound both joy and grief, the recognition of what is familiar, the separation from companions, the want of food, and numberless other emotions. The aquatic animals, however, are not only voiceless, but also incapable of being tamed or taught or trained for any participation in the life of men. 'The ox knoweth his owner, and the ass his master's crib';[4] but the fish could not recognize the one who feeds him. The ass knows the familiar voice. He knows the road which he has frequently walked, and what is more, he at times becomes the guide for the man who goes astray.

---
4 Isa. 1.3.

No other of the land animals is said to possess the keen hearing of this animal. And which of the sea animals would be able to imitate the resentment of camels, their fierce wrath, and their persistence in anger? If some time previously a camel has been struck, he saves up his wrath for a long time, but, when he finds a suitable opportunity, he repays the evil. Hear, you sullen men who pursue vengeance as though it were a virtue, who it is that you resemble when you harbor for so long a time your resentment against your neighbor like a spark hidden in ashes, until finding material, you kindle your wrath like a flame.

(2) 'Let the earth bring forth a living creature.' Why does the earth bring forth a living creature? In order that you may learn the difference between the soul of a beast and that of a man. A little later you will come to know how the soul of man was formed; now, hear about the soul of the irrational animals. Since, as it is written, the life of every creature is its blood,[5] and the blood, when congealed, is wont to change into flesh, and the flesh, when corrupted, decomposes into earth, reasonably, the soul of animals is something earthy. Therefore, 'Let the earth bring forth a living creature.' See the relation of soul to blood, of blood to flesh, of flesh to earth; and again, after having resolved it into its elements, return through the same steps from earth to flesh, from flesh to blood, from blood to soul, and you will find that the soul of beasts is earth. Do not think that it is antecedent to the essence of their bodies or that it remains after the dissolution of the flesh. Shun the idle talk of the proud philosophers, who are not ashamed to regard their own soul and that of dogs as similar, who say that they were at some time women, or bushes, or fish of the sea.[6] I certainly would not say that they were

---
5 Cf. Lev. 17.11: 'Because the life of the flesh is in the blood.'
6 Cf. Empedocles, *Fragments:* 'Once already have I as a youth been born. as a maiden, Bush, and winged bird, and silent fish in the waters.' (Translation of W. C. Lawton in Warner's *Library of the World's Best Literature*).

ever fish, but that they were more irrational than fish when they were writing those things, and I would maintain it most vigorously.

'Let the earth bring forth living creatures.' Perhaps, many wonder why, when my sermon was hurrying along without a break, I was silent for a long time. It is not, however, the more studious of my audience who are ignorant of the cause of my speechlessness. Why should they be, who by their glances and nods to each other had turned my attention toward them and had led me on to the thought of things omitted? For, I had forgotten an entire class of creatures, and this by no means the least; moreover, my discourse was nearly finished, leaving that class almost entirely uninvestigated.

'Let the waters bring forth crawling creatures of different kinds that have life and winged creatures that fly above the earth under the firmament of the heavens.'[7] We talked about the aquatic animals last evening as long as time permitted; today we have changed over to an examination of land animals. But, the winged creatures between the two escaped us. Therefore, like forgetful travelers who, when they leave something important behind, even if they have gone forward a great distance on the journey, return again the same way, enduring the trouble of the journey as a penalty deserved for their carelessness, so we too, must, as it seems, go back again over the same road. In fact, the part omitted is not to be contemned, but seems to be the third part of the animal creation, if, indeed, there are three kinds of animals, the land, the winged, and the aquatic. 'Let the waters bring forth,' He says, 'crawling creatures of different kinds that have life, and winged creatures of different kinds that fly above the earth under the firmament of the heavens.' Why did He give winged creatures also their origin from the waters? Because the flying animals have a certain relationship, as it were, with those that swim. For, just as the fish cut the water, going

---
7 Gen. 1.20.

forward with the motion of their fins and guiding their turns and forward movements by the change of their tails, so also in the case of birds, they can be seen moving through the air on wings in the same manner. Therefore, since one characteristic common to both is swimming, one certain relationship has been provided for them through their generation from the waters. But, none of the winged creatures is without feet, because food for all of them comes from the earth and all necessarily require the assistance of feet. To the birds of prey sharp pointed claws have been given for catching their prey; but for the rest the service of feet has been granted as an indispensable means for procuring their food as well as for the other needs of life. A few of the birds have poor feet, not suitable for walking nor for seizing the prey, like the swallows, which are able neither to walk nor to seize prey, and the so-called swifts, for whom food is provided from insects borne about in the air. However, the flight of the swallow, which is close to the ground, serves them as a substitute for feet.

(3) There are also numberless varieties of species among the birds, and if one will go through these varieties in the same manner as we applied ourselves in part to the examination of the fish, he will find one name for the winged creatures but numberless variations among them in size and form and color; also an indescribably great difference among them in regard to their lives, their actions, and their customs. In fact, some have already tried to use coined names, so that the characteristic of each kind might be known through the unaccustomed and strange name as if through a certain brand. Some they called Schizoptera, as the eagles; others, Dermoptera, as the bats; others, Ptilota,[8] as the wasps; and others, Coleoptera,[9]

---

[8] I.e. by Aristotle; cf. *History of Animals* 1.5.490a: 'Of animals that can fly some are furnished with feathered wings [Schizoptera], as the eagle and the hawk; some are furnished with membranous wings [Ptilota], as the bee and cockchafer; others are furnished with leathern wings [Dermoptera], as the flying fox and the bat.'

[9] Cf. *Ibid.* 1.5.490a: 'Of creatures that can fly and are bloodless some are coleopterous or sheath-winged.'

as the beetles and the insects which, generated in certain chests and clothes, split their shell and free themselves for flight.

Common usage, however, is a sufficient indication to us of the specific character of the species, as well as the distinctions made by the Scripture concerning the clean and unclean creatures. For instance, the class of carnivora is of one kind and their constitution is of a type suitable to their manner of life, sharp claws, a curved beak, and a swift wing, so that the prey is easily seized and, being torn to pieces, becomes the food for its captor.[10] Different from this is the constitution of seed-picking birds; and different, that of those which are nourished by everything they find. Even among these there are the greatest diversities. Some of them are gregarious, except the birds of prey, which have no social relationship except the mating by pairs. Numberless others, however, adopt the collective form of life, for example, pigeons, cranes, starlings, and jackdaws. Again, among them some are without a commander and are, as it were, autonomous; but others, as the cranes, permit themselves to be ruled by a leader.[11] There is still a certain other difference among them, by which some are nonmigratory and native to the country, and others are accustomed to fly very far away and for the most part to migrate as winter approaches.

The majority of the birds that are reared become tame and domesticated, except the weak ones, which because of their excessive timidity and fear do not endure the continual annoyance of handling. Some of the birds also like the companionship of man, accepting the same dwellings as we; others love the mountains and solitude. But, the greatest difference is

---

10 Cf. *Ibid.* 8.3.592a: 'Of birds, such as have crooked talons are carnivorous without exception, and cannot swallow corn or bread-food, even if it be put in their bills in tit-bits.'
11 Cf. *Ibid.* 9.10.614b: "They [cranes], furthermore, have a leader in their flight, and patrols that scream on the confines of the flock so as to be heard by all.'

the peculiarity in the tones of each. Some of the birds twitter and chatter; others are silent. Some species have melodious and varied tones; others are quite inharmonious and without song. Some are imitative, either being naturally able to imitate, or acquiring the ability by training; others utter one sole and unchangeable sound. The cock possesses an exulting tone; the peacock, one that seeks honor; the pigeons and domestic birds are amorous in tone, mating at every opportunity. The partridge has a treacherous and jealous voice, maliciously assisting the hunters to seize the prey.

(4) Innumerable, as we have said, are the differences in their actions and their lives. Some of the irrational creatures are like members of a state, if, indeed, it is characteristic of citizenship that the activities of the individuals tend to one common end. This may be seen in the case of bees. Their dwelling is common, their flight is shared by all, and the activity of all is the same; but, the most significant point is that they engage in their work subject to a king and to a sort of commander, not taking it upon themselves to go to the meadows until they see that the king is leading the flight.[12] In their case, the king is not elected; in fact, the lack of judgment on the part of the people has frequently placed the worst man in office. Their king does not hold a power acquired by lot; the chances of lot, which frequently confer the power on the worst of all, are absurd. Nor is he placed on the throne through hereditary succession; for the most part, even such men through softness and flattery become rude and ignorant of all virtue. But, he holds the first place among all by nature, differing in size and appearance and in the gentleness of his disposition. The king has a sting, but he does not

---

12 Cf. *Ibid.* 9.40.624a: 'They say that, if a young swarm go astray, it will turn back upon its route and by the aid of scent seek out its leader. It is said that if he is unable to fly he is carried by the swarm, and that, if this swarm outlives the king for a while and constructs combs, no honey is produced and the bees soon die out.'

use it for vengeance.¹³ There is this positive unwritten law of nature, that they who are placed in the highest positions of power should be lenient in punishing. Those bees, however, which do not follow the example of the king, quickly repent of the indiscretion, because they die after giving a prick with their sting.¹⁴ Let the Christians heed, who have received the command to 'render to no man evil for evil,' but to 'overcome evil with good.'¹⁵

Imitate the character of the bee, because it constructs its honeycomb without injuring anyone or destroying another's fruit. It gathers the wax openly from the flowers, then, sucking in with its mouth the honey, a dewlike moisture sprinkled in the flowers, it injects this into the hollows of the wax. At first, therefore, it is liquid, then in time being matured, it attains its proper consistency and sweetness. The bee itself has won honorable and becoming praise from the Proverb, which calls it wise and industrious.¹⁶ It gathers its food so laboriously ('Whose labors,' it is said, 'kings and private men set before them for their health.'¹⁷), and devises so wisely its storehouses for the honey (stretching the wax into a thin membrane, it builds numerous cells adjacent to each other), that the great number of the connecting walls of the very tiny cells supports the whole. Each cell fastens upon the other, separated from and at the same time joined to it by a thin partition. Then these compartments are built up on each other two and three stories. The bee avoids making one unbroken cavity lest the liquid, because of its weight, should break through and escape to the outside. Notice how

---

13 Cf. *Ibid.* 9.40 626a: 'The kings are the least disposed to show anger or to inflict a sting.'
14 Cf. *Ibid.* 9.40.626a: 'Bees that sting die from their inability to extract the sting without at the same time extracting their intestines. True, they often recover, if the person stung takes the trouble to press the sting out; but once it loses its sting the bee must die.'
15 Rom. 12.17, 21.
16 Cf. Prov. 6.8a (Septuagint version).
17 Prov. 6.8b (Septuagint version).

the discoveries of geometry are merely incidental to the very wise bee. The cells of the honeycombs are all hexagonal and equilateral, not resting upon each other in a straight line, lest the supports, coinciding with the empty cells, might meet with disaster; but, the corners of the hexagons below form a base and support for those resting upon them, so that they safely sustain the weights above them and hold the liquid separate in each cell.

(5) How could I possibly make an accurate review of the peculiarities in the lives of birds? How the cranes[18] in turn accept the responsibility of outposts at night, and while some sleep, others, making the rounds, provide every safety for those asleep; then, when the time of watching has been completed, the guard, having called out, goes to sleep and another, succeeding, provides in his turn the safety which he has enjoyed. You will see this discipline also in their flight, a different one takes up the task of guiding at different times and, after having led the flight for a certain appointed time, goes around to the rear, transferring the leadership of the journey to the one behind him.

The conduct of the storks is not far from reasoning intelligence; thus they all reside in these regions at the same time, and likewise all depart at one signal. Our crows attend them as bodyguards and escort them, as it seems to me, providing a certain auxiliary force against hostile birds. And a proof is, first, that the crows do not appear at all during that time; then, that, returning with wounds, they carry clear proofs of their protective and defensive alliance. Who prescribed the laws of hospitality among them? Who threatened them with an indictment for military desertion, so that no one deserts the escort? Let the inhospitable listen, who close their doors

---

18 Cf. Aristotle, *Ibid.* 9.10.614b: 'When they, the cranes, settle down, the main body go to sleep with their heads under their wing, standing first on one leg and then on the other, while their leader with his head uncovered, keeps a sharp look out, and when he sees anything of importance signals it with a cry.'

and do not share shelter in winter and at night with travelers. The solicitude of the storks for their old would suffice to make our children devoted to their fathers, if they were willing to heed it. For, surely, no one at all is so lacking in intelligence as not to judge it deserving of shame to be inferior in virtue to irrational birds. They, surrounding their father when from old age he has shed his feathers, warm him through with their own feathers; they also procure food in abundance for him[19] and furnish powerful aid on the flight, gently lifting him on each side upon their wings. This fact has been so commonly proclaimed among all that already some call the repayment of benefactions 'antipelárgōsis.'

Let no one bewail his poverty; let no one who possesses little at home despair of his life, when he looks at the inventiveness of the swallow. When building her nest, she carries the dry twigs in her beak, and not being able to raise the mud in her claws, she moistens the tips of her wings with water, then, rolling in the very fine dust, she thus contrives to secure the mud. After gradually fastening the twigs of wood to each other with mud as with some glue, she raises her young in this nest.[20] If anyone stabs the eyes of these young, she possesses a natural remedy, through which she restores to soundness the sight of her children.[21] Let this warn you not to turn to evil-doing because of poverty, nor in the harshest suffering to cast aside all hope and remain idle and inactive, but to flee to God; for, if He bestows such things upon the

---

19 Cf. *Ibid.* 9.13 615b: 'It is a common story of the stork that the old birds are fed by their grateful progeny.' Cf. also Pliny, *Natural History* 10 32.
20 Cf. *Ibid.* 9.7.612b: 'Preeminent intelligence will be seen more in small creatures than in large ones, as is exemplified in the case of birds by the nest building of the swallow. In the same way as men do, the bird mixes mud and chaff together; if it runs short of mud, it souses its body in water and rolls about in the dry dust with wet feathers.'
21 Cf. *Ibid.* 6.5.563a :'If you pick out the eyes of swallow chicks while they are yet young, the birds will get well again and will see by and by.'

swallow, how much more will He give to those who call upon Him with their whole heart?

The halcyon is a sea bird. It is accustomed to build its nest along the very shores, depositing its eggs in the sand itself; and it builds its nest almost in the middle of winter, a time when the sea is being dashed against the land by many violent windstorms. Nevertheless, all the winds are calmed and the waves of the sea become quiet for seven days when the halcyon is sitting upon her eggs. In exactly that number of days it hatches its young. But, since there is need of food for the nestlings so that they may grow, the bountiful God provides for the tiny creatures seven more days. As all the sailors know this, they call these the halcyon days.[22] These laws divine Providence has ordained concerning the irrational creature to encourage you to ask from God what pertains to your salvation. What wonders could not be performed for you, who have been made according to the image of God, when, indeed, for the sake of a bird so small the great and fearful sea is held in check, submitting to the command to be calm in the midst of winter?

(6) They say that the turtledove, when once separated from her mate, no longer accepts union with another, but, in memory of her former spouse, remains widowed, refusing marriage with another.[23] Let the women hear how the chastity of widowhood, even among the irrational creatures, is preferred to the unseemly multiplicity of marriages.

The eagle is most unjust in the rearing of her offspring. When she has brought forth two nestlings, she drops one of them to the ground, thrusting it out by blows from her wings; and, taking up the other one, she claims it alone as her own.

---

22 Cf. *Ibid.* 5.8.542b: 'The halcyon breeds at the season of the winter solstice. Accordingly, when this season is marked with calm weather, the name of "halcyon days" is given to the seven days preceding, and to as many following, the solstice.'
23 Cf. *Ibid.* 9.7.613a: 'The turtledove and the ringdove both have but one mate, and let no other come nigh.'

Because of the labor of rearing it, she rejects one which she has hatched.[24] The lammergeyer, however, as it is said, does not allow it to perish, but, taking it up, rears it along with her own nestlings.[25] Such are those parents who expose their children on a pretext of poverty, or who are unfair to their offspring in the distribution of the inheritance. For, just as they have given existence equally to each, so it is just also to provide them with opportunities for livelihood equally and impartially. Do not imitate the cruelty of the birds with crooked talons, who, when they see their own nestlings already attempting flight, throw them out of the nest, striking and thrusting with their wings, and for the future take no care of them. The love of the crow for its offspring is laudable. She even accompanies them when they have begun to fly and feeds and nurtures them for a very long time.

Many kinds of birds do not need the union with the males for conception; but, in other kinds, eggs produced without copulation [wind eggs] are sterile. It is said that the vultures hatch without coition a very great number of young, and this, although they are especially long-lived; in fact, their life generally continues for a hundred years. Consider this as my special observation from the history of the birds, in order that, if ever you see any persons laughing at our mystery, as though it were impossible and contrary to nature for a virgin to give birth while her virginity itself was preserved immaculate, you may consider that God, who is pleased to save the faithful by the foolishness of our preaching,[26] first set forth innumerable reasons from nature for our beliefs in His wonders.

---

24 Cf. *Ibid.* 6.6 563a: 'The eagle lays three eggs and hatches two of them, as it is said in the verses ascribed to Musaeus: "That lays three, hatches two, and cares for one." This is the case in most instances.'
25 Cf. *Ibid.* 9.34.619b: 'The so-called phene or lammergeier, . . . rears its own young and those of the eagle as well; for when the eagle ejects its young from the nest, this bird catches them up as they fall and feeds them. For the eagle, by the way, ejects the young birds prematurely, before they are able to feed themselves, or to fly.'
26 Cf. 1 Cor. 1.21.

(7) 'Let the waters bring forth crawling creatures that have life and winged creatures that fly above the earth under the firmament of the heavens.' They were ordered to fly above the earth because the earth provides nourishment for all, but under the firmament of the heavens, because, as we previously defined, the air there is called 'ouranos,' the 'heavens,' derived from 'orāsthai,' 'to be seen,'[27] and it is called 'firmament' because the air above our heads in comparison with the ether is somewhat denser and is made thicker by the vapors rising from below.

You have, therefore, the heavens adorned, the earth beautified, the sea abounding in its proper offspring, and the air full of the birds which fly through it. Everything, which by the command of God was brought forth from nonexistence into existence, and whatever my discourse has omitted at the present time so as to avoid a longer delay on these matters and so that it might not seem to extend beyond measure, may you who are studious review by yourselves, learning the wisdom of God in all things, and may you never cease from admiration nor from giving glory to the Creator for every creature.

You have species of birds which live their life in the darkness of night, and those which fly about in the light of day. Of those which feed by night there are bats, owls, and night ravens. Therefore, at any time when sleep does not come, a reflection on these birds and an examination of their individual qualities will suffice to cause you to give glory to the Creator. How the nightingale keeps awake when she sits on her eggs, since she does not cease from singing the whole night through.[28] How the bat is at the same time a quadruped and a fowl. How alone of the birds it makes use of teeth and produces offspring like the quadrupeds, yet travels through the air, raising itself not by wings, but by a kind of skin mem-

---
27 Wrong etymology. Cf. n. 33, Homily 3.
28 Cf. Pliny, *op. cit.* 10.43: 'The song of the nightingale is to be heard without intermission for fifteen days and nights continuously when the foliage is thickening, as it bursts from the bud.'

brane. How bats have by nature a mutual love, and like a chain cling to each other and hang one from the other, a thing which is not easily accomplished among us men; for, separation and solitude are preferred by the majority to community and union. How like to the eyes of the owl are they who devote themselves to vain wisdom. At night its vision is keen but, when the sun is shining, it grows dim. So the understanding of these men is very sharp for the contemplation of foolishness, but is absolutely blind in the consideration of the true light.

In the daytime it is very much easire for you to admire the Creator in all things. How our domestic fowl, calling out with his shrill voice and informing you that the sun is already approaching from afar off, wakens you for your labors, and rises early with the travelers and leads the farmers out to harvest. How vigilant are the geese and how very sharp in their perception of hidden dangers. At one time, in fact, they saved the imperial city by making known that some enemies were already about to seize the citadel of Rome through secret underground passages.[29] In what bird does nature not show some marvel peculiar to it? Who announces beforehand to the vultures the death of men when they are marching against each other? You may see countless flocks of vultures attending the army, guessing at the result from the warlike preparation. Now, this is not far from human reasoning. How shall I describe for you the terrible invasions of the locusts, which, rising in a mass at one signal and encamping along the whole width of a region, do not touch the fruits before the divine command is given them? And how the rose-colored starling,

---

29 Cf Livy, 5 47.2 ff.: 'The geese with their gabbling and clapping of their wings woke Marcus Manlius,—consul of three years before and a distinguished soldier,—who, catching up his weapons and at the same time calling the rest to arms, strode past his bewildered comrades to a Gaul who had already got a foothold on the crest and dislodged him with a blow from the boss of his shield . . . and presently the whole company lost their footing and were flung down headlong to destruction.'

the remedy for the plague, follows, with its boundless capacity for devouring them, our benevolent God in His kindness to man having made its nature insatiable? And what method of singing the cicada has? How it is, that, though the sound is produced by air which they inhale in dilating the chest, they are more musical at midday? But, in truth, I seem to be left farther behind in my explanation of the wonders of the winged creatures than if I had attempted to attain to their speed on foot.

Whenever you see those winged creatures called insects, such as the bees and wasps (they have been called insects because they appear cut into segments all around), consider that they do not have respiration or lungs but are completely nourished in all parts of their bodies by the air. Therefore, if they are drenched with oil, they perish, since their pores are stopped up;[30] but, if vinegar is immediately poured on them, the passages are opened and life is restored again. Our God has produced neither anything beyond need nor a deficiency of the necessities of life for any creature. Again, if you observe those creatures which are fond of water, you will find that they are differently constituted. Their feet are not divided like those of the crow nor hooked like those of the carnivora, but are broad and membranous so that they may easily swim upon the water, pushing through the water with the webs of their feet as if with oars. Now, if you notice how the swan, putting its neck down into the deep water, brings up food for itself from below, then you will discover the wisdom of the Creator, in that He gave it a neck longer than its feet for this reason, that it might, as if lowering a sort of fishing line, procure the food hidden in the deep water.[31]

---

30 Cf. Aristotle, *Ibid.* 8.27.605b: 'All insects, without exception, die if they be smeared over with oil.'
31 Cf. Aristotle, *On the Parts of Animals* 4.12.693a: 'In web-footed birds, . . . the neck is elongated, so as to be suitable for collecting food from the water. . . . For most birds of this kind . . . live by preying on some of the smaller animals that are to be found in water, and use these parts for their capture, the neck acting as a fishing rod, and the beak representing the line and hook.'

(8) The words of Scripture, if simply read, are a few short syllables: 'Let the waters bring forth winged creatures that fly above the earth under the firmament of the heavens'; but, when the meaning in the words is explained, then the great marvel of the wisdom of the Creator appears. How many varieties of winged creatures He has provided for! How different He has made them from each other in species! With what distinct properties He has marked each kind! The day is failing me while I relate to you the wonders in the air.

The land, ready in turn to exhibit creatures rivaling the plants, the swimming species, and the winged creatures, calls us to present wild beasts and reptiles and herds. 'Let the earth bring forth living creatures, cattle and wild animals and crawling creatures of different kinds.'[32] What do you say, you who mistrust Paul concerning the transformation made at the resurrection,[33] when you see many creatures of the air changing their forms? What stories are told about the Indian silkworm, the horned one! First, it changes into a caterpillar, then goes on to become a buzzing insect; however, it does not remain in this shape, but clothes itself with light, wide metallic wings. Whenever, therefore, you women sit unwinding the product of these, the threads, I mean, which the Chinese send to you for the preparation of soft garments,[34] recall the metamorphoses in this creature, conceive a clear idea of the resurrection, and do not refuse to believe the change which Paul announces for all men.

But, I perceive that my speech is going beyond due limits. When, indeed, I look at the great number of matters discussed, I see that I am being borne beyond bounds; but, again, when I take into consideration the variety of the wisdom

---

32 Gen. 1.24.
33 Cf. Col. 3.4: 'When Christ, your life, shall appear, then you too will appear with him in glory.'
34 Cf. Aristotle, *History of Animals* 5.19.551b: 'A class of women unwind and reel off the cocoons of these creatures, and afterwards weave a fabric with the threads thus unwound.'

manifested in the works of creation, I acknowledge that I have not even begun my explanation. At the same time it was not useless to detain you so long. For, what could anyone do during this time until evening? Guests are not pressing you; banquets are not awaiting you. Therefore, if it seems good to you, let us avail ourselves of the bodily fast for the joy of our souls. Since you have frequently served the flesh for pleasure, today persevere in the service of the soul. 'Delight in the Lord, and he will give thee the requests of thy heart.'[35] If you are eager for riches, you have spiritual riches, 'The judgments of the Lord are true, justified in themselves, more to be desired than gold and many precious stones.'[36] If you are devoted to enjoyment and pleasure, you have the eloquent words of God, which are 'sweeter than honey and the honeycomb'[37] to a man who is sound in his spiritual sense. If I shall dismiss you and put an end to the assembly, there are some who will run to the gaming tables. There oaths and cruel contentions and pangs of avarice are to be found. The demon stands by, inflaming the passions with dotted bones and changing the same money from one side of the table to the other, now leading this one on by victory and throwing that one into despair; again, causing the first to bear himself proudly and the latter to be covered with shame. What is the benefit of fasting in our body while filling our souls with innumerable evils? He who does not play at dice, but spends his leisure otherwise, what nonsense does he not utter? What absurdities does he not listen to? Leisure without the fear of God is, for those who do not know how to use time, the teacher of wickedness. Perhaps, some profit will be found in what I have said; but, if not, at least, because you have been kept occupied here, you have not sinned. Therefore, to detain you longer is to withdraw you for a longer time from evils.

---

35 Ps. 36.4.
36 *Ibid.* 18.10.
37 *Ibid.* 18.11.

What I have said will suffice for a reasonable judge, if he looks, not at the wealth of creation, but at the weakness of our power and at what is sufficient for the pleasure of those assembling. The earth welcomed you with its own plants, the sea with its fish, the air with its birds. The dry land in turn is ready to exhibit treasures equal to these. But, let this be the end of the morning feasting, lest satiety make you too dull for the enjoyment of the evening banquet. May He who has filled all things with His creation and has left us in all things clear memorials of His wondrous works fill your hearts with all spiritual joy, in Christ Jesus our Lord, to whom be glory and power forever. Amen.

# HOMILY 9

## Creation of Land Animals

(ON THE HEXAEMERON)

How did my morning repast of words appeal to you? Indeed, it has occurred to me that I should compare my talk with the kindness of a certain poverty-stricken host, who was ambitious to be among those that offer a good table, but, lacking costly foods, annoyed his guests by laying his poor fare upon the table in such abundance that his ambition was changed in him into disgraceful lack of taste. Well, such has been our method, unless you say differently. Yet, however it was, you must not disregard it. Elisha was by no means rejected as a poor host by his contemporaries, in spite of the fact that he feasted his friends on wild plants.

I know the laws of allegory, although I did not invent them of myself, but have met them in the works of others. Those who do not admit the common meaning of the Scriptures say that water is not water, but some other nature, and they explain a plant and a fish according to their opinion. They describe also the production of reptiles and wild animals, changing it according to their own notions, just like the dream interpreters, who interpret for their own ends the appearances seen in their dreams. When I hear 'grass,' I think of grass, and in the same manner I understand everything as it is said, a plant, a fish, a wild animal, and an ox. 'Indeed, I am not ashamed of the gospel.'[1] And, although those who have written about the world have argued much about the shape of the earth, whether the earth is a sphere, or a cylinder, or

---

1 Rom. 1.16.

is similar to a disk and is rounded off equally on all sides, or whether it is like a winnowing fan and hollowed out in the center[2] (the cosmographers have suggested all these notions, each one overthrowing the ideas of the other), I shall not be persuaded to say that our version of the creation is of less value because the servant of God, Moses, gave no discussion concerning the shape and did not say that its circumference contains one hundred and eighty thousand stades, nor measured how far its shadow spreads in the air when the sun passes under the earth, nor explained how, when this shadow approaches the moon, it causes the eclipses. Since he left unsaid, as useless for us, things in no way pertaining to us, shall we for this reason believe that the words of the Spirit are of less value than their foolish wisdom? Or shall I rather give glory to Him who has not kept our mind occupied with vanities but has ordained that all things be written for the edification and guidance of our souls? This is a thing of which they seem to me to have been unaware, who have attempted by false arguments and allegorical interpretations to bestow on the Scripture a dignity of their own imagining. But, theirs is the attitude of one who considers himself wiser than the revelations of the Spirit and introduces his own ideas in pretense of an explanation. Therefore, let it be understood as it has been written.

(2) 'Let the earth bring forth living creatures; cattle and wild beasts and crawling creatures.'[3] Consider the word of God moving through all creation, having begun at that time, active up to the present, and efficacious until the end, even to the consummation of the world. As a ball, when pushed by someone and then meeting with a slope, is borne downward

---

[2] Cf. Aristotle, *On the Heavens* 2.13.293b, and 294b: 'Some think that it is spherical, others that it is flat and drum-shaped. . . . Anaximenes and Anaxagoras and Democritus give the flatness of the earth as the cause of its staying still.' 2.14.297a: 'Its shape must necessarily be spherical.'

[3] Cf. Gen. 1.24: 'Let the earth bring forth all kinds of living creatures: cattle, crawling creatures and wild animals.'

by its own shape and the inclination of the ground and does not stop before some level surface receives it, so, too, the nature of existing objects, set in motion by one command, passes through creation, without change, by generation and destruction, preserving the succession of the species through resemblance, until it reaches the very end. It begets a horse as the successor of a horse, a lion of a lion, and an eagle of an eagle; and it continues to preserve each of the animals by uninterrupted successions until the consummation of the universe. No length of time causes the specific characteristics of the animals to be corrupted or extinct, but, as if established just recently, nature, ever fresh, moves along with time.

'Let the earth bring forth living creatures.' This command remains in the earth and the earth does not cease serving the Creator. Some things, in fact, are produced from the successors of those which existed previously, while others are shown to be engendered, even at present, from the earth itself, which not only causes the grasshoppers to spring forth in the abundant rains and other countless species of winged insects which are borne about in the air, of which the majority are nameless because of their ethereal nature, but also generates from itself mice and frogs. Somewhere or other, around the Egyptian Thebes, when a furious rain beats down in the burning heat of the day, the country is filled with field mice. And as for the eels, we do not see that they come into existence otherwise than from the slime, since neither an egg nor any other method effects their reproduction, but their generation is from the earth.[4]

---

[4] Cf. Aristotle, *History of Animals* 6.16.570a: 'There is no doubt, then, that they [eels] proceed neither from pairing nor from an egg. Some writers, however, are of opinion that they generate their kind, because in some eels little worms are found, from which they suppose that eels are derived. But this opinion is not founded on fact. Eels are derived from the so-called "earth's guts" that grow spontaneously in mud and in humid ground; in fact, eels have at times been seen to emerge out of such earthworms, and on other occasions have been rendered visible when the earthworms were laid open by either scraping or cutting.'

'Let the earth bring forth living creatures.' The herds are earthy and are bent toward the earth, but man is a heavenly creature who excels them as much by the excellence of his soul as by the character of his bodily structure. What is the figure of the quadrupeds? Their head bends toward the earth and looks toward their belly and pursues its pleasure in every way. Your head stands erect toward the heavens; your eyes look upward, so that, if ever you dishonor yourself by the passions of the flesh, serving your belly and your lowest parts, 'you are compared to senseless beasts, and are become like to them.'[5] A different solicitude is becoming to you, namely, to 'seek the things that are above, where Christ is,'[6] and with your mind to be above earthly things. As you have been molded, so dispose your own life. Keep your citizenship in heaven.[7] Your true country is Jerusalem above, your fellow citizens and fellow countrymen are the 'first-born who are enrolled in the heavens.'[8]

(3) 'Let the earth bring forth living creatures.' Therefore, the soul of brute beasts did not emerge after having been hidden in the earth, but it was called into existence at the time of the command. But, there is only one soul of brute beasts, for, there is one thing that characterizes it, namely, lack of reason. Each of the animals, however, is distinguished by different characteristics. The ox is steadfast, the ass sluggish; the horse burns with desire for the mare; the wolf is untamable and the fox crafty; the deer is timid, the ant industrious; the dog is grateful and constant in friendship. As each animal was created, he brought with him a distinctive characteristic of nature. Courage was brought forth with the lion, also the tendency to a solitary life and an unsocial attitude toward

---

5 Cf. Ps. 48 13. St. Basil changes the verb from the third person to the second.
6 Col. 3.1.
7 Cf. Phil. 3 20: 'But our citizenship is in heaven.'
8 Cf. Heb. 12.22, 23: 'But you have come to . . . the heavenly Jerusalem, . . . and to the Church of the firstborn who are enrolled in the heavens.'

those of his kind. Like a sort of tyrant of brute beasts, because of his natural arrogance, he does not admit an equal share of honor for the many. By no means does he accept yesterday's food or return to the remains of his prey. In him, also, nature has placed such powerful organs of voice that frequently many animals that surpass him in swiftness are overcome by his mere roaring. The leopard is violent and impetuous in attack. He has a body fitted for agility and lightness in accord with the movements of his spirit. The nature of the bear is sluggish and his ways peculiar to himself, treacherous and deeply secretive. He has been clothed with a body of the same type, heavy, compact, not distinctly articulated, truly fit for chilly hibernating in caves.

If we consider how much care, natural and inborn, these brute beasts take of their lives, either we shall be roused to watch over ourselves and to have forethought for the salvation of our souls, or we shall be absolutely condemned, when we are found to be failing even in the imitation of irrational animals. Frequently a bear, when suffering with very deep wounds, heals himself by packing the wounds through all sorts of devices with that mullein which has astringent properties. You might also see a fox healing himself with the sap of the pine. A tortoise, having taken his fill of the flesh of vipers, escapes injury from the venom through the antidote of marjoram;[9] and a serpent heals an injury in his eyes by feeding on fennel.

But, what rational prudence do not their forecasts of the changes in the atmosphere conceal? Everywhere the sheep, when winter approaches, ravenously devour the fodder, as if providing themselves with food against the coming scarcity.

---

9 Cf. Aristotle, *Ibid.* 9.6.612a· 'The tortoise, when it has partaken of a snake, eats marjoram; this action has been actually observed. A man saw a tortoise perform this operation over and over again, and every time it plucked up some marjoram go back to partake of its prey; he, thereupon pulled the marjoram up by the roots, and the consequence was the tortoise died.'

And the cattle, long enclosed during the winter season, when finally spring approaches, recognizing the change by their natural sensation, look from within the stables toward the exits, all turning their heads as by one agreement. Some alert persons have observed that the hedgehog has devised two vents for its hole and, when the north wind is about to blow, it blocks up the northern entrance, but, when the south wind again follows, it passes back to the northerly one.[10] Now, what are we men taught by these acts? Not only that the solicitude of our Creator extends through all things, but also that there is among brute beasts a certain sense perception of the future, so that we should not cling to our present life but should preserve all our zeal for future time. Will you not be industrious for your own self, O man? Will you not, after having observed the example of the ant, lay up in the present age rest to be enjoyed in the future? In the summertime the ant hoards up a supply of food for the winter and it does not, when the inconveniences of winter are not yet at hand, while away its time in idleness, but with a sort of relentless zeal it urges itself on to labor until it has stored up sufficient food in the storehouses. And it does not do even this indifferently but contrives by a certain wise inventiveness to cause the food to hold out as long as possible. It cuts through the middle of the grains with its claws so that they may not germinate and thereby become useless as food. Moreover, if it perceives that they are wet, it dries them. It does not expose them in every kind of weather, but only whenever it foresees that the air will continue at a mild temperature. At any rate, you will not see rain falling from the clouds as long as the food has been set out by the ants.

What words can express these marvels? What ear can

---

10 Cf. *Ibid.* 9.12.612b. 'In regard to the instinct of hedgehogs, it has been observed in many places that, when the wind is shifting from north to south, and from south to north, they shift the outlook of the earth-holes, and those that are kept in domestication shift over from one wall to the other.'

understand them? What time can suffice to say and to explain all the wonders of the Creator? Let us also say with the prophet: 'How great are thy works, O Lord? thou hast made all things in wisdom.'[11] The fact, then, that we were not taught by books what was useful is not a sufficient defense for us, who have understood how to choose what is advantageous by the untaught law of nature. Do you know what good you should do for your neighbor? What you wish him to do for you. Do you know what is evil? What you yourself would not choose to suffer from another. No skill in gathering roots or acquaintance with herbs procured for the irrational animals the knowledge of what was useful, but each of the animals is able naturally to make provisions for its own safety and it possesses a certain inexplainable attraction toward that which is according to its nature.

We also possess natural virtues toward which there is an attraction of soul not from the teaching of men, but from nature itself. Thus, no lesson teaches us to hate disease, but we have of ourselves an aversion to suffering; so, too, a certain untaught rejection of evil exists in our soul. Every evil is a sickness of soul, but virtue offers the cause of its health. Some have indeed rightly defined health as the good order of natural functions. If one uses this definition also in referring to a good condition in the soul, he will not err. Therefore, the soul, without being taught, strives for what is proper to it and conformable to its nature. For this reason self-control is praised by all, justice is approved, courage is admired, and prudence is greatly desired. These virtues are more proper to the soul than health is to the body. Children, love your parents.[12] Parents, 'do not provoke your children to anger.'[13] Does not nature itself say these things? Paul recommends nothing new but he binds more tightly the bonds of nature. If the lioness loves her offspring and the wolf fights for her

---
11 Ps. 103.24.
12 Cf. Eph. 6.1: 'Children, obey your parents.'
13 Eph. 6.4.

whelps, what can man say when he disregards the command and debases his nature, or when a son dishonors the old age of his father, or a father through a second marriage neglects the children of his first marriage?

(4) Among irrational animals the love of the offspring and of the parents for each other is extraordinary because God, who created them, compensated for the deficiency of reason by the superiority of their senses. Really, how is it that among countless sheep a lamb, leaping out from the fold, knows the appearance and voice of its mother, hurries toward her, and seeks its own source of milk? Even if it finds the maternal udder dry, it is satisfied with it, running past many that are heavy with milk. And how does the mother know her own among the countless lambs? They have one voice, the same appearance, a like odor among all, as much as reaches our sense of smell, but, nevertheless, they have a certain sense impression that is keener than our perception, through which the recognition of its own offspring is possible for each animal. The puppy does not yet have teeth, and nevertheless, he defends himself with his mouth against anyone that teases him. The calf has not yet horns, but he knows where nature has implanted his weapons. These facts support the evidence that the instincts of all animals are untaught, that nothing is without order or moderation in all that exists, but that all things bear traces of the wisdom of the Creator, showing in themselves that they were created prepared to assure their own preservation.

The dog is without reason but, nevertheless, he has sense reactions equivalent to reason. In fact, the dog appears to have been taught by nature what the wise of the world, who occupy themselves during life with much study, have solved with difficulty, I mean the complexities of inference. In tracking down a wild beast, if he finds the tracks separated in many directions, he traverses the paths leading each way and all but utters the syllogistic statement through his actions: 'Either the wild beast went this way,' he says, 'or this, or in that direction; but, since it is neither here nor there, it remains that he set out in that direction.' Thus, by the elimination of the false he finds the true way. What more do those do who settle down solemnly to their theories, draw lines in the dust, and then reject two of the three premises, finding the true way in the one that is left?

Does not the gratitude of the dog put to shame any man who is ungrateful to his benefactors? In fact, many dogs are said to have died beside their masters, murdered in a lonely place. In the case of recent murder some dogs have actually become guides for those seeking the murderer and have caused the evildoer to be brought to justice. What can they say who not only fail to love the Lord who created and nourishes them, but even treat as friends men who use offensive language against God, share the same table with them, and even at the meal itself permit blasphemies against Him who provides for them.

(5) Let us, however, return to the contemplation of creation. The more easily the animals are captured the more prolific they are. Therefore, hares and also wild goats produce many offspring, while wild sheep bear twins, that the species, which is devoured by carnivorous animals, may not fail. But, the beasts of prey bring forth few offspring. Whence the lioness with difficulty becomes the mother of only one lion.[14] For,

---

14 Cf. Herodotus, 3.108: 'The lioness, a very strong and bold beast, bears offspring but once in her life, and then but one cub; for the uterus comes out with the cub in the act of birth. This is the reason of it:— when the cub first begins to stir in the mother, its claws, much sharper than those of any other creature, tear the uterus, and as it grows, much more does it scratch and tear, so that when the hour of birth is near seldom is any of the uterus left whole.' Aristotle denies this in his *History of Animals* 6.31.579b: 'The lioness brings forth in the spring, generally two cubs at a time, and six at the very most; but sometimes only one. The story about the lioness discharging her womb in the act of parturition is a pure fable, and was merely invented to account for the scarcity of the animal; . . . The Syrian lion bears cubs five times: five cubs at the first litter, then four, then three, then two, and lastly one; after this the lioness ceases to bear for the rest of her days.'

it comes forth, as it is said, by tearing the womb to pieces with its pointed claws. And serpents are born after having eaten through the womb, making a proper return to the one who bore them.[15] Thus, everything in existence is the work of Providence, and nothing is bereft of the care owed to it. If you observe carefully the members even of the animals, you will find that the Creator has added nothing superfluous, and that He has not omitted anything necessary. Carnivorous animals He has fitted with sharp teeth; there was need of such for the nature of their food. Those which are only half equipped with teeth, He provided with many varied receptacles for the food. Because the food is not ground sufficiently fine the first time, He has given them the power to chew again what has already been swallowed. Thus, having been finely ground by the chewing of the cud, it is assimilated by the animal that is feeding. The first, second, third, and fourth stomachs in the ruminants do not remain idle, but each fulfills a necessary function.[16]

The camel's neck is long in order that it may be brought to the level of his feet and he may reach the grass on which he lives. The bear's neck and also that of the lion, tiger, and the other animals of this family, is short and is buried in the shoulders, because their food does not come from the grass and they do not have to bend down to the ground. They are carnivorous and secure their food by preying upon animals.

But what is the reason for the elephant's trunk? Because

---

15 Cf. Herodotus, 3.109: 'When serpents pair, and the male is in the very act of generation, the female seizes him by the neck, nor lets go her grip till she have devoured him. Thus the male dies; but the female is punished for his death; the young avenge their father, and eat their mother while they are yet within her; nor are they dropped from her till they have devoured her womb. Other snakes that do no harm to men, lay eggs and hatch out a vast number of young.'

16 Cf. Aristotle, *ibid.* 2.17.507a: 'However, animals present diversities in the structure of their stomachs. In the first place, of the viviparous quadrupeds, such of the horned animals as are not equally furnished with teeth in both jaws are furnished with four such chambers. These animals, by the way, are those that are said to chew the cud.' Cf. also *On the Parts of Animals* 3.14.674b.

the huge creature, the largest of land animals, produced for the consternation of those encountering it, had to have a very fleshy and massive body. If an immense neck proportionate to his legs had been given to this animal, it would have been hard to manage, since it would always be falling down because of its excessive weight. As it is, however, his head is attached to his backbone by a few vertebrae of the neck and he has the trunk which fulfills the function of the neck and through which he procures nourishment for himself and draws up water. His legs, which are not jointed, support his weight like joined columns. If loose and flexible limbs supported him, the bending of his joints would be continuous, since they would not suffice to bear his weight whether he was attempting to kneel or rise. As a matter of fact, a short knucklebone is set under the foot of the elephant, but there is no joint for an ankle or for a knee. Indeed, the sliding motion of joints could not support the enormous, swaying mass of flesh. Hence, there was need of that trunk reaching down to the feet. Have you not seen them in wars, leading the way for the phalanx like living towers? Or cutting through the close shield formation of the opponents with an attack that is irresistible? Unless his lower parts were in proportion, the animal would not endure these tasks for any length of time. At present, however, it is recorded that the elephant lives even three hundred years and more.[17] For this reason, also, its legs are solid and unjointed. As we have said, the trunk, which is serpentlike and rather flexible by nature, carries the food up from the ground. Thus the statement is true that nothing superfluous or lacking can be found in creation. Yet, this animal, which is so immense in size, God has made subject to us so that, when taught, it understands, and when struck, it submits. By this He clearly teaches that He has placed all things under us because we have been made to the image of the Creator. Not

---

17 Cf. *ibid.* 8.9.596a: 'The elephant is said by some to live for about two hundred years; by others, for three hundred.'

only among the large animals is it possible to see His inscrutable wisdom, but even among the smallest it is possible to find no less marvels. Just as I do not have greater admiration for the great mountain peaks which, because they are near the clouds, preserve the wintry cold with its violent gusts, than for the deep depressions of the valleys, which not only escape the harsh windiness of the heights, but retain always the warm breezes, so too, in the constitution of the animals I do not admire the huge elephant more than the mouse, which is formidable to the elephant, or than the very fine sting of the scorpion, which the Craftsman hollowed out like a tube so that through it the poison is injected into those stung. And, let no one bring a charge against the Creator because He has produced venomous animals, destructive and hostile to our life; or one might with equal reason make charges against a teacher when he brings the levity of youth into order, chastening the undisciplined one with rods and whips.

(6) Wild animals are a proof of our faith. Have you trusted in the Lord? 'Thou shalt walk upon the asp and the basilisk; and thou shalt trample under foot the lion and the dragon.'[18] You have the power through faith to walk upon serpents and scorpions. Or, do you not observe that the viper which fastened onto Paul when he was gathering sticks inflicted no harm because the holy man was found to be full of faith?[19] Yet, if you are incredulous, fear not the wild beast more than your own lack of faith, through which you have made yourself an easy prey to every form of corruption. I notice, however, that I have long been asked explanations about the

---
18 Ps. 90.13.
19 Cf. Acts 28.3-6: 'Now Paul gathered a bundle of sticks and laid them on the fire, when a viper came out because of the heat and fastened on his hand. When the natives saw the creature hanging from his hand, they said to one another, "Surely this man is a murderer, for though he has escaped the sea, Justice does not let him live." But he shook off the creature into the fire and suffered no harm. Now they were expecting that he would swell up and suddenly fall down and die; but after waiting a long time and seeing no harm come to him, they changed their minds and said that he was a god.'

creation of men, and I seem almost to hear my audience clamoring out, 'We are taught the nature of our possessions, but we are ignorant of ourselves.' Therefore, we must put aside the hesitation which delays us and discuss it.

In truth, to know oneself seems to be the hardest of all things. Not only our eye, which observes external objects, does not use the sense of sight upon itself, but even our mind, which contemplates intently another's sin, is slow in the recognition of its own defects. Therefore, even at present our speech, after eagerly investigating matters pertaining to others, is slow and hesitant in the examination of our own nature. Yet, it is not possible for one, intelligently examining himself, to learn to know God better from the heavens and earth than from our own constitution, as the prophet says: 'Thy knowledge is become wonderful from myself';[20] that is, having carefully observed myself, I have understood the superabundance of wisdom in You.

'And God said, "Let us make mankind." '[21] Where, I pray, is the Jew, who in times past, when the light of theology was shining as through windows, and the Second Person was being indicated mystically, but not yet clearly revealed, fought against the truth and said that God was speaking to Himself? For, He Himself spoke, it is said, and He Himself made. 'Let there be light,' and there was light.[22] Therefore, the wickedness in their words was obvious even at that time. What coppersmith or carpenter or shoemaker, sitting down alone among the tools of his craft, with no one helping him, says to himself: 'Let us make a sword,' or 'Let us construct a plow,' or 'Let us make a shoe'? Does he not rather accomplish the work undertaken in silence? Truly, it is utter nonsense for anyone to sit down and command and watch over himself, and imperiously and vehemently urge himself on. Since they do not shrink

---

20 Ps. 138.6.
21 Gen. 1.26.
22 *Ibid.* 1.13.

from calumniating the Lord Himself, what would they not say with a tongue so trained to falsehood? The present word, however, completely blocks their mouth. 'And God said, "Let us make mankind." '[23] Tell me, is then the Person only one? The command was not written, 'Let mankind be made,' but 'Let us make mankind.' As long as the one to be taught had not yet appeared, the preaching of theology was deeply hidden; now, when the creation of mankind was expected, faith was revealed, and the doctrine of truth was more clearly disclosed. 'Let us make mankind.' You, O enemy of Christ, hear Him addressing the companion of His creative activity, 'By whom also he made the world; who . . . upholds all things by the word of his power.[24]

Not in silence, however, does mankind accept the word of true religion but, just as the wild beasts, which fiercely hate mankind, when they are enclosed in cages, roar about the enclosures, displaying the meanness and savagery of their nature without being able to satisfy their fury, so also the Jews, a race hostile to truth, being straightened, say that there are many to whom the word of God is directed. He says to the angels standing beside Him, 'Let us make mankind.' It is Jewish fiction, a frivolous fable derived from these words. That they may not admit one Person, they introduce numberless persons. And denying the Son, they attribute to the servants the honor of counsel and make our fellow slaves the lords of our creation. Man, when perfected, is lifted up to the dignity of angels. But, what creature can be equal to the Creator?

Consider the following words also: 'In our image.'[25] What do you say to this? Surely, the image of God and of the angels is not the same. Now, it is absolutely necessary for the form of the Son and of the Father to be the same, the form being

---
23 *Ibid.* 1.26.
24 Heb. 1.2, 3.
25 Gen. 1.26.

understood, of course, as becomes the divine, not in a bodily shape, but in the special properties of the Godhead. You also, who are of the recent mutilation,[26] who, under a pretense of Christianity, cultivate Judaism, listen. To whom does He say: 'In our image'? To whom else, I say, than to the 'brightness of his glory and the image of his substance,'[27] who is 'the image of the invisible God'?[28] Therefore, to His own living image who says: 'I and the Father are one,'[29] and 'He who sees me sees also the Father,'[30] to this image He says: 'Let us make mankind in our own image.' Where there is one image, where is the dissimilarity? 'And God created Man.'[31] Not 'they created.' Here He avoided the plurality of persons. Teaching the Jew by the former words and preventing error in the Gentile by the latter, he returned safely to the singular form, in order that you might understand the Son with the Father and avoid the risk of polytheism. 'In the image of God he created him.'[32]

Again, the Person of the co-worker was introduced. For, He did not say, 'In His own image,' but 'In the image of God.' We shall tell later, if God permits, in what respect man is in the image of God and how he shares in His likeness. At present, let us say this much: if there is one image, whence did it come to your mind to utter an intolerable blasphemy, saying that the Son is unlike the Father? O the ingratitude! Do you refuse to share with the Benefactor the likeness which you received? And do you think that the gifts of grace presented to you remain your own, and yet, do not permit the Son to have a likeness from nature with His Father?

But now, evening, having long ago sent the sun to its setting, again imposes silence upon us. Let us, therefore, at this

---

26 Phil. 3.2.
27 Heb. 1.3.
28 Col. 1.15.
29 John 10.30.
30 *Ibid.* 14.9.
31 Gen. 1.27.
32 *Ibid.*

point, be content with what has been said and lay our words to rest. We have at present employed our speech to arouse your zeal as much as possible, but, with the help of the Spirit, we shall later add a more perfect examination of the facts lying before us. Depart, I beg of you, rejoicing, O Christ-loving assembly, and arrange your modest tables with a remembrance of what I have said, instead of with expensive foods and varied delicacies. Let the Anomoean be covered with confusion; let the Jew feel shame; let the pious rejoice in the dogmas of truth; let the Lord be glorified, to whom be glory and power forever. **Amen.**

# HOMILY 10

## *A Psalm of the Lot of the Just Man*

### (ON PSALM 1)

ALL SCRIPTURE IS INSPIRED by God and is useful,[1] composed by the Spirit for this reason, namely, that we men, each and all of us, as if in a general hospital for souls, may select the remedy for his own condition. For, it says, 'care will make the greatest sin to cease.'[2] Now, the prophets teach one thing, historians another, the law something else, and the form of advice found in the proverbs something different still. But, the Book of Psalms has taken over what is profitable from all. It foretells coming events; it recalls history; it frames laws for life; it suggests what must be done; and, in general, it is the common treasury of good doctrine, carefully finding what is suitable for each one. The old wounds of souls it cures completely, and to the recently wounded it brings speedy improvement; the diseased it treats,

---

1 2 Tim. 3.16. St. Basil begins here his prologue in praise of the psalms, which includes the first four paragraphs. This prologue is also found in many manuscripts and editions of St. Augustine's commentaries on the psalms and was by many attributed to St. Augustine. However, it has now been shown that the prologue as found in St. Augustine's works is the prologue of St. Basil's homilies as translated by Rufinus. It is probably because of this prologue that St. Basil omitted the superscription of the Psalm 1, which reads: 'The Happiness of the Just and the Evil State of the Wicked.' The superscriptions of the Psalms usually indicated both their literary type and their authorship, occasion of delivery, or musical accompaniment. Cf. C. J. Callan, *The New Psalter*, pages 3-7.
2 Eccles. 10.4.

and the unharmed it preserves. On the whole, it effaces, as far as is possible, the passions, which subtly exercise dominion over souls during the lifetime of man, and it does this with a certain orderly persuasion and sweetness which produces sound thoughts.

When, indeed, the Holy Spirit saw that the human race was guided only with difficulty toward virtue, and that, because of our inclination toward pleasure, we were neglectful of an upright life, what did He do? The delight of melody He mingled with the doctrines so that by the pleasantness and softness of the sound heard we might receive without perceiving it the benefit of the words, just as wise physicians who, when giving the fastidious rather bitter drugs to drink, frequently smear the cup with honey. Therefore, He devised for us these harmonious melodies of the psalms, that they who are children in age or, even those who are youthful in disposition might to all appearances chant but, in reality, become trained in soul. For, never has any one of the many indifferent persons gone away easily holding in mind either an apostolic or prophetic message, but they do chant the words of the psalms, even in the home, and they spread them around in the market place, and, if perchance, someone becomes exceedingly wrathful, when he begins to be soothed by the psalm, he departs with the wrath of his soul immediately lulled to sleep by means of the melody.

(2) A psalm implies serenity of soul; it is the author of peace, which calms bewildering and seething thoughts. For, it softens the wrath of the soul, and what is unbridled it chastens. A psalm forms friendships, unites those separated, conciliates those at enmity. Who, indeed, can still consider as an enemy him with whom he has uttered the same prayer to God? So that psalmody, bringing about choral singing, a bond, as it were, toward unity, and joining the people into a harmonious union of one choir, produces also the greatest of blessings, charity. A psalm is a city of refuge from the demons; a means

of inducing help from the angels, a weapon in fears by night, a rest from toils by day, a safeguard for infants, an adornment for those at the height of their vigor, a consolation for the elders, a most fitting ornament for women. It peoples the solitudes; it rids the market place of excesses; it is the elementary exposition of beginners, the improvement of those advancing, the solid support of the perfect, the voice of the Church. It brightens the feast days; it creates a sorrow which is in accordance with God. For, a psalm calls forth a tear even from a heart of stone. A psalm is the work of angels, a heavenly institution, the spiritual incense.

Oh! the wise invention of the teacher who contrived that while we were singing we should at the same time learn something useful; by this means, too, the teachings are in a certain way impressed more deeply on our minds. Even a forceful lesson does not always endure, but what enters the mind with joy and pleasure somehow becomes more firmly impressed upon it. What, in fact, can you not learn from the psalms? Can you not learn the grandeur of courage? The exactness of justice? The nobility of self-control? The perfection of prudence? A manner of penance? The measure of patience? And whatever other good things you might mention? Therein is perfect theology, a prediction of the coming of Christ in the flesh, a threat of judgment, a hope of resurrection, a fear of punishment, promises of glory, an unveiling of mysteries; all things, as if in some great public treasury, are stored up in the Book of Psalms. To it, although there are many musical instruments, the prophet adapted the so-called harp, showing, as it seems to me, that the gift from the Spirit resounded in his ears from above. With the cithara and the lyre the bronze from beneath responds with sound to the plucking, but the harp has the source of its harmonic rhythms from above, in order that we may be careful to seek the things above and not be borne down by the sweetness of the melody to the passions of the flesh. And I believe this, namely, that the words of prophecy are made clear to us in a profound and wise manner through the structure of the instrument, because those who are orderly and harmonious in soul possess an easy path to the things above. Let us now see the beginning of the psalms.

(3) 'Blessed is the man who hath not walked in the counsel of the ungodly.'[3] When architects raise up immensely high structures, they put under them foundations proportionate to the height; and when shipbuilders are constructing a merchantman that carries 10,000 measures, they fix the ship's keel to correspond with the weight of the wares it is capable of carrying. Even in the generation of living animals, since the heart is the first organ formed by nature,[4] it receives a structure from nature proportionate to the animal destined to be brought into existence. Therefore, since the body is built around in proportion to its own beginnings, the differences in the sizes of animals are produced. Like the foundation in a house, the keel in a ship, and the heart in the body of an animal, this brief introduction seems to me to possess that same force in regard to the whole structure of the psalms.

When David intended to propose in the course of his speech to the combatants of true religion many painful tasks involving unmeasured sweats and toils, he showed first the happy end, that in the hope of the blessings reserved for us we might endure without grief the sufferings of this life. In the same way, too, the expectation of suitable lodging for them lightens the toil for travelers on a rough and difficult road, and the desire for wares makes mechants dare the sea, while the prom-

---

[3] Ps. 1.1. Also, note the way a man grows hardened in sin—he walks in the ways of the ungodly, stands in the way of sinners, and sits among the wicked. Cf. n.7 *infra*.

[4] Cf. Aristotle, *On the Parts of Animals* 3.4.665a: 'For, in sanguineous animals both heart and liver are visible enough when the body is only just formed, and while it is still extremely small.' Also 666a: 'For no sooner is the embryo formed, than its heart is seen in motion as though it were a living creature, and this before any of the other parts, it being, as thus shown, the starting-point of their nature in all animals that have blood.'

ise of the crop steals away the drudgery from the labors of the farmers. Therefore, the common Director of our lives, the great Teacher, the Spirit of truth, wisely and cleverly set forth the rewards, in order that, rising above the present labors, we might press on in spirit to the enjoyment of eternal blessings. 'Blessed is the man who hath not walked in the counsel of the ungodly.' What is truly good, therefore, is principally and primarily the most blessed. And that is God. Whence Paul also, when about to make mention of Christ, said: 'According to the manifestation of our blessed God and Savior Jesus Christ.'[5] For, truly blessed is Goodness itself toward which all things look, which all things desire, an unchangeable nature, lordly dignity, calm existence; a happy way of life, in which there is no alteration, which no change touches; a flowing fount, abundant grace, inexhaustible treasure. But, stupid and worldly men, ignorant of the nature of good itself, frequently bless things worth nothing, riches, health, renown; not one of which is in its nature good, not only because they easily change to the opposite, but also because they are unable to make their possessors good. What man is just because of his possessions? What man is self-controlled because of his health? On the contrary, in fact, each of these possessions frequently becomes the servant of sin for those who use them badly. Blessed is he, then, who possesses that which is esteemed of the greatest value, who shares in the goods that cannot be taken away. How shall we recognize him? 'He who hath not walked in the counsel of the ungodly.'

But, before I explain what it is 'not to walk in the counsel of the ungodly,' I wish to settle the question asked at this point. Why, you say, does the prophet single out only man and proclaim him happy? Does he not exclude women from happiness? By no means. For, the virtue of man and woman is the same, since creation is equally honored in both; there-

---

[5] Cf. Tit. 2:13: 'Looking for the blessed hope and glorious coming of our great God and Savior, Jesus Christ.'

fore, there is the same reward for both. Listen to Genesis. 'God created man,' it says, 'in the image of God he created him. Male and female he created them.' They whose nature is alike have the same reward. Why, then, when Scripture had made mention of man, did it leave woman unnoticed? Because it believed that it was sufficient, since their nature is alike, to indicate the whole through the more authoritative part.

'Blessed, therefore, is the man who hath not walked in the counsel of the ungodly.' Notice the exactness of the wording, how each single word of the statement is fulfilled. It did not say, 'who does not walk in the counsel of the ungodly,' but 'who hath not walked.' He who happens to be in this life, is not yet blessed, because of the uncertainty of his departure. But, he who has fulfilled what has fallen to his share and has closed his life with an end that cannot be gainsaid, that one is already safely proclaimed blessed. Why, then, are they who are walking in the law of the Lord blessed? Here Scripture regards as blessed not those who have walked, but those who are still walking, because they who are doing good receive approval in the work itself; and they who are fleeing evil are to be praised, not if, perhaps, they shun the sin once or twice, but if they are able to escape the experience of evil entirely. From the train of my reasoning another difficulty has presented itself to us. Why does Scripture proclaim as blessed, not him who is successfully performing a good act, but him who did not commit sin? Because in that case the horse and ox and stone will be considered blessed. For, what inanimate object has 'stood in the way of sinners'? Or what irrational creature has 'sat in the chair of pestilence'?[6] Now, if you will wait a little, you will find the solution. It continues: 'But his will

---

6 Ps. 1.1. *Chair of pestilence* in Hebrew terminology implies a circle or assembly of those who scoff at religion. Cf. M. Britt, *Dictionary of the Psalter*, p. 201. St. Basil translated the expression with the meaning of 'pestilence' but gave it an allegorical interpretation.

is in the law of the Lord.'⁷ However, the practice of the divine law falls only upon him who possesses intelligence. And we say this, that the starting point in acquiring the good is the withdrawal from evil. 'Decline from evil,' it says, 'and do good.'⁸

(4) Therefore, leading us on wisely and skilfully to virtue, David made the departure from evil the beginning of good. If he had put forth for you immediately the final perfections, you would have hesitated at the undertaking, but, as it is, he accustoms you to things more easily gained in order that you may have courage for those which follow. I would say that the exercise of piety resembles a ladder, that ladder which once the blessed Jacob saw,⁹ of which one part was near the earth and reaching to the ground, the other extended above, even to the very heavens. Therefore, those who are being introduced to a life of virtue must place their foot upon the first steps and from there always mount upon the next, until by gradual progress they have ascended to the height attainable by human nature. As withdrawal from the earth is the first step on the ladder, so in a manner of life in harmony with God the departure from evil is the first. Actually, idleness is in every way easier than any action whatsoever, as for instance, 'Thou shalt not kill; thou shalt not commit adultery; thou shalt not steal.'¹⁰ Each of these demands idleness and inactivity. 'Thou shalt love thy neighbor as thyself.'¹¹ and 'Sell what thou hast, and give to the poor,'¹² and 'If anyone forces thee to go for one mile, go with him two,'¹³ are activities worthy of athletes, and requiring for success a soul already vigorous. Therefore, admire the wisdom of him who leads us

---

7 *Ibid.* 1.2.
8 *Ibid.* 36.27.
9 Cf. Gen. 28.12: 'He dreamed that a ladder was set up on the ground with its top reaching to heaven.'
10 Exod. 20.13-15.
11 Matt. 19.19.
12 *Ibid.* 19.21.
13 *Ibid.* 5.41.

on to perfection through things that are rather easy and more readily gained.

He put before us three acts which must be guarded against: walking in the counsel of the ungodly, standing in the way of sinners, sitting on the chair of pestilences. In accordance with the nature of things, he set up this order by his words. First, we take counsel with ourselves; next, we strengthen our resolution; then, we continue unchanged in what has been determined. Primarily, therefore, the purity of our mind is to be deemed blessed, since the resolution in the heart is the root of the actions of the body. Thus, adultery, first enkindled in the soul of the lover of pleasure, causes destruction through the body. Whence, also, the Lord says that the things that defile a man are from within.[14] And, since impiety is properly called the sin against God, may it never happen that we admit doubts concerning God through want of faith. It is 'walking in the counsel of the ungodly,' if you should say in your heart, 'Is it really God who governs all things? Is God actually in the heavens, managing each individual thing? Is there a judgment? Is there a reward for each according to his work? Why, then, are the just poor, and sinners rich? Why are these sick, and those in good health? These dishonored, and those held in esteem? Is not the world borne along without visible cause, and do not some unaccountable circumstances allot the lives for each without any order?' If you have had these thoughts, you have walked in the counsel of the ungodly. Blessed, therefore, is he who has not admitted any doubt concerning God, who did not become weak in soul concerning the present, but awaits that which is promised, who did not hold any disloyal suspicion about Him who created us.

'And blessed is that man who has not stood in the way of sinners.' Life, then, is called a way because each being that

---

[14] Cf. Matt. 15.18: 'But the things that proceed out of the mouth come from the heart, and it is they that defile a man.'

enters into life hastens toward its end. Just as those who are sleeping in ships are carried by the wind through its own force to the harbors, even though they themselves do not perceive it but the course hurries them on to the end, so we also, as the time of our life flows on, are hurried along as if by some continuous and restless motion on the unheeded course of life, each one toward his proper end. For example, you sleep, and time runs past you; you are awake, and you are busily engaged in mind. All the same, life is spent, even though it has escaped our notice. We run a certain course, each and every man urged on to his proper end; for this reason we are all on the way. And thus you should understand the meaning of 'the way.' You are placed as a traveler in this life; you pass by all things, and everything is left behind you. You saw a plant or grass or water on the way, or any other worthwhile sight. You enjoyed it a little, then you passed on. Again, you came upon stones, gullies, peaks, cliffs, and palisades, or perhaps, even wild beasts, reptiles, thorns, and other troublesome objects; you were a little distressed, then you left them behind. Such is life, which holds neither lasting pleasures nor permanent afflictions. The way is not yours, neither are the present affairs yours. Among travelers, as soon as the first moves his foot, immediately the one after him takes a step, and after that one, he who follows him.

(5) Consider also the circumstances of life, whether they are not very much the same. Today you have cultivated the earth, tomorrow another will do so, and after him another. Do you see these fields and these costly houses? How many times has each of them already changed its name since it came into existence? They were said to be this man's; then, the name was changed for another; then they passed on to that man; and now, finally, they are said to belong to still another. Is not our life a way, receiving one man after another sucessively and keeping all following one another? 'Blessed, therefore, is he who has not stood in the way of sinners.'

Now, what does the expression 'has not stood' mean? While we men were in our first age, we were neither in sin nor in virtue (for the age was unsusceptible of either condition); but, when reason was perfected in us, then that happened which was written: 'But when the commandment came, sin revived, and I died.'[15] Wicked thoughts, which originate in our minds from the passions of the flesh, rise up. In truth, if, when the command came, that is, the power of discernment of the good, the mind did not prevail over the baser thoughts but permitted its reason to be enslaved by the passions, sin revived, but the mind died, suffering death because of its transgressions. Blessed, therefore, is he who did not continue in the way of sinners but passed quickly by better reasoning to a pious way of life. For, there are two ways opposed to each other, the one wide and broad, the other narrow and close.[16] And there are two guides, each attempting to turn the traveler to himself. Now, the smooth and downward sloping way has a deceptive guide, a wicked demon, who drags his followers through pleasure to destruction, but the rough and steep way has a good angel, who leads his followers through the toils of virtue to a blessed end.

As long as each of us is a child, pursuing the pleasure of the moment, he has no care for the future; but, when he has become a man, after his judgment is perfected, he seems, as it were, to see his life divided for him between virtue and evil, and frequently turning the eye of his soul upon each, he separates the analogous traits that belong to each. The life of the sinner shows all the pleasures of the present age; that of the just reveals in a slight measure the blessings of the future alone. And, insofar as the future promises beautiful rewards, to that extent does the way of those saved offer the present toilsome works; on the contrary, the pleasant and

---

15 Rom. 7.9.
16 Cf. Matt. 7.13. 'For wide is the gate and broad is the way that leads to destruction.'

undisciplined life does not hold out the expectation of later delights, but those already present. So, every soul becomes dizzy and changes from one side to the other in its reasonings, choosing virtue when things eternal are in its thoughts, but, when it looks to the present, preferring pleasure. Here it beholds the comforts of the flesh, there the enslavement of the flesh; here drunkenness, there fasting; here intemperate laughter, there abundant tears; in this life dancing, in that prayer; here flutes, there groans; here incontinence, there virginity. While, therefore, that which is truly good can be apprehended by the reason through faith (it has been banished far and the eye did not see it nor the ear hear it), yet, the sweetness of sin has pleasure ready and flowing through every sense. Blessed is he who is not turned aside to his destruction through its incitements to pleasure, but eagerly awaits the hope of salvation through patient endurance, and in his choice of one of the two ways, does not go upon the way leading to the lower things.

(6) 'Nor sat in the chair of pestilence.'[17] Does he mean these chairs upon which we rest our bodies? What is the association of wood with sin, so that I flee the chair occupied before by the sinner as being harmful? Or, should we not think that a steady and lasting persistence in the choice of evil is called a chair? This we must guard against because the practice of assiduously occupying ourselves with sins engenders in our souls a certain condition that can scarcely be removed. An inveterate condition of the soul and the exercise of evil strengthened by time, are hard to heal, or even are entirely incurable, since, for the most part, custom is changed into nature. Indeed, not to attach ourselves to evil is a request worth praying for. But there remains a second way: immediately after the temptation to flee it as if it were a venomous sting, according to words of Solomon concerning the wicked woman: 'Do not set your eye upon her, but leap back; do not

---
17 Cf. Ps. 1.1. Also n. 6 above.

delay.'[18] Now, I know that some in their youth have sunk down into the passions of the flesh and have remained in their sins until their old age because of the habit of evil. As the swine rolling about in the mire always smear more mud on themselves, so these bring upon themselves more and more each day the shame of pleasure. Blessed is it, therefore, not to have had evil in your mind; but, if through the deceit of the enemy, you have received in your soul the counsels of impiety, do not stay in your sin. And, if you have experienced this, do not become established in evil. So then, 'do not sit in the chair of pestilence.'

If you have understood what Scripture calls a chair, that it means lasting persistence in evil, examine now of what pestilences it speaks. Those who are skilled in these matters say that the pestilence, when it touches one man or animal, is communicated to all those who are near at hand; for, the nature of the disease is such that all are infected with the sickness by one another. Of some such kind are the workers of iniquity. Since one gives the disease to one and another gives it to another, they are all sick together and perish at the same time. Or, do you not see the licentious persons sitting in the market place, who laugh at the chaste, relate their shameful acts, the works of darkness, and recount their disgraceful passions as deeds of prowess or some other manly virtues? These are the pestilences who are striving to bring their own evil upon all, and who vie emulously that many be made to resemble them, in order that by fellowship through evils they may escape censure. In fact, neither can a fire, which has seized upon material that is easily enkindled, be prevented from passing through all of it, especially if it meets with a favorable breeze that carries the flame, nor can the sin which has fastened upon one be prevented from going through all, if the winds of wickedness have kindled it. For, the spirit of impurity does not allow the disgrace to remain in the one, but,

---

18 Cf. Prov 9 18a (only in Septuagint version).

immediately, comrades of the same age are called in; carousels, strong drink, and shameful tales; a harlot drinking with them, smiling upon this one, goading that one on, and inflaming all to the same sin.

Is this pestilence, indeed, a small thing, or is the spreading of evil something small? But, surely, did not the emulator of the avaricious man or of one possessed of civil authority who is conspicuous for some other wickedness, or of him who holds the power among his people, or commands armies, and who then is contaminated with shameful passions, did not he, I say, admit the pestilence into his soul, making his own the evil of the person emulated? For, the distinctions acquired in life make the lives of those who are distinguished conspicuous; and soldiers strive, for the most part, to be like military commanders, and the common people in the cities emulate those in power. And in general, whenever the evil of the one has been considered deserving of imitation by the many, properly and fitly the pestilence of souls will be said to prevail in life. Even renown won in the midst of evil draws many of the unsteady to the same ambition. Since, therefore, one is filled with corruption by this man, and another by that one, let such be said to have the pestilence in their souls. Do not, therefore, sit in the chair of pestilence, nor participate in the council of seducers and corrupters, nor persist in counsels badly given.

My speech, however, is still in its introduction, yet, I see that its extent exceeds due proportions, so that it is not easy either for you to retain more, nor for me to continue my lecture because of the natural weakness of my voice which is failing me. Although my words are incomplete, since flight from evil has been taught, but perfection through good works omitted, nevertheless, in commending the present matters to attentive hearers, we promise, if God permits, to complete the omissions, if only we do not experience complete silence henceforth. May the Lord grant us the reward for our words, and you the fruit of what you have heard, by the grace of

Christ Himself, because to Him is glory and power forever. Amen.

## HOMILY 11

*A Psalm of David which He Sang to the Lord, for the Words of Chusi, the Son of Jemini*[1]

(ON PSALM 7)

THE INSCRIPTION of the Seventh Psalm seems in a way to be opposed to the history of the kingdoms where the facts about David are recorded.[2] For in the history, Chusi is mentioned as the chief companion of David and the son of Arachi, but in the psalm, Chusi is the son of Jemini. Neither he nor any other of those appearing in the history was the son of Jemini. Perhaps, he was called the son of Jemini for this reason, because he displayed great valor and manliness through a mere pretense of friendship, going over, as he pretended, to Absalom, but, in reality, thwarting the plans of Achitophel, a very skilled man, well trained in military affairs, who was giving his counsel. 'The son of Jemini' is interpreted 'the son of the right hand.' By his proposals he prevented the acceptance of the plan of Achitophel—that no time should intervene in the affairs but that an attack should be made immediately on the father while he was unprepared—'in order that,' as Scripture says, 'the Lord might bring all evils upon Absalom.'[3] At all events, he seemed to them to introduce more plausible reasons for postponement and delay, while his real purpose was to give time to David to gather his forces. Because

---
1 Ps. 7.1.
2 Cf. 2 Kings 15-18.
3 2 Kings 17.14.

of his counsel he was acceptable to Absalom, who said: 'The counsel of Chusi the Arachite is better than the counsel of Achitophel.'[4]

However, Chusi informed David through the priests Sadoc and Abiathar of the decision and bade him not to camp in Araboth in the desert, but urged him to cross it.[5] Since, then, he was on the right hand of David through his good advice, he obtained the name from his brave deed. Surely, it is because of this that he is called 'son of Jemini,' that is, 'son of the right hand.' It is a custom of Scripture not only to give those who are more wicked a name from their sin rather than from their fathers, but also to call the better sons from the virtue characterizing them. Accordingly, the Apostle calls the devil the son of perdition. 'Unless the impious one is revealed, the son of perdition.'[6] And in the Gospel the Lord called Judas the son of perdition. 'And not one of them perished,' it says, 'except the son of perdition.'[7] But, He calls those formed in the knowledge of God children of wisdom, 'For, wisdom,' He says, 'is justified by her children.'[8] He also says: 'If a son of peace be there.'[9] It should not, then, seem strange that the father of his body was not mentioned, and that the chief companion of David was called the son of his right hand, receiving a title belonging to him because of his deeds.

(2) 'O Lord my God, in thee have I put my trust; save me.'[10] Although the saying, 'O Lord my God, in thee have I put my trust; save me,' is thought to be a simple prayer and one that can be offered up rightly by anyone, perhaps such is not the case. For, he who puts his trust in man or is buoyed up by some other concerns of life, such as power, or possessions, or

---

4 *Ibid.*
5 Cf. 2 Kings 17.15, 16.
6 Cf. 2 Thess. 2.3: 'Unless the man of sin is revealed, the son of perdition.'
7 John 17.12.
8 Matt. 11 19.
9 Luke 10.6.
10 Ps. 7.2.

any of the things considered by the many to be glorious, is not able to say, 'O Lord my God, in thee have I put my trust.' In fact, there is a command that we should not put our trust in rulers, and 'Cursed be the man that trusteth in man.'[11] As it is proper not to worship anything else besides God, so also is it proper not to trust in any other except God the Lord of all things. 'The Lord' it is said, 'is my hope and my praise.'[12]

How is it that at first David prays to be saved from his persecutors, and then, to be delivered? An explanation will make the statement clear. 'Save me from all them that persecute me, and deliver me, lest at any time he seize upon my soul like a lion.'[13] Now, what is the difference between being saved and being delivered? Properly speaking, those who are weak need safety, but those who are held in captivity need deliverance. Therefore, he who has some weakness in himself, but possesses faith in himself, is disposed by his own faith to be saved. 'For, thy faith,' it is said, 'has saved thee';[14] and 'So be it done to thee as thou hast believed.'[15] But, he who must be delivered, awaits a price which must be paid in his name from the outside. Accordingly, being under sentence of death, knowing that there is one who saves and one who delivers, 'In thee have I put my trust,' he says, 'save me' from weakness, and 'deliver me' from captivity. I think that the noble athletes of God, who have wrestled considerably with the invisible enemies during the whole of their lives, after they have escaped all of their persecutions and reached the end of life, are examined by the prince of the world in order that, if they are found to have wounds from the wrestling or any stains or effects of sin, they may be detained; but, if they are found unwounded and stainless, they may be brought by

---
11 Jer. 17.5.
12 St. Basil seems to have confused Ps. 70.5: 'For thou art my patience, O Lord: my hope, O Lord, from my youth,' and Ps. 117.14: 'The Lord is my strength and my praise.'
13 Ps. 7.2, 3.
14 Luke 7.50.
15 Matt. 8.13.

Christ into their rest as being unconquered and free. Therefore, he prays for his life here and for his future life. For, he says: 'Save me' here 'from them that persecute me; deliver me' there in the time of the scrutiny 'lest at any time he seize upon my soul like a lion.' You may learn this from the Lord Himself who said concerning the time of His passion: 'Now the prince of this world is coming, and in me he will have nothing.'[16] He who had committed no sin said that he had nothing; but, for a man it will be sufficient, if he dares to say: 'The prince of this world is coming, and in me he will have few and trivial penalties.' And there is a danger of experiencing these penalties, unless we have some one to deliver us or to save us. For, the two tribulations set forth, two petitions are introduced. 'Save me from the multitude of them that persecute me, and deliver me, lest at any time I be seized as if there were no one to redeem me.'[17]

(3) 'O Lord my God, if I have done this thing, if there be iniquity in my hands; if I have rendered to them that repaid me evils, let me deservedly fall empty before my enemies. Let the enemy pursue my soul, and take it.'[18] It is usual for Scripture to use the word 'repaying' not only in the case of customary acts, as when some good or evil is already in existence, but also in the case of acts beginning, as in the case of 'Repay thy servant.'[19] Instead of 'give,' it says 'repay.' A giving is the beginning of beneficence; but payment is the reciprocal measuring out of equal value on the part of him who has received benefits; repayment is a sort of second beginning and cycle of benefits or evils stored up for certain ones. In my opinion, since the expression, making, as it were, a re-petition in place of a petition, requests repayment, it presents some such meaning as this: the debt of care necessarily owed through nature to children by their parents, this provide for me. Indeed,

---

16 John 14.30.
17 Ps. 7.2, 3.
18 *Ibid.* 7.4-6.
19 Ps. 118.17.

care for their livelihood is owed to children by a father through natural love. 'For the parents,' it is said, 'should save up for the children,'[20] in order that in addition to life, they may still provide for them the means for their livelihood. Such is frequently the offering or repayment found in Scripture in initial activities. But here, he who is speaking seems to have confidence because he has not rendered to those repaying evils, nor repaid the like. 'If I have done this thing, and if I have rendered to them that repaid me evils, let me deservedly fall empty before my enemies.'[21] He falls empty before his enemies who falls from grace, which is the fullness of Christ. 'Let the enemy pursue my soul, and take it, and tread down my life on the earth.'[22] The soul of the just man, severing itself from affection for the body, has its life hidden with Christ in God, so that it can say like the Apostle: 'It is now no longer I that live, but Christ lives in me. And the life that I now live in the flesh, I live in faith.'[23] But, the soul of the sinner and of him who lives according to the flesh and is defiled by the pleasures of the body is wrapped up in the passions of the flesh as in mud; and the enemy, trampling upon this soul, strives to pollute it still more and, as it were, to bury it, treading upon him who has fallen, and with his feet trampling him into the ground, that is, trampling the life of him who has slipped into his body.

'And bring down my glory to the dust.'[24] The glory of the saints who possess citizenship in heaven and who store up for themselves good things in the everlasting treasuries is in heaven; but the glory of earthly men and those living according to the flesh is said to settle in the dust. He who has gloried in earthly wealth and who pursues the short-lived honor of

---

20 Cf. 2 Cor. 12 14: 'For the children should not save up for the parents, but the parents for the children.'
21 Ps. 7 5.
22 *Ibid.* 7.6.
23 Gal. 2.20.
24 Ps. 7.6.

men and has put his trust in corporeal advantages possesses a glory for himself which does not look up to heaven but remains in the dust.

(4) 'Rise up, O Lord, in thy anger: and be exalted in the borders of my enemy.'[25] The prophet prays that the mystery of the Resurrection be accomplished now, or the elevation on the cross, which was to take place after the wickedness of the enemies had mounted to its uttermost limits. Or the expression, 'And be thou exalted in the borders of my enemy,' suggests some such meaning as this: to whatever peak the evil shall ascend, even if it shall go on, pouring out to an immeasurable and unlimited degree, you are able in the abundance of your power, like a good physician, anticipating the limits of its spreading, to stop the disease which is increasing as it creeps along, and to break off its course by corrective blows.

'And arise, O Lord my God, in the precept which thou hast commanded.'[26] This saying can also be referred to the mystery of the Resurrection, since the prophet is exhorting the Judge to arise in order to avenge every sin and to bring to fulfillment the commands previously laid on us. It can also be accepted in reference to the state at that time of the affairs of the prophet, who was exhorting God to rise in order to avenge the precept which He had enjoined. There was a command, 'Honor thy father and thy mother,'[27] given by God, which indeed his son had transgressed. Therefore, he urges God, for the correction of that son himself and for the restraint of the many, not to be long-suffering, but to rise in anger and, having risen up, to avenge His own command. 'For You will not avenge me,' he says, 'but Your own despised precept, which You Yourself enjoined.'

'And a congregation of people shall surround thee.'[28] It is evident that, if one unjust man is chastened, many will be

---
25 *Ibid.* 7.7.
26 *Ibid.*
27 Exod. 20.12.
28 Ps. 7.8.

converted. Punish, therefore, the wickedness of this man, in order that a great congregation of people may surround You. 'And for their sakes return thou on high.'[29] For the sake of the congregation surrounding You, which You acquired by Your condescension through grace and by Your Incarnation, return to the heights of glory, which You had before the world was made.

'The Lord will judge the people.'[30] Words about judgment are scattered in many places in Scripture, as most cogent and essential for the teaching of true religion to those who believe in God through Jesus Christ. Since the words concerning the judgment are written with various meanings, they seem to hold some confusion for those who do not accurately distinguish the meanings. 'He who believes in me is not judged; but he who does not believe is already judged.'[31] But, if he who does not believe, is the same as an impious man, how has it been said that the impious will not rise up in judgment? And, if those who believe have been made sons of God through faith, and for this reason are worthy of being called gods themselves, how does God stand in a congregation of gods, and in the midst will judge gods? Well, it seems that the word 'judge' is at times employed by Scripture in place of 'approve,' as in the expression, 'Judge me, O Lord, for I have walked in my innocence,' for, it continues there, 'Prove me, O Lord, and try me';[32] and for 'condemn' as in the expression, 'But if we judged ourselves, we should not thus be judged.'[33] If we examine ourselves well, it says, we would not be subjected to condemnation. Again, it says that the Lord will enter into judgment with all flesh,[34] that is, in the examination of the actions in the lives of each He sub-

---

29 *Ibid.*
30 Ps. 7.9.
31 Cf. John 3.18: 'He who believes in him is not judged; but he who does not believe is already judged.'
32 Ps. 25.12.
33 1 Cor. 11.31.
34 Cf. Jer. 25.31: 'He entereth into judgment with all flesh.'

jected Himself to judgment and compared His own precepts with the actions of sinners, defending Himself with proofs that He has done all things depending upon Him for the salvation of those judged, in order that the sinners, being persuaded that they are liable to punishment for sins and acknowledging the divine justice, may willingly accept the penalty falling to their lot.

(5) There is still another meaning for the word 'judge,' as when the Lord says: 'The queen of the South will rise up in the judgment and will condemn this generation.'[35] He says that those who refuse the divine teaching and are without love for the noble and good, and who abandon completely the doctrines which tend to teach wisdom, by comparison and contrast with those of their own generation who excel in zeal for the noble and good, receive a more severe condemnation in the matters which they neglected. But, I believe that all who have received this earthy body will not be judged in the same manner by the just Judge since outside influences, which are far different for each of us, cause the judgment in the case of each to vary. For the combination of circumstances not in our power, but involuntary, either makes our sins more grievous, or even lightens them. Suppose that the matter to be judged is fornication. But, one who was trained from the beginning in evil practices committed this sin. Now, he was not only brought into life by licentious parents but also was reared with bad habits, with drunkenness and revelings and shameful tales. On the other hand, if another who had many challenges to the most excellent things, education, teachers, hearing of more divine words, salutary reading, advice of parents, tales which mold to seriousness and self-control, an ordered manner of life, if he, then, was carried away into a like sin as the other and gives an account of his life, how is it possible that such a one will not rightly be considered deserving of a heavier penalty in comparison with the former?

---
35 Matt. 12.42.

The one will be accused only on the ground that he did not use rightly the salutary inclinations implanted among his thoughts, but the other, in addition to this, because, although he obtained much assistance for salvation, through want of self-control and of attention, in a very short time he betrayed himself. Similarly also, he who has been trained from the beginning in piety and has escaped all perversion in the doctrines concerning God, and who has been brought up in the law of God which attacks every sin and invites to the opposite, will not have the same excuse for idolatry as he who was educated by lawless parents and by people taught from the beginning to worship idols.

'The Lord will judge the people.' In one way the Jew, and in another the Scythian. The first, indeed, rests content in the law and glories in God and approves the better things. Since he has been instructed by the law, and in addition to the general concepts has been taught the prophetic and legal writings by song and by training, if he is found to have made a false step contrary to the law, he will have far more grievous sins imputed to him. But, as for the Scythian nomads, who have been brought up with wild and inhuman practices, accustomed to robbery and acts of violence against each other, with no control of their temper and easily roused to bitter wrath against each other, accustomed, moreover, to judge all rivalry by the sword, and taught to put an end to fights with blood, if ever they show any humanity or goodness toward each other, they procure a more severe penalty for us because of their own virtuous actions.

(6) 'Judge me, O Lord, according to my justice, and according to my innocence in me.'[36] These words seem to contain some boastfulness and to be very much like the prayer of the Pharisee who was exalting himself, but, if one considers them reasonably, the prophet will be seen to be far from such a disposition. 'Judge me, O Lord,' he says, 'according to my

---
36 Ps. 7.9.

justice.' 'There are many sayings about justice,' he says, 'and the limits of perfect justice are hard to reach.' For, there is a justice of the angels, which transcends that of men, and, if there is any power above the angels, it has also a supremacy of justice proportionate to its greatness; and there is the justice of God Himself, which exceeds all understanding, which is inexpressible, and is incomprehensible to all created nature. 'Judge me, therefore, O Lord, according to my justice,' that is, according to that attainable by men and possible for those living in the flesh. 'And according to my innocence in me.' Thus especially, the disposition of the speaker proves to be very far from pharisaical arrogance; for, he names his innocence as if it were simplicity and ignorance of things useful to know according to the saying in the Proverbs: 'The innocent believeth every word.'[37] Since, therefore, we men through ignorance fall unguardedly into many sins, he entreats God and asks to meet with pardon because of his innocence. From this it is evident that these words show the humility of the speaker rather than arrogance. 'Judge me,' he says, 'according to my justice, and judge me according to the innocence which is in me.' Comparing my justice with human frailty, thus judge me, and understanding the simplicity of my character, do not, as though I were shrewd or circumspect in the affairs of the world, at once condemn me as a sinner.

'Let the wickedness of sinners be brought to nought.'[38] He who says this prayer is obviously a disciple of the evangelical precepts. He prays for those who treat him maliciously, asking that the wickedness of the sinners be circumscribed by a definite limit and boundary. Just as if some one, when praying for those who are suffering in body, would say, 'Let the disease of those who are suffering come to an end.' In order that the sin slowly creeping farther may not spread like cancer,[39] since

---

37 Prov. 14.15.
38 Ps. 7.10.
39 Cf. 2 Tim. 2.17: 'And their speech spreads like a cancer.'

he loves his enemy and wishes to do good to those who hate him, and for this reason prays for those who treat him maliciously, he begs of God that the further outpouring of sin may cease and have definite bounds.

'And thou shalt direct the just.'[40] The just man is called righteous, and the heart which has been set straight is righteous. What, then, does the prophet's prayer mean here? For, he prays that one who already possesses righteousness be set right. One certainly would not say that there is anything crooked in a just man nor distorted nor twisted. But, perhaps, the prayer is necessary for the just man in order that his rightness in purpose and integrity of will may be directed by the guiding hand of God, so that he shall never through weakness turn aside from the canon, as it were, of truth, nor be misled by the enemy of truth through perverted doctrines.

'The searcher of hearts and reins is God.'[41] Since Scripture in many places accepts the heart for the principal part of the body, and the reins for the affective part of the soul, here also this same expression signifies: 'O God, judge me for the teachings concerning piety which I hold and for the movements of my affections; for, You are the One who searches the hearts and the reins.' A search is properly an inquiry with all manner of tortures brought upon those who are examined by the judges, in order that persons who conceal on themselves things sought may by the force of their sufferings restore the hidden object to sight. In the undeceivable inquiries of the Judge our thoughts are examined and our deeds are examined. Let no one, therefore, anticipate the true Judge, and let no one judge before time, 'until the Lord comes, who will both bring to light the things hidden in darkness and make manifest the counsels of hearts.'[42] In searching the hearts and the reins God shows His justice. Now, the heart of Abraham was

---

40 Ps. 7.10.
41 *Ibid.*
42 1 Cor. 4.5.

searched to see if he loved God with his whole soul and his whole heart, when he was commanded to offer Isaac as a holocaust, in order that he might show that he did not love his son above God. And Jacob, who was the object of the plots of his brother, was searched, in order that his brotherly love might shine forth undimmed amidst such great sins of Esau. Therefore, the hearts of these were searched; but, the reins of Joseph were searched when, although the licentious mistress was madly in love with him, he preferred the honor of chastity to shameful pleasure. Moreover, he was searched for this reason, that the witnesses of the judgment of God might agree that honor was justly bestowed on him, because his chastity shone so very brightly in great trials.

(7) 'My help is from God.'[43] In wars those who are fighting rightly seek aid against the attacks of their opponents. And so here he who is aware of invisible enemies and who sees the danger near him from enemies encamped around him says: 'My help is not from wealth nor from corporal resources nor from my own power and strength nor from human ties of kinship, but "My help is from God." ' What assistance the Lord sends to those who fear Him, we have learned elsewhere in a psalm which says: 'The angel of the Lord shall encamp round about them that fear him: and shall deliver them.'[44] And in another place: 'The angel who has delivered me.'[45]

'Who saveth the upright of heart.'[46] He is upright in heart who does not have his mind inclined to excess nor to deficiency, but directs his endeavors toward the mean of virtue. He who has turned aside from valor to something less is perverted through cowardice; but, he who has strained on to greater things inclines toward temerity. Therefore, the Scripture calls those 'crooked' who go astray from the mean by excess or by deficiency. For, as a line becomes crooked when its

---
43 Ps. 7.11.
44 *Ibid.* 33.8.
45 Gen. 48.16.
46 Ps. 7.11.

straightforward direction is deflected, now convexly, now concavely, so also a heart becomes crooked when it is at one time exalted through boastfulness, at another dejected through afflictions and humiliations. Wherefore Ecclesiastes says: 'The perverted will not be kept straight.'[47]

'God is a just judge, strong and patient: he is not angry every day.'[48] The prophet seems to say this, alluding to those who are always disturbed at what happens, as if calming the confusion of men, lest at any time they mistrust His providence concerning the universe, when they see a father unavenged at the rebellion of his son and the wickedness of Absalom prospering in whatever he proposed. Correcting, therefore, the foolishness in their thoughts, he testified to them: 'God is a just judge, strong and patient: he is not angry every day.' Not indiscriminately does any of the things that happen take place, but God measures out in turn to each person with the measures with which He first measured out the actions of their life. When I have committed a sin, I receive in return according to my desert. 'Speak not, then, iniquity against God,'[49] for God is a just Judge. Do not be so poorly disposed toward God as to think that He is too weak to avenge, for He is also strong. What reason is there, then, that swift vengeance is not inflicted on the sinner? Because He is patient, 'He is not angry every day.'

'Except you will be converted, he will polish his sword.'[50] It is a threatening saying, urging on to conversion those who are slow to repent. He does not immediately threaten wounds and blows and death, but, the polishing of arms and a certain preparation, as it were, for vengeance. Just as men who are polishing up their arms indicate by this action the attack in war, so Scripture, wishing to bespeak a movement of God toward vengeance, says that He polishes His sword. 'He hath

---

47 Cf. Eccles. 1.15: 'The perverse are hard to be corrected.'
48 Ps. 7.12 (Septaugint version).
49 *Ibid.* 74.6.
50 *Ibid.* 7.13.

bent his bow, and made it ready, and in it he hath prepared the instruments of death.'[51] There is no bowstring which stretches the bow of God, but a punitive power, now strained tight, again loosened. Scripture threatens the sinner that future punishments are prepared for him, if he remains in his sin. 'And in the bow he hath prepared the instruments of death.' The instruments of death are the powers which destroy the enemies of God.

'He hath made ready his arrows for them that burn.'[52] As fire was produced by the Creator for material that burns—it certainly was not created for steel which is not melted by fire, but for wood which burns up—so also arrows were made by God for souls which are easily enkindled, whose great amount of material, worldly and suitable for destruction, has been collected. Those, then, who have accepted beforehand and hold in themselves the burning arrows of the devil, are the ones who receive the arrows of God. For this reason Scripture says: 'He hath made ready his arrows for them that burn.' Carnal loves burn the soul, and so do desires for money, fiery wraths, griefs which inflame and melt the soul, and fears which estrange from God. He who is unharmed by the arrows of the enemy and who has put on the armor of God[53] remains untouched by the death-bringing arrows.

(8) 'Behold he hath been in labor with injustice; he hath conceived sorrow, and brought forth iniquity.'[54] The passage seems to be confused in its order, since they who are pregnant first conceive, then are in labor, and finally bring forth. But here, first comes the travail, then the conception, and lastly the delivery. However, this is most vivid for the conception by the heart. Indeed, the irrational impulses of the licentious, the insane and frenzied lusts have been called travails because they are engendered in the soul with suddenness and pain.

---

51 *Ibid.* 7.13, 14.
52 *Ibid.* 7.14.
53 Cf. Eph. 6.11: 'Put on the armor of God.'
54 Ps. 7.15.

Through such an impulse he who has not command over his wicked practices, has begotten iniquity. David seems ashamed to say this because he is the father of a lawless son. 'He is not my son,' he says, 'but he has become the son of the father to whom he gave himself in adoption through sin.' Therefore, according to John, 'He who commits sin is of the devil.'[55] Behold then, the devil was in labor with him through injustice, and he conceived him, as if he drew him within his innermost parts beneath the vitals of his own passion and was pregnant of him, then brought him forth, having made manifest his iniquity because his rebellion against his father was proclaimed to all.

'He hath opened a pit and dug it.'[56] We do not find the name of 'pit' (lákkos) ever assigned in the divine Scriptures in the case of something good, nor a 'well' of water (phréar) in the case of something bad. That into which Joseph was thrown by his brothers is a pit (lákkos).[57] And there is a slaughter 'From the firstborn of Pharao unto the firstborn of the captive woman that was in the prison (lákkon).'[58] And in the psalms: 'I am counted among them that go down to the pit (lákkon).'[59] And in Jeremia it is said: 'They have forsaken me, the fountain of living water, and have digged to themselves cisterns (lákkous), broken cisterns, that can hold no water.'[60] Moreover, in Daniel[61] the lions' den (lákkos), into which Daniel was thrown, is described. On the other hand, Abraham[62] digs a well (phréar); so do the sons of Isaac;[63] and Moses,[64] coming to a well (phréar), rested. We

---
55 1 John 3.8.
56 Ps. 7.16.
57 Gen. 37.24.
58 Exod. 12.29.
59 Ps. 87.5.
60 Jer. 2.13.
61 Cf. Dan. 6.
62 Cf. Gen. 26.15: 'They stopped up at that time all the wells that the servants of his father Abraham had digged.'
63 Cf. Gen. 26.17-22.
64 Exod. 2.15.

also receive the order from Solomon[65] to drink water from our own cisterns (angeíon) and from the streams of our wells (phreáton). And beside the well (pēgé) the Savior conversed with the Samaritan woman concerning the divine mysteries.[66] As to the reason for the pits being assigned among the worse things and the wells among the better, we think it is this. The water in the pit is something acquired, having fallen from the sky; but, in the wells streams of water, buried before the places were dug out, are revealed when the heaps of earth covering them and the material of any sort whatsoever, lying upon them, which is also all earth, have been removed. Now, it is as if there were a pit in souls in which the better things, changed and debased, fall down, when a person, having resolved to have nothing good and noble of his own, puts to flight the thoughts of the good and noble that have slipped into it, twisting them to evil-doing and to contradictions of truth. And again, there are wells, when a light and a stream of water unimpaired in word and in doctrines break forth after the baser materials which had been covering it are removed. Therefore, it is necessary for each one to prepare a well for himself, in order that he may guard the command mentioned previously, which says, 'Drink water out of thy own cistern, and the streams of thy own well.'[67] Thus we shall be called the sons of those who have dug the wells, Abraham, Isaac, and Jacob. But, a pit must not be dug lest we fall into the hole, as it is said in this place, and so fail to hear the words written in Jeremia in reproach of sinners, for, God says concerning them what we have briefly mentioned before: 'They have forsaken me, the fountain of living water, and have digged to themselves cisterns, broken cisterns, that can hold no water.'[68]

---

65 Prov. 5.15.
66 Cf. John 4.6: 'Now Jacob's well was there. Jesus, therefore, wearied as he was from the journey, was sitting at the well.'
67 Prov. 5.15.
68 Jer. 2.13.

## HOMILY 12

*A Psalm of David against Usurers*

(ON PSALM 14)

YESTERDAY, WHEN WE WERE DISCUSSING with you the Fourteenth Psalm,[1] the time did not permit us to reach the end of our talk. Now, we have come as considerate debtors to pay the debt of our deficiency. There is a small part still to be heard, so it seems, and probably, it escaped the notice of most of you, so that you do not think that any of the psalm was omitted. Since we understand the great power in the affairs of life that this brief text possesses, we did not think that we ought to neglect the advantage of a close scrutiny. The prophet, describing in the text the perfect man who is about to arrive at the unchangeable life, enumerated among his noble deeds, the fact that he did not put his money out at interest.[2] This sin has been censured in many places in Scripture. Indeed, Ezechiel[3] places it among the greatest of evils to take interest or any profit, and the law expressly forbids it. 'Thou shalt not lend at interest to thy brother, and to thy neighbor.'[4] Again it says: 'Deceit upon deceit, and interest upon interest.'[5] And concerning a city which is

---

1 This is St. Basil's second homily on Psalm 14.
2 Cf. Ps. 14.5: 'He that hath not put out his money to usury.'
3 Cf. Ezech. 22.12: 'Thou hast taken usury and increase, and hast covetously oppressed thy neighbor.'
4 Cf. Deut. 23.19: 'Thou shalt not lend to thy brother money to usury, nor corn, nor any other thing.'
5 Jer. 9.6 (Septuagint version).

flourishing with a multitude of evils, what does the psalm say? 'Usury and deceit have not departed from its streets.'[6] Now, the prophet also has taken over this same practice as characteristic of perfection in man when he says: 'He hath not put out his money to usury.'[7]

Truly, the act involves the greatest inhumanity, that the one in need of necessities seeks a loan for the relief of his life, and the other, not satisfied with the capital, contrives revenues for himself from the misfortunes of the poor man and gathers wealth. The Lord has laid a clear command on us, saying: 'And from him who would borrow of thee, do not turn away.'[8] But, the avaricious person, seeing a man by necessity bent down before his knees as a suppliant, practicing all humility, and uttering every manner of petition, does not pity one who is suffering misfortune beyond his desert; he takes no account of his nature; he does not yield to his supplications; but, rigid and harsh he stands, yielding to no entreaties, touched by no tears, persevering in his refusal. Calling down curses on himself and swearing that he is entirely without money, and is himself looking around to see if he can find someone who lends money out at interest, he is believed in his lie because of his oaths, and incurs the guilt of perjury as the evil gains of his inhumanity. But, when he who is seeking the loan makes mention of interest and names his securities, then, pulling down his eyebrows, he smiles and remembers somewhere or other a family friendship, and calling him associate and friend, he says, 'We shall see if we have any money at all reserved. There is a deposit of a dear friend who entrusted it to us for matters of business. He has assigned a heavy interest for it, but we shall certainly remit some and give it at a lower rate of interest.' Making such pretenses, and fawning upon and enticing the wretched man with such words, he binds him with

---

6 Ps. 54.12. The Septuagint version here uses 'kopos' in place of 'tokos.'
7 *Ibid.* 14.5.
8 Matt. 5.42.

contracts; then, after having imposed on the man the loss of his liberty in addition to his oppressing poverty, he departs. As the borrower has made himself responsible for the interest, of whose full payment he has no idea, he accepts a voluntary servitude for life.

Tell me, do you seek money and means from a poor man? If he had been able to make you richer, why would he have sought at your doors? Coming for assistance, he found hostility. When searching around for antidotes, he came upon poisons. It was your duty to relieve the destitution of the man, but you, seeking to drain the desert dry, increased his need. Just as if some physician, visiting the sick, instead of restoring health to them would take away even their little remnant of bodily strength, so you also would make the misfortunes of the wretched an opportunity of revenue. And, just as farmers pray for rains for the increase of their crops, so you also ask for poverty and want among men in order that your money may be productive for you. Do you not know that you are making an addition to your sins greater than the increase to your wealth, which you are planning from the interest? He who is seeking the loan stops in the midst of his difficulties and despairs of the payment whenever he considers his poverty, but makes a rash bid for the loan when he considers his present need. And so, the one is overcome, yielding to his need; and the other departs, having safeguarded himself with securities and contracts.

(2) He who has received the money is at first bright and cheerful, gladdened by another's prosperity and showing it by the change in his life. His table is lavish, his clothing more costly, his servants changed in dress to something more brilliant; there are flatterers, boon companions, innumerable dining-hall drones. But, as the money slips away, and the advancing time increases the interest due, the nights bring him no rest, the day is not bright, nor is the sun pleasant, but he is disgusted with life, he hates the days which hasten

on toward the appointed time, he fears the months, the parents, as it were, of his interest. If he sleeps, he sees in his sleep the money-lender standing at his head, an evil dream; if he is awake, his whole thought and care is the interest. 'The poor man and the creditor,' it is said, 'have met one another: the Lord makes a visitation of both of them.'[9] The one, like a dog, is greedy for the quarry; the other, like a prey ready at hand, cowers at the encounter. Poverty takes away from him his confidence in speaking. Both have the reckoning on the tips of their fingers, since the one is rejoicing at his increased interest, and the other lamenting his added misfortune.

'Drink water out of thy own cistern.'[10] that is, examine your own resources, do not go to the springs belonging to others, but from your own streams gather for yourself the consolations of life. Do you have metal plates, clothing, beasts of burden, utensils of every kind? Sell them; permit all things to go except your liberty. 'But I am ashamed,' he says, 'to put them out in public.' Why, pray tell me, seeing that a little later another will bring them forth, and, selling your possessions at an auction, will dispose of them at a price too low in your eyes? Do not go to another's doors. 'For truly another's well is narrow.'[11] It is better to relieve the necessity gradually by various devices, than, after having been suddenly lifted up by others' resources, to be later deprived of all your belongings at once. If, therefore, you have anything by means of which you may pay, why do you not put an end to your present need from those resources? If you are without means for the payment, you are treating evil with evil. Do not take on a creditor to pester you. Do not endure, like a prey, to be hunted and tracked down. Borrowing is the beginning of falsity; an opportunity for ingratitude, for senseless pride, for

---

9 Prov. 29.13 (Septuagint version).
10 *Ibid.* 5.15.
11 *Ibid.* 23.27 (Septuagint version).

perjury. The words of a man when he is borrowing are of one kind, those when payment is being demanded are of another. 'Would that I had not met you, I would have found opportunity to deliver myself from my necessity. Did you not put the money into my hand, although I was unwilling? Your gold was mixed with copper and your coin was counterfeit.' If, then, your creditor is a friend, do not suffer the loss of his friendship; if he is an enemy, do not come under the control of a hostile person.

After you have gloried for a little while in another's possessions, you will later be giving up your patrimonial possessions. You are poor now, but free. When you have borrowed, you will not be rich, and you will be deprived of freedom. He who borrows is the slave of his creditor, a slave serving for pay, who endures unmerciful servitude. Dogs, when they have received something, are pacified, but the money-lender, on receiving something, is further provoked. He does not stop railing, but demands more. If you swear, he does not trust; he examines your family affairs; he meddles with your transactions. If you go forth from your chamber, he drags you along with him and carries you off; if you hide yourself inside, he stands before your house and knocks at the door. In the presence of your wife he puts you to shame; he insults you before your friends; in the market place he strangles you; he makes the occurrence of a feast an evil; he renders life insupportable for you. 'But the necessity was great,' you say, 'and there were no other means of revenue.' Well, what advantage is there from deferring the day? Poverty like a good runner[12] will again overtake you, and the same necessity with an increase will be present. For, the loan does not provide complete deliverance, but a short delaying of your hardship. Let us suffer the difficulties from want today and not put it off until tomorrow. If you do not borrow, you will be poor today and likewise for the future; but, if you borrow, you will be more cruelly

---

12 Cf. Prov. 24.34: 'And poverty shall come to thee as a runner.'

tormented, since the interest has increased your poverty still more. At present no one brings a charge against you because you are poor; for, this is an involuntary evil; but, if you are liable for interest, there is no one who will not blame your imprudence.

(3) Let us not in addition to our involuntary evils bring on through our folly a self-chosen evil. It is the act of a childish mind not to adapt oneself according to present circumstances, but, turning to uncertain hopes, to make trial boldly of a visible and undeniable evil. Plan now how you will make the payment. Is it from this money which you are receiving? And, if you reckon the interest, how will you multiply your money to such an extent, that on the one hand, it will take care of your need, and on the other, will make up the complete capital and produce besides the interest. But, you will not pay off the loan from what you receive. From elsewhere, then? Let us not wait for those hopes and let us not go like fish after the bait. As they swallow down the hook with the food, so we also through the money are entangled in the interest. Poverty is no cause of shame. Why, then, do we bring upon ourselves the disgrace of being in debt? No one treats wounds with another wound, nor cures an ill with another ill, nor corrects poverty by means of interest.

Are you rich? Do not borrow. Are you poor? Do not borrow. If you are prospering, you have no need of a loan; if you have nothing, you will not repay the loan. Do not give your life over to regret, lest at some time you may esteem as happy the days before the loan. Let us, the poor, surpass the rich in this one thing, namely, freedom from care. Let us laugh at them lying awake while we sleep, and always engaged and anxious while we are free from care and at ease. Yet, he who owes is both poor and full of care, sleepless by night, sleepless by day, anxious at all times; now he is putting a value on his own possessions, now on the costly houses, the fields of the rich, the clothing of chance comers, the table-furnishings of those entertaining. 'If these were mine,' he says, 'I would sell them for such and such a price, and I would be free from the interest.' These things settle in his heart by night, and by day they occupy his thoughts. If you knock at his door, the debtor hides under the couch. If some one ran in quickly, his heart pounded. Does the dog bark? He drips with perspiration; he suffers anguish; he looks around to see where he can flee. When the appointed time draws near, he is anxious about what falsehood he shall tell, what pretext he shall invent so as to evade his creditor. Do not think of yourself only as receiving, but also as being dunned.

Why do you yoke yourself with a prolific wild beast? They say that hares bring forth and at the same time both rear young and become doubly pregnant.[13] So also with moneylenders, the money is lent out and, at the same time, it reproduces from itself and is in a process of growth. You have not yet received it in your hands and you have been required to pay out the interest for the present month. And this, lent out again, has nourished another evil, and that another, and so the evil is endless. Therefore, this form of avarice is considered deserving of this name. For, it is called 'tókos' (parturition), as I think, because of the fecundity of the evil. In fact, from where else would it receive its name? Or, perhaps, it is called 'tókos' (parturition) because of the anguish and distress which it is accustomed to produce in the souls of the borrowers. As travail comes to the one who is giving birth, so the appointed day comes to the debtor. There is interest upon interest, the wicked offspring of wicked parents. Let these offspring of interest be called broods of vipers. They say that vipers are born by gnawing through the womb of the mother.[14]

---

13 Cf. Aristotle, *History of Animals* 6.33.579b f.: 'Hares breed and bear at all seasons, superfetate during pregnancy, and bear young every month. They do not give birth to their young ones all together at one time, but bring them forth at intervals over as many days as the circumstances of each case may require. The female . . . is capable of conception while suckling her young.'
14 Cf. Hexaemeron, Homily 9, n.15.

And the interests are produced by eating up the houses of the debtors. Seeds spring up in time; and animals in time bring their offspring to perfection; but the interest is produced today, and today again begins its breeding. Those of the animals which give birth early, early cease from bearing; but money, which speedily begins to bear interest, takes on an endless increase which becomes greater and greater. Everything that increases, when it reaches its proper size, stops increasing; but the money of avaricious men always increases progressively with time. The animals, after transmitting to the offspring the power of bearing, desist from conception; both the money of the money-lenders and the accruing interest produce, and the capital is redoubled. Do not, then, make trial of this unnatural beast.

(4) You see that the sun is free. Why do you begrudge freedom of life to yourself? No boxer avoids the blows of his antagonist as much as the debtor avoids a meeting with his creditor, hiding his head behind pillars and walls. 'Well, how could I be fed?' he says. You have hands; you have skill; put yourself out for hire; do service; there are many devices for earning a livelihood, many opportunities. But, you are unable to do it? Beg from those who have possessions. Is begging a shameful act? It is certainly more disgraceful to refuse payment of borrowed money. And I say this, assuredly, not to enact a law, but to show that any methods are more endurable than borrowing. The ant is able, neither begging nor borrowing, to nourish itself; and the honey bee bestows upon kings the remains of its own nourishment; yet to these, nature has given neither hands nor arts. But, will you, a man, an inventive animal, not find one device for the guidance of your life? And yet, we see that it is not those in need of the necessities who come for a loan (for, they do not find any who trust them), but, that men who devote themselves to unrestrained expenses and fruitless extravagances and who are slaves to effeminate luxuries, are the borrowers. 'I need for myself,' he

says, 'costly clothing and gold plate, for my sons decent garments as an ornament for them, also for my servants bright-colored and varied attire, and for my table abundance of food.' He who does such things for a woman goes to a money-changer and, before he has spent what he has received, he changes one master for another; and always fastening to himself one lender after another, he thus endeavors to escape the evidence of his need by the continuous succession of evils. As those who suffer from dropsy are thought to be fat, so also he lives with an appearance of wealth, always receiving and always giving, settling the first debts by those following, acquiring for himself the apparent trustworthiness required for getting money by the continuous succession of evil. Then, just as those with cholera, who are always vomiting what was taken previously, and who, before they are entirely purged, are swallowing down another meal, again give it up with pain and convulsions; in the same way, these also, who substitute interest for interest and who, before they are cleared of the first, bring on another loan and glory for a little while in another's wealth, later bewail their own affairs.

O, how many have been destroyed by the possessions of other men? How many men, after building castles in the air, have as their only benefit, a loss beyond measure? 'But many,' he says, 'grow rich from loans.' But more, I think, fasten themselves to halters. You see those who have become rich, but you do not count those who have been strangled, who, not enduring the shame incurred by their begging, preferred death through strangling to a shameful life. I have seen a piteous sight, free sons dragged to the market place to be sold because of the paternal debt. You are not able to leave money to your sons? Do not deprive them as well of their dignity. Preserve for them this one thing, the possession of their liberty, the sacred trust which you received from your parents. No one has ever been prosecuted for the poverty of his father, but a father's debt leads into prison. Do not leave a bond, a paternal curse, as it were, descending upon the sons and grandsons.

(5) Listen, you rich men, to what we advise the poor because of your inhumanity: rather to persevere in their terrible situations than to accept the misfortunes which come from the payment of interest. But, if you obey the Lord, what need is there of these words? What is the counsel of the Master? 'Lend to those from whom you do not hope to receive in return.'[15] 'And what sort of a loan is this,' he says, 'to which there is no hope of a return attached?' Consider the force of the statement, and you will admire the kindness of the Lawmaker. Whenever you have the intention of providing for a poor man for the Lord's sake, the same thing is both a gift and a loan, a gift because of the expectation of no repayment, but a loan because of the great gift of the Master who pays in his place, and who, receiving trifling things through a poor man, will give great things in return for them. 'He that hath mercy on the poor, lendeth to God.'[16] Do you not wish to have the Lord of the universe answerable to you for payment? Or, if one of the rich men in the city would promise you the payment for the others, would you accept his pledge? But, you do not accept God as the surety for the poor. Give the money, since it is lying idle, without weighing it down with additional charges, and it will be good for both of you. There will be for you the assurance of its safety because of his custody; for him receiving it, the advantage from its use. And, if you are seeking additional payment, be satisfied with that from the Lord. He Himself will pay the interest for the poor. Expect kindly acts from Him who is truly kind. This interest, which you take, is full of extreme inhumanity. You make profit from misfortune, you collect money from tears, you strangle the naked, you beat the famished; nowhere is there mercy, no

---

15 Cf. Luke 6.35: 'But love your enemies; and do good, and lend, not hoping for any return.'
16 Prov. 19.17.

thought of relationship with the sufferer; and you call the profits from these things humane! Woe to you who say that the bitter is sweet and the sweet bitter,[17] and who call inhumanity by the name of humanity. The riddles of Sampson, which he propounded to his fellow-drinkers, were not of such a kind: 'Out of the eater came forth meat, and out of the strong came forth sweetness,'[18] and from inhumanity came forth humanity. 'Men do not gather grapes from thorns, or figs from thistles,'[19] nor humanity from interest. Every 'bad tree bears bad fruit.'[20] Some are collectors of a hundredfold and some collectors of tenfold, names horrible indeed to hear; monthly exactors, they attack the poor according to the cycles of the moon, like those demons which cause epileptic fits. It is wicked lending for both, for the giver and for the receiver, bringing loss to the one in money and to the other in soul. The farmer, when he has taken his ear of corn, does not search for the seed again under the root; but, you have the fruits and you do not give up claim to the principal. Without land you produce, without sowing you reap. It is not evident for whom you collect. It is indeed apparent who he is who weeps because of the interest, but it is doubtful who he is who is to enjoy the abundance that comes from it. In fact, it is uncertain whether you will not leave to others the gift of wealth, but the evil of injustice you have treasured up for yourself. 'And from him who would borrow of thee, do not turn away,'[21] and do not give your money at interest, in order that, having been taught what is good from the Old and the New Testament, you may depart to the Lord with good hope, receiving there the interest from your good deeds, in Christ Jesus our Lord, to whom be glory and power forever. Amen.

---

17 Cf. Isa. 5.20: 'Woe to you that call evil good, and good evil: that put darkness for light, and light for darkness: that put bitter for sweet, and sweet for bitter.'
18 Judges 14.14.
19 Matt. 7.16.
20 *Ibid* 7.17.
21 *Ibid.* 5.42.

# HOMILY 13

*A Psalm of David at the Finishing of the Tabernacle*

(ON PSALM 28)

THE TWENTY-EIGHTH PSALM has a general title, for it says, 'A psalm of David,' and it has something specific also, since it adds, 'at the finishing of the tabernacle.' But, what is this? Let us consider what the finishing is and what the tabernacle is, in order that we may be able to meditate on the meaning of the psalm. Now, as regards the history, it will seem that the order was given to the priests and Levites who had acquitted themselves of the work to remember what they ought to prepare for the divine service. Scripture, furthermore, solemnly declares to those going out and departing from the tabernacle what it is proper for them to prepare and to have for their assembly on the following day: namely, 'offspring of rams, glory and honor, glory to his name'; likewise it declares that nowhere else is it becoming to worship except in the court of the Lord and in the place of holiness.[1] But, according to our mind which contemplates the sublime and makes the law familiar to us through a meaning which is noble and fitted to the divine Scripture, this occurs to us: the ram does not mean the male among the sheep; nor the tabernacle, the building constructed from this inanimate material; and

---

1 Cf Ps. 28.1, 2: 'Bring to the Lord, O ye children of God: bring to the Lord the offspring of rams. Bring to the Lord glory and honor: bring to the Lord glory to his name: adore ye the Lord in his holy court.'

the going out from the tabernacle does not mean the departure from the temple; but, the tabernacle for us is this body, as the Apostle taught us when he said: 'We who are in this tabernacle sigh.'[2] And again, the psalm: 'Nor shall the scourge come near thy dwelling.'[3] And the finishing of the tabernacle is the departure from this life, for which Scripture bids us to be prepared, bringing this thing and that to the Lord, since, indeed, our labor here is our provision for the future life. And that one who here bears glory and honor to the Lord through his good works will treasure up for himself glory and honor according to the just requital of the Judge.

In many copies we find added the words, 'Bring to the Lord, O ye children of God.'[4] And, since indeed not everyone's gift is acceptable to God, but only his who brings it with a pure heart, for Scripture says: 'The vows of a hired courtesan are not pure';[5] and again, Jeremia says: 'Shall not your vows and the holy flesh take away from you your crimes, or shall you be pure on account of these?'[6] therefore, the psalm first wants us to be the children of God, then to seek to carry our gifts to God, and not just any gifts, but whatever ones He Himself has appointed. First, say 'Father,' then ask for what follows from that. Examine from what kind of life you have presented yourself; whether you are worthy to call the Holy God your Father. Through holiness we have affection for the Holy One. If you wish to be always the son of the Holy One, let holiness adopt you as a son. Therefore, 'bring to the Lord,' not you who are just any persons nor who are sons of just any persons, but you who are children of God. You may be sure that He demands great gifts; therefore, He chooses great men to offer them. In order that he may not cast your thoughts down to earth, and make you seek a ram, that irrational beast and

---

2 2 Cor. 5.4.
3 Ps. 90.10.
4 *Ibid.* 28 1.
5 Prov. 19.13 (Septuagint version).
6 Jer. 11.15 (Septuagint version).

bleating animal, as if you expected to appease God by sacrificing it, he says: 'Bring to the Lord, O ye children of the Lord.' There is no need of a son that you may offer the son himself, but, if a son is something great, it is proper for the offering to be something great and worthy of the affection of a son and of the dignity of the Father. He says: 'Bring the offspring of rams,' that, when they are offered by you, they may be changed from the state of offspring of rams into that of children of God.

(2) The ram is an animal capable of leading, one which guides the sheep to nourishing pastures and refreshing waters, and back again to the pens and farmhouses. Such are those who are set over the flock of Christ, since they lead them forth to the flowery and fragrant nourishment of spiritual doctrine, water them with living water, the gift of the Spirit, raise them up and nourish them to produce fruit, but guide them to rest and to safety from those who lay snares for them. Scripture wishes, then, the children of these to be led forth to the Lord by the children of God. If the leaders of the rest are the rams, their children would be those formed to a life of virtue through zeal for good works by the teaching of the leaders. Therefore, 'Bring to the Lord, O ye children of God; bring to the Lord the offspring of rams.' Have you learned to whom it was addressed? Have you learned concerning whom he spoke?

'Bring to the Lord,' he says, 'glory and honor.'[7] Now, how do we, dust and ashes,[8] offer glory to the great Lord? And how honor? Glory, through our good works, when our works shine before men, so that men seeing our works give glory to our Father in heaven.[9] And through temperance and holiness which is incumbent upon those who profess piety it is possible

---
7 Ps. 28.2.
8 Cf. Gen. 18.27: 'Abraham answered, "I have ventured to speak to the Lord though I am but dust and ashes."'
9 Cf. Matt. 5.16. 'Even so let your light shine before men, in order that they may see your good works and give glory to your Father in heaven.'

to give glory to God, according to the admonition of Paul, who said: 'Glorify God in your members.'[10] The Lord also demands this glory from those who believe in Him and who have been honored with the gift of the adoption of sons. 'The son' it is said, 'honoreth the father,' and, 'if then I be a father, where is my honor?'[11] He truly bears honor to God, who according to the proverb honors God by his just labors and offers to Him the first fruits of his justice.[12] Everyone who discusses divine matters in an orderly way so as always to hold the correct opinion concerning the Father, the Godhead of the Only-begotten, and the glory of the Holy Spirit, brings glory and honor to the Lord. And, because His providence penetrates even to the smallest things, he increases the glory who is able to give the reasons for which all things were created and for which they are preserved, and also for which, after this present stewardship, they will be brought to judgment. He who is able himself to contemplate each individual creature with clear and unconfused thoughts and, after having contemplated them himself, is able to present to others also the facts concerning the goodness of God and His just judgment, he is the one who brings glory and honor to the Lord and who lives a life in harmony with this contemplation. For, the light of such a man shines before men,[13] since by word and work and through manly deeds of every kind the Father in heaven is glorified.

He does not bring glory and honor to the Lord who becomes passionately stirred over human glory, nor he who prizes money, nor he who sets great store on the pleasures of the body, nor he who regards with admiration strange religious beliefs. Just as through good works we bring glory to the Lord, so through wicked works we do the opposite. What, indeed, does He say to sinners? 'My name is blasphemed

---
10 1 Cor. 6.20 (Septuagint version with 'mélesin' substituted for 'somati').
11 Mal. 1.6.
12 Cf. Prov. 3.9: 'Honor the Lord with thy substance, and give him of the first of all thy fruits.'
13 Cf. Matt. 5.16.

through you among the Gentiles.'¹⁴ Again, the Apostle says: 'Dost thou dishonor God by transgressing the Law?'¹⁵ For, contempt and disregard of the laws is an insult to the Lawgiver. When a house is badly managed, and in it are found passion and screaming, insolence and mocking laughter, wantonness and profligacy, impurity and licentiousness, the disgrace and shame of what happens fall upon him who is its master. Consequently, we believe that, as in good works God is honored, so in wicked works the enemy is honored. When 'I shall take the members of Christ and make them members of a harlot,'¹⁶ I have transferred the glory from Him who saved me to him who destroys me. The unbeliever 'changes the glory of the incorruptible God for an image made like to corruptible man and to birds and four-footed beasts and creeping things' on earth.¹⁷ And he who worships and serves the creature more than the Creator does not bring glory to God, but to the creatures. Therefore, let him who says that a creature is some great thing and then worships it, know with what party he himself will be placed.

Let us fear lest, by bringing glory and occasions of exultation to the devil through our sins, we may be handed over to everlasting shame with him. That our sin becomes glory for him who effects it in us, understand by a similitude. When two generals make an attack upon each other, and one army wins, its commander receives the glory; but, when the opposing one is victorious, the honor is in turn transferred to him. Thus, the Lord is the One honored in your good deeds, but in your contrary acts His opponent is honored. Do not, I pray, consider that the enemy is far from you, and do not look at the leaders from afar, but examine yourself and you will find all the truth of the similitude. For, when the mind

---

14 Cf. Rom. 2.24: ' "For the name of God," as it is written, "is blasphemed through you among the Gentiles." '
15 Rom. 2.23.
16 1 Cor. 6.15.
17 Rom. 1.23.

wrestles with passion, if, indeed, it prevails through vigor and attention, it wins the prize of victory over the passion and by its own means, as it were, it crowns God. But, when it becomes soft and stoops to pleasure, being made a slave and captive of sins, it gives to the enemy a cause of boasting and conceit and an opportunity for pride.

(3) 'Adore ye the Lord in his holy court.'[18] After the offerings requested have been brought, adoration is necessary, and an adoration which is not outside of the church, but is paid in the very court of God. 'Do not,' He says, 'devise for me private courts or synagogues.' There is only one holy court of God. The synagogue of the Jews was formerly a court, but, after the sin against Christ, their habitation was made desolate.[19] For this reason also the Lord said: 'And other sheep I have that are not of this fold.'[20] In saying that some from among the Gentiles were predestined for salvation, He shows His own court in addition to that of the Jews. Accordingly, it is not proper to adore God outside of this holy court, but only within it, lest anyone who is outside of it and is attracted by those outside of it, might lose the right to be in the court of the Lord. Many assume an attitude of prayer, but they are not in the court because of the wandering of their mind and the distraction of their thoughts coming from vain solicitude. It is possible to consider the court in a still loftier sense as the heavenly way of life. Therefore, 'They that are planted' here 'in the house of the Lord,' which is the Church of the living God, there 'shall flourish in the courts of our God.'[21] But, he who makes his belly a god, or glory, or money, or anything else which he honors more than all things, neither adores the Lord, nor is in the holy court, even though he seems to be worthy of the visible assemblies.

---

18 Ps. 28.2.
19 Cf. Ps. 68.26: 'Let their habitation be made desolate.'
20 John 10.16. 'Aulês,' translated 'court' in Ps. 28.2, is here translated 'fold.'
21 Ps. 91.14.

'The voice of the Lord is upon the waters.'[22] In many places you might find the word 'voice' occurring. Therefore, for the sake of understanding what the voice of the Lord is, we should gather, as far as we are able, from the divine Scripture what has been said about the voice; for instance, in the divine warning to Abraham: 'And immediately the voice came to him: He shall not be your heir.'[23] And in Moses: 'And all the people saw the voice and the flames.'[24] Again, in Isaia: 'The voice of one saying: Cry.'[25] With us, then, voice is either air which has been struck or some form which is in the air against which he who is crying out wishes to strike. Now, what is the voice of the Lord? Would it be considered the impact on the air? Or air, which has been struck reaching the hearing of him to whom the voice comes? Or neither of these, but that this is a voice of another kind, namely, an image formed by the mind of men whom God wishes to hear His own voice, so that they have this representation corresponding to that which frequently occurs in their dreams? Indeed, just as, although the air is not struck, we keep some recollection of certain words and sounds occurring in our dreams, not receiving the voice through our hearing, but through the impression on our heart itself, so also we must believe that some such voice from God appeared in the prophets.

'The voice of the Lord is upon the waters.' As, indeed, in regard to the sensible creation, since the clouds, when they are full of water, produce sound and noise, striking against each other, 'The voice' it is said, 'of the Lord is upon the waters.' Then, too, if there should be the noise of waters breaking against some barrier, and if the sea, thrown into confusion by the winds, should seethe and send forth a mighty sound, these inanimate creatures have voice from the Lord,

---

22 *Ibid.* 28.3.
23 Gen. 15.4.
24 Exod. 20.18.
25 Isa. 40.6.

since Scripture shows that every creature all but cries out, proclaiming the Creator. If the thunder crashes from the clouds, we need believe only that the God of majesty has thundered and that He who by Himself preserves the moisture is the Lord.

'The Lord is upon many waters.'[26] We have learned in the creation of the world that there is water above the heavens, again, water of the deep, and yet again, the gathered waters of the seas. Who, then, is He who holds together these waters, not allowing them to be borne downward by their physical weight, except the Lord who established Himself upon all things, who holds sway over the waters? Perhaps, even in a more mystic manner the voice of the Lord was upon the waters, when a voice from above came to Jesus as He was baptized, 'This is my beloved Son.'[27] At that time, truly, the Lord was upon many waters, making the waters holy through baptism; but, the God of majesty thundered from above with a mighty voice of testimony. And over those to be baptized a voice left behind by the Lord is pronounced: 'Go, therefore,' it says, 'baptize in the name of the Father, and of the Son, and of the Holy Spirit.'[28] Therefore, 'The voice of the Lord is upon the waters.'

Thunder is produced when a dry and violent wind, closed up in the hollows of a cloud and violently hurled around in the cavities of the clouds, seeks a passage to the outside. The clouds, offering resistance under the excessive pressure produce that harsh sound from the friction of the wind. But, when, like bubbles distended by the air, they are unable to resist and endure any longer, but are violently torn apart and give the air a passage to the outer breeze, they produce the noises of the thunder. And this is wont to cause the flash of

---

26 Ps. 28.3.
27 Matt. 3.17.
28 *Ibid.* 28.19.

lightning.[29] Therefore, it is the Lord who is upon the waters and who arouses the mighty noises of the thunder, causing such an exceedingly great noise in the delicate element of air. It is also possible for you, according to ecclesiastical diction to call by the name of thunder the doctrine which after baptism is in the souls of those already perfect by the eloquence of the Gospel. That the Gospel is thunder is made evident by the disciples who were given a new name by the Lord and called Sons of Thunder.[30] Therefore, the voice of such thunder is not in any chance person, but only in one who is worthy to be called a wheel. 'The voice of thy thunder,' it says, 'in a wheel.'[31] That is, whoever is stretching forward, like a wheel, touching the earth with a small part of itself, and really such as that wheel was, about which Ezechiel said: 'I saw and behold there was one wheel on the earth attached to the four living creatures, and their appearance and their form was as the appearance of Tharsis.'[32]

(4) 'The God of majesty hath thundered, the Lord is upon many waters.' The waters are also the saints, because rivers flow from within them,[33] that is, spiritual teaching which refreshes the souls of the hearers. Again, they receive water which springs up to eternal life, wherefore, it becomes in those who receive it rightly 'a fountain of water, springing up unto

---

29 Cf. Aristotle's theory in *Meteorology* 2.9.369a and b: 'Now the heat in the clouds that escapes disperses to the upper region. But if any of the dry exhalation is caught in the process as the air cools, it is squeezed out as the clouds contract, and collides in its rapid course with the neighboring clouds, and the sound of this collision is what we call thunder. . . . The variety of the sound is due to the irregularity of the clouds and the hollows that intervene where their density is interrupted. . . . It usually happens that the exhalation that is ejected is inflamed and burns with a thin and faint fire: this is what we call lightning.'
30 Cf. Mark 3.17: 'And James the son of Zebedee, and John the brother of James (these he surnamed Boanerges, that is, Sons of Thunder).'
31 Ps. 76.19.
32 Cf. Ezech. 1.15 (Septuagint version).
33 Cf. John 7.38: 'He who believes in me, as the Scripture says, "From within him there shall flow rivers of living water."'

life everlasting.'³⁴ Upon such waters, then, is the Lord. Remember also the story of Elias, when the heavens were closed three years and six months; when, although there was clear weather on the summit of Carmel, he heard a voice of many waters; then there followed thunder coming from the clouds and water pouring down.³⁵ The Lord, therefore, is upon many waters.

'The voice of the Lord is in power.'³⁶ As there is a voice in a wheel, so the voice of the Lord is in power. For, he who prevails over all things in Christ who strengthens him,³⁷ he it is who hears the commands of the Lord and does them. Therefore, the voice of the Lord is not in the weak and dissolute soul, but in that which vigorously and powerfully achieves the good.

'The voice of the Lord in magnificence.'³⁸ Magnificence is virtue extraordinarily great. He who performs great actions becomingly, such a one hears himself called magnificent. When the soul is not enslaved by the pride of the flesh, but assumes a greatness and dignity proper to it because of its awareness of its attributes received from God, in this soul is the voice of the Lord. Therefore, they who entertain noble thoughts of God, contemplating sublimely the reasons for creation, and being able to comprehend to a certain extent at least the goodness of God's providence, and who besides are unsparing in their expenditures and are munificent in supplying the needs of their brothers, these are the magnificent men in whom the voice of the Lord dwells. In truth the magnificent man despises all bodily things, judging them deserving of no account in comparison with the unseen world. No difficult conditions will grieve the magnificent man; nor,

---

34 John 4.14.
35 Cf. 3 Kings 18.41-45.
36 Ps. 28.4.
37 Cf. 1 Tim. 1.12: 'I give thanks to Christ Jesus our Lord, who has strengthened me.'
38 Ps. 28.4.

in short, will any suffering greatly trouble him, nor will the sins of paltry and contemptible little men move him, nor the impurity of the flesh humble him. He is difficult of access to the humiliating passions, which cannot even look upon him because of the loftiness of his mind. There is mentioned also a certain magnificence of God, according to the saying: 'Thy magnificence is elevated above the heavens.'[39] Those, then, who give great glory to God, elevate His magnificence.

(5) 'The voice of the Lord breaketh the cedars.'[40] The cedar is at times praised by Scripture as a stable tree, free from decay, fragrant, and adequate for supplying shelter, but at times it is attacked as unfruitful and hard to bend, so that it offers a representation of impiety. 'I have seen the wicked highly exalted, and lifted up like the cedars of Libanus.'[41] In this sense it is now accepted. For 'the voice of the Lord breaketh the cedars.' As this even happens in a magnificent soul, so He is said to break those vainly puffed up and magnifying themselves in the things of this world which are considered exalting, wealth, glory, power, beauty of body, influence, or strength. 'Yea, the Lord breaks the cedars of Libanus.'[42] They who trample upon others' affairs and from that gather false glory for themselves, they are cedars of Libanus. Just as the cedars, which are lofty in themselves, because they are produced on a high mountain become more conspicuous through the added height of the mountain, so also those leaning upon the perishable things of the world are cedars indeed through their false glory and vanity of mind; and they are called cedars of Libanus because they are glorying in the elevation which belongs to another and are raised up to their false glory by the earth and earthly circumstances, as if by the summit of Libanus.

However, the Lord does not break all the cedars, but those

---
39 *Ibid.* 8.2.
40 *Ibid.* 28.5.
41 *Ibid.* 36.35.
42 *Ibid.* 28.5.

of Libanus. Since Libanus is a place of idolatry, the souls which lift themselves up, opposing the means of knowing God, are called cedars of Libanus and they deserve to be broken. There are also some cedars of God, which are covered by the branches of the vine transferred from Egypt, as we have learned in psalms: 'The shadow of it covered the hills; and the branches thereof the cedars of God.'[43]

Then, among other concepts of Christ, our Lord is said to be a vine: 'I am the vine,' He says, 'you are the branches.'[44] The cedars are God's, which for a time were unfruitful and fit for burning, but, coming under the protection of Christ and, as it were, clothed in Him, by the grace coming from Him they veil the unfruitfulness of their life. The fruitful branches, embracing, guard the cedars of God; but, the cedars of Libanus the Lord breaks: 'And he shall reduce them to pieces, as a calf of Libanus.'[45]

Remember the calf in Exodus, which they fashioned through idolatry, which Moses beat to powder and gave to the people to drink.[46] In a manner similar to that calf, He will utterly destroy all Libanus and the practice of idolatry prevailing in it. 'And as the beloved son of unicorns.'[47] The only-begotten Son, He who gives His life for the world whenever He offers Himself as a sacrifice and oblation to God for our sins, is called both Lamb of God and a Sheep. 'Behold,' it is said, 'the lamb of God.'[48] And again: 'He was led like a sheep to slaughter.'[49] But, when it is necessary to take vengeance and to overthrow the power attacking the race of men, a certain wild and savage force, then He will be called the Son

---

43 *Ibid.* 79 11.
44 John 15.5.
45 Ps. 28 6
46 Cf. Exod. 32 20: 'And laying hold of the calf which they had made, he burnt it, and beat it to powder, which he strowed into the water, and gave thereof to the children of Israel to drink.'
47 Ps. 28.6
48 John 1.29.
49 Acts 8.32; Isa. 53.7.

## HOMILY 13

of unicorns. For, as we have learned in Job, the unicorn is a creature, irresistible in might and unsubjected to man. 'For, thou canst not bind him with a thong,' he says, 'nor will he stay at thy crib.'[50] There is also much said in that part of the prophecy about the animal acting like a free man and not submitting to men. It has been observed that the Scripture has used the comparison of the unicorn in both ways, at one time in praise, at another in censure. 'Deliver,' he says, 'my soul from the sword . . . and my lowness from the horns of the unicorns.'[51] He said these words complaining of the warlike people who in the time of passion rose up in rebellion against him. Again, he says, 'My horn shall be exalted like that of the unicorn.'[52] It seems that on account of the promptness of the animal in repelling attacks it is frequently found representing the baser things, and because of its high horn and freedom it is assigned to represent the better. On the whole, since it is possible to find the 'horn' used by Scripture in many places instead of 'glory,' as the saying: 'He will exalt the horn of his people,'[53] and 'His horn shall be exalted in glory,'[54] or also, since the 'horn' is frequently used instead of 'power,' as the saying: 'My protector and the horn of my salvation,'[55] Christ is the power of God; therefore, He is called the Unicorn on the ground that He has one horn, that is, one common power with the Father.

(6) 'The voice of the Lord divideth the flame of fire.'[56] According to the story of the three children in Babylon[57] the flame of fire was divided, when the furnace poured forth the fire forty-nine cubits high and burned up all those around; but, the flame, divided by the command of God, admitted the

---
50 Job 39.10.
51 Ps. 21.21, 22.
52 *Ibid.* 91.11.
53 *Ibid.* 148.14.
54 *Ibid.* 111.9.
55 *Ibid.* 17.3.
56 *Ibid.* 28.7.
57 Cf. Dan. 3.47-50.

wind within itself, providing for the boys a most pleasant breeze and coolness as in the shade of plants in a tranquil spot. For, it was, it is said, 'like the blowing of a wind bringing dew.'[58] And it is far more wonderful for the element of fire to be divided than for the Red Sea to be separated into parts. Nevertheless, the voice of the Lord divides the continuity and unity in the nature of fire. Although fire seems to human intelligence to be incapable of being cut or divided, yet by the command of the Lord it is cut through and divided. I believe that the fire prepared in punishment for the devil and his angels[59] is divided by the voice of the Lord, in order that, since there are two capacities in fire, the burning and the illuminating, the fierce and punitive part of the fire may wait for those who deserve to burn, while its illuminating and radiant part may be allotted for the enjoyment of those who are rejoicing. Therefore, the voice of the Lord divideth the fire and allots it, so that the fire of punishment is darksome, but the light of the state of rest remains incapable of burning.

'The voice of the Lord shaketh the desert.'[60] The shaking of the desert is dispensed as a benefit to it from the Lord, in order that, having changed from its desolate state, it may become an inhabited land and, having laid aside the reproach of barrenness, it may receive the praise of fecundity ('For many are the children of the desolate, more than of her that hath a husband.'[61]), and being filled with the spirit of the waters, that which before was desert may be made into pools of standing water. 'The Lord shall shake the desert of Cades.'[62] Now, the Lord will not shake every desert, but that of Cades, that is, sanctification. For, Cades is interpreted 'sanctification.'

'The voice of the Lord prepareth the stags.'[63] The words

---

58 Dan. 3.50.
59 Cf. Matt. 25.41: ' "Depart from me, accursed ones, into the everlasting fire which was prepared for the devil and his angels." '
60 Ps 28.8.
61 Isa. 54.1.
62 Ps. 28.8.
63 *Ibid.* 28.9.

concerning the preparation of the stags, which was made by the voice of the Lord, must be explained with the same esteem as those previously mentioned. Accordingly, since the stag obtained such a preparation that it is unharmed by the bite of serpents;[64] on the contrary, that the meat of the viper is even a purgative for it, as they say who have observed these things, and since all poisonous animals are accepted for the representation of the wicked and contrary powers (for, the Lord says: 'I have given you power to tread upon serpents and scorpions, and over all the power of the enemy.'[65] and again, the psalm promises to the prophet: 'Thou shalt walk upon the asp and the basilisk,'[66]), it is necessary, whenever we hear the word 'stag' in the Scripture, to take the word for the representation of the better power. 'The high hills are for the harts,'[67] and 'The hart panteth after the fountains of water.'[68] Since, then, every just man has his abode on the heights 'pressing on toward the goal, to the prize of the heavenly call,'[69] he returns to the fresh fountains, searching for the first sources of theology. But, the hart draws out with the breathing of his mouth the hidden venomous animals, and leads them out from their hiding places by the force of his breath. Just as the holy man is called an eagle because he walks on high and because he is separated very far from the earth, and a sheep because of his gentleness and the free gift of what he possesses, and a ram because of his authority, and a dove because of his innocence, so also, he is called the hart because of his opposition to wickedness. Therefore Solomon says: 'Let thy dearest hind and most agreeable fawn consort with

---

64 Aristotle, in *History of Animals* 9.5.611b, says that, if a stag is stung by a venom-spider or similar insect, it gathers crabs and eats them; however, he does not mention the bite of the serpent.
65 Luke 10.19.
66 Ps. 90.13.
67 *Ibid.* 103.18.
68 *Ibid.* 41.2.
69 Phil. 3.14.

thee,'⁷⁰ showing us that the harts, as mentioned previously, are suitable in the teaching of theology.

(7) 'The voice of the Lord prepareth the stags.' When, then, we see some man of God perfect and prepared, we seek for profit from intercourse with him. Wherever a stag is present, all the evil of serpents is banished. The venomous animals do not endure the odor of this animal and, in truth, when its horns are burnt for fumigation, they withdraw elsewhere. 'And he will discover the thick woods.'⁷¹ First, the voice of the Lord prepares the stags, then it discovers the thick woods, natural spots made dense with wild and unfruitful material, to which, especially, the venomous animals are wont to flee. Since, therefore, the stag has already been perfected by the preparation made by the Lord, the just man, made like to it, discovers the thick woods, so that, uncovered and ready, the corruptors of our life may be delivered up. And because 'every tree that is not bringing forth good fruit is to be cut down by the axe and thrown into the fire,'⁷² necessarily, the thick woods, the woody souls in which, like some wild beasts, the varied passions of sins lurk, are cleared out by that word, which is 'keener than any two-edged sword.'⁷³ When many men, laden with the cares of life, keep their souls like some thorn-producing land and do not allow them to be trained to bear the fruit of the word, the Lord discovers the thick woods, that is, the deformity and unseemliness and harmfulness of the cares of this life, in order that, when the place of good and evil has been made plain, men may not through ignorance hold perverse judgments concerning their affairs. Many think that the good, when it is painful, is evil, and they pursue the bad, because of the pleasure attached to it, as good. The misconception about such things among men is unspeakably great. Therefore, the fruitful woods and all cedars, which also receive

---

70 Prov. 5.19 (Septuagint version).
71 Ps. 28.9.
72 Matt. 3.10.
73 Heb. 4.12.

praise, belong to the nature of the good; but, the thick woods, which the voice of God discovers and reveals in order that those who think that they will find some useful fruit in them may not be deceived, belong to the nature of the bad.

'And in his temple all shall speak his glory.'[74] Let those who give themselves to long conversations hear the words of the psalm and take heed. What does the psalm say? He who is in the temple of God does not speak out abuse nor folly nor words full of shameful matters, but, 'in his temple all shall speak his glory.' Holy angels stand by, who write the words; the Lord is present, who sees the affections of those entering. The prayer of each is manifested to God; one seeks heavenly things affectionately and one seeks them learnedly; one utters his words perfunctorily with the tips of his lips, but his heart is far from God.[75] Even though he prays, he seeks the health of his flesh, material wealth, and human glory. None of these should be sought, as Scripture teaches, but, 'in his temple all shall speak his glory.' 'The heavens show forth the glory of God.'[76] The praise of God is a duty belonging to angels. This one duty, referring glory to the Creator, belongs to every army of heavenly creatures. Every creature, whether silent or uttering sound, whether celestial or terrestrial, gives glory to the Creator. But, wretched men, who leave their homes and run to the temple, as if to enrich themselves somewhat, do not lend their ears to the words of God; they do not possess a knowledge of their nature; they are not distressed, although they have previously committed sin; they do not grieve at remembering their sins, nor do they fear the judgment; but, smiling and shaking hands with one another, they make the house of prayer a place of lengthy conversations, pretending not to hear the psalm which solemnly protests and says: 'In the temple of God all shall speak his glory.' You not only do not speak

---

74 Ps. 28.9.
75 Cf. Matt. 15.8 and Isa. 29.13: 'This people honors me with their lips, but their heart is far from me.'
76 Ps. 18.2.

His glory, but, you even become a hindrance to the other, turning his attention to yourself and drowning out the teaching of the Spirit by your own clamor. See to it that you do not at some time leave condemned along with those blaspheming the name of God instead of receiving a reward for glorifying Him. You have a psalm, you have a prophecy, the evangelical precepts, the preachings of the apostles. Let the tongue sing, let the mind interpret the meaning of what has been said, that you may sing with your spirit, that you may sing likewise with your mind. Not at all is God in need of glory, but He wishes you to be worthy of winning glory. Therefore, 'What a man sows, he will also reap.'[77] Sow glorification, that you may reap crowns and honors and praises in the kingdom of heaven. This statement, 'In his temple all shall speak his glory,' was made not unfittingly in a digression, because some in the temple of God talk endlessly until their tongue aches; and these enter without profit. Would that it might be only without profit and not with harm!

(8) 'The Lord maketh the flood to dwell.'[78] A flood is an overflow of water which causes all lying below it to disappear and cleanses all that was previously filthy. Therefore, he calls the grace of baptism a flood, so that the soul, being washed well of its sins and rid of the old man, is suitable henceforward as a dwelling place of God in the Spirit. Further, what is said in the Thirty-first Psalm agrees with this. For, after he has said: 'I have acknowledged my sin, and my injustice I have not concealed,' and also, 'For this shall every one that is holy pray to thee,' he brought in, 'And yet in a flood of many waters, they shall not come nigh unto him.'[79] Indeed, the sins shall not come nigh to him who received baptism for the remission of his transgressions through water and the Spirit. Something akin to this is found in the prophecy of Michea:

---

77 Gal. 6.7.
78 Ps. 28.10.
79 *Ibid.* 31.5, 6.

'Because he delighteth in mercy, he will turn again and have mercy on us, he will put away our iniquities, and will cast them into the bottom of the sea.'[80]

'And the Lord shall sit king forever.'[81] God is sitting in the soul which shines from its washing, as if He were making it a throne for Himself. 'The Lord will give strength to his people: the Lord will bless his people with peace.'[82] From His erring people the Lord will take away the strong man and the strong woman,[83] but to him who acts honestly He gives strength. Therefore, 'to everyone who has shall be given.'[84] He who is confirmed in the performance of good works becomes worthy of the blessing of God. Peace, which is a certain stability of mind, seems to be the most perfect of blessings, so that the peaceful man is distinguished by the calmness of his character, but, he who is attacked by his passions has not yet participated in the peace from God, which the Lord gave to His disciples, and which, surpassing all understanding, will keep the souls of the worthy.[85] For this, the Apostle also prays for the churches, saying: 'Grace and peace be multiplied to you.'[86] May it be granted to us, after we have struggled nobly and subdued the spirit of the flesh, which is an enemy to God, when our soul is in a calm and tranquil state, to be called the sons of peace, and to share the blessing of God in peace, in Christ Jesus our Lord, to whom be glory and power, now and always, and forever. Amen.

---

80 Mich. 7.19.
81 Ps. 28.10.
82 *Ibid.* 28.11.
83 Cf. Isa. 3.1: 'For behold the sovereign the Lord of hosts shall take away from Jerusalem, and from Juda the valiant and the strong.'
84 Matt. 25.29.
85 Cf. Phil. 4.7: 'And may the peace of God which surpasses all understanding guard your hearts and your minds in Christ Jesus.'
86 I Peter 1.2.

# HOMILY 14

## *A Psalm of a Canticle on the Dedication of the House of David*

(ON PSALM 29)

THE PHYSICAL STRUCTURE of the body is, speaking figuratively, a harp and an instrument harmoniously adapted for the hymns of our God; and the actions of the body, which are referred to the glory of God are a psalm, whenever in an appropriate measure we perform nothing out of tune in our actions. Whatever pertains to lofty contemplation and theology is a canticle. Therefore, the psalm is a musical sermon when it is played rhythmically on the instrument with harmonic sounds. But the canticle is a melodious utterance expressed harmoniously without the accompaniment of the instrument. Accordingly, since this was entitled, 'A psalm of a canticle.'[1] we believe that the expression suggests action following contemplation. This psalm of a canticle, according to the title, embraces certain words of the dedication of the house. And the speech, in its material form, seems to have been delivered in the time of Solomon, when the renowned temple was raised, and to have been adapted to the harp; but, in its spiritual meaning, the title seems to signify the Incarnation of the Word of God and to make known the dedication of a house, which same house had been constructed in a novel and incredible manner. We have found many

---
1 Ps. 29.1.

things in this psalm announced by the Lord in person. Or, perhaps, it is proper to consider the house as the Church built by Christ; just as Paul writes in his letter to Timothy: 'In order that thou mayest know how to conduct thyself in the house of God, which is the Church of the living God.'[2] The dedication of the Church must be understood as the renewal of the mind, which takes place through the Holy Spirit in each, individually, of those who make up the body of the Church of Christ. It is a divine and musical harmony, not which includes words that gladden the ear, but those that calm and soften the wicked spirits which trouble souls that are exposed to harm.

'I will extol thee, O Lord, for thou hast upheld me: and hast not made my enemies to rejoice over me.'[3] How is He who dwells on high extolled by those who have as their portion the lowly places? For, if God is in heaven above and you on the earth below, in what manner could you extol God? What, then, does this message mean to the prophet? Or, is He, perhaps, said to be extolled by those who are able to have noble and holy thoughts about Him and to live for the glory of God? Therefore, he who with understanding is hastening toward bliss extols God, but, he who is turning the opposite way, which rightly should not even be mentioned, abases God as much as lies in his power.

(2) We attribute to God, as it were, every state that corresponds to our circumstances. For this reason, when we are half asleep and behaving slothfully, God, since He judges us unworthy of His observant watchfulness over us, is said to be asleep. But, when, after noticing at some time the harm that comes from the sleep, we shall say, 'Arise, why sleepest thou, O Lord?'[4] 'Behold he shall neither slumber nor sleep at that time, that keepeth Israel.'[5] Some others, as it were, turn their

---

2 1 Tim. 3.15.
3 Ps. 29.2
4 *Ibid.* 43.23.
5 *Ibid.* 120.4 (Septuagint version).

eyes away from God because of their shameful deeds and their acts unworthy of the eyes of God; these, on repenting, say: 'Why turnest thou thy face away?'[6] Besides these, there are others who have cast out the memory of God and, as it were, are producing in Him forgetfulness of themselves, and these say: 'Why forgettest thou our want and our trouble?'[7] In a word, men do the very things that are humanly spoken about God, making God in their own regard such as each has formerly made himself. Therefore, 'I will extol thee, O Lord, for thou hast upheld me: and hast not made my enemies to rejoice over me.' And I will suffer nothing low or abject in my life.

Why is the power of extolling present in me? Because You have first upheld me. Very clearly David said, 'Thou hast upheld,' instead of, 'Thou hast raised me up,' and You have made me superior to those rising up against me, just as if some one, taking by the hand a child who was inexperienced in swimming, would draw him up above the water. He, then, who by the help of God has raised himself up from a fall, through gratitude promises God glorification by his good works. Or, as if someone, by supporting a certain weak wrestler from a possible fall and making him superior to his antagonist, provides for the one an opportunity of victory but deprives the other of the pleasure of his fall. It is not the afflictions, which are sent upon the saints for a trial, that procure happiness for our invisible enemies, but, when we refuse afflictions and our thoughts are anxious, because we have grown weary of our frequent sufferings, then they are made glad and they clap and rejoice. Such it was in the case of Job.[8] He lost his possessions; he was bereft of his children; his flesh oozed forth putrid matter and worms. This was not yet, however, a pleasure to the antagonist. But, if, yielding to his

---

6 *Ibid.* 43.24.
7 *Ibid.*
8 Cf. Job 1 and 2.

sufferings, he had uttered any blasphemous word according to the advice of his wife, then the enemy would have rejoiced over him. It is the same in the case of Paul, who was hungry and thirsty, naked, buffeted, wearied, and never at rest; the enemy did not rejoice. On the contrary, the enemy was crushed, seeing him enduring the conflicts, so that Paul said with disdain: 'Who shall separate us from the love of Christ?'[9]

(3) 'O Lord my God, I have cried to thee, and thou hast healed me.'[10] Blessed is he who knows his own interior wound so that he can approach the physician and say: 'Heal me, O Lord, for my bones are troubled,'[11] and 'I said: O Lord, be thou merciful to me: heal my soul, for I have sinned against thee.'[12] Here, however, there is thanksgiving for the healing that has been conferred; for he says, 'O Lord my God.' God is not the God of all, but of those who are united with Him through love. He is the God of Abraham, and the God of Isaac, and the God of Jacob.'[13] If He were the God of all, He would not have borne this witness to them as something special. Again, Jacob says: 'My God has helped you.'[14] And Thomas, embracing the Lord with the fullest assurance, says: 'My Lord and my God.'[15] The expression, then, 'O Lord my God,' is spontaneous, and is proper to the state of the prophets. 'I have cried to thee, and thou hast healed me.' There was no interval between my voice and your grace, but at the same time that I cried out the healing came to me. While you are still calling, it is said, 'I shall say, "Behold I am here."' [16] In praying to God, therefore, we should speak loudly, in order that a speedy healing may be sent forth to us.

'Thou hast brought forth, O Lord, my soul from hell.'[17]

9 Rom. 8.35.
10 Ps. 29.3.
11 *Ibid.* 6 3.
12 *Ibid.* 40.5.
13 Exod. 3.6.
14 *Ibid.* 49.25 (Septuagint version).
15 John 20.28.
16 Isa. 58.9 (Septuagint version).
17 Ps. 29.4.

For this healing, he who was going down from illness into hell but was led up from hell through the power of Him who overthrows for our sake the ruler of death, gives thanks to God. 'Thou hast saved me from them that go down into the pit.'[18] Frequently, underground ditches which have been made into a prison for captives are called pits. Thus, there is the expression in Exodus: 'From the firstborn of Pharao, unto the firstborn of the captive woman who was in the pit.'[19] But, they even threw Jeremia also into a pit;[20] and his brothers through jealousy confined Joseph in a pit without water.[21] Each act, therefore, either draws us downward by oppressing us with sin, or lifts us upward by raising us on wings toward God. Therefore, You have saved me, who formerly lived a wicked life, and have separated me from those who go down to the dark and frigid region. This is the meaning of the words: 'Thou hast upheld me.' That is to say, 'You have led me back from my downward course, so as not to give my enemies an occasion to rejoice over me.' Now, this he said in another place: 'Who hath made my feet like the feet of harts: and who setteth me upon high places.'[22] He calls the deliverance from the pit and the uplifting, the return to high places.

'Sing to the Lord, O ye his saints.'[23] Not if someone utters the words of the psalm with his mouth, does that one sing to the Lord; but, all who send up the psalmody from a clean heart, and who are holy, maintaining righteousness toward God, these are able to sing to God, harmoniously guided by the spiritual rhythms. How many stand there, coming from fornication? How many from theft? How many concealing in their hearts deceit? How many lying? They think they are

---
18 *Ibid.*
19 Exod. 12.29.
20 Cf. Jer. 37.15: 'So Jeremia went into the house of the prison, and into the dungeon: and Jeremia remained there many days.'
21 Cf. Gen. 37.24: 'They seized him and threw him into the cistern, which was empty and dry.'
22 Ps. 17.34.
23 *Ibid.* 29.5.

singing, although in truth they are not singing. For, the Scripture invites the saint to the singing of psalms. 'A bad tree cannot bear good fruit,'[24] nor a bad heart utter words of life. Therefore, 'make the tree good and its fruits good.'[25] Cleanse your hearts, in order that you may bear fruit in the spirit and may be able, after becoming saints, to sing psalms intelligently to the Lord.

(4) 'And give praise to the memory of his holiness.'[26] David did not say: 'Give praise to His holiness,' but, 'to the memory of his holiness'; that is, 'Give thanks.' Indeed, the singing of praises here is accepted in place of giving thanks. Give thanks, therefore, that you were mindful of His holiness, since formerly, because you were sinking deep in evil and were polluted with the uncleanness of the flesh, you had become forgetful of the holiness of Him who made you. For the atonement of your sins, confess your former actions which were not rightly performed.

'For wrath is in his indignation; and life in his good will.'[27] First, he mentioned something depressing, wrath in the indignation of God; then, something brighter, life in His good will. This seems to be tautology to those who are not able to attain to an exact understanding of the meanings, since the prophet says that wrath is in the indignation of God, as if wrath and indignation were the same thing; but, there is a very great difference. Indignation is the decision to inflict some particular sad punishments upon a man deserving of them; but wrath is the suffering and the punishment already being inflicted by the just Judge according to the measure of the wrong done. What I say will become clearer from an example. The doctor, having diagnosed the swollen and festering part, judges that an incision is necessary for the sufferer. This, Scripture calls indignation. But, after the decision of the

---

24 Matt. 7.18.
25 *Ibid.* 12.33.
26 Ps. 29.5.
27 *Ibid.* 29.6.

doctor on the remedy, the operation then follows, bringing the remedies decided upon to accomplishment; and the knife, cutting in, also causes pain for the one who is being cut. This is called the wrath of God. Come, then, to the proposition, and you will find the consequence of this opinion. 'For wrath is in his indignation,' a penalty, according to the just judgment of God; but, 'life in his good will.' What, then, does he say? That what God wills is this, that all share His life; and misfortunes are not wrought by His will but are brought on by the just deserts of those who have sinned. Therefore, God grants life to each one according to His own will, and each one stores up wrath for himself 'On the day of wrath and of the revelation and of the just judgment of God.'[28] It is customary for Scripture to place sad conditions before the more auspicious ones, because the pleasure is sweeter when grief has gone before it. 'I will kill,' it says, 'and I will make to live.'[29] He Himself causes the suffering and again restores; He struck, and His hands healed.[30] The afflictions precede, in order that the graces may be lasting, since we then exert ourselves exceedingly for the preservation of what has been given.

'In the evening weeping shall have place, and in the morning gladness.'[31] Recall the time of the passion of the Lord, and you will find the meaning. For, in the evening, weeping overwhelmed the disciples of the Lord when they saw Him hanging on the cross; but, in the morning, gladness, when after the Resurrection they ran about with joy, giving each other the good tidings of the appearance of the Lord. Or, perhaps, even in general this time is called evening in which those who have wept blessedly will be consoled when morning comes. 'Blessed are they who mourn, for they shall be com-

---

28 Rom. 2.5.
29 Deut. 32.39.
30 Cf. *Ibid.*
31 Ps. 29.6.

forted.'³² 'Blessed are they who weep, for they shall laugh.'³³ They, therefore, who spend the days of their life, which is already at its consummation and declining toward its setting, in weeping for their sins, these will be glad in that true morning which is approaching. 'They that sow in tears shall reap in joy,'³⁴ of course, in the future.

(5) 'And in my abundance I said: I shall never be moved.'³⁵ As the prosperity of a city is dependent upon the supply of goods for sale in the market, and as we say that a country is prosperous which produces much fruit, so also there is a certain prosperity of the soul when it has been filled with works of every kind. It is necessary first for it to be laboriously cultivated, and then to be enriched by the plentiful streams of heavenly waters, so as to bear fruit thirtyfold, sixtyfold, and a hundredfold,³⁶ and to obtain the blessing which says: 'Blessed shall be thy barns and blessed thy stores.'³⁷ He, therefore, who is conscious of his own constancy, will say with sure confidence and will strongly maintain that he will not be turned away by any opponent, like a full field which the Lord has blessed.

'O Lord, in thy favor, thou gavest strength to my beauty.'³⁸ They who are engaged in the examination of the reason for virtues, have said that some of the virtues spring from contemplation and some are noncontemplative; as for instance, prudence springs from contemplation in the sphere of things good and evil, but self-control from the contemplation of things to be chosen or avoided, justice, of things to be assigned or not to be assigned, and valor, of those that are dangerous or not dangerous; but beauty and strength are noncontemplative

---

32 Matt. 5.5.
33 Luke 6.21.
34 Ps. 125.5.
35 Ibid. 29.7.
36 Cf. Matt. 13.23: 'He bears fruit and yields in one case a hundredfold, in another sixtyfold, and in another thirtyfold.'
37 Deut. 28.5.
38 Ps. 29.8.

virtues, since they follow from the contemplative. From the fitness and harmony of the contemplations of the soul, some wise men have perceived beauty; and from the effectiveness of the suggestions from the contemplative virtues, they have become aware of strength. But, for this, namely, that beauty may exist in the soul, and also the power for the fulfillment of what is proper, we need divine grace. As, therefore, he said above: 'Life is in his good will,' so, now, he extols God through his thanksgiving, saying: 'In thy favor, thou gavest strength to my beauty.' For, I was beautiful according to nature, but weak, because I was dead by sin through the treachery of the serpent. To my beauty, then, which I received from You at the beginning of my creation, You added a strength which is appropriate for what is proper. Every soul is beautiful, which is considered by the standard of its own virtues. But beauty, true and most lovely, which can be contemplated by him alone who has purified his mind, is that of the divine and blessed nature. He who gazes steadfastly at the splendor and graces of it, receives some share from it, as if from an immersion, tingeing his own face with a sort of brilliant radiance. Whence Moses also was made resplendent in face by receiving some share of beauty when he held converse with God.[39] Therefore, he who is conscious of his own beauty utters this act of thanksgiving: 'O Lord, in thy favor, thou gavest strength to my beauty.'

Just as the noncontemplative virtues, both beauty and strength, follow from the contemplative virtues, so there are certain noncontemplative vices, shameful conduct and weakness. In fact, what is more unbecoming and uglier than a passionate soul? Observe, I beg you, the wrathful man and his fierceness. Look at the man who is distressed, his abasement and dejection of soul. Who could endure to look at him who is sunk in sensuality and gluttony or who is alarmed by fears? For, the feelings of the soul affect even the extremities of the

---

39 Cf. Exod. 34.29 (Septuagint version).

body, just as also the traces of the beauty of the soul shine through in the state of the saint. Accordingly, we must have regard for beauty, in order that the Bridegroom, the Word, receiving us, may say: 'Thou art all fair, O my love, and there is not a spot in thee.'[40]

(6) 'Thou turnedst away thy face from me, and I became troubled.'[41] 'As long as the rays of the sun of Your watchfulness shone upon me,' he says, 'I lived in a calm and untroubled state, but, when You turned Your face away, the agitation and confusion of my soul was exposed.' God is said to turn away His face when in times of troubles He permits us to be delivered up to trials, in order that the strength of him who is struggling may be known. Therefore, 'if the peace which surpasses all understanding will guard our hearts,'[42] we shall be able to escape the tumult and confusion of the passions. Since perversion is opposed to the will of God, and disorder to beauty and grace and strength, the disorder would be a deformity and weakness of the soul, present in it because of its estrangement from God. We pray always for the face of God to shine upon us, in order that we may be in a state becoming to a holy person, gentle and untroubled in every way, because of our readiness for the good. 'I am ready,' he says, 'and am not troubled.'[43]

'To thee, O Lord, will I cry: and I will make supplication to my God.'[44] Frequently, the statement is made in regard to crying out to the Lord that it is the privilege of him alone who desires great and heavenly things to cry out. But, if anyone asks God for trifling and earthly things, he uses a small and low voice, which does not reach to the height nor come to the ears of the Lord.

---

40 Cant. 4.7.
41 Ps. 29.8.
42 Cf. Phil. 4.7: 'And may the peace of God which surpasses all understanding guard your hearts and your minds in Christ Jesus.'
43 Ps. 118.60.
44 *Ibid.* 29.9.

'What profit is there in my blood, whilst I go down to corruption?'[45] 'Why,' he says, 'have I cried out? And for what have I prayed to You, my Lord and my God? What need is there for me,' he says, 'of bodily comfort and much blood, since presently my body will be handed over to the general dissolution.' 'But I chastise my body and bring it into subjection,'[46] lest at any time, because my blood is in good condition and overheated, my corpulence may become an occasion of sin. Do not flatter your flesh with sleep and baths and soft coverings, but say always these words: 'What profit is there in my blood, whilst I go down to corruption?' Why do you treat with honor that which a little later shall perish? Why do you fatten and cover yourself with flesh? Or, do you not know that the more massive you make your flesh, the deeper is the prison you are preparing for your soul?

'Shall dust confess to thee, or declare thy truth?'[47] How, indeed, shall man, made of clay and flesh, confess to You, his God? And how will he declare the truth, who has never given time to learning and has buried his mind in such a mass of flesh? For this reason, therefore, I waste away my flesh and I am unsparing of my blood which, indeed, is wont to be converted into flesh, that there may be no obstacle to me for confession or for the knowledge of truth.

(7) 'The Lord hath heard, and hath had mercy on me: the Lord became my helper.'[48] After relating what it was that he cried out to God, immediately sensible of the assistance of God, he encourages us to ask for the same things, saying: 'The Lord hath heard, and hath had mercy on me: the Lord became my helper.' Let us also pray, therefore, and cry out with a spiritual cry, demanding great things, not seeking after the flesh ('For they who are carnal cannot please God'[49]), in order that the

---

45 *Ibid.* 29.10.
46 1 Cor. 9.27.
47 Ps. 29.10.
48 *Ibid.* 29.11.
49 Rom. 8.8.

Lord may hear us, having mercy on our weakness, and that we also, rejoicing in the divine assistance, may say, 'Thou hast turned for me my mourning into joy.'[50] The joy of God is not found in just any soul but, if some one has mourned much and deeply his own sin with loud lamentations and continual weepings, as if he were bewailing his own death, the mourning of such a one is turned into joy. That it is praiseworthy to mourn is evident from the boys who sit in the market place, saying: 'We have sung dirges, and you have not wept; we have piped to you, and you have not danced.'[51] The flute is a musical instrument which needs wind for the melody. Wherefore, I think that every holy prophet was called figuratively a flute because of the inspiration of the Holy Spirit. For this reason he says: 'We have piped to you, and you have not danced.' The prophetical words, indeed, urge us on to the rhythmic action of the holy prophecy, which is called dancing. But, the prophets make lamentation for us, summoning us to mourn, in order that, becoming aware from the prophetic words of our own sins, we may bewail our destruction, afflicting our flesh with hardships and toils. By such a person, the mourning garment, which he put on when bewailing his sin, is rent, and the tunic of joy is placed around him and the cloak of salvation, those bright wedding garments, with which, if one is adorned, he will not be cast out from the bridal chamber.

'Thou hast cut my sackcloth, and hast compassed me with gladness.'[52] The sackcloth is a help to penance, since it is a symbol of humility. 'They would have repented long ago,' it is said, 'sitting in sackcloth and ashes.'[53] Now, since the Apostle 'with face unveiled is transformed into his very image

---

50 Ps. 29.12.
51 Luke 7.32.
52 Ps. 29.12.
53 Luke 10.13.

from glory to glory,'⁵⁴ he calls the grace given to him by the Lord his own glory.

(8) 'To the end that my glory may sing to thee.'⁵⁵ The glory of the just man is the Spirit which is in him. Therefore, let him who sings by the Spirit say: 'To the end that my glory may sing to thee, and I may not regret.' He means, 'No longer shall I do things which deserve the pricking and piercing of my heart at the remembrance of my sins.' 'O Lord my God, I will give praise to thee for ever.'⁵⁶ This is instead of 'I will give thanks.' For, when You granted me pardon because of my repentance and led me back into glory, taking away the shame of my sins, for this I shall give praise to You for all eternity. In fact, what space of time could be so great, that it could produce in my soul forgetfulness of such mighty benefits?

---

54 Cf 2 Cor. 3.18: 'But we all, with faces unveiled, reflecting as in a mirror the glory of the Lord, are being transformed into his very image from glory to glory.'
55 Ps. 29.13.
56 *Ibid.*

# HOMILY 15

## *A Psalm in Praise of the Power and Providence of God*

### (ON PSALM 32)

**R**EJOICE IN THE LORD, O ye just; praise becometh the upright.[1]
The voice of exultation is familar in the Scripture, betokening a very bright and happy state of soul in those deserving of happiness. 'Rejoice,' therefore, 'in the Lord, O ye just,' not when the interests of your home are flourishing, not when you are in good health of body, not when your fields are filled with all sorts of fruits, but, when you have the Lord—such immeasurable Beauty, Goodness, Wisdom. Let the joy that is in Him suffice for you. He who exults with joy and happiness in anything that is much desired, seems thus to rejoice in Him. Therefore, Scripture urges the just to be aware of their dignity, because they have been considered worthy to be the servants of so great a Master, and to glory in His service with inexpressible joy and exultation, since the heart is, as it were, bounding with ecstasy of love of the good. If at any time a light, for example, falling upon your heart, produced a continuous thought of God and illumined your soul, so that you loved God and despised the world and all things corporeal, understand from that faint and brief resemblance the whole state of the just, who are enjoying God

---

[1] Ps. 32.1.

steadily and uninterruptedly. At some rare times by the dispensation of God that transport of joy seizes you in order that through a little taste He may remind you of what you have been deprived. But, for the just man the divine and heavenly joy is lasting, since the Holy Spirit dwells in him once for all. 'But the firstfruit of the Spirit is: charity, joy, peace.'[2] Therefore, 'rejoice in the Lord, O ye just.' The Lord is like a place capable of containing the just, and there is every reason for one who is in Him to be delighted and to make merry. Moreover, the just man becomes a place for the Lord, when he receives Him in himself. He who sins gives place to the devil, taking no heed of him who said: 'Do not give place to the devil,'[3] nor to Ecclesiastes, 'If the spirit of him that hath power, ascend upon thee, leave not thy place.'[4] Let us, then, who are in the Lord and who, as much as we are able, observe closely His wonders, so draw joy to our hearts from the contemplation of them.

'Praise becometh the upright.'[5] As a crooked foot does not fit into a straight sandal, so neither is the praise of God suited to perverted hearts. For this reason, I think, since speech concerning the Savior is not becoming in the mouth of the demons, He takes away their power, in order that they may not make Him known. And Paul rebuked the divining spirit in order that the Holy One might not be praised by an unclean person.[6] Such also is this saying: 'But to the sinner God hath said: Why dost thou declare my justices?'[7] Let us earnestly endeavor, therefore, to flee every crooked and tortuous act, and let us keep our mind and the judgment of our soul as straight as a rule, in order that the praise of the Lord may

---

2 Gal. 5.22.
3 Eph. 4.27.
4 Eccles. 10.4.
5 Ps. 32.1.
6 Cf. Acts 16 18: 'This she did for many days; until Paul, being very much grieved, turned and said to the spirit, "I order thee in the name of Jesus Christ to go out of her." '
7 Ps. 49.16.

be permitted to us since we are upright. In the same way the serpent, which is the author of sin, is called crooked, and the sword of God is drawn against the dragon, the crooked serpent,[8] which makes many twists and turns in its progress. As the coiling movement of the serpent trails along, it is traced unevenly on the ground, since, if it were otherwise, the first parts would hasten along, the next follow transversely and the tail bend aside in the opposite direction. Therefore, he who follows the serpent shows that his life is crooked, uneven, and filled with contrarieties; but, he who follows after the Lord makes his paths straight and his footprints right. For, 'the Lord our God is righteous, and his countenance hath beheld righteousness.'[9] If two rulers are compared with each other, their straightness is in agreement with each other, but, if a distorted piece of wood is compared with a ruler, the crooked one will be found at variance with the straight. Since, therefore, the praise of God is righteous, there is need of a righteous heart, in order that the praise may be fitting and adapted to it. But, if 'no one can say "Jesus is Lord," except in the Holy Spirit,'[10] how would you give praise, since you do not have the right spirit in your heart?

(2) 'Give praise to the Lord on the harp; sing to him with the psaltery, the instrument of ten strings.'[11] First, it is necessary to praise the Lord on the harp; that is, to render harmoniously the actions of the body. Since, indeed, we sinned in the body, 'when we yielded our members as slaves of sin, unto lawlessness,'[12] let us give praise with our body, using the same instrument for the destruction of sin. Have you reviled?

---

8 Cf. Isa. 27.1: 'In that day the Lord with his hard, and great, and strong sword shall visit leviathan the bar serpent, and leviathan the crooked serpent.'
9 Ps. 91.16; 10.8.
10 1 Cor. 12.3.
11 Ps. 32.2.
12 Cf. Rom. 6.19: 'For as you yielded your members as slaves of uncleanness and iniquity unto iniquity, so now yield your members as slaves of justice unto sanctification.'

Bless. Have you defrauded? Make restitution. Have you been intoxicated? Fast. Have you made false pretensions? Be humble. Have you been envious? Console. Have you murdered? Bear witness, or afflict your body with the equivalent of martyrdom through confession. And then, after confession you are worthy to play for God on the ten-stringed psaltery. For, it is necessary, first, to correct the actions of our body, so that we perform them harmoniously with the divine Word and thus mount up to the contemplation of things intellectual. Perhaps, the mind, which seeks things above, is called a psaltery because the structure of this instrument has its resonance from above. The works of the body, therefore, give praise to God as if from below; but the mysteries, which are proclaimed through the mind, have their origin from above, as if the mind was resonant through the Spirit. He, therefore, who observes all the precepts and makes, as it were, harmony and symphony from them, he, I say, plays for God on a ten-stringed psaltery, because there are ten principal precepts, written according to the first teaching of the Law.

'Sing to the Lord a new canticle.'[13] That is, not in the antiquity of written word, but in the newness of the spirit serve God. He who understands the law not in a corporeal sense, but who becomes acquainted with its spiritual meaning is the one who sings the new canticle. For, the ancient aged testament has passed and the new renewed canticle of the teaching of the Lord has succeeded, which revives our youth like an eagle, when we destroy the exterior man and are renewed day by day. But, he who 'strains forward to what is before,'[14] always becomes newer than he was formerly. Therefore, becoming always newer than he was, he sings a newer canticle to God. But according to custom, that is said to be newer which is admirable or which has recently come into existence. If, then, you relate the wondrous manner and the

---
13 Ps. 32.3.
14 Phil. 3.13.

whole surpassing nature of the Incarnation of the Lord, you will sing a newer and an unusual canticle; and, if you go on through the regeneration and renewal of the whole world which had grown old under its sin, and proclaim the mysteries of the Resurrection, you thus sing a canticle both new and recent.

(3) 'Sing well unto him with a loud noise.'[15] Hear the command. 'Sing well,' with unwavering mind, with sincere affection. 'Sing with a loud noise.' Like certain brave soldiers, after the victory against the enemy, pour forth hymns to the Author of the victory. 'Take courage,' it is said, 'I have overcome the world.'[16] What man is capable of fighting against the evil one, unless, fleeing to the protection of the power of our Commander in chief, by our faith in Him we smite our enemy and shoot him with arrows? Therefore, 'sing well with a loud noise.' But, the loud noise is a certain inarticulate sound, when those who are fighting side by side in a war shout out in unison with each other. Sing, then, in harmony and in agreement and in union through charity. Now, what should those say who are singing? 'That the word of the Lord is right.'[17] Therefore, he first summons the righteous to praise, since the Word of the Lord is righteous and is destined to be glorified, who 'was in the beginning with God and was God.'[18] The Father, then, is righteous; the Son is righteous; the Holy Spirit is righteous.

'And all his works are done with faithfulness.'[19] What does this mean? His work is the heavens, His work is the earth, His work is the sea, the air, all things inanimate, animate, rational, and irrational. How, then, are all things done with faithfulness? What sort of faith is there in inanimate objects? What is the faith of the brute beasts? What faith is there in

---
15 Ps. 32.3.
16 John 16.33.
17 Ps. 32.4.
18 John 1.1.
19 Ps. 32.4.

a stone? What faith in a dog? Neither the inanimate object nor the beast is in faith. Nevertheless, the assertion excludes nothing, but includes all things when it says: 'All his works are done with faithfulness.' What, then, does this mean? 'If you see the heavens,' he says 'and the order in them, they are a guide to faith, for through themselves they show the Craftsman; and, if you see the orderly arrangement about the earth, again through these things also your faith in God is increased. In fact, it is not by acquiring knowledge of God with our carnal eyes that we believe in Him, but by the power of the mind we have perceived the invisible God through visible things. Therefore, 'all his works are done with faithfulness.' Even if you consider the stone, it also possesses a certain proof of the power of its Maker: likewise, if you consider the ant or the gnat or the bee. Frequently in the smallest objects the wisdom of the Creator shines forth. He who unfolded the heavens and poured out the boundless expanses of the seas, He it is who hollowed out the very delicate sting of the bee like a tube, so that through it the poison might be poured out. Therefore 'all his works are done with faithfulness.' Do not say: 'This happened by chance' and 'that occurred accidentally.' Nothing is casual, nothing indeterminate, nothing happens at random, nothing among things that exist is caused by chance. And do not say 'It is a bad mishap,' or 'it is an evil hour.' These are the words of the untaught. 'Are not two sparrows sold for a farthing? And yet not one of them will fall'[20] without the divine will. How many are the hairs of your head? Not one of them will be forgotten.[21] Do you see the divine eye, how none of the least trifles escapes its glance?

The Lord 'loveth mercy and judgment; the earth is full of the mercy of the Lord.'[22] If the judgment of God, who renders

---

20 Matt. 10.29.
21 Cf. Matt. 10.30. 'But as for you, the very hairs of your head are all numbered.'
22 Ps. 32.5.

precisely according to our deserts what is due to us for our deeds, should be by itself, what hope would there be? Who of all mankind would be saved? But, as it is, 'He loveth mercy and judgment.' It is as if He had made mercy a coadjutor to Himself, standing before the royal throne of His judgment, and thus He leads each one to judgment. 'If thou, O Lord, wilt mark iniquities: Lord, who shall stand it?'[23] Neither is mercy without judgment, nor judgment without mercy. He loves mercy, therefore, before judgment, and after mercy He comes to judgment. However, these qualities are joined to each other, mercy and judgment, lest either mercy alone should produce presumption, or judgment alone cause despair. The Judge wishes to have mercy on you and to share His own compassion, but on condition that He finds you humble after sin, contrite, lamenting much for your evil deeds, announcing publicly without shame sins committed secretly, begging the brethren to labor with you in reparation; in short, if He sees that you are worthy of pity, He provides His mercy for you ungrudgingly. But, if He sees your heart unrepentant, your mind proud, your disbelief of the future life, and your fearlessness of the judgment, then He desires the judgment for you, just as a reasonable and kind doctor tries at first with hot applications and soft poultices to reduce a tumor, but, when he sees that the mass is rigidly and obstinately resisting, casting away the olive oil and the gentle method of treatment, he prefers henceforth the use of the knife. Therefore, He loves mercy in the case of those repenting, but He also loves judgment in the case of the unyielding. Isaia says some such thing, too, to God: 'Thy mercy in measure.'[24] For, he compares the mercy with the judgment of Him who gives compensation by scale and number and weight according to the deserts of each.

(4) 'The earth is full of the mercy of the Lord.'[25] Here mercy is separated from judgment. The earth is full of only

---
23 *Ibid.* 129.3.
24 Isa. 28.17.
25 Ps. 32.5.

the mercy of the Lord, since His judgment is stored up for the appointed time. Here, then, mercy is apart from judgment; indeed, He did not come 'in order that He might judge the world, but that He might save the world.'[26] But there, judgment is not apart from mercy because man could not be found clean from stain, not even if he had lived for only one day.[27] And so, if anyone sees the evil spreading daily and the mortal race of man, so far as it merits for its sins, deserving of countless deaths, he will admire the riches of the goodness of God and of His forbearance and patience. Of course, while we are on earth, we need mercy. Those in heaven, indeed, merit to be called happy, not to be pitied. Or, the explanation is, perhaps, that, because of the sentence laid upon us for sin, it is we who are called earth, since we hear from God, 'Earth you are, and unto earth you shall return,'[28] we, who are full of the mercies of God. For, 'when we were dead by reason of our' offenses and 'sins,' God, having mercy, 'brought us to life together with Christ.'[29]

'By the word of the Lord the heavens were established; and all the power of them by the spirit of his mouth.'[30] Where are those who set at naught the Spirit? Where are those who separate It from the creative power? Where are those who dissever It from union with the Father and Son? Let them hear the psalm which says: 'By the word of the Lord the heavens were established; and all the power of them by the spirit of his mouth.' The term 'Word,' will not be considered as this common form of diction which consists of names and expressions, nor will the Spirit be considered as vapor poured out in the air; but as the Word, which was in the beginning with God,[31] and as the Holy Spirit, which has obtained this

---

26 Cf. John 3.17: 'For God did not send his Son into the world in order to judge the world, but that the world might be saved through him.'
27 Cf. Job 14.4, 5 (Septuagint version).
28 Gen. 3.9.
29 Eph. 2.5.
30 Ps. 32.6.
31 John 1.1.

appellation as Its own. As, then, the Creator, the Word, firmly established the heavens, so the Spirit which is from God, which proceeds from the Father, that is, which is from His mouth (that you may not judge that It is some external object or some creature, but may glorify It as having Its substance from God) brings with It all the powers in Him. Therefore, all the heavenly power was established by the Spirit; that is, it has from the assistance of the Spirit the solidity and firmness and constancy in holiness and in every virtue that is becoming to the sacred powers. In this place, therefore, the Spirit was described as from His mouth; we shall find elsewhere that the Word also was said to be from His mouth, in order that it may be understood that the Savior and His Holy Spirit are from the Father. Since, then, the Savior is the Word of the Lord, and the Holy Spirit is the Spirit from His mouth, both joined with Him in the creation of the heavens and the powers in them, and for this reason the statement was made: 'By the word of the Lord the heavens were established; and all the power of them by the spirit of his mouth.' For, nothing is made holy, except by the presence of the Spirit. The Word, the Master Craftsman and Creator of the universe, gave entrance into existence to the angels; the Holy Spirit added holiness to them. The angels were not created infants, then perfected by gradual exercise and thus made worthy of the reception of the Spirit; but, in their initial formation and in the material, as it were, of their substance they had holiness laid as a foundation. Wherefore, they are turned toward evil with difficulty, for they were immediately steeled by sanctity, as by some tempering, and possessed steadfastness in virtue by the gift of the Holy Spirit.

(5) 'Gathering together the waters of the sea, as a vessel; laying up the depths in storehouses.'[32] He did not say, 'Gathering together the waters of the sea as in a vessel,' but, 'as a vessel,' thus 'gathering together the waters of the sea.' Con-

---
32 Ps. 32.7.

sider, I beg of you, the nature of a vessel, now inflated, when the skin is stretched tight by the enclosed air; now reduced, when that which is stretching it yields. In this way, therefore, the sea at times swells and, becoming wild and swollen with the winds, it seethes; again, at other times, in a calm, it is reduced to a lower level. As a vessel, then, the Lord thus gathers together and reduces the water of the sea. However, we have found in certain copies, 'Gathering together as in a vessel the waters of the sea,' where Scripture refers us to ancient history, when the Red Sea, although no one was dividing it nor enclosing it, of itself stood firm, as if held in some vessel,[33] because the divine command did not permit it to be poured forth.

'Laying up the depths in storehouses.' It would be more consistent as regards the general notion to say: 'Placing storehouses in the depths,' that is, enclosing its wealth in mystery. But, now he says that the depths are like certain treasures worthy of the divine storehouses. Are, then, the words concerning the divine judgment, which are unutterable and incomprehensible to human understanding, never called depths, since the reasons according to which He dispenses all things individually are stored up only in the knowledge of God? In fact, we learned in another psalm, which said, 'Thy judgments are a great deep,'[34] that the judgments made about each one are called a deep. Therefore, if you seek to know why the life of a sinner is continued, but the days of sojourning of the just man are cut short; why the unjust man thrives, but a just man is afflicted; why the young child is snatched away before coming to maturity; whence are wars; why there are shipwrecks, earthquakes, droughts, heavy rains; why things destructive of men are created; why one man is a slave, another, free, one is rich, another is poor (and the difference in sins and in

---

33 Cf. Exod 14 22: 'And the children of Israel went in through the midst of the sea dried up: for the water was as a wall on their right hand and on their left.'
34 Ps. 35.7.

virtuous actions is great; she who was sold to a brothelkeeper is in sin by force, but she who immediately obtained a good master grows up with virginity); why this one is treated with kindness, and that one condemned; and what is the reward in the case of each of these from the Judge; taking all these questions into your mind, consider that the judgments of God are the depths and, because they are enclosed in the divine storehouses, are not easily grasped by those encountering them. To him who believes, a promise is given by God: 'I will give thee hidden treasures, unseen ones.'[35] When we have been deemed worthy of knowledge face to face, we shall see also the depths in the storehouses of God. If you will gather together the sayings in Scripture about vessels, you will better comprehend the prophetic meaning. Those, then, who are renewed day by day and who take new wine from the true vine, are said in the Gospel to be new vessels. But, they who have not yet put off the old man are old vessels, unable to be trusted for the reception of new wine. For, no one puts new wine into old wineskins, lest the wine be spilt, and those skins be entirely ruined, inasmuch as they are considered worthy of no excuse hereafter, if they spill the good new wine. New wine must be poured into fresh skins.[36] The new and spiritual wine and that which is glowing with the Holy Spirit, the perception of truth which never becomes old, must be put in the new man, who, because 'he always bears about in his body the dying of Jesus,'[37] might justly be said to be a new vessel.

(6) 'Let all the earth fear the Lord, and let all the inhabitants of the world be in awe of him.'[38] Since the fear of the Lord is the beginning of knowledge, let those who are earthly minded be taught through fear. In fact, fear is necessarily

---

35 Isa. 45.3.
36 Cf. Matt. 9.17: 'Nor do people pour new wine into old wine-skins, else the skins burst, the wine is spilt, and the skins are ruined. But they put new wine into fresh skins.'
37 Cf. 2 Cor. 4.10: 'Always bearing about in our body the dying of Jesus.'
38 Ps. 32.8.

employed as introductory to true religion, but love, now taking over, brings to perfection those who have been prepared by a fear that is capable of knowledge. To the whole earth, therefore, Scripture advises fear. 'Let all the inhabitants of the world,' it says, 'be in awe of him.' Let them make every movement, as it were, whether effected by the mind or by bodily action, according to the will of God. At least I understand the words, 'Let them be in awe of him,' in this way. For example, let neither the eye be moved without God, nor the hand be put in motion without God, nor the heart think on things not well pleasing to God. In short, let them be in awe of no one else, and let nothing move them except the fear of God.

'For he spoke and they were made: he commanded and they were created.'[39] To the two preceding statements: 'Let all the earth fear,' and 'Let all the inhabitants of the world be in awe,' he added two more, 'He spoke and they were made; he commanded and they were created.' Since man is composed of an earthy form and a soul indwelling in a body, that which was formed from earth is called earth; for the soul which obtains as its lot a life in the flesh is called the inhabitant of the world. Appropriately, therefore, the saying, 'He spoke and they were made,' is assigned to the earth. In the case of our form which was made from the earth, 'they were made,' but, in the case of the part created according to the image of God, 'they were created,' since the creation is frequently understood in the transformation and improvement, as the expression, 'If any man is in Christ, he is a new creature,'[40] and also, 'That of the two he might create one new man.'[41] Perhaps also, 'they were made' is spoken in the case of the first begetting of man, and 'they were created' in the case of the second regeneration through the grace of Christ. As a com-

---

39 *Ibid.* 32.9.
40 2 Cor. 5.17.
41 Eph. 2.15.

mand of God excels a mere word, to the same extent does creation excel generation.

'The Lord bringeth to nought the counsels of nations; and he rejecteth the devices of people.'[42] This is an explanation of the preceding statement of how God created those who believe in Him in consequence of His bringing to nought the foolish counsels which the people held about idolatry and all vanity, and in consequence of His rejection of the counsels of princes. And it is possible to refer these things to the time of His passion when they thought that they were crucifying the King of Glory, but He through the economy of the cross was renewing humanity. For, in the Resurrection the counsel of nations, of Pilate and his soldiers, and of whoever was active in the matter of the cross, was brought to nought; the counsels of the princes were rejected, and also those of the high priests and scribes and kings of the people. In fact, the Resurrection destroyed their every device. If you will read the things in each history which God did to the faithless nations, you will find that the statement has much force even according to our corporeal intelligence. When Joram, son of Achaab, was king in Israel, then his son Ader, King of Syria, carrying on a war with a great force and a heavy hand, besieged Samaria, so that even the necessaries of life were wanting to them, and the head of an ass was sold for fifty shekels of silver,[43] and the fourth part of a cabe[44] of pigeon's dung for five shekels of silver.[45] At that time, therefore, in order that the promise of Elisha might be fulfilled, the counsels of Syria were brought to nought, and abandoning their tents and all their supplies, they fled, leaving such a great abundance in Samaria that a

---
42 Ps. 32.10.
43 The silver shekel had the same value as a stater, approximately seventy-two and a half cents.
44 A cabe was about four pints.
45 Cf. 4 Kings 6.25: 'And there was a great famine in Samaria; and so long did the siege continue, till the head of an ass was sold for fourscore pieces of silver, and the fourth part of a cabe of pigeon's dung, for five pieces of silver.'

measure of fine flour and two measures of barley were sold for one shekel.⁴⁶ Thus, then, the Lord knew how to bring to nought the counsels of nations. We learned in the time of Achitophel how He cast away the counsels of the princes, when David prayed, saying: 'Infatuate the counsel of Achitophel.'⁴⁷ Therefore, when you hear some one making great threats and announcing that he will bring upon you all sorts of ill-treatment, losses, blows, or death, look up to the Lord who brings to nought the counsels of nations and rejects the devices of the people.

(7) 'But the counsel of the Lord standeth for ever: the thoughts of his heart to all generations.'⁴⁸ Do you not see the teachings of the nations, this empty philosophy, how subtle and farfetched they are concerning the inventions of their teachings, both in the rational speculations and in the moral injunctions, and in certain natural sciences and the other so-called esoteric teachings? How all things have been scattered and rendered useless, and the truths of the Gospel alone now hold place in the world? For, many are the counsels in the hearts of men, but the counsel of the Lord has prevailed. And it is necessary, at least if the counsel from God is to remain in our souls firm and steadfast, for the human thoughts which we formerly held, first to be rejected. Just as he who intends to write on wax, first smooths it down and thus puts on whatever forms he wishes, so also the heart which is to admit clearly the divine words must be made clean of the opposite thoughts. 'The thoughts of his heart to all generations.' Since, then, there are two chosen peoples, and two testaments were given to them according to the saying, 'The thoughts of his heart to all generations (eis geneàn kaí geneán),' since 'generation' is named twice, there can be understood also two thoughts, the one, according to which we

---

46 Cf. 4 Kings 7.16: 'and a bushel of fine flour was sold for a stater, and two bushels of barley for a stater, according to the word of the Lord.'
47 2 Kings 15.31.
48 Ps. 32.11.

received the previous testament, but the second, bestowing upon us the new and saving teaching of Christ.

'Blessed is the nation whose God is the Lord: the people whom he hath chosen for his inheritance.'[49] No one considers the people of the Jews blessed, but, as that people which was chosen according to merit from all the peoples. For, we are the nation of whom the Lord is our God; we are also the people whom He chose[50] as an inheritance for Himself; the nation, for we have been selected from many nations; the people, because we have been summoned in place of the rejected people. And, since 'Many are called, but few are chosen,'[51] he does not pronounce him blessed who is called, but him who is chosen. Blessed is he whom He chose. What is the cause of the pronouncement of blessedness? The expected inheritance of everlasting blessings. Or, does he, perhaps, according to the Apostle, since, when the full number of nations will have entered, then all Israel will be saved, first proclaim blessed, the full number of nations, then later, Israel, which is saved? Certainly, not just anyone will be saved, but only the remnant which is according to the election of grace. Therefore, he says: 'The people whom he hath chosen for his inheritance.'

(8) 'The Lord hath looked from heaven: he hath beheld all the sons of men from his habitation which he hath prepared.'[52] The Lord looks from above on those who stand fast in their proper dignity and perform the duties that belong to human nature. But, He regards differently those who fall into the utmost evils because He Himself came down. 'Because,' He said, 'the outcry against Sodom and Gomorrah is great, and their sin is very grave, I will go down to see whether they have done all that the outcry which has come

---
49 *Ibid.* 32.12.
50 Cf. 1 Peter 2.9: 'You, however, are a chosen race, a royal priesthood, a holy nation, a purchased people.'
51 Matt. 20.16.
52 Ps. 32.13, 14.

to me indicates.'[53] And again, 'He came down to see the city and the tower which men had built.'[54] But here it says, 'The Lord hath looked from heaven: he hath beheld all the sons of men.' Consider the lofty spectator; consider Him who is bending down regarding the affairs of mankind. Wherever you may go, whatever you may do, whether in the darkness or in the daytime, you have the eye of God watching. 'From his habitation which he hath prepared.' The gates are not being opened, the curtains are not being drawn together, the habitation of God is ready for viewing. He looks upon all the sons of men. No one escapes His sight; no darkness, no concealing walls, nothing is a hindrance to the eyes of God. He is so far from failing to look upon each individually, that He even looks into the hearts, which He Himself formed without any admixture of evil. God, the creator of men, made the heart simple according to His own saving image; but later we made it, by union with passions of the flesh, a complicated and manifold heart, destroying its likeness to God, its simplicity, and its integrity. Since He is the Maker of hearts, therefore, He understands all our works. But, we call both words and thoughts and, in general, every movement of man, his works. With what feelings or for what purpose they are, whether to please men or to perform the duties of the commands given us by God, He alone knows, who understands all our works. Therefore, for every idle word we give an account.[55] Even for a cup of cold water, we do not lose our reward,[56] because the Lord understands all our works.

(9) 'The king is not saved by a great army.'[57] Not the extent of the military force, not the walls of cities, not an infantry phalanx, not cavalry troops, not equipment of naval power, will procure safety for the king. For, the Lord estab-

---

53 Gen. 18.20, 21.
54 *Ibid.* 11.5.
55 Matt. 12.36.
56 *Ibid.* 10.42.
57 Ps. 32.16.

lishes kings and removes them, and 'there exists no authority, except that appointed by God.'[58] Therefore, the king is saved, not through much power, but through divine grace. So that the saving is true for them also: 'By grace you have been saved.'[59] So also, a farmer does not obtain his portion of harvest as much through his agricultural diligence as through God, who causes the crops to grow. For 'neither he who plants is anything, nor he who waters, but God who gives the growth.'[60] And if 'the heart of the king is in the hand of God,'[61] he will not be saved through power of arms, but through the divine guidance. Now, not any random person is in the hand of God, but he who is worthy of the name of king. And some have defined the kingly office as lawful authority, or the universal control that is not liable to sin.

'Nor shall the giant be saved by his own great strength.'[62] He calls him a giant who uses physical power and bodily force. Therefore, neither the king has aid enough from his soldiery, nor is the strong man able to suffice for himself against everything. All things that are at once human, when compared with the true power are weakness and infirmity. Therefore, 'The weak things of the world has God chosen to put to shame the strong,'[63] and 'out of the mouths of infants and of sucklings He has perfected praise, that He may destroy the enemy and the avenger.'[64] Divine grace operating in the infants and the unintelligent is especially conspicuous.

'Useless is the horse for safety; neither shall he be saved by the abundance of his strength.'[65] The horse has been excluded from the use of holy men. Neither does Israel, when

---

58 Rom. 13.1.
59 Eph. 2.5.
60 1 Cor. 3.7.
61 Prov. 21.1.
62 Ps. 32.16.
63 1 Cor. 1.27.
64 Ps. 8.3. St. Basil uses the verb in the third person in place of the second.
65 Ps. 32.17.

she was successful in wars, seem to have used cavalry forces nor did any one of the holy men accept the private use of horses as proper for them. Pharaoh used a cavalry, and the arrogant Sennacherib took pride in the great number of his horses. Wherefore, He cast into the sea Pharaoh's cavalry and the riders;[66] and all the horsemen of Sennacherib slept.[67] Whence, also, the law given by Moses, which ordains the duties of kings, says: 'He shall not multiply horses to himself.'[68] 'Neither shall he be saved by the abundance of his strength.' 'For when I am weak, then I am strong.'[69] For the abundance of bodily strength is a hindrance to the safety of the spirit.

(10) 'Behold the eyes of the Lord are on them that fear him.'[70] Elsewhere, it says, 'The eyes of the Lord are upon the just,'[71] but here, 'on those that fear him.' When we look upon the Lord and our eyes are on Him, so that we say, 'Behold as the eyes of the servants are on the hands of their masters, so are our eyes unto the Lord our God,'[72] then, we, as it were, draw the eye of the Lord to watch over us.

'And on them who hope in his mercy.'[73] The humility of those who serve the Lord indicates how they hope in His mercy. He who does not trust in his own good deeds nor expects to be justified by his works has, as his only hope of salvation, the mercies of God. For, when he considers that the expression, 'Behold the Lord and his reward,'[74] refers to each according to his work, and when he ponders his own evil deeds, he fears the punishment and cowers beneath the threats.

---

66 Cf. Exod. 14.28: 'And the waters returned, and covered the chariots and the horsemen of all the army of Pharaoh, who had come into the sea after them.'
67 Cf. 4 Kings 19.35: 'And it came to pass that night that an angel of the Lord came, and slew in the camp of the Assyrians a hundred and eighty-five thousand.' Cf. also Isa. 37.36.
68 Deut. 17.16.
69 2 Cor. 12.10.
70 Ps. 32.18.
71 *Ibid.* 33.16.
72 *Ibid.* 122.2.
73 *Ibid.* 32.18.
74 Isa. 40.10.

# HOMILY 15 245

There is good hope which gazes steadfastly at the mercies and kindness of God lest it be swallowed up by grief. He hopes that his soul will be delivered from death and will be fed by Him in famine.[75]

'Our soul waiteth for the Lord: for he is our helper and protector.'[76] This word contains an exhortation to endurance, so that, even if we are seized by one of those who are oppressing us, we do not depart from the love of God which is in Christ Jesus, but with our whole soul endure the sufferings, awaiting help from God.

'For in him our heart shall rejoice; and in his holy name we have trusted.'[77] This agrees with the words in the beginning of the psalm: 'Rejoice in the Lord, O ye just.' And 'For in him our heart shall rejoice.' And it seems to me that consistently with these words the Apostle said: 'In all these things we overcome because of him who has loved us,'[78] and 'Not only this, but we exult in tribulations also.'[79] For, the psalmist in saying: 'Our soul waiteth for the Lord,' in order that he might show that it was not through force nor because he was oppressed by afflictions that he displayed patience, but that with all joy he accepts the ill-treatment for the name of the Lord, says, 'Not only do we endure, but also "In him our heart shall rejoice, and in his holy name we have trusted."' It is sufficient for us to be named Christians to escape all abuse from our adversaries. The name of God is said to be holy, not entirely because it has a certain sanctifying power in its syllables, but because the whole specific character of God and the thought contained in what is specially contemplated concerning Him is holy and pure.

'Let thy mercy, O Lord, be upon us, as we have hoped in

---

75 Cf. Ps. 32.19: 'To deliver their souls from death; and feed them in famine.'
76 Ps. 32.20.
77 *Ibid.* 32.21.
78 Rom. 8.37.
79 *Ibid.* 5.3.

thee.'[80] Do you see how wisely he prayed? He has made a proper disposition the measure of the number of God's mercies. 'To such an extent,' he says, 'let thy mercy be upon us, as we have previously hoped in thee.' All our hope is to return to eternal rest, in order that, after the body of our lowly condition has been changed, we may realize that this same body has been made like to the glorified Body of Christ.

---

80 Ps. 32.22.

# HOMILY 16

*A Psalm of David When He Changed His Countenance before Abimelech and Being Dismissed by Him Went Away*[1]

(ON PSALM 33)

THE SUBJECT OF THE PSALM draws us to two premises. Both the actions of David in Nobe, the city of the priests, and those in Geth at the home of Achis, the king of the foreign nations, seem to be in agreement with the inscription. For, he changed his countenance when he conversed with Abimelech, the priest, concealing his flight and pretending to be zealous to perform the royal command and, then, took the loaves of proposition and the sword of Goliath. Moreover, he also changed his countenance when, seized in the midst of the enemy, he perceived that they were conversing with each other and preparing for vengeance. Scripture says: 'The servants of Achis said to each other: Is not this David the king of the land? Did they not sing to him in their dances, saying: David has slain his tens of thousands, and Saul his thousands? And David,' it says, 'was exceedingly afraid at the face of Achis, and he changed his countenance before them.'[2]

Now, how is it that the inscription names Abimelech, but history mentions Achis, as king of the Gethites? We have some such reason as this that comes to us from tradition, namely that the kings of the foreign peoples had the common

---

1 Cf. 1 Kings 21.
2 1 Kings 21.11-13.

name Abimelech, but besides that, each was called by his own name. It is possible to see this in the case of the Roman empire, the Augustuses were also commonly called Caesars, but they still kept their own personal names. The name Pharaoh is of the same kind among the Egyptians. He appears to have been called Pharaoh who ruled in the time of Joseph;[3] and there was a Pharaoh who was established as king of Egypt in the time of Moses,[4] four generations later; and a Pharaoh, during the time of Solomon: 'For, he took,' it says, 'the daughter of Pharaoh.'[5] Moreover, he who ruled during the time of the prophecy of Jeremia was called Pharaoh.[6] So, too, there was an Abimelech during the time of Abraham: 'And Abimelech and Hochozath, the leader of his bride, and Philoch the general of his army, speaking, said to Abraham.'[7] And again, concerning Isaac: 'And when very many days were passed, and he abode there, Abimelech king of the Philistines looking out through a window, saw Isaac playing with Rebecca.'[8] In the same way, therefore, here also in the time of David the common title of the kingly office, Abimelech, is used in the inscription. But, the name was handed down in history as Achis, which was given to him personally from birth.

In the presence of this man, therefore, he changed his countenance, carried along between the hands of the servants, knocking against the gates of the city and driveling his spittle upon his beard, so that Achis said to his servants: 'Why have you brought him to me? Am I in need of madmen, that you have brought in this fellow to play the madman in my

---

3 Cf. Gen. 39.1: 'When Joseph was taken down to Egypt, Phutiphar, an Egyptian, one of Pharao's officers, . . . bought him.'
4 Cf. Exod. 2.5: 'And behold the daughter of Pharao came down to wash herself in the river.'
5 Cf. 3 Kings 3.1: 'And the kingdom was established in the hand of Solomon, and he made affinity with Pharao the king of Egypt.'
6 Cf. Jer. 37.6: 'Behold the army of Pharao, which is come forth to help you.'
7 Gen. 21.22 (Septuagint version). St. Basil uses 'Philoch' for 'Phichol.'
8 *Ibid.* 26.8.

presence?'⁹ Having caused himself to be dismissed from there by these means, he came safely through, Scripture says, to the cave of Odollam.

Then, because he had been delivered from great danger, he sent up this prayer of thanksgiving to God who had rescued him. 'I will bless the Lord at all times.'¹⁰ Having escaped death, as if he were setting up norms for his life, he molded his soul to an exact manner of living, so that he ceased at no time from praise, but referred the beginning of affairs, great and small, to God. 'I will not think,' he says, 'that anything was done through my own diligence nor happened through spontaneous chance but, "I will bless the Lord at all times," not only in prosperity of life, but also in precarious times.' The Apostle, learning from this, says: 'Rejoice always. Pray without ceasing. In all things give thanks.'¹¹ Do you not see how great was the love of the man? He did not cease through impatience at the continuous succession of evils, when he was not only driven out of his country, away from his relatives, friends, and possessions, but also when he was handed over to the enemy by force and was on the point of being torn to pieces by them.¹² He did not say: 'How long will these continuous evils last?' He did not cease through impatience at the long stretch of tribulations, knowing 'that tribulation works out endurance, and endurance tried virtue, and tried virtue hope.'¹³ In truth, tribulations are, for those well prepared, like certain foods and exercises for athletes which lead the contestant on to the hereditary glory, if, when we are reviled, we bless; maligned, we entreat; ill-treated, we give thanks; afflicted, we glory in our afflictions.¹⁴ It is indeed shameful

---

9 1 Kings 21.14, 15. St. Basil uses the first person singular instead of the plural.
10 Ps. 33.2.
11 1 Thess. 5.16-18.
12 Cf. 1 Kings 19-26.
13 Rom. 5.3, 4.
14 Cf. 1 Cor. 4.12, 13: 'We are reviled and we bless, we are persecuted and we bear with it, we are maligned and we entreat.'

for us to bless on propitious occasions, but to be silent on dark and difficult ones. On the contrary, we must bless even more at that time, knowing that 'whom the Lord loves, he chastises; and he scourges every son whom he receives.'[15]

'His praise shall be always in my mouth.'[16] The prophet seems to promise something impossible. For, how can the praise of God be always in the mouth of man? When he engages in the ordinary conversations pertaining to daily life, he does not have the praise of God in his mouth. When he sleeps, he will keep absolute silence. And how will the mouth of one who is eating and drinking produce praise? We answer to this that there is a certain spiritual mouth of the interior man by which he is fed when he partakes of the word of life, which is the bread that comes down from heaven.[17] Concerning that mouth the prophet also says: 'I opened my mouth and panted.'[18] The Lord even urges us to have it open wide so as to receive plentifully the food of truth. 'Open thy mouth wide,' He says, 'and I will fill it.'[19] The thought of God, therefore, having been once for all molded and, as it were, sealed in the authoritative part of the soul, can be called praise of God, since it is always present in the soul. Moreover, according to the counsel of the Apostle, the zealous man can do all things for the glory of God, so that every act and every word and every work has in it power of praise. Whether the just man eats or drinks, he does all for the glory of God.[20] The heart of such a one watches when he is sleeping, according to him who said in the Canticle of Canticles: 'I sleep, and my heart watcheth.'[21] For, on many occasions the visions seen during sleep are images of our thoughts by day.

---

15 Heb. 12.6.
16 Ps. 33.2.
17 Cf. John 6.33: 'For the bread of God is that which comes down from heaven and gives life to the world.'
18 Ps. 118.131.
19 *Ibid.* 80.11.
20 1 Cor. 10.31.
21 Cant. 5.2.

## HOMILY 16

(2) 'In the Lord shall my soul be praised.'²² 'Let no one,' David says, 'praise my intelligence, through which I was preserved from dangers.' For, not in the power of man, nor in wisdom, but in the grace of God is salvation. 'Let not,' it is said, 'the rich man glory in his riches, nor the wise man in his wisdom, nor the strong man in his strength, but let him that glorieth glory in this, that he understandeth and knoweth' the Lord his God.²³ Do you see how the Apostle praises the helpers of the Gospel? He who is 'your fellow servant and minister in the Lord.'²⁴ If, however, someone is praised for beauty of body or renowned parentage, his soul is not praised in the Lord, but each person of such a kind is occupied with vanity. The ordinary professions, in fact, those of governor, doctor, orator, or architect who constructs cities, pyramids, labyrinths, or any other expensive or ponderous masses of buildings, do not merit to be truly praised. They who are praised for these things do not keep their soul in the Lord. It suffices us for every dignity to be called servants of such a great Lord. Certainly, one who ministers to the King will not be high-minded because he has been assigned to this particular rank of the ministry, and having been considered worthy to serve God, he will not contrive for himself praises from elsewhere, will he, as if the call of the Lord did not suffice for all pre-eminence of glory and distinction?

Therefore, 'in the Lord shall my soul be praised: let the meek hear and rejoice.'²⁵ Since with the help of God, by deceiving my enemies, he says, I have successfully obtained safety without war, by only the changing of my countenance, 'Let the meek hear' that it is possible even for those at peace to erect a trophy, and for those not fighting to be named victors. 'And let them rejoice,' being strengthened to embrace

---

22 Ps. 33.3.
23 Jer. 9.23, 24. St. Basil changed the order of the words somewhat.
24 Cf. Col. 4.7. 'Our dearest brother and faithful minister and fellow-servant in the Lord.'
25 Ps. 33.3.

meekness by my example. I received this gift from God because I completely realized meekness. 'O Lord, remember David, and all his meekness.'²⁶ Meekness is indeed the greatest of the virtues; therefore, it is counted among the beatitudes. 'Blessed are the meek,' it is said, 'for they shall possess the earth.'²⁷ For, that earth, the heavenly Jerusalem, does not become the booty of those who fight, but is appointed as the inheritance of the patient and meek. Moreover, the expression, 'Let the meek hear,' means the same as 'Let the disciples of Christ hear.' Perhaps, the wonder of the beneficence of God toward him is meant prophetically to pass over to us. In fact, let those hear, who many generations later will become disciples of Christ. For, he called those meek to whom the Lord said: 'Learn from me, for I am meek and humble of heart.'²⁸ Those of calm character and so free from all passion that they have no confusion present in their souls, they are the ones called meek. Wherefore, Moses is acknowledged to be meeker than all men on the earth.

(3) 'O magnify the Lord with me.'²⁹ He adopts a refrain that is becoming to him for glorifying the Lord. Let no one who is confused, no one who is disturbed, no one who is provoking his soul with the passions of the flesh, be united with me; but you, the meek, who have successfully attained to stability and firmness of soul, and who shake off sluggishness and drowsiness in the performance of your duties, you 'magnify the Lord with me.' But, he magnifies the Lord who endures trials for the sake of piety with keen understanding and an exulting and exalted spirit. Then, he also does, who observes with keen understanding and most profound contemplation the greatness of creation, so that from the greatness and beauty of the creatures he may contemplate their Creator. The deeper one penetrates into the reasons for which things

---
26 *Ibid.* 131.1.
27 Matt. 5.4.
28 *Ibid.* 11.29.
29 Ps. 33.4.

## HOMILY 16

in existence were made and are governed, the more he contemplates the magnificence of the Lord and, as far as lies in him, magnifies the Lord. Since, therefore, one mind and the attention of one man do not suffice even for a brief time for the comprehension of the splendors of God, he associates with himself all the meek for a participation in this activity. It is necessary, in fact, to achieve complete tranquility from outside confusions, and bringing about an entire silence in the hidden recesses of the heart, thus to devote oneself to the contemplation of the truth. Do you hear what he says when he confesses his sin? 'My eye is troubled through indignation.'[30] Yet, not only indignation, but also concupiscence and cowardice and envy trouble the eye of the soul; and, on the whole, all the passions are confounding and disturbing to the clearsightedness of the soul. As it is not possible for a disturbed eye to apprehend accurately visible objects, so neither is it possible for a disturbed heart to devote itself to a consideration of the truth. It is necessary, then, to withdraw from the affairs of the world and, neither through the eyes nor the ears nor through any other means of perception, to introduce alien thoughts into the soul. The wars which arise from the pride of the flesh fill the interior with noises that are never silent and with irreconcilable discords.

'I sought the Lord, and he heard me.'[31] Let the meek hear these things, he says, that in that difficult time when all the wrath of the malicious was roused against me and every hand was armed against me, and I, stripped and unarmed, was exposed to the enemy, ready for every outrage, even at that time I was not confounded in my thoughts through fear; I was not distracted from the thought of God; I did not despair of my safety; but, I sought the Lord. I not only asked with a kind of simple and temporal hope in the Lord, but I sought. Indeed, the meaning of the word 'sought' signifies something

---
30 *Ibid.* 6.8.
31 *Ibid.* 33.5.

more than the word 'ask,' just as a search is more than an inquiry. 'For those searching have failed in their search.'[32] Therefore, these words suggest much leisure and calmness throughout the search.

(4) 'And he delivered me from all my troubles.'[33] The whole life of the just man is filled with affliction. 'How narrow and strait the road';[34] and 'Many are the afflictions of the just.'[35] For this reason the Apostle said: 'In all things we suffer tribulations';[36] and 'That through many tribulations we must enter the kingdom of God.'[37] But, God delivers His saints from their afflictions. Though He does not leave them without trial, yet He bestows on them patient endurance. For, if 'tribulation works out endurance, and endurance tried virtue,'[38] he who excludes tribulation from himself deprives himself of his tried virtue. As no one is crowned without an adversary, so also he cannot be declared tried except through tribulations. Therefore, 'he delivered me from all my troubles,' not permitting me to be afflicted, but with the temptation giving me a way out that I might be able to bear it.[39]

'Come ye to him and be enlightened: and your faces shall not be confounded.'[40] He urges those who sit in darkness and in the shadow of death to come to the Lord and to approach the rays of His Godhead, in order that, illuminated with the truth by this nearness, they may through grace take His light unto themselves. As the present sensible light does not appear equally to all, but to those who have eyes and are awake and able to enjoy the presence of the sun without any obstacle,

---

32 *Ibid.* 63.7.
33 *Ibid.* 33.5.
34 Matt. 7.14.
35 Ps. 33.2.
36 2 Cor. 4.8.
37 Acts 14.21.
38 Rom. 5.3.
39 Cf. 1 Cor. 10.13: 'God is faithful and will not permit you to be tempted beyond your strength, but with the temptation will also give you a way out that you may be able to bear it.'
40 Ps. 33.6.

so also the Sun of justice,⁴¹ 'the true light that enlightens every man who comes into the world,'⁴² does not bestow His brightness on all, but on those who live in a manner worthy of Him. 'Light,' it is said, 'is risen,' not to the sinner, but 'to the just.'⁴³ For, as the sun is risen, but not for the bats nor for any other creatures that feed by night, so also the light is by its own nature bright and capable of brightening. However, all do not share in its brightness. Thus also, 'Everyone who does evil hates the light and does not come to the light, that his deeds may not be exposed.'⁴⁴ 'Come ye, therefore, to him and be enlightened: and your faces shall not be confounded.'⁴⁵ Blessed is he, who on the day of the righteous judgment of God, when the Lord comes to bring to light the things hidden in darkness and to make manifest the counsels of hearts, has dared to be subjected to that light of scrutiny and has returned without cause for shame because of a conscience undefiled by evil deeds. They, indeed, who do evil deeds will rise to reproach and to shame, beholding in themselves the ugliness and the likenesses of their sins. And, perhaps, that shame with which the sinners are going to live forever will be more fearful than the darkness and the eternal fire, since they have always in their eyes the traces of sin in their flesh like certain indelible stains, which remain perpetually in the memory of their soul. Yet, it is the privilege of few to approach to the true Light and to reveal the things hidden and after the revelation to go away with face not confounded.

(5) 'This poor man cried, and the Lord heard him.'⁴⁶ Poverty is not always praiseworthy, but only that which is practiced intentionally according to the evangelical aim. Many

---

41 Mal. 4.2.
42 John 1.9.
43 Ps. 96.11.
44 John 3.20.
45 Ps. 33.6.
46 *Ibid.* 33.7.

are poor in their resources, but very grasping in their intention; poverty does not save these; on the contrary, their intention condemns them. Accordingly, not he who is poor is by all means blessed, but he who has considered the command of Christ better than the treasures of the world. These the Lord also pronounces blessed, when He says: 'Blessed are the poor in spirit,'[47] not those poor in resources, but those who from their soul have chosen poverty. For, nothing that is not deliberate is to be pronounced blessed. Therefore, every virtue, but this one especially before all others, is characterized by the action of the free will. So it is said: 'This poor man cried.' By the demonstrative word for the man who was poor because of God, and hungry and thirsty and naked, he calls forth your understanding; 'This poor man,' all but pointing with his finger; this disciple of Christ. It is possible also to refer this expression to Christ, who being rich by nature, because all things belonging to the Father are His, became poor for our sakes in order that by His poverty we might become rich.[48] Nearly every work that leads to the blessing, the Lord Himself began, setting Himself forth as an example to His disciples. Return to the blessings and you will find on examining each that He anticipated the teaching contained in the words by His deeds. 'Blessed are the meek.'[49] How, then, shall we learn meekness? 'Learn from me, for I am meek and humble of heart.'[50] 'Blessed are the peacemakers.'[51] Who will teach us the beauty of peace? The Peacemaker Himself, who makes peace and reconciles two men into one new man;[52] who made peaceful by the blood of His cross both things of heaven and

---

47 Matt. 5.3.
48 Cf. 2 Cor. 8.9: 'For you know the graciousness of our Lord Jesus Christ—how, being rich, he became poor for your sakes, that by his poverty you might become rich.'
49 Matt. 5.5.
50 *Ibid.* 11.29.
51 *Ibid.* 5.9.
52 Cf. Eph. 2.15: 'that of the two he might create in himself one new man.'

those of earth. 'Blessed are the poor.'[53] He Himself is the one who was poor and who emptied Himself in the form of a slave[54] in order that 'of his fullness we might all receive, grace for grace.'[55] If anyone, then, led by the holy and benevolent Spirit, not being presumptuous, but humbling himself in order that he may exalt the others, should call upon the Spirit, offering great prayers, and should utter nothing base or lowly because he is seeking terrestrial and worldly things, the cry of such a man will be heard by the Lord. What, therefore, is the aim of the prayer heard? To be delivered from all troubles, unwounded, unbent, and unenslaved by the pride of the flesh. Now, what is the manner in which the poor man is delivered?

'The angel of the Lord shall encamp round about them that fear him: and shall deliver them.'[56] He explained whom he reckons as the poor man—him who fears the Lord. Therefore, he who fears is still in the rank of the slave. But, he who had been made perfect by love now mounted quickly to the dignity of son. Hence the slave is said to be also poor, because he has nothing of his own; but the son is said to be already rich, because he is the heir of the paternal goods. 'The angel of the Lord,' therefore, 'shall encamp round about them that fear him.' An angel attends everyone who believes in the Lord if we never chase him away by our evil deeds. As smoke puts the bees to flight,[57] and a foul smell drives away the doves, so also the lamentable and foul sin keeps away the angel, the guardian of our life. If you have in your soul works worthy of angelic custody, and if a mind rich in the contemplation of truth dwells within you, because of the wealth of your

---

53 Matt. 5.3.
54 Cf. Phil. 2.7: 'but he emptied himself, taking the nature of a slave and being made like unto men.'
55 John 1.16.
56 Ps. 33.8.
57 Cf. Virgil, *Georgics* IV. 227-230: 'If now their narrow home thou wouldst unseal, And broach the treasures of the honey-house, With draught of water first foment thy lips, And spread before thee fumes of trailing smoke.' (Translation of James Rhoades).

esteemed works of virtue God necessarily establishes guards and custodians beside you and fortifies you with the guardianship of angels. Consider what the nature of the angels is, that one angel is compared to a whole army and a crowded encampment. So, through the greatness of him who guards you the Lord bestows upon you an encampment; and through the strength of the angel He surrounds you on all sides with His protection as with a wall. For, this is what the word 'round about' signifies. Just as the encircling walls, put round about all the cities, keep off the attacks of the enemies on all sides, so also the angel shields from the front and guards the rear and does not leave the two sides unprotected. For this reason, 'A thousand shall fall at thy side, and ten thousand at thy right hand; but' the stroke of the enemy 'shall not come nigh thee,'[58] because He will give commands to His angels concerning you.

(6) 'O taste, and see that the Lord is sweet.'[59] Frequently we have noticed that the faculties of the soul are called by the same name as the external members. Since our Lord is true Bread and His flesh is true Meat, it is necessary that the pleasure of the enjoyment of the Bread be in us through a spiritual taste. As the nature of honey can be described to the inexperienced not so much by speech as by the perception of it through taste, so the goodness of the heavenly Word cannot be clearly taught by doctrines, unless, examining to a greater extent the dogmas of truth, we are able to comprehend by our own experience the goodness of the Lord. 'Taste' he said, but not 'be filled,' because now we know in part and through a mirror and in an obscure manner we see the truth;[60] but the time will come when the present pledge and this taste of grace will attain to the perfection of enjoyment for us. Just

---

58 Ps. 90.7.
59 *Ibid.* 33.9.
60 Cf. 1 Cor. 13.12: 'We see now through a mirror in an obscure manner, but then face to face. Now I know in part, but then I shall know even as I have been known.'

as those who are suffering from a disordered stomach and from loss of appetite, and who turn away from food, are cured of this annoyance by the doctors, who stir up their appetites through special attention to the food, so that, when their taste is provoked by the savory cooking, their appetites will increase always more and more, so also in the case of the word of truth, experience itself will always, he says, excite in you an insatiable desire. Therefore, he says, 'Taste,' in order that you, hungering and thirsting after justice, may always be blessed. 'Blessed is the man that hopeth in him.'[61] He who always has a desire of the Word will put his hope in nothing else than in the Lord.

'Fear the Lord, all ye his saints: for there is no want to them that fear him.'[62] Unless fear disciplines our life, it is impossible successfully to attain holiness in body. 'Pierce thou my flesh with thy fear.'[63] As those who are pierced by nails have the members of their bodies immovable for any activity, so those who are possessed by the divine fear in their soul escape all annoyance from sinful passions. In him who fears there is not want, that is, he is failing with regard to no virtue who is prevented by fear from every absurd act, since he falls short of nothing good that belongs to human nature. As he is not perfect in body who is lacking in any necessary part, but is imperfect because of what he lacks, so also he who is disposed contemptuously about one of the commands, because he is wanting in it, is imperfect in that in which he lacks. But, he who has assumed perfect fear and through piety shrinks beneath all things will commit no sin because he despises nothing; he will not experience any want because he will possess fear sufficiently in all things.

(7) 'The rich have wanted, and have suffered hunger; but they that seek the Lord shall not be deprived of any good.'[64]

---

61 Ps. 33.9.
62 *Ibid.* 33.10.
63 *Ibid.* 118.120.
64 *Ibid.* 33.11.

Let this word, which teaches the unreliability of excessive wealth, edify us even to the contempt of corporal riches. For, wealth is unstable and like a wave accustomed to change hither and thither by the violence of the wind. Perhaps he says that the people of Israel are rich, who have the adoption of sons and divine worship, the promises, and the fathers. They, however, have been poor because of their sin against the Lord. 'But they that seek the Lord shall not be deprived of any good.' They have wanted in a certain way and have suffered hunger. For, when they had put to death the Bread of life, a hunger for the Bread came upon them, and the chastisement from the thirst was imposed on them; but 'the hunger was not for sensible bread nor the thirst, for water, but a hunger to hear the word of God.'[65] Therefore, 'they have wanted and have suffered hunger.'

They, however, who have learned from the Gentiles to seek the Lord have not suffered the loss of every good. God Himself is absolute Good, and they who seek Him will not be without Him. Let no uninstructed person who considers the position concerning good and evil indistinguishable call him good who has a pleasure that is temporary and that departs with the death of the body. He who reduces bodily wealth and bodily advantages to the order of good draws down to matters cheap and not deserving of account a name that is holy and proper to God alone, and at the same time encounters the most serious contradiction. Either he will say that the apostles did not obtain bodily goods because they did not seek the Lord; or, if they did seek Him and failed to obtain such goods, he will bring a charge against the Scripture itself which says that they who seek the Lord do not suffer the loss of good. But, the saints also sought the Lord, and they did not fail in the knowledge of Him who was sought, nor were they deprived of the blessings stored up in the eternal rest. Con-

---

65 Cf. Amos 8.11: 'And I will send forth a famine into the land: not a famine of bread, nor a thirst of water, but of hearing the word of the Lord.'

cerning them one might say 'of every good.' For, bodily joys have more pain than pleasure; marriages involve childlessness, widowhood, corruption; agriculture, fruitlessness; trade, shipwrecks; wealth, plots; luxuries and satiety and continual pleasures, a variety of diseases, as well as sufferings of many kinds. Paul also sought the Lord and no blessing was wanting to him. And yet, who could enumerate the annoyances of the body, in which he lived during his whole life? 'Thrice he was scourged, once he was stoned, thrice he suffered shipwreck, a night and a day he was adrift on the sea, in journeyings often . . . in hunger and thirst, in fastings often, in labor and hardships,'[66] in distresses frequently. A man hungering and thirsting and being naked and buffeted even to his last hour, surely, was suffering the loss of bodily blessings. Lift up your mind, I pray, to what is truly good in order that you may recognize the harmonious agreement of the Scripture, and may not let yourself fall into uncertainty of thought.

(8) 'Come, children, hearken to me: I will teach you the fear of the Lord.'[67] It is the voice of the devoted teacher, encouraging you to learn through his paternal mercy. In fact, the disciple is the spiritual child of the teacher. That one who receives from another formation in piety is, as it were, molded by him and is brought into existence, just as the fetus formed within her is brought into existence by one who is pregnant. For this reason Paul also taking up again the whole Church of the Galatians, which had fallen from its earlier teachings and which was abortive, as it were, and forming Christ in them anew, called them little children; and, when with pain and affliction he corrected those who had erred, he said that he was in labor in soul because of his grief at those who had fallen away. 'My dear children, with whom I am in labor again, until Christ is formed in you.'[68] Therefore, 'Come, children, hearken to me.'

---

66 2 Cor. 11.25, 27. St. Basil substitutes the third person for the first.
67 Ps. 33.12.
68 Gal. 4.19.

What, really, does our spiritual father intend to teach? 'I will teach you the fear of the Lord.' When he ordered us above to fear the Lord, he also showed the profit that comes from fear, saying: 'There is no want to them that fear him.'[69] At present also, they hand down to us a certain teaching of divine fear. Now, it is in the power of every one, even of the private individual, to say that it is necessary to be healthy; but, to say how health must be obtained, that certainly belongs to him who understands the art of medicine. Every fear is not a good and saving feeling, but there is also a hostile fear, which the prophet prays may not spring up in his soul, when he says: 'Deliver my soul from the fear of the enemy.'[70] Fear of the enemy is that which produces in us a cowardliness with regard to death and misleads us to cower before distinguished persons. How, in fact, will he who fears these things be able in time of martyrdom to resist sin even to death and to pay his debt to the Lord, who died and rose again for us? He also, who is easily scared by the demons, has the fear of the enemy in him. On the whole, such a fear seems to be a passion born of unbelief. For, no one who believes that he has at hand a strong helper is frightened by any of those who attempt to throw him into confusion.

The fear, however, which is salutary and the fear which is productive of holiness, fear which springs up in the soul through devotion and not through passion, what kind would you have me say it is? Whenever you are about to rush headlong into sin, consider that fearful and intolerable tribunal of Christ, in which the Judge is seated upon a certain high and sublime throne, and every creature stands trembling beside His glorious presence,[71] and we are about to be led forth, one by one, for the examination of the actions of our life. And

---

69 Ps. 33.10.
70 *Ibid.* 63.2.
71 Cf. Matt. 25.31, 32: 'But when the Son of Man shall come in his majesty, and all the angels with him, then he will sit on the throne of his glory; and before him will be gathered all the nations.'

beside him who has done many wicked deeds throughout his life certain horrible and dark angels stand, flashing fire from their eyes and breathing fire because of the bitterness of their wills, and with a countenance like the night because of their dejection and their hatred of man. Then, there is the deep pit and the darkness[72] that has no outlet and the light without brightness, which has the power of burning in the darkness but is deprived of its splendor. Next is the poisonous and flesh-devouring class of worms,[73] which eat greedily and are never satiated and cause unbearable pains by their voracity; and lastly, the severest punishment of all, that eternal reproach and shame. Fear these things, and being taught by this fear, check your soul, as with a bit, from its desire for wickedness.

The father promised to teach us this fear of the Lord, and not to teach indiscriminately, but to teach those who wish to heed him; not those who have long fallen away, but those who run to him through a desire of being saved; not 'strangers to the covenants,'[74] but those who are reconciled through baptism by the word of the adoption of sons. Therefore, he says, 'Come,' that is, 'because of your good deeds approach me, children,' since you are considered worthy because of your regeneration to become sons of light. You, who have the ears of your heart open, hear; I shall teach you fear of the Lord, that fear which a little while ago our sermon described.

(9) 'Who is the man that desireth life: who loveth to see good days?'[75] If anyone wishes life, he says, he does not live this common life, which brute beasts also live, but the true life which is not cut short by death. 'For, now,' it is said, 'you have died and your life is hidden with Christ in God. When Christ, your life, shall appear, then you too will appear with him in

---

72 Cf. Matt. 8.12: 'But the children of the kingdom will be put forth into the darkness outside.'
73 Cf. Isa. 66.24: 'Their worm shall not die, and their fire shall not be quenched.'
74 Eph. 2.12.
75 Ps. 33.13.

glory.'⁷⁶ Therefore, Christ is, in truth, life; and our way of life in Him is true life. In like manner, also, the other days are good, which the prophet set forth in the promise. 'Who is the man that desireth life: who loveth to see good days?' For, the days of this life are evil, since this life, being the measure of the world, concerning which there is the saying: 'The whole world is in the power of the evil one,'⁷⁷ is made quite like the nature of the world which it measures. But, these days are parts of this time. Therefore, the Apostle says: 'Making the most of your time, because the days are evil.'⁷⁸ Likewise Jacob says: 'The days of my pilgrimage are short and wretched.'⁷⁹ We are not, then, in life, but in death. And so the Apostle prayed, saying: 'Who will deliver me from the body of this death?'⁸⁰ There is, however, a certain other life, to which these words call us; and, although at present our days are evil, yet some others are good, which night does not interrupt; for God will be their everlasting light, shining upon them with the light of His glory.⁸¹ Consequently, when you hear of the good days, do not think that your life here is set forth in the promises. In fact, these are the destructible days, which the sensible sun produces; but, nothing destructible could suitably be a gift for the indestructible. Now, if the soul is indestructible, its gifts are also indestructible. 'This world as we see it is passing away.'⁸² If the law has some shadow of the good things to come, consider I pray, certain sabbaths pleasant, holy, brought from the eternal days, new

---

76 Col. 3.3, 4.
77 1 John 5.19.
78 Eph. 5.16.
79 Cf. Gen. 47.9: 'The length of my pilgrimage has been one hundred and thirty years; short and wretched has been my life.'
80 Rom. 7.24.
81 Cf. Apoc. 22.5: 'And night shall be no more, and they shall have no need of light of lamp, or light of sun, for the Lord God will shed light upon them; and they shall reign forever and ever.'
82 1 Cor. 7.31.

moons, festivals; but, consider, I pray you, in a manner proper to the spiritual law.[83]

'Keep thy tongue from evil, and thy lips from speaking guile.'[84] If you wish to live in the good days, if you love life, fulfill the precept of life. 'He who loves me,' He says, 'will keep my commands.'[85] The first command is, 'Keep thy tongue from evil, and thy lips from speaking guile.' The most common and varied sin is that committed through the tongue. Were you provoked to anger? The tongue is already running on. Are you possessed by concupiscence? Before all things you have a tongue, a sort of pimp and promoter, as it were, assistant to the sin, subduing your neighbors by histrionic arts. Your tongue is also a weapon for your injustice, not uttering the words from the heart, but bringing forth those inspired by deceit. But, what need is there to put in words all the sins committed through the tongue? Our life is filled with faults due to the tongue. Obscenity, scurrility, foolish talk, unbecoming words, slanders, idle conversation, perjuries, false testimony, all these evils, and even more than these, are the work of the tongue. But, they who open their mouth against the glory of God and talk of injustice on high, do they perform their act of impiety by some other instrument and not through the instrumentality of the tongue? Since, then, 'by thy words thou wilt be justified, and by thy words thou wilt be condemned,'[86] check your tongue from evil, and do not fabricate empty treasures with a deceitful tongue. Stop also your lips from speaking guile; instead, let the whole organ, which was given to you for the service of speech, have nothing to do with wicked deeds. Guile is hidden wrongdoing brought to bear against the neighbor under a pretense of better things.

---

83 Cf. Col. 2.16, 17: 'Let no one, then, call you to account for what you eat or drink or in regard to a festival or a new moon or a Sabbath. These are a shadow of things to come.'
84 Ps. 33.14.
85 Cf. John 14.23: 'If anyone love me, he will keep my word.'
86 Matt. 12.37.

(10) 'Turn away from evil and do good, seek after peace and pursue it.'[87] These counsels are elementary and are channels to piety; they describe accurately how to prevail over the tongue, how to refrain from deceitful schemes, how to turn away from evil. Mere abstinence from evil is not a characteristic of a perfect man; but, for one recently instructed in basic principles it is fitting to turn aside from the impulse to evil and, being delivered from the habits of a depraved life as from a bad road, to pursue the performance of good. In fact, it is impossible to cleave to the good unless one has withdrawn entirely and turned away from the evil, just as it is impossible to repair one's health unless one rids himself of the disease, or for one who has not completely checked a chill to be in a state of warmth; for, these are inadmissible to each other. So also, it is proper for him who intends to live a good life to depart from all connection with evil. 'Seek after peace and pursue it.' Concerning this peace the Lord has said: 'Peace I leave with you, my peace I give to you; not as the world gives peace do I give to you.'[88] Seek, therefore, after the peace of the Lord and pursue it. And you will pursue not otherwise than running toward the goal to the prize of the heavenly calling.[89] For, the true peace is above. Yet, as long as we were bound to the flesh, we were yoked to many things which also troubled us. Seek, then, after peace, a release from the troubles of this world; possess a calm mind, a tranquil and unconfused state of soul, which is neither agitated by the passions nor drawn aside by false doctrines that challenge by their persuasiveness to an assent, in order that you may obtain 'the peace of God which surpasses all understanding and guards your heart.'[90] He who seeks after peace, seeks Christ, because 'he himself is our peace,' who has made two men into

---

87 Ps. 33.15.
88 John 14.27.
89 Phil. 3.14.
90 Cf. Phil. 4.7: 'And may the peace of God which surpasses all understanding guard your hearts.'

one new man,⁹¹ making peace, and 'making peace through the blood of his cross, whether on earth or in the heavens.'⁹²

(11) 'The eyes of the Lord are upon the just: and his ears unto their prayers.'⁹³ Just as the saints 'are the body of Christ, member for member, and God indeed has placed some in the Church,'⁹⁴ as eyes, some as tongues, others taking the place of hands, and still others that of feet; so also some of the holy spiritual powers and those which are about the heavenly places are called the eyes because they are entrusted with our guardianship, and others ears, because they receive our petitions. Now, therefore, he said that the power which watches over us and that which is aware of our prayers are eyes and ears. So, 'the eyes of the Lord are upon the just: and his ears unto their prayers.' Since every act of the just man is worthy in the sight of God, and every word, because no just man speaks idly, is active and efficacious, for this reason these words say that the just man is always watched over and always heard.

'But the countenance of the Lord is against them that do evil things: to cut off the remembrance of them from the earth.'⁹⁵ By the countenance I think is meant the open and manifest coming of the Lord in the judgment. Therefore, the eyes of the Lord, as of one still observing us from afar, are said to look upon the just man; but, the countenance itself, it is said, will appear for the purpose of wiping out entirely from the earth all remembrance of wickedness. Do not think, I beg of you, that the countenance of God is molded in bodily form, since in that case the words of Scripture will seem to be unreasonable, and there will seem to be eyes by themselves which shine upon the just, and again the countenance by itself

---

91 Cf. Eph. 2.14: 'For he himself is our peace, he it is who has made both one.'
92 Col. 1.20.
93 Ps. 33.16.
94 1 Cor. 12.27, 28.
95 Ps. 33.17.

which threatens the wicked. And yet, the eyes are neither apart from the countenance, nor is the countenance bereft of eyes. Now, 'No man shall see the face of the Lord and live,'[96] but, 'the angels' of the little ones in the Church 'always behold the face of our Father in heaven.'[97] Wherefore, it is impossible for us now to be capable of the sight of the glorious appearance because of the weakness of the flesh which envelops us. The angels, however, since they do not have any such covering as our flesh, are prevented in no way from continually fastening their gaze upon the face of the glory of God. We also, after we have been made 'sons of the resurrection,'[98] will be considered worthy of the knowledge face to face. At that time the just will be deemed worthy of the sight of His countenance in glory, but the sinners, of the sight in judgment, since all sin is going to be utterly destroyed by the just judgment of God.

(12) 'The just cried, and the Lord heard them: and delivered them out of all their troubles.'[99] The cry of the just is a spiritual one, having its loudness in the secret recess of the heart, able to reach even to the ears of God. Indeed, he who makes great petitions and prays for heavenly favors, he cries out and sends up a prayer that is audible to God. Therefore, 'the just cried.' They sought after nothing petty, nothing earthly, nothing lowly. For this reason the Lord received their voice, and He delivered them from all their tribulations, not so much freeing them from their troubles as making them victorious over the circumstances.

'The Lord is nigh unto them that are of a contrite heart: and he will save the humble of spirit.'[100] By His goodness He is near to all; but, we go far away through sin. 'For behold,'

---

96 Cf. Exod. 33.20: 'Thou canst not see my face: for man shall not see me and live.'
97 Matt. 18.10.
98 Luke 20.36.
99 Ps. 33.18.
100 *Ibid.* 33.19.

he says, 'they that go far from thee shall perish.'[101] Therefore, Moses is said to approach to God;[102] and, if anyone else is like him through manly deeds and good actions he comes near to God. These words hold openly the prophecy of the coming of the Lord and are in agreement with the preceding. For, there it was said: 'The countenance of the Lord is against them that do evil things'; that is, His appearance in the judgment will be for the destruction of all evil. 'The Lord is nigh unto them that are of a contrite heart.' He announces beforehand the coming of the Lord in the flesh, which is already near at hand and not far distant. Let this saying from the prophecy of Isaia be trustworthy to you: 'The spirit of the Lord is upon me, because the Lord hath anointed me: he hath sent me to preach to the meek, to heal the contrite of heart, to preach release to the captives and sight to the blind.'[103] Since, indeed, as a doctor he was sent to the contrite of heart, he says, 'The Lord is near,' I say to you, lowly and contrite in spirit, cheering you and leading you on to patience in the joy of what is expected. Contrition of heart is the destruction of human reckonings.

He who has despised present things and has given himself to the word of God, and is using his mind for thoughts which are above man and are more divine, he would be the one who has a contrite heart and has made it a sacrifice which is not despised by the Lord. For, 'a contrite and humbled heart, O God, thou wilt not despise.'[104] Therefore, 'the Lord is nigh unto them that are of a contrite heart: and he will save the humble of spirit.' He who has no vanity and is not proud of anything human, he is the one who is contrite in heart and humble of spirit. He is humble also, who is walking in sin, because sin is of all things most humiliating. Wherefore, we say that she is humbled who is corrupted and has lost the holi-

---

101 *Ibid.* 72.27.
102 Cf. Exod. 24.2: 'And Moses alone shall come up to the Lord.'
103 Isa. 61.1.
104 Ps. 50.19.

ness of virginity. So, Amnon, it is said, rising up against Thamar 'humbled' her.[105] Those, then, who have destroyed the majesty and elevation of their soul, being cast down to the earth by sin and beaten flat, as it were, are bent over, crawling along like the serpent, absolutely unable to be restored; these, in truth, are humbled, but not in spirit; for, their humility is not praiseworthy. But, whoever, having the gift of the Holy Spirit, willingly humble themselves under their inferiors, saying according to the Apostle that they are the servants of those in Christ,[106] and 'the offscouring of all, even until now,'[107] and again, 'We have become as the refuse of this world,'[108] these use humility in a spiritual way, making themselves the last of all, in order that they may be first in the kingdom of heaven. The Lord also proclaims them blessed, saying: 'Blessed are the poor in spirit.'[109]

'Many are the afflictions of the just; but out of them all will the Lord deliver them.'[110] 'In all things we suffer tribulation, but we are not distressed.'[111] For this reason the Lord also says to His disciples: 'In the world you have affliction. But take courage, I have overcome the world.'[112] So that, whenever you see the just with diseases, with maimed bodies, suffering loss of possessions, enduring blows, disgraces, all defect and need of the necessities of life, remember that, 'Many are the afflictions of the just; but out of them all will the Lord deliver them.' And he who says the affliction is not proper to a just man says nothing else than that an adversary is not proper for the athlete. But, what occasions for crowns will the athlete have who does not struggle? Four times already in this Psalm it has

---

105 Cf. 2 Kings 13.22: 'For Absalom hated Amnon because he had ravished his sister Thamar.'
106 Cf. 2 Cor. 4.5: 'For we preach not ourselves, but Jesus Christ as Lord, and ourselves merely as your servants in Jesus.'
107 1 Cor. 4.13.
108 *Ibid.*
109 Matt. 5.3.
110 Ps. 33.20.
111 2 Cor. 4.8
112 John 16.33.

been told in what manner the Lord delivers from affliction whomever He wishes to deliver. First, 'I sought the Lord, and he heard me; and he delivered me from all my troubles.' Second, 'This poor man cried, and the Lord heard him: and saved him out of all his troubles.' Third, 'The just cried, and the Lord heard them: and delivered them out of all their troubles.' And lastly, 'Many are the afflictions of the just; but out of them all will the Lord deliver them.'

(13) 'The Lord keepeth all their bones, not one of them shall be broken.'[113] Is it necessary to hold fast to the word and to be satisfied with the thought which readily falls upon our ears, that these bones of the just, the props of the flesh, will not be broken because of the protection given to them by the Lord? Or, will only the bones of the just man who is alive and engaged in life be guarded unbroken? Or, when the bonds of the body have been loosened, will it happen that there will be no cause of breaking for the just man? And truly, we have learned by experience that many bones of the just have been broken, when some among them handed themselves over to all forms of punishment for the sake of giving testimony for Christ. Already the persecutors have broken the legs of some and have frequently pierced hands and heads with nails. And yet, who will deny that of all, it is the most just who were brought to perfection in the testimony?

Perhaps, just as the term man is used for the soul and the human mind, so also his members are similarly named in accordance with the members of the flesh; thus, frequently Scripture names the members of the inner man, for example, 'The eyes of a wise man are in his head,'[114] that is, the hidden part of the wise man is foreseeing and farseeing. And again, it means equally the eyes both of the soul and of the flesh, not only in that saying which we have set forth, but also in the statement that 'the commandment of the Lord is light-

---
113 Ps. 33.21.
114 Eccles. 2.14.

some and enlightening the eyes.'[115] But, what should we say concerning this: 'He who has ears to hear, let him hear'?[116] It is evident, indeed, that some possess ears better able to hear the words of God. But, to those who do not have those ears, what does he say? 'Hear, ye deaf, and, ye blind, behold.'[117] Also 'I opened my mouth, and panted,'[118] and 'Thou hast broken the teeth of sinners.'[119] All these things were said in reference to the faculties which render service for spiritual food and spiritual doctrines. Such also is this saying, 'My bowels, my bowels are in pain,'[120] and this, 'And the foot' of the wise man 'shall not stumble.'[121] All such expressions are used in reference to the inner man.

According to the same reasoning there should also be certain bones of the inner man in which the bond of union and harmony of spiritual powers is collected. Just as the bones by their own firmness protect the tenderness of the flesh, so also in the Church there are some who through their own constancy are able to carry the infirmities of the weak. And as the bones are joined to each other through articulations by sinews and fastenings which have grown upon them, so also would be the bond of charity and peace, which achieves a certain natural junction and union of the spiritual bones in the Church of God. Concerning those bones which have been loosened from the frame and have become, as it were, dislocated, the prophet says: 'Our bones are scattered by the side of hell.'[122] And, if at any time disturbance and agitation seizes upon them, he says in prayer: 'Heal me, O Lord, for my bones are troubled.'[123] When, however, they preserve their

---

115 Ps. 18.9.
116 Luke 8.8.
117 Isa. 42.18.
118 Ps. 118.131.
119 *Ibid.* 3.8.
120 Jer. 4.19.
121 Prov. 3.23.
122 Ps. 140.7.
123 *Ibid.* 6.3.

own systematic arrangement, protected by the Lord, not one of them will be broken, but they will be worthy to offer glory to God. For, he says: 'All my bones shall say: Lord, Lord, who is like to thee?'[124] Do you know the nature of intellectual bones? Perhaps, in reference to the mystery of our resurrection, the Church might use this expression, 'All my bones shall say.' Indeed, it is said: 'Thus saith the Lord to these bones: Behold, I will send spirit of life into you, and I will lay sinews upon you, and will cause flesh to grow over you, and you shall live, and you shall know that I am the Lord.'[125] So, these bones, having taken on life and giving thanks for their resurrection, will say, 'Lord, Lord, who is like to thee?'

(14) Accurately has the statement been added: 'The death of the wicked is very evil,'[126] because there is a certain death of the just, not evil by nature, but good. In fact, those who die together with Christ have come into a good death; and those who have died to sin have died a good and salutary death. However, 'the death of the wicked is very evil.' Punishment follows after them, as also after the rich man who 'clothed himself in purple and fine linen, and who feasted every day in splendid fashion.'[127]

'And they that hate the just shall be guilty.'[128] They also, who, since they are living in sin, hate the just, are thus convicted by the ways of the just man because of their proximity to the better, as by the straightness of a rule. Since they are living in sin, they conduct themselves hatefully toward the just man, being in fear of reproach; and because they hate, they again involve themselves in sins. Many are the pretexts on which the just man might be hated, outspokenness, for instance, in his reproofs. They hate the man who reproves

---

124 *Ibid.* 34.10.
125 Ezech. 37.5, 6.
126 Ps. 33.22.
127 Luke 16.19.
128 Ps. 33.22.

them in the gate,[129] and they loathe holy speech. Also, love for the first place and love of power have roused many to hatred of the rulers; sometimes, even ignorance of the reputation of the just man and of who is a just man. 'The death of the wicked is very evil.' Or, he even calls all life death, because the Apostle called this flesh death, when he said: 'Who will deliver me from the body of this death?'[130] Those who use this body wickedly and make it the servant of sin prepare an evil death for themselves.

'The Lord will redeem the souls of his servants: and none of them that trust in him shall offend.'[131] Since those who were created to serve the Lord were being held fast by the captivity of the enemy, He will redeem their souls by His precious blood. Therefore, no one of those who hope in Him will be found in sin.

---

129 Cf. Isa. 29.21: 'That made men sin by word, and supplanted him that reproved them in the gate, and declined in vain from the just.'
130 Rom. 7.24.
131 Ps. 33.23.

# HOMILY 17

*Unto the End[1] for Those Who Shall be Changed, for the Sons of Core[2] for Understanding*

(ON PSALM 44)

THIS PSALM SEEMS TO BE one that is adapted to perfecting human nature and that provides assistance for attaining the prescribed end for those who have elected to live in virtue. Indeed, in order that those advancing may attain perfection, there is need of the teaching which is provided by this psalm with the inscription, 'Unto the end, for those that shall be changed.' It really says in an obscure manner, 'For men.' For, we especially of all rational beings are subject to variations and changes day by day and almost hour by hour. Neither in body nor in mind are we the same, but our body is in perpetual flux and disintegration; it is in motion and transition, either increasing from smaller to larger, or reducing from perfection to deficiency. The child now frequenting the school and fit to acquire the arts and sciences is not the same as the newly born infant; and again, the adoles-

---

1 'Unto the end, or, as St. Jerome renders it, "*victori, to him that overcometh*," which some understand of *the chief musician*, to whom they suppose the psalms, which bear the title, were given to be sung; we rather understand the psalms thus inscribed to refer to Christ, who is the "end of the law," and the "great conqueror" of death and hell, and to the New Testament.' Rheims-Douay Bible, Ps. 4, n.1.
2 The sons of Core did not perish with their father in his rebellion against Moses (cf. Num. 26.11), and later they and their descendants were appointed to sing before the tabernacle of the Lord (cf. 1 Par. 6.31, 37; also 2 Par. 9.19).

cent is admittedly different from the child, since he is already able to join with the young men. And beyond the adolescent is another man, one with firmness and great stature of body and perfection of reasoning. Having come to the peak of his vigor and attained the stability of manhood, he again begins little by little to reduce to a smaller man as the condition of his body imperceptibly declines and his bodily energies are lessened, until, bent down by age, he waits for the last withdrawal of strength. Accordingly, we are the ones who are changing and the psalm wisely alludes to us men through these words.

Angels do not admit any change. No one among them is a child, nor a young man, nor an old man, but in whatever state they were created in the beginning, in that state they remain, their substance being preserved pure and inviolate for them. But, we change in our body, as has been shown, and in our soul and in the inner man, always shifting our thoughts with the circumstances. In fact, we are one sort of person when we are cheerful and when all things in our life are moving forward with the current; but, we are another sort in precarious times, when we stumble against something that is not according to our wishes. We are changed through anger, assuming a certain savage state. We are also changed through our concupiscences, becoming like beasts through a life of pleasure. 'They are become as amorous horses,' madly in love with their neighbors' wives.[3] The deceitful man is compared to a fox, as Herod was;[4] the shameless man is called a dog, like Nabel the Carmelian.[5] Do you see the variety and diversity of our change? Then, admire him who has fittingly adapted this title to us.

---

3 Cf. Jer. 5.8: 'They are become as amorous horses and stallions: every one neighed after his neighbor's wife.'
4 Cf. Luke 13.32: 'Certain Pharisees came up, saying to him, "Depart and be on thy way, for Herod wants to kill thee." And he said to them, "Go and say to that fox." '
5 Cf. 1 Kings 25.3 (Septuagint version).

(2) For this very reason, a certain one of the interpreters[6] seems to me to have handed over beautifully and accurately the same thought through another title, saying, 'For the lilies,' in place of, 'For them that shall be changed.' He thought that it was appropriate to compare the transitoriness of human nature with the early death of flowers. But, since this word has been inflected in the future tense, (it is said: 'For them that shall be changed,' as if at some time later this change will be shown to us), let us consider whether there is suggested to us the doctrine of the resurrection, in which a change will be granted to us, but a change for something better and something spiritual. 'What is sown in corruption,' he says, 'rises in incorruption.' Do you see the change? 'What is sown in weakness rises in power; what is sown a natural body rises a spiritual body,'[7] when every corporeal creature will change together with us. Also, 'The heavens shall grow old like a garment and as a vesture' God 'shall change them, and they shall be changed.'[8] Then, according to Isaia, 'The sun will be sevenfold, and the moon like the present size of the sun.'[9]

Since the sayings of God have not been written for all, but for those who have ears according to the inner man, he wrote the inscription, 'For them that shall be changed,' as I think, for those who are careful of themselves and are always advancing through their exercises of piety toward something better. This is surely the best change which the right hand of the most High will bestow; of which the blessed David also had an understanding when, having tasted the blessings of

---

6 The Benedictine editors believe that St. Basil is speaking of the translator, Aquila, who has this title in the Hexapla for this Psalm: 'Tôi nikopoiôi epi tôis krínois tôn uiôn Koré, epistemonos âisma prosfilías.'
7 1 Cor. 15.42-44.
8 Ps. 101.27.
9 Cf. Isa. 30.26: 'And the light of the moon shall be as the light of the sun, and the light of the sun shall be sevenfold.'

virtue, he strained forward to what was before.[10] For, what does he say? 'And I said, Now I have begun: this is the change of the right hand of the most High.'[11] Therefore, one who is advancing in virtue is never unchanged. 'When I was a child,' it is said, 'I spoke as a child, I felt as a child, I thought as a child. Now that I have become a man, I have put away the things of a child.'[12]

Again, when he had become a man, he did not rest from his work, but 'forgetting what was behind, he strained forward to what was before, he pressed on towards the goal to the prize of the heavenly calling.'[13] There is a change, therefore, of the inner man who is renewed day by day.

Since he, the prophet, is about to announce to us what concerns the Beloved, who for our sake took upon Himself the dispensation of the Incarnation, for those who are worthy of this grace he says that he has given this canticle for the sons of Core. For it is a canticle and not a psalm; because it is sung with harmonious modulation by the unaccompanied voice and with no instrument sounding in accord with it. And it is a canticle for the Beloved. Shall I describe to you whom the Scripture says the Beloved is? Or do you know, even before our words, recalling the voice in the Gospel? 'This is my beloved Son, in whom I am well pleased; hear him.'[14] The Beloved is to the Father as the Only-begotten One; and to every creature as a kind Father and a good Ruler. The same thing is by nature both beloved and good. Wherefore, some have rightly given the definition, saying that 'good' is what all things desire.

It is not the privilege of any chance person to go forward to the perfection of love and to learn to know Him who is truly

---

10 Cf. Phil. 3.13, 14: 'But one thing I do: forgetting what is behind, I strain forward to what is before, I press on towards the goal, to the prize of God's heavenly call.'
11 Ps. 76.11.
12 1 Cor. 13.11.
13 Cf. Phil. 3.13. Cf. n. 10 supra.
14 Matt. 17.5.

beloved, but of him who has already 'put off the old man, which is being corrupted through its deceptive lusts, and has put on the new man,'[15] which is being renewed that it may be recognized as an image of the Creator. Moreover, he who loves money and is aroused by the corruptible beauty of the body and esteems exceedingly this little glory here, since he has expended the power of loving on what is not proper, he is quite blind in regard to the contemplation of Him who is truly beloved. Therefore, it is said: 'Thou shalt love the Lord thy God with thy whole heart, and with thy whole soul, and with thy whole mind.'[16] The expression, 'With thy whole,' admits of no division into parts. As much love as you shall have squandered on lower objects, that much will necessarily be lacking to you from the whole. Because of this, of all people few have been called friends of God, as Moses has been described as a friend;[17] likewise, John: 'But the friend' he says, 'of the bridegroom, who stands, rejoices exceedingly,'[18] that is to say, he who has a steadfast and immovable love for Christ, he is worthy of His friendship. Therefore, the Lord said to His disciples who were already perfect: 'No longer do I call you servants,' but friends; 'because the servant does not know what his master does.'[19] Accordingly, it is the privilege of a perfect man truly to recognize the Beloved. In reality, only holy men are the friends of God and friends to each other, but no one of the wicked or stupid is a friend. The beauty of friendship does not fall into a depraved state, since nothing shameful or incongruous can be capable of the harmonious union of friendship. Evil is contrary not to the good only, but also to itself. But, now let us proceed to an examination of the words.

---

15 Eph. 4.22, 24.
16 Mark 12.30.
17 Cf. Exod. 33.11: 'And the Lord spoke to Moses face to face, as a man is wont to speak to his friend.'
18 John 3.29.
19 *Ibid.* 15.15.

(3) 'My heart hath uttered a good word.'[20] Some have already thought that these words were spoken from the Person of the Father concerning the Word who was with Him from the beginning, whom He brought forth, they say, as it were, from His Heart and His very Vitals; and from a good Heart there came forth a good Word. But, it seems to me that these words refer to the person of the prophet, since what follows the saying no longer makes the explanation concerning the Father equally smooth for us. The Father would not say concerning His own tongue: 'My tongue is the pen of a scrivener that writeth swiftly. Thou art beautiful above the sons of men.'[21] Not, indeed, by a comparison with men does He possess a superiority of beauty. And continuing, he says: 'Therefore God, thy God hath anointed thee with the oil of gladness.'[22] He did not say: 'I, God, anointed you,' but, 'He anointed you,' so that it is shown from this that the one speaking is another person. What else is this, therefore, than the prophet spreading the action of the Holy Spirit which has come upon him? 'My heart hath uttered a good word,' he says. Now, since belching is hidden breath which is blown upwards when the bubbles due to the effervescence of the food burst, he who is fed with the 'living bread which came down from heaven and gives life to the world'[23] and who is filled 'by every word that comes forth from the mouth of God,'[24] according to the customary allegorical interpretation of the Scripture, this soul, I say, nourished with the divine learning, sends forth an utterance proper to its food. Therefore, since the food was rational and good, the prophet uttered a good word. For 'the good man from the good treasure' of his heart brings forth the

---

20 Ps. 44.2.
21 *Ibid*. 44.2, 3.
22 *Ibid*. 44.8.
23 Cf. John 6.51, 52: 'I am the living bread that has come down from heaven. . . . and the bread that I will give is my flesh for the life of the world.'
24 Matt. 4.4.

good.²⁵ Let us ourselves, therefore, seek after the nourishment from the Word for the filling of our souls ('The just,' it is said, 'eateth and filleth his soul'²⁶), in order that, in correspondence with what we are fed, we may send up, not some vulgar word, but a good one. The wicked man, nourished by unsound doctrines, utters in his heart a wicked word. Do you not see what sort of words the mouths of heretics pour forth? How harsh and foul, indicating some serious disease in the innermost part of the wretched ones? 'The evil man from the evil treasure' of his heart brings forth evil.²⁷ 'Do not, therefore, having itching ears, heap up for yourself teachers'²⁸ who are able to produce disease in your vitals and to procure for you the utterance of evil words for which you are going to be judged on the day of judgment. 'For by thy words thou wilt be justified,' he said, 'and by thy words thou wilt be condemned.'²⁹

'I speak my works to the king.'³⁰ These words also lead us especially to understand the person of the prophet. 'I speak my works to the king,' that is, I will confess to the judge and get ahead of the accuser by reporting my own deeds. Certainly, we have received the command which says: 'Tell first your transgressions that you may be justified.'³¹

'My tongue is the pen of a scrivener that writeth swiftly.'³² As the pen is an instrument for writing when the hand of an experienced person moves it to record what is being written, so also the tongue of the just man, when the Holy Spirit moves it, writes the words of eternal life in the hearts of the faithful,

---

25 Cf. Matt. 12.35: 'The good man from his good treasure brings forth good things.'
26 Prov. 13.25.
27 Cf. Matt. 12.35: 'and the evil man from his evil treasure brings forth evil things.'
28 Cf. 2 Tim. 4.3: 'But having itching ears, they will heap up to themselves teachers according to their own lusts.'
29 Matt. 12.37.
30 Ps. 44.2.
31 Isa. 43.26 (Septuagint version).
32 Ps. 44.2.

dipped 'not in ink, but in the Spirit of the living God.'[33] The scrivener, therefore, is the Holy Spirit, because He is wise and an apt teacher of all; and swiftly writing, because the movement of His mind is swift. The Spirit writes thoughts in us, 'Not on tablets of stone but on fleshy tablets of the heart.'[34] In proportion to the size of the heart, the Spirit writes in hearts more or less, either things evident to all or things more obscure, according to its previous preparation of purity. Because of the speed with which the writings have been finished all the world now is filled with the Gospel.

It seemed best to us to interpret the next expression as beginning with itself and not to join it with the preceding, but to associate it with what follows. For the words, 'Thou art ripe in beauty' we think are spoken to the Lord by way of apostrophe.

(4) 'Thou art ripe in beauty, above the sons of men: grace is poured abroad in thy lips.'[35] Both Aquila and Symmachus[36] introduce us to this thought; the first saying, 'Thou art adorned with beauty above the sons of men,' and Symmachus, 'Thou art beautiful with a beauty above the sons of men.' Now, he [David] calls the Lord ripe in beauty when he fixes his gaze on His divinity. He does not celebrate the beauty of the flesh. 'And we have seen him, and he had no sightliness, nor beauty, but his appearance was without honor and lacking above the sons of men.'[37] It is evident, then, that the prophet, looking upon His brilliancy and being filled with the splendor there, his soul smitten with this beauty, was moved to a divine love of the spiritual beauty, and when this appeared in the human soul all things hitherto loved seemed shameful and abominable. Therefore, even Paul, when he

---

[33] 2 Cor. 3.3.
[34] *Ibid.*
[35] Ps. 44.3.
[36] Aquila and Symmachus were two early translators of the Old Testament into Greek. Their versions were included by Origen in the Hexapla.
[37] Isa. 53.2, 3 (Septuagint version).

saw His ripe beauty 'counted all things as dung that he might gain Christ.'[38] Those outside the word of truth, despising the simplicity of expression in the Scriptures, call the preaching of the Gospel folly; but we, who glory in the cross of Christ, 'to whom the gifts bestowed on us by God were manifested through the Spirit, not in words taught by human wisdom,'[39] know that the grace poured out by God in the teachings concerning Christ is rich. Therefore, in a short time the teaching passed through almost the whole world, since grace, rich and plentiful, was poured out upon the preachers of the Gospel, whom Scripture called even the lips of Christ. Moreover, the message of the Gospel in its insignificant little words possesses great guidance and attraction toward salvation. And every soul is overcome by the unalterable doctrines, being strengthened by grace to an unshaken faith in Christ. Whence the Apostle says: 'Through whom we have received grace and apostleship to bring about obedience to faith.'[40] And again: 'I have labored more than any of them, yet not I, but the grace of God with me.'[41]

(5) 'Grace is poured abroad in thy lips; therefore hath God blessed thee forever.'[42] In the Gospel it has been written: 'They marvelled at the words of grace that came from his mouth.'[43] The psalm, wishing to bring forward vividly the great amount of grace in the words spoken by our Lord, says: 'Grace is poured abroad in thy lips,' because of the abundance of grace in the words. 'God hath blessed thee forever,' it says. It is evident that these words refer to His human nature, as it advances 'in wisdom and age and grace.'[44] According to this

---

38 Phil. 3.8.
39 Cf. 1 Cor. 2.12, 13: 'Now we have received not the spirit of the world, but the spirit that is from God, that we may know the things that have been given us by God. These things we also speak, not in words taught by human wisdom, but in the learning of the Spirit.'
40 Rom. 1.5.
41 1 Cor. 15.10.
42 Ps. 44.3.
43 Luke 4.22.
44 *Ibid.* 2.52.

we clearly perceive that grace has been given to Him as the prize for His brave deeds. Similar to this is the saying: 'Thou hast loved justice and hated iniquity: therefore God, thy God, hath anointed thee with the oil of gladness above thy fellows.'[45] The saying of Paul to the Philippians is also much like to this: 'He humbled himself, becoming obedient to death, even to death on a cross. Therefore God also has exalted him.'[46] So that it is clear that these words were spoken concerning the Savior as a man. Or, there is this explanation. Since the Church is the body of the Lord, and He Himself is the head of the Church, just as we have explained that those ministering to the heavenly Word are the lips of Christ (even as Paul, or anyone else much like to him in virtue, had Christ speaking in himself[47]), so also we, as many of us as are believers, are the other members of the body of Christ. Now, if anyone refers to the Lord the praise given to the Church, he will not sin. Therefore, the saying: 'God hath blessed thee'; that is to say, He has filled thy members and thy body with blessings from Himself for eternity, that is to say, for time without end.

'Gird thy sword upon thy thigh, O thou most mighty. With thy ripeness and thy beauty.'[48] We believe that this refers figuratively to the living Word of God, so that He is joined with the flesh, who is 'efficient and keener than any two-edged sword, and extending even to the division of soul and spirit, of joints also and of marrow, and a discerner of the thoughts and intentions of the heart.'[49] For, the thigh is a symbol of efficiency in generation. 'For these,' he says, 'are the souls that came out of Jacob's thigh.'[50] As, then, our Lord Jesus Christ

---

45 Ps. 44.8.
46 Phil. 2.8.
47 Cf. 2 Cor. 13.3: 'Do you seek a proof of the Christ who speaks in me?'
48 Ps. 44.4.
49 Heb. 4.12.
50 Cf. Exod. 1.5: 'And all the souls that came out of Jacob's thigh were seventy.'

is a life and a way,[51] and bread,[52] and a grapevine,[53] and a true light,[54] and is also called numberless other names, so, too, He is a sword that cuts through the sensual part of the soul and mortifies the motions of concupiscence. Then, since God the Word was about to unite Himself to the weakness of flesh, there is added beautifully the expression, 'thou most mighty,' because the fact that God was able to exist in the nature of man bears proof of the greatest power. In fact, the construction of heaven and earth, and the generation of sea and air and the greatest elements, and whatever is known above the earth and whatever beneath the earth, do not commend the power of the Word of God as much as His dispensation concerning the Incarnation and His condescension to the lowliness and weakness of humanity.

'With thy ripeness and thy beauty.' Ripeness differs from beauty, because ripeness is said to be the attainment at a suitable time to its own flowering, as the grain is ripe which is already mature for the harvest; and the fruit of the vine is ripe which receives the proper maturing for its own perfection through the season of the year and is fit for enjoyment. On the other hand, beauty is the harmony in the composition of the members, and it possesses a grace that blooms in it. Therefore, 'Gird thy sword upon thy thigh, O thou most mighty. With thy ripeness and thy beauty.' 'With thy ripeness,' that is to say, in the fullness of time; 'and thy beauty,' the divinity which can be known through contemplation and reason. For, that is truly beautiful which exceeds all human apprehension and power and can be contemplated by the mind alone. The disciples to whom He privately explained the parables knew His beauty. Peter and the Sons of Thunder saw His beauty on

---

51 Cf. John 14.6: 'Jesus said to him, "I am the way, and the truth, and the life." '
52 Cf. *Ibid.* 6.35: 'But Jesus said to them, "I am the bread of life." '
53 Cf. *Ibid.* 15.5: 'I am the vine, you are the branches.'
54 Cf. *Ibid.* 1.9: 'It was the true light that enlightens every man who comes into the world.'

the mountain,[55] surpassing in splendor the brilliance of the sun, and they were considered worthy to perceive with their eyes the beginning of His glorious coming.

'Set out, proceed prosperously, and reign.'[56] That is to say, having begun your care of men through the flesh, make that care earnest and lasting and never weakening. This will provide a way and a course for the preaching, and will subject all to your power. Let it not astonish us that the expression, 'proceed prosperously,' is spoken in the imperative mood, because of the custom of Scripture which always arranges its expressions of desire in this way. For example, 'Thy will be done,'[57] instead of, 'May Thy will be done.' And 'Thy kingdom come,'[58] instead of 'May Thy kingdom come.'

(6) 'Because of truth and meekness and justice: and thy right hand shall conduct thee wonderfully.'[59] In the same way again, this saying is fashioned figuratively, just as if the Lord were receiving as a reward these favors, namely, to proceed prosperously and to reign, because of His truth and meekness and justice. We must understand it in this way: since things human have been distorted by deceit, rule among men who are governed by sin in order that You may sow the truth again, for You are the Truth. And, 'because of meekness,' in order that by Your example all may be led forth to clemency and goodness. Wherefore, the Lord also said: 'Learn from me, for I am meek and humble of heart.'[60] And He showed this meekness in His works themselves; 'when he was reviled, he was silent;'[61] when He was scourged, He endured. 'And thy

---

55 Cf. Matt. 17.1, 2: 'Now after six days Jesus took Peter, James and his brother John, and led them up a high mountain by themselves, and was transfigured before them. And his face shone as the sun, and his garments became white as snow'
56 Ps. 44.5.
57 Matt. 6.10.
58 *Ibid.*
59 Ps. 44.5.
60 Matt. 11.29.
61 1 Peter 2.23.

right hand shall conduct thee wonderfully.' Not a pillar of cloud, nor the illumination of fire, but Thy right hand itself.

'Thy arrows are sharp, O thou most mighty.'[62] The sharp arrows of the Mighty One are the well-aimed words which touch the hearts of the hearers, striking and wounding their keenly perceptive souls. 'The words of the wise,' it is said, 'are as goads.'[63] The psalmist, therefore, praying to be delivered at some time from the deceitful men of his time, seeks after the sharp arrows of the Mighty One for the cure of the deceitful tongue. He wishes for 'coals that lay waste'[64] to be at hand, so that punishment, which he called 'coals that lay waste,' may be ready for those upon whom through blindness of heart the rational arrows do not fasten. For those who have made themselves destitute of God the preparation of coals that lay waste is necessary. Now, therefore, 'Thy arrows are sharp.' The souls which have received the faith are wounded by these arrows, and those inflamed with the highest love of God say with the spouse, 'I languish with love.'[65] Indescribable and inexpressible are the beauty of the Word and the ripeness of the wisdom and of the comeliness of God in His own image. Blessed, therefore, are those who are fond of contemplating true beauty. As if bound to Him through love, and loving the celestial and blessed love, they forget relatives and friends; they forget home and all their abundance; and forgetful even of the bodily necessity to eat and drink, they have clung only to the divine and pure love. You will understand the sharp arrows also as those sent out to sow the Gospel in the whole world, who, because they had spurred themselves on, shone with works of justice, and they crept subtly into the souls of those who were being instructed; for, these arrows, sent out everywhere, were preparing the people to fall under Christ. However, the phrase seems to me to be restored more con-

---

62 Ps. 44.6 (Septuagint version).
63 Eccles. 12.11.
64 Ps. 119.4.
65 Cant. 2.5.

sistently by a transposition of words, so that the meaning is this: 'Set out, proceed prosperously, and reign, and Thy right hand shall conduct Thee wonderfully, and under Thee people shall fall; because Thy arrows are sharp in the hearts of the King's enemies.' No one who is fighting against God and is boastful and arrogant falls under God, but they who accept subjection through faith. The arrows, falling in the hearts of those who were at some time enemies of the King, draw them to a love for the truth, draw them to the Lord, so that they who were enemies to God are reconciled to Him through its teachings.

(7) 'Thy Throne, O God, is forever and ever; the sceptre of thy kingdom is a sceptre of uprightness. Thou hast loved justice and hated iniquity; therefore God, thy God, hath anointed thee with the oil of gladness above thy fellows.'[66] After he has directed his attention to mankind and discoursed much about it, he now elevates his sermon to the heights of the glory of the Only-begotten. 'Thy Throne,' he says, 'O God, is forever and ever,' that is to say, Thy Kingdom is beyond the ages and older than all thought. And beautifully after the subjection of the people does he celebrate the magnificence of the kingdom of God. 'The sceptre of thy kingdom is a sceptre of uprightness.' For this reason also he gave Him His own name, clearly proclaiming Him God: 'Thy Throne, O God.' The sceptre of God is punitive, and while correcting, it brings forth upright and not perverse judgments. Therefore, the sceptre of uprightness is called the sceptre of His Kingdom. 'And if his children forsake my law, and walk not in my judgments, I will visit their iniquities with a rod.'[67] Do you see the just judgment of God? He does not make use of it in the case of chance persons, but of sinners. It is also called a rod of consolation: 'Thy rod,' he says, 'and thy staff, they have comforted me.'[68] It is a rod of affliction, too: 'Thou shalt rule

---

66 Ps. 44.7, 8.
67 *Ibid.* 88.31, 33.
68 *Ibid.* 22.4.

them with a rod of iron, and shalt break them in pieces like a potter's vessel.'[69] Things of earth and clay are broken in kindness toward those who are governed, as it is handed down, 'for the destruction of the flesh, that his spirit may be saved.'[70]

(8) 'Therefore God, thy God, hath anointed thee with the oil of gladness above thy fellows.'[71] Since it was necessary to give form to the typical anointing, and the typical high priests and kings, the flesh of the Lord was anointed with the true anointing, by the coming of the Holy Spirit into it, which was called 'the oil of gladness.' And He was anointed above His fellows; that is to say, all men who are members of Christ. Therefore, a certain partial sharing of the Spirit was given to them, but the Holy Spirit descending upon the Son of God, as John says, 'abode upon him.'[72] Rightly is the Spirit called the 'oil of gladness,' inasmuch as one of the fruits produced by the Holy Spirit is joy. Since the account concerning the Savior is mixed because of the nature of the divinity and the dispensation of the Incarnation, looking again at the humanity of God he says: 'Thou hast loved justice and hated iniquity,' meaning 'the rest of men frequently achieve by labor and practice and diligence a disposition toward virtue and a disinclination to vice; but You have a certain natural attraction to the good and an aversion for iniquity.' Yet, it is not hard for us, if we wish it, to take up a love for justice and a hatred for iniquity. God has advantageously given all power to the rational soul, as that of loving, so also that of hating, in order that, guided by reason, we may love virtue but hate vice. It is possible at times to use hatred even praiseworthily. 'Have I not hated them, O Lord, that hated thee: and pined away because of thy enemies? I have hated them with a perfect hatred.'[73]

(9) 'Myrrh and aloes and cassia perfume thy garments, from

---

69 *Ibid.* 2.9.
70 1 Cor. 5.5.
71 Ps. 44.8.
72 John 1.32.
73 Ps. 138.21, 22.

the ivory houses: out of which the daughters of Kings have delighted thee in thy glory.'[74] The statement of the prophet, descending gradually and consistently and mentioning first all those things which pertain to the dispensation of the Incarnation, by a strong breath of the Spirit which reveals to him hidden things, came to the passion. 'Myrrh,' he says, 'and aloes and cassia perfume thy garments.' Now, the fact that myrrh is a symbol of burial even the evangelist John taught us when he said that He was prepared for burial by Joseph of Arimathea with myrrh and aloes.[75] Aloes itself is also a very refined form of myrrh. When the aromatic herb is squeezed, whatever part of it is liquid is separated as aloes, but the denser part which is left is called myrrh. Surely, then, the sweet odor of Christ gives forth the fragrance of myrrh because of His passion and of aloes because He did not remain motionless and inactive for three days and three nights but descended to the lower world to distribute the graces of the Resurrection, in order that He might fulfill all things which have reference to Him. And it breathes forth the fragrance of cassia because cassia is a certain very delicate and fragrant bark which is tightly stretched around a woody stalk. Perhaps, Scripture profoundly and wisely intimated to us through the name of cassia the suffering of the cross undertaken in kindness to every creature. Therefore, you have myrrh because of burial; aloes, because of the passage down to the lower world (since every drop is borne downward); and cassia, because of the dispensation of the flesh upon the wood. For this reason he says: 'the daughters of kings have delighted thee in thy glory.' But, who would be the daughters of kings except the generous and great and kingly souls? Those which, after they had learned to know Christ through His descent to a human state 'delighted Him in His glory,' in true faith and perfect charity,

---

[74] *Ibid.* 44.9.
[75] Cf. John 19 38, 39: 'Joseph of Arimathea, . . . besought Pilate that he might take away the body of Jesus. And there also came Nicodemus . . . bringing a mixture of myrrh and aloes.'

giving glory to His divinity. And these aromatic herbs, he says, are not sparingly present in the garments of Christ (that is to say, the parable of the sermons and the preparation of the doctrines), but are brought from all the buildings. He says that the largest of the dwellings are houses, and that these are constructed of ivory, because the prophet is teaching, I think, the wealth of the love of Christ for the world.

'The queen stood on thy right hand, arrayed in gilded clothing, embroidered with varied colors.'[76] Now he is speaking about the Church, about which we have learned in the Canticle that it is the one perfect dove of Christ,[77] which admits those who are known for their good works to the right side of Christ, separating them from the bad, just as the shepherd separates the sheep from the goats.[78] Therefore, the queen, that is, the soul which is joined with the Word, its Bridegroom, not subjected by sin but sharing the kingdom of Christ, stands on the right hand of the Savior in gilded clothing, that is to say, adorning herself charmingly and religiously with spiritual doctrines, interwoven and varied. Since, however, the teachings are not simple, but varied and manifold, and embrace words, moral and natural and the so-called esoteric, therefore, the Scripture says that the clothing of the bride is varied.

(10) 'Hearken, O daughter, and see, and incline thy ear: and forget thy people and thy father's house. And the king shall greatly desire thy beauty, for he is thy Lord, and him they shall adore.'[79] He summons the Church to hear and observe the precepts and, addressing her as daughter, associates her with himself through this title, as if he had adopted her through love. 'Hearken, O daughter, and see.' He teaches

---

76 Ps. 44.10.
77 Cf. Cant. 6.8: 'One is my dove, my perfect one.'
78 Cf. Matt. 25.32: 'And before him will be gathered all the nations, and he will separate them one from another, as the shepherd separates the sheep from the goats; and he will set the sheep on his right hand, but the goats on the left.'
79 Ps. 44.11, 12.

that she has a mind trained to contemplation through the word, 'see.' Observe well, he says, the creation, and, aided by the order in it, thus ascend to the contemplation of the Creator. Then bending her lofty and proud neck, he says: 'Incline thy ear.' Do not run away to stories from the outside, but accept the humble voice in the evangelical account. 'Incline thy ear' to this teaching in order that you may forget those depraved customs and the lessons of your fathers. Therefore, 'forget thy people and thy father's house.' For, everyone 'who commits sin is of the devil.'[80] Cast out, I pray you, he says, the teachings of the evil spirits, forget sacrifices, nocturnal dances, tales which inflame to fornication and to every form of licentiousness. For this reason have I called you my own daughter, that you may hate the parent who previously begot you for destruction. If through such forgetfulness you erase the blemishes of your depraved learning, assuming your own proper beauty, you will appear desirable to your Spouse and King. 'Because he is thy Lord, and him they shall adore.' He intimates the need of submission by the expression: 'He is thy Lord. Him they shall adore,' that is, every creature. Therefore, 'at the name of Jesus Christ every knee shall bend of those in heaven, on earth and under the earth.'[81]

'And the daughter of Tyre with gifts, yea, all the rich among the people, shall entreat thy countenance.'[82] Idolatry seems to have been practiced excessively in the Chanaanite country. The metropolis of Chanaan is Tyre. Scripture, then, urging the Church on to obedience, says: 'And the daughter of Tyre will come at some time with gifts. And the rich among the people will entreat thy countenance with gifts.' He did not say: 'They will entreat you with gifts,' but, 'thy countenance.' For, the Church will not be adored, but Christ, the head of the Church, whom Scripture called the 'countenance.'

---

80 1 John 3.8.
81 Phil. 2.10.
82 Ps. 44.13.

(11) 'All the glory of the king's daughter is within, invested and adorned with golden borders. After her shall virgins be brought to the king.'[83] After she had been cleansed of the former doctrines of wickedness, and was heeding the instruction and forgetting her people and her father's house, the Holy Spirit relates what pertains to her. And since He saw the cleanliness deeply hidden, He says: 'All the glory of the king's daughter,' that is to say, of Christ's bride, who has become henceforth through adoption daughter of the king, 'is within.' The assertion urges us to penetrate to the inmost mysteries of ecclesiastical glory, since the beauty of the bride is within. He who makes himself ready for the Father who sees in secret, and who prays and does all things, not to be seen by men, but to be known to God alone,[84] this man has all his glory within, even as the king's daughter. And the golden borders with which the whole is invested and adorned are within.

Seek nothing with exterior gold and bodily adornment; but consider the garment as one worthy to adorn him who is according to the image of his Creator, as the Apostle says: 'Stripping off the old man, and putting on the new, one that is being renewed unto perfect knowledge "according to the image of his Creator." '[85] And he who has put on 'the heart of mercy, kindness, humility, patience, and meekness,'[86] is clothed within and has adorned the inner man. Paul exhorts us to put on the Lord Jesus,[87] not according to the exterior man, but in order that our remembrance of God may cover over our whole mind. But, I believe that the spiritual garment is woven when the attendant action is interwoven with the word of doctrine. In fact, just as a bodily garment is woven

---

83 *Ibid.* 44.14, 15.
84 Cf. Matt. 6.1-6.
85 Col. 3.9, 10.
86 *Ibid.* 3.12.
87 Cf. Rom. 13.14: 'But put on the Lord Jesus Christ, and as for the flesh, take no thought for its lusts.'

when the woof is interwoven with the warp, so when the word is antecedent, if actions in accordance with the word should be produced, there would be made a certain most magnificent garment for the soul which possesses a life of virtue attained by word and action. But, the borders hang down from the garment, these also spiritual; therefore, they too are said to be golden. Since, indeed, the word is greater than the deed, there is, as it were, a certain border which remains over from the woven robe according to the action. Certain souls, since they have not accepted seeds of false doctrines, follow the spouse of the Lord and because they are following His spouse they will be led to the King. Let those also who have vowed virginity to the Lord hear that virgins will be led to the King, but virgins who are close to the Church, who follow after her, and who do not wander away from the ecclesiastical discipline.

The virgins 'shall be brought with gladness and rejoicing: they shall be brought into the temple of the king.'[88] Not those who through constraint assume virginity, nor those who accept the chaste life through grief or necessity, but those who in gladness and rejoicing take delight in so virtuous an act, these will be brought to the King, and they will be brought not into some insignificant place, but into the temple of the King. For, the sacred vessels, which human use has not defiled, will be brought into the holy of holies and they will have the right of entrance into the innermost shrines, where unhallowed feet do not walk about. And how great a matter it is to be brought into the temple of the King, the prophet shows when he prays for himself and says: 'One thing I have asked of the Lord, this will I seek after; that I may dwell in the house of the Lord all the days of my life. That I may see the delight of the Lord, and may visit his temple.'[89]

(12) 'Instead of thy fathers, sons are born to thee: thou shalt make them princes over all the earth.'[90] Since she was

---
88 Ps. 44.16.
89 *Ibid.* 26 4.
90 *Ibid.* 44.17.

ordered above to forget her people and her father's house, in exchange for her obedience she now receives instead of fathers, sons who are conspicuous for such great qualities that they are established as 'princes over all the earth.' Who, then, are the sons of the Church? Surely, the sons of the Gospel, who rule all the earth. 'Their sound hath gone forth,' he says, 'into all the earth,'[91] and 'They shall sit on twelve thrones, and they shall judge the twelve tribes of Israel.'[92] And if anyone accepts the patriarchs as the fathers of the bride, even thus the explanation of the apostles does not fail. For, instead of them there were born to her through Christ sons, who do the works of Abraham and, therefore, are deemed equal in honor with them, because they have done the same things for which the fathers were considered worthy of great honors. In truth, the saints are the princes of all the earth because of their attraction for the good, since the nature itself of good bestows upon them the first place, as it bestowed upon Jacob the rights of Esau. For, it is said: 'Be master of your brother.'[93] Accordingly, they who have been made equal in honor with their fathers and have received in addition the pre-eminence in all things through the exercise of virtue, are both sons of the bride of Christ and are established by their own mother as princes over all the earth. Consider, I pray you, how great is the power of the queen, that she appoints princes over all the earth.

'I shall remember thy name throughout all generations. Therefore shall people praise thee forever: yea forever and ever.'[94] After all things else the Scripture, as if in the person of the Church, says: 'I shall remember thy name throughout all generations.' And what is the remembrance of the Church? The praise of the people.

---

91 *Ibid.* 18.5.
92 Matt. 19.28.
93 Gen. 27.29.
94 Ps. 44.18. St. Basil substitutes the first person singular for the third person in the verbs.

## HOMILY 18

*A Psalm for the Sons of Core*

(ON PSALM 45)

UNTO THE END, for the sons of Core, 'a Psalm for the hidden.'[1]

This psalm seems to me to contain the prophecy concerning the end of time. Paul, having knowledge of this end, says: 'Then comes the end, when he delivers the kingdom to God the Father.'[2] Or, since our actions lead us to the end, each one to the end proper to itself, the good leading toward happiness, and the base toward eternal condemnation, and since the counsels delivered by the Spirit in this psalm lead those obeying them to the good end, therefore it has been entitled: 'Unto the end,' inasmuch as it is the record of the teachings for the happy end of human life. 'For the sons of Core.' This psalm is also said to be for the sons of Core, whom the Holy Spirit does not separate, since, as with one soul and one voice, with complete harmony toward each other, they utter the words of prophecy, while no one of them prophesies anything at all contrary to the others, but the gift of prophecy is given to them equally because of the equality of their mutual affection for the good. Moreover, the psalm is said to be 'for the hidden,' that is to say, for secret things, and those buried in mystery. Having meditated on the expressions of the psalm

---

1 Ps. 45.1.
2 1 Cor. 15.24.

in turn, you will learn the hidden meaning of the words, and that it is not the privilege of any chance person to gaze at the divine mysteries, but of him alone who is able to be a harmonious instrument of the promise, so that his soul is moved by the action of the Holy Spirit in it instead of by the psaltery.

'Our God is our refuge and strength: a helper in troubles, which have found us exceedingly.'[3] Because of the weakness present in him from nature, every man has need of much assistance, if many troubles and labors befall him. Seeking a refuge, therefore, from all precarious situations, like one fleeing to a place of sanctuary or having recourse to some sharp summit surrounded by a strong wall because of the attack of the enemy, so he flees to God, believing that a dwelling in Him is his only rest. Therefore, because flight to God was agreed upon by all, the enemy produced great illusion and confusion concerning the choice of the Savior. Plotting as an enemy, again he deceives the victims of his plots into thinking that they should flee to him as to a protector. Consequently, a twofold evil surrounds them, since they are either seized by force or destroyed by deceit. Therefore, the unbelievers flee to demons and idols, having the knowledge of the true God snatched away by the confusion which is produced in them by the devil.

They who recognize God err in the judgment of their affairs, making demands for useful things foolishly, asking for some things as good, which frequently are not for their advantage, and fleeing others as evil, though at times they bring great assistance to them. For example, is someone sick? Because he is fleeing the pain from the sickness, he prays for health. Did he lose his money? He is exceedingly pained by the loss. Yet, frequently the disease is useful when it will restrain the sinner, and health is harmful when it becomes the means for sin to one who possesses it. In the same manner, money also has already served some for licentiousness, while

---
3 Ps. 45.2.

poverty has taught self-control to many who had begun badly. Do not flee, then, what you do not need to flee, and do not have recourse to him to whom it is unnecessary. But, one thing you must flee, sin; and one refuge from evil must be sought, God. Do not trust in princes; do not be exalted in the uncertainty of wealth; do not be proud of bodily strength; do not pursue the splendor of human glory. None of these things saves you; all are transient, all are deceptive. There is one refuge, God. 'Cursed be the man that trusteth in man,'[4] or in any human thing.

(2) Therefore, 'God is our refuge and strength.' To him who is able to say: 'I can do all things in him,' Christ, 'who strengthens me,'[5] God is strength. Now, it is the privilege of many to say: 'God is our refuge,' and 'Lord, thou hast been our refuge.'[6] But, to say it with the same feelings as the prophet is the privilege of few. For, there are few who do not admire human interests but depend wholly upon God and breathe Him and have all hope and trust in Him. And our actions convict us whenever in our afflictions we run to everything else rather than to God. Is a child sick? You look around for an enchanter or one who puts superstitious marks on the necks of the innocent children; or finally, you go to a doctor and to medicines, having neglected Him who is able to save. If a dream troubles you, you run to the interpreter of dreams. And, if you fear an enemy, you cunningly secure some man as a patron. In short, in every need you contradict yourself— in word, naming God as your refuge; in act, drawing on aid from useless and vain things. God is the true aid for the righteous man. Just as a certain general, equipped with a noble heavy-armed force, is always ready to give help to an oppressed district, so God is our Helper and an Ally to everyone who is waging war against the wiliness of the devil, and He sends out

---

4 Jer. 17.5.
5 Phil. 4.13.
6 Ps. 89.1.

ministering spirits for the safety of those who are in need. Moreover, affliction will find every just man because of the established way of life. He who avoids the wide and broad way and travels the narrow and close one[7] will be found by tribulations. The prophet formed the statement vividly when he said: 'In troubles which have found us exceedingly.' For, they overtake us like living creatures, 'working out endurance, and through endurance tried virtue, and through tried virtue hope.'[8] Whence also, the Apostle said: 'Through many tribulations we must enter the kingdom of God.'[9] And 'Many are the afflictions of the just.'[10] But, he who generously and calmly endures the trial of affliction will say: 'In all these things we overcome because of him who has loved us.'[11] And he is so far from refusing and shrinking from the afflictions that he makes the excessive evils an occasion of glory, saying: 'And not only this, but we exult in tribulations also.'[12]

(3) 'Therefore we will not fear, when the earth shall be troubled; and the mountains shall be removed into the heart of the sea.'[13] The prophet shows the great strength of his confidence in Christ, because, even if all things are turned upside down, and the earth, being troubled, is overturned, and if the mountains, leaving their proper sites, are removed to the middle of the sea, 'We will not fear,' seeing that we have 'God as our refuge and strength and helper in troubles which have found us exceedingly.' Whose heart is so undaunted, whose thoughts are so untroubled, as in such great confusion to direct

---

7 Cf. Matt 7.13, 14: 'For wide is the gate and broad is the way that leads to destruction, and many there are who enter that way. How narrow the gate and close the way that leads to life.'
8 Cf. Rom. 5 3, 4: 'But we exult in tribulations also, knowing that tribulation works out endurance, and endurance tried virtue, and tried virtue hope.'
9 Acts 14.22.
10 Ps. 33.20.
11 Rom. 8.37.
12 *Ibid.* 5.3.
13 Ps. 45.3.

his mind toward God, and through hope in Him to be astounded at nothing that happens? We, however, do not endure the anger of man; if a dog runs at us, or some other animal, we do not look to God for help in our trouble, but, panic-stricken we turn our attention toward ourselves.

'Their waters roared and were troubled.'[14] He had said that there was a disturbance of the earth and a transposition of mountains. Now he says that there is a tossing and an upheaval of the sea, since the mountains are falling into the midst of the seas. 'Their waters roared and were troubled,' the waters of the seas, of course. Furthermore, the mountains themselves make a disturbance in the waters, since they are not established in the sea, but are producing a great turmoil in the waters by their own tossing. Accordingly, when the earth is troubled, and the waters of seas roar and are boiled up from the depths, and the mountains are removed and endure much disturbance through the surpassing power of the Lord, then, he says, our heart is undaunted because it has safe and firm hopes in God.

'The mountains were troubled with his strength.'[15] You are also able to understand the meaning of this statement figuratively, calling those persons mountains who are arrogant because of their own greatness but who are ignorant of the strength of God and exalt themselves exceedingly against the knowledge of God, and who then, conquered by men preaching the word of wisdom with virtue and wisdom, in the consciousness of their poverty fear the Lord and humble themselves under His strength. Or perhaps, even the rulers of this world and the fathers of wisdom that perishes, are themselves called mountains, being troubled at the strength of Christ which He showed in the contest of the cross against him who had the power of death. Just as if a certain noble contestant, 'Disarming the Principalities and Powers,' overthrew them,

---
14 *Ibid.* 45.4.
15 *Ibid.*

and 'displayed them openly, leading them away in triumph by force of the cross.'[16]

(4) 'The streams of the river make the city of God joyful.'[17] The briny seawaters, being exceedingly disturbed by the winds, roar and are troubled, but the streams of the river, proceeding noiselessly and flowing in silence to those worthy of receiving them, make the city of God joyful. And now the just man drinks the living water and later will drink more plentifully, when he has been enrolled as a citizen in the city of God. Now he drinks through a mirror and in an obscure manner[18] because of his gradual perception of the divine objects of contemplation; but then he will welcome at once the flooded river, which is able to overwhelm all the city of God with joy. Who could be the river of God except the Holy Spirit, who comes into those worthy because of the faith of the believers in Christ? 'He who believes in me, as the Scripture says, "From within him there shall flow rivers." '[19] And again, 'If anyone drinks of the water which I give, it will become in him a fountain of water, springing up unto life everlasting.'[20] This river, accordingly, makes all the city of God at once joyful, that is to say surely, the Church of those who hold to a heavenly manner of life. Or, every creature endowed with intelligence, from celestial powers even to human souls, must be understood as the city made joyful by the inflowing of the Holy Spirit.

Some give the definition that a city is an established community, administered according to law. And, the definition that has been handed down of the city is in harmony with the celestial city, Jerusalem above. For, there it is a com-

---

16 Col. 2.15.
17 Ps. 45.5
18 1 Cor. 13.12.
19 John 7.38.
20 *Ibid.* 4.13, 14.

munity of the first-born who have been enrolled in heaven,[21] and this is established because of the unchanging manner of life of the saints, and it is administered according to the heavenly law. Therefore, it is not the privilege of human nature to learn the arrangement of that city and all its adornment. Those are the things 'Eye hath not seen nor ear heard, nor has it entered into the heart of man, what things God has prepared for those who love him,'[22] but there are myriads of angels there, and an assembly of saints, and a Church of the first-born that are enrolled in heaven.[23] Concerning that David said: 'Glorious things are said of thee, O city of God.'[24] To that city through Isaia God has promised: 'I will make thee to be an everlasting glory, a joy unto generation and generation, and there shall not be wasting nor destruction in thy borders, and salvation shall possess thy walls.'[25] Therefore, having raised the eyes of your soul, seek, in a manner worthy of things above, what pertains to the city of God. What could anyone consider as deserving of the happiness in that city, which the river of God makes joyful, and of which God is the Craftsman and Creator?

'The most High hath sanctified his own tabernacle.'[26] Perhaps, he is saying that the God-bearing flesh is sanctified through the union with God. From this you will understand that the tabernacle of the most High is the manifestation of God through the flesh.

(5) 'God is in the midst thereof, it shall not be moved: God will help it in the morning early.'[27] Since God is in the midst of the city, He will give it stability, providing assistance for

---

21 Cf. Heb. 12.23: 'But you have come to Mount Sion, and to the city of the living God, the heavenly Jerusalem, and to the company of many thousands of angels, and to the Church of the firstborn who are enrolled in the heavens.'
22 1 Cor. 2.9.
23 See note 21 above.
24 Ps. 86.3.
25 Isa. 60.15, 18.
26 Ps. 45.5.
27 *Ibid.* 45.6.

it at the first break of dawn. Therefore, the word, 'of the city,' will fit either Jerusalem above or the Church below, 'The most High hath sanctified his own tabernacle' in it. And through this tabernacle, in which God dwelt, He was in the midst of it, giving it stability. Moreover, God is in the midst of the city, sending out equal rays of His providence from all sides to the limits of the world. Thus, the justice of God is preserved, as He apportions the same measure of goodness to all. 'God will help it in the morning early.' Now, the perceptible sun produces among us the early morning when it rises above the horizon opposite us, and the Sun of justice[28] produces the early morning in our soul by the rising of the spiritual light, making day in him who admits it. 'At night' means we men are in this time of ignorance. Therefore, having opened wide our mind, let us receive 'the brightness of his glory,' and let us be brightly illumined by the everlasting Light, 'God will help it in the morning early.' When we have become children of light, and 'the night is far advanced for us, and the day is at hand,'[29] then we shall become worthy of the help of God. Therefore, God helps the city, producing in it early morning by His own rising and coming. 'Behold a man,' it is said, 'the Orient is his name.'[30] For those upon whom the spiritual light will rise, when the darkness which comes from ignorance and wickedness is destroyed, early morning will be at hand. Since, then, light has come into the world in order that he who walks about in it may not stumble, His help is able to cause the early morning. Or perhaps, since the Resurrection was in the dim morning twilight, God will help the city in the morning early, who on the third day, early on the morning of the Resurrection gained the victory through death.

(6) 'Nations were troubled, and kingdoms were bowed

---

28 Cf. Mal. 4.2: 'But unto you that fear my name, the Sun of justice shall arise.'
29 Rom. 13.12.
30 Zach. 6.12. St. Basil uses 'ánthrōpos' in place of 'anér.'

down:' the most High 'uttered his voice, the earth trembled.'[31] Consider, I pray you, that a certain city is the object of plots by the enemy who are making war on it, while in the meantime, many nations are settled around it and the kings are dividing by lot the sceptres of each nation; then, that a certain general, unconquerable in might, appears all at once to help this city; he breaks the siege, scatters the gathering of nations, forces the kings into flight simply by calling upon them with power, and he terrifies their hearts by the firmness of his voice. How much disturbance was probably aroused when the nations were being pursued and the kings were being turned into flight! Is it not likely that some indistinct rumbling and incessant noise was sent up from their confused flight, and all the place was full of those driven out because of their cowardice, so that a commotion sprang up everywhere in the cities and villages that received them? Now, he presents such succor for the city of God from the Savior in his words: 'Nations were troubled, and kingdoms were bowed down: the most High uttered his voice, the earth trembled.'

'The Lord of armies is with us: the God of Jacob is our protector.'[32] He saw the incarnate God, he saw Him who was born of the Holy Virgin, 'Emmanuel, which is, interpreted, "God with us," '[33] and for this reason he cries out in prophetic words: 'The Lord of armies is with us,' showing that it is He who was manifested by the holy prophets and patriarchs. Our protector, he says, is not another God besides Him who was handed down by the prophets; but the God of Jacob, who spoke in an oracle to His servant, 'I am the God of Abraham, the God of Isaac, and the God of Jacob.'[34]

(7) 'Come and behold ye the works of God: what wonders he hath done upon earth, making wars to cease even to the

---

31 Ps. 45.7.
32 *Ibid.* 45.8.
33 Matt. 1.23.
34 Exod. 3.6.

end of the earth.'[35] The Scripture invites those who are far from the word of truth to nearness through knowledge, saying: 'Come and behold.' Just as in the case of bodily eyes great distances make the perception of visible objects dim, but the nearer approach of those viewing offers a clear knowledge of the objects seen, so also in the case of objects of contemplation in the mind, he who has not been made familiar with God through His works nor has drawn near to Him is not able to see His works with the pure eyes of his mind. Therefore, 'Come,' first approach, then see the works of the Lord which are prodigious and admirable, by which He struck down and converted to quiet peacefulness nations, formerly warlike and factious. 'Come, children, hearken to me,'[36] and 'Come, all you who labor and are burdened.'[37] It is the paternal voice of One with outstretched arms calling to Himself those who until then were rebelling. He who has heard the call and has approached and cleaves to the One commanding, will see Him who through the cross made all things peaceful 'whether on the earth or in the heavens.'[38]

'He shall destroy the bow, and break the weapons; and the shield he shall burn in the fire.'[39] Do you see the peaceful spirit of the Lord of armies, that He has with Him invisible forces of angelic hosts? Do you see the courage and at the same time the kindliness of the Commander in chief of the armies? Though He is indeed the Lord of armies and has all the companies of angelic hosts, nowhere does He slay any one of the enemies, He overthrows no one, He touches no one; but, He destroys the bows and the weapons, and the shields He burns in the fire. He destroys the bow so that no longer will the burnt missiles be thrown among them, and He will break the weapons, those with which they fight hand to hand, so that

---

35 Ps. 45.9, 10.
36 *Ibid.* 33.12.
37 Matt. 11.28.
38 Col. 1.20.
39 Ps. 45.10.

those near at hand cannot be plotted against and wounded. And the shields He will burn in the fire, stripping the adversaries of their defenses and doing all things in kindness to the enemy.

(8) 'Be still and see that I am God.'[40] As far as we are engaged in affairs outside of God, we are not able to make progress in the knowledge of God. Who, anxious about the things of the world and sunk deep in the distractions of the flesh, can be intent on the words of God and be sufficiently accurate in such mighty objects of contemplation? Do you not see that the word which fell among the thorns is choked by the thorns?[41] The thorns are the pleasures of the flesh and wealth and glory and the cares of life. He who desires the knowledge of God will have to be outside of all these things, and being freed from his passions, thus to receive the knowledge of God. For, how could the thought of God enter into a soul choked by considerations which preoccupied it? Even Pharao knew that it was proper for one to seek God when he was unoccupied, and for this reason he reproached Israel: 'You are unoccupied, you are idle, and you say, "We shall offer prayers to the Lord, our God." '[42] Now, leisure itself is good and useful to him who is unoccupied, since it produces quiet for the acquisition of salutary doctrines. But, the leisure of the Athenians was evil, 'who used to spend all their leisure telling or listening to something new.'[43] Even at the present time some imitate this, misusing the leisure of life for the discovery of some newer teaching. Such leisure is dear to unclean and wicked spirits. 'When the unclean spirit,' it is said, 'has gone out of a man, he says, "I will return to my

---

40 *Ibid.* 45.11.
41 Cf. Matt. 13.7, 22: 'And other seeds fell among thorns; and the thorns grew up and choked them. . . . And the one sown among the thorns, that is the man who listens to the word; but the care of this world and the deceitfulness of riches choke the word and it is made fruitless.'
42 Cf. Exod. 5.17: 'And he said: You are idle, and therefore you say: Let us go and sacrifice to the Lord.'
43 Acts 17.21.

house which I left." And when he has come, he finds the place unoccupied and swept.'[44] May it not be that we make our leisure a time for the adversary to enter, but let us occupy our house within, causing Christ to dwell in us beforehand through the Spirit. At all events, after giving peace to those who were up to this time troubled by the enemies, then he says, 'Have nothing to do with the enemies disturbing you, in order that in silence you may contemplate the words of truth.' For this reason also the Lord says: 'Everyone who does not renounce all that he possesses, cannot be my disciple.'[45] It is necessary, then, to be free from the works of marriage, in order that we may have leisure for prayer; to be unoccupied with the pursuit of wealth, with the desire for this little glory, with the lust for pleasure, with envy and every form of wickedness against our neighbor, in order that, after our soul has found peace and is disturbed by no passion, the illumination of God, as if in a mirror, may become clear and unobscured.

'I will be exalted among the nations, and I will be exalted in the earth.'[46] Clearly the Lord says these words concerning His own Passion, just as it has been written in the Gospel: 'And I, if I be lifted up, will draw all to myself.'[47] 'And as Moses lifted up the serpent in the desert, even so must the Son of Man be lifted up'[48] upon the earth. Since, then, for the sake of the nations He was to be lifted up on the cross and for the sake of all the earth to accept that elevation, therefore, He says: 'I will be exalted among the nations, and I will be exalted in the earth.'

'The Lord of armies is with us: the God of Jacob is our protector.'[49] Exulting in the help of God, twice he called out the same words: 'The Lord of armies is with us,' as if trampling

---

44 Matt. 12.43, 44, with slight changes.
45 Luke 14.33.
46 Ps. 45.11.
47 John 12.32, with slight changes.
48 *Ibid.* 3.14.
49 Ps. 45.12.

and leaping upon the enemy, inasmuch as he would suffer nothing from him because of his perfect trust in the Savior of our souls. 'If God is for us, who is against us.'[50] He who gave the victory to Jacob and after the contest designated him as Israel,[51] He it is who is our Protector; He fights for us. But we are silent, because 'He himself is our peace, he it is who has made both one, that of the two he might create one new man.'[52]

---

50 Rom. 8.31.
51 Cf. Gen. 32.29: 'You shall no longer be called Jacob, but Israel, because you have contended with God and men, and have triumphed.'
52 Eph 2.14, 15.

# HOMILY 19

*Unto the End, a Psalm for the Sons of Core on the Prosperity of the Wicked*[1]

(ON PSALM 48)

EVEN AMONG THE GENTILES certain men have formed ideas concerning the end of man and have arrived at various opinions about the end. Some declared that the end was knowledge; others, practical activity; others, a different use of life and body; but the sensual men declared that the end was pleasure. For us, however, the end for which we do all things and toward which we hasten is the blessed life in the world to come. And this will be attained when we are ruled by God. Up to this time nothing better than the latter idea has been found in rational nature, and to it the Apostle stirs us when he says: 'Then comes the end, when he delivers the kingdom to God the Father.'[2] This same thing Sophonia likewise set forth in prophecy, saying in the person of God: 'For my judgment is to assemble the Gentiles, to receive the kings, to pour out upon them my indignation. For in the fire of my jealousy shall all the earth be devoured; because then I will restore for many peoples a tongue for its generation, that all may call upon the name of the Lord and may serve him under one yoke.'[3] To this end, therefore, I think the advantages from the psalms refer, since they have

---
1 Ps. 48.1.
2 1 Cor. 15.24.
3 Soph. 3.8, 9 (Septuagint version).

311

this heading. Those persons also are in accord with this idea, who have written, 'For a Victory,' or 'A Song of Victory,' or 'To the Victor,' for, since 'Death is swallowed up in victory,'[4] and it has been utterly destroyed by Him who says, 'I have overcome the world,'[5] and since all things have been conquered by Christ, and 'At his name every knee shall bend of those in heaven, on earth and under the earth,'[6] perhaps, the Holy Spirit is proclaiming beforehand in triumphal odes what things are reserved for us.

'Hear these things, all ye nations; give ear, all ye inhabitants of the world. All you that are earthborn, and you sons of men: both rich and poor together.'[7] The place of assembly is very great since the psalm summons to the hearing all the nations as well as all who fill the world with their dwellings. With this lofty proclamation it attracts, I believe, not only the earthborn and the sons of men, but also the rich and the poor, and invites them to listen. What sort of a watchtower stands up so high over all the earth, as to see all the nations from afar off and to embrace all the world with the eyes? What herald is so loud-voiced as to shout out so as to be heard by so many ears at the same time? What place is able to hold those assembling? How great and how wise is the teacher, that he finds instructions worthy of so great an assembly? Wait a little and you will learn that what follows is worthy of the promise. For, He who is assembling and summoning all by the proclamation is the Paraclete, the Spirit of truth, who brings together through prophets and apostles those who are saved; of whom, since 'Their sound hath gone forth into all the earth; and their words unto the ends of the world,'[8] therefore, it says: 'Hear, all ye nations, and all ye inhabitants of the world.' Wherefore, the Church has been collected from all

---

[4] 1 Cor. 15.54.
[5] John 16.33.
[6] Phil. 2.10.
[7] Ps. 48.2, 3.
[8] *Ibid* 18.5.

classes of life, in order that no one may be left without its aid.

There are three pairs of groups called, in which every race of men is included—pagans and the inhabitants of the world, earthborn and the sons of men, rich and poor. Whom, then, has it left out of the audience? Those who are outsiders to the faith were called through the calling of the pagans. Those who are inhabitants of the world are those who are in the Church. The earthborn are they who are wise in earthly matters and cleave to the pleasures of the flesh. The sons of men are they who exercise some care for and who train their reason, for reasoning is characteristic of man. The rich and the poor have their identity known from themselves: the first, exceeding in the possession of the necessities of life; the second, standing in want of them.

Since the Physician of souls did not come to call the just, but the sinners to repentance,[9] in his summons he placed first in each pair the group that was condemned. For, the pagans are worse than the inhabitants of the world, but nevertheless, they were preferred in the summons in order that those who were ill might first share the aid of the Physician. Again, the earthborn were placed before the sons of men, and the rich before the poor. The group which was despaired of and which held salvation difficult was summoned before the poor. Such is the kindness of the Physician; He gives a share of aid to the weaker first.

At the same time the sharing of the summons is a uniting in peace, so that those who were, up to this time, opposed to each other because of customs might, through gathering together, become habituated to each other in love. Let the rich man know that he has been summoned by the same proclamation as the poor man. 'Both rich and poor together,' he says. Leaving outside the superiority toward the more needy and the insolence of wealth, in this way enter into the Church of God. Let not the rich, then, treat the poor man disdainfully, nor

---
9 Cf. Matt. 9.13: 'For I have come to call sinners, not the just.'

the poor man cower beneath the power of the prosperous. And let not the sons of men despise the earthborn, nor again, the earthborn alienate themselves from them. Let the pagans become accustomed to the inhabitants of the world, and let the inhabitants of the world through charity take them to themselves as guest friends by covenants.

(2) 'My mouth shall speak wisdom: and the meditation of my heart understanding.'[10] Since, according to the Apostle, 'With the heart a man believes unto justice, and with the mouth profession of faith is made unto salvation,'[11] truly, the action of both in men suggests perfection; therefore, the sentence has brought the two together in the same place, the action of the mouth and the attention of the heart. If, indeed, goodness had not been stored up beforehand in the heart, how would he who did not possess it in secret bring forth the treasure through his mouth? And if, having good things in his heart, he would not make them public by speech, it will be said to him: 'Wisdom that is hid, and treasure that is not seen: what profit is there in them both?'[12] Therefore, for the profit of others let my mouth speak wisdom, and for our own progress let my heart meditate prudence.

'I will incline my ear to a parable; I will open my proposition on the psaltery.'[13] The prophet still introduces his own person, in order that his words may not be despicable as if brought forward from human invention. The things that I teach, he says, from the Spirit, these I proclaim to you, saying nothing of my own, nothing human; but, since I have been hearkening to the propositions of the Spirit, who hands down in mystery to us the wisdom of God, I am opening for you and am making manifest the proposition; moreover, I am opening not otherwise than through the psaltery. The psaltery is a musical instrument which gives out its sounds harmoniously

---

10 Ps 48.4.
11 Rom. 10.10
12 Ecclus. 20.32.
13 Ps. 48.5.

with the melody of the voice. Accordingly, the rational psaltery is opened especially at that time when actions in harmony with the words are displayed. And he is a spiritual psaltery who has acted and has taught. He it is who opens the proposition in the psalms, setting forth the possibility of the teaching from his own example. As, therefore, he is conscious that there is nothing incongruous or out of tune in his life, so with confidence he utters the following words: 'Why shall I fear in the evil day? The iniquity of my heel shall encompass me.'[14] By the evil day he means the day of judgment, concerning which it is said: 'The day of the Lord, an incurable day, will come upon all the nations.'[15] 'in which,' says the prophet, 'his own devices will beset each.'[16] At that time, then, because I have done nothing lawless on the way of life, I shall not fear the evil day. For, the signs of sinners will not stand around me nor beset me, in silent accusation bringing the proof against me. No one else will stand as accuser except yourself, or your deeds themselves, each standing near in its own form—adultery, theft, fornication—with the night, with the manner, with the peculiar circumstances characterizing it, and in general, each sin with its own character will be at hand bearing a clear reminder. The signs of sinners, then, will not beset me, 'because I inclined my ear to a parable, I opened my proposition on the psaltery.'

(3) 'They that trust in their own strength, and glory in the multitude of their riches.'[17] This sentence is directed by the prophet to two types of persons: to the earthborn and to the rich. He speaks to the first to overthrow their false notions due to their power; to the second, their pride due to the abundance of their possessions. You, he says, who trust in your

---
14 *Ibid.* 48.6.
15 Cf. Isa. 13.9: 'Behold, the day of the Lord shall come, a cruel day, and full of indignation, and of wrath, and fury, to lay the land desolate, and to destroy the sinners thereof out of it.'
16 Cf. Osee 7.2: 'Their own devices now have beset them about, they have been done before my face.'
17 Ps. 48.7.

own strength. These are the earthborn, who put their trust in strength of body and believe that human nature is sufficient for ably accomplishing what they wish. And you, he says, who trust in the uncertainty of riches, listen. You have need of ransoms that you may be transferred to the freedom of which you were deprived when conquered by the power of the devil, who taking you under his control, does not free you from his tyranny until, persuaded by some worthwhile ransom, he wishes to exchange you. And the ransom must not be of the same kind as the things which are held in his control, but must differ greatly, if he would willingly free the captives from slavery. Therefore, a brother is not able to ransom you. For, no man can persuade the devil to remove from his power him who has once been subject to him, not he, at any rate, who is incapable of giving God a propitiatory offering even for his own sins. How, then, will he have power to do this for the other? And what could he possess so great in this world that he would have a sufficient exchange price for a soul which is precious by nature, since it was made according to the image of its Creator? What labor of the present age is sufficient for the human soul as a means and provisions for the future life?

So far we have considered these things rather simply. Even if he seems to be one of the very powerful men in this life, even if he is surrounded with a great number of possessions, these words teach him to descend from such a notion and to humble himself under the mighty hand of God,[18] not to trust to a reputed power, and not to glory in the multitude of his riches. Nevertheless, it is possible to mount a little higher in thought, and for those who are trusting in their own power and those glorying in the multitude of their riches to take thought concerning the powers of the soul, inasmuch as not even the soul is complete in itself for salvation. For, if there should be anyone perfect among the sons of men, if the wisdom

---

18 Cf. 1 Peter 5.6· 'Humble yourselves, therefore, under the mighty hand of God, that he may exalt you in the time of visitation.'

of God is lacking, he will be reputed as nothing. Even if he will have acquired for himself a multitude of theories from the wisdom of the world, and have obtained by lot some wealth of knowledge, let him hear the whole truth of the matter: that every human soul has bowed down under the evil yoke of slavery imposed by the common enemy of all and, being deprived of the very freedom which it received from the Creator, has been led captive through sin. Every captive has need of ransoms for his freedom. Now, neither a brother can ransom his brother, nor can anyone ransom himself, because he who is ransoming must be much better than he who has been overcome and is now a slave. But, actually, no man has the power with respect to God to make atonement for a sinner, since he himself is liable for sin. 'All have sinned and have need of the glory of God. They are justified freely by his grace through the redemption which is in Christ Jesus'[19] our Lord.

(4) 'He shall not give to God his ransom, nor the price of the redemption of his soul.'[20] Do not, then, seek your brother for your ransoming, but Him who surpasses your nature, not a mere man, but the Man God Jesus Christ, who alone is able to give ransom to God for all of us, because 'God has set him forth as a propitiation by his blood through faith.'[21] Moses was the brother of Israel, and yet he was not able to redeem him. How, then, will any ordinary man be ransomed? Wherefore, the one sentence declares: 'No brother can redeem,' and the other with gravity adds interrogatively: 'Will man redeem?'[22] Moses did not free his people from sin, but he begged from God the exemption of the punishment due to sin. However, he was not able to give his own ransom when he was in sin, because, after the many and great wonders and signs which he saw, he uttered those words expressive of doubt: 'Hear me, ye rebellious and incredulous: Can we bring you

---
19 Rom. 3.23, 24.
20 Ps 48.8, 9.
21 Rom. 3.25.
22 Ps. 48.8 (Septuagint version).

forth water out of this rock?'[23] Therefore, the Lord, because of this word, said to Moses and Aaron: 'Because you have not believed me to sanctify me before the children of Israel, you shall not bring these people into the land which I have given them.'[24] 'He shall not, then, give to God his ransom.'

In fact, what can man find great enough that he may give it for the ransom of his soul? But, one thing was found worth as much as all men together. This was given for the price of ransom for our souls, the holy and highly honored blood of our Lord Jesus Christ, which He poured out for all of us; therefore, we were bought at a great price.[25] If, then, a brother does not redeem, will man redeem? But, if man cannot redeem us, He who redeems us is not a man. Now, do not assume, because He sojourned with us 'in the likeness of sinful flesh,'[26] that our Lord is only man, failing to discern the power of the divinity, who had no need to give God a ransom for Himself nor to redeem His own soul because 'He did no sin, neither was deceit found in his mouth.'[27] No one is sufficient to redeem himself, unless He comes who turns away the captivity of the people, not with ransoms nor with gifts, as it is written in Isaia,[28] but in His own blood.

Although we are not His brothers, but have become His enemies by our transgressions, He, who is not mere man, but God, after the freedom which He bestowed on us, also calls us His brothers. 'I will declare thy name,' He says, 'to my brethren.'[29] Now, He who has redeemed us, if you examine His nature, is neither brother nor man; but, if you examine His condescension to us through grace, He calls us brothers and descends to our human nature, who 'shall not give to God

---

23 Num. 20 10.
24 *Ibid.* 20.12.
25 Cf. 1 Cor. 6.20: 'For you have been bought at a great price.'
26 Rom. 8.3.
27 1 Peter 2.22.
28 Cf. Isa. 52.3: 'For thus saith the Lord: You were sold gratis, and you shall be redeemed without money.'
29 Ps. 21.23. St. Basil uses 'apangelô' in place of 'diēgésomai.'

his own ransom,' but that of the whole world. He does not need a ransom, but He Himself is the propitiation. 'For it was fitting that we should have such a high priest, holy, innocent, undefiled, set apart from sinners, and become higher than the heavens. He does not need to offer sacrifices daily (as the other priests did), first for his own sins, and then for the sins of the people.'[30] Then he says: 'And he labored forever, and shall live unto the end.'[31] His self-existence, His might, His untiring nature labored in this life, when 'wearied from the journey, he was sitting at the well.'[32]

(5) 'He shall not see destruction, when he shall see the wise dying'[33] (for, the Father will not permit His Holy One to see corruption[34]), when they shall die who boast of their wisdom which is ceasing. But, if you wish to take the words in reference to just men, remember the saying of Job: 'Man is born to labor,'[35] and again, that of the Apostle: 'I have labored more than any of them,'[36] and also: 'In many more labors.'[37] He, then, who has labored in this life will live unto the end; but he who spends his time in softness and all laxity because of his luxurious living, 'who is clothed in purple and fine linen, and feasting every day in splendid fashion,'[38] and flees the labors imposed by virtue, has neither labored in this life nor will he live in the future, but he will see life afar off, while being racked in the fire of the furnace. But, he who has sweated in numberless contests for the sake of virtue, and who, to attain it, has been proved in many more labors, he is the

---

30 Heb. 7.26, 27.
31 Ps. 48.9, 10.
32 John 4.6.
33 Ps. 48.11.
34 Cf. Ps. 15.10: 'Nor wilt thou give thy holy one to see corruption.' Cf. also Acts 2.27.
35 Job 5.7.
36 1 Cor. 15.10.
37 2 Cor. 11.23.
38 Cf. Luke 16.19: 'There was a certain rich man who used to clothe himself in purple and fine linen, and who feasted every day in splendid fashion.'

one who is going to live unto the end, just as Lazarus,[39] who labored much in afflictions, and just as Job, who was very weary in the contests against the adversary. 'For, there,' he says, 'the wearied are at rest.'[40] Therefore, the Lord calls to rest those who labor and are burdened.[41]

Now, how are those who are laboring in good works said to be burdened? Because 'Going they went and wept, casting their seeds. But coming they shall come with joyfulness, carrying their sheaves'[42] full of fruits, which were rendered to them in the proportion in which they were sown. So they are said to be burdened, who, because 'they sow bountifully, also reap bountifully,'[43] and with everlasting joy lay upon their shoulders the sheaves of spiritual fruits. He, then, who has been redeemed by God who gave the ransom for him, labored for this life, but, after this he will live unto the end. He also 'shall not see destruction, when he will see the wise dying.'[44]

He who chose the narrow and wearisome road instead of the smooth and open one, at the time of the visitation of God, when those who did not believe in the words of God, but went after the desires of their vain hearts, will be led away to everlasting punishment, he, I say, will not see the everlasting destruction, the eternal misery. But he says, indeed, that the wise are skilled in knavery, and Jeremia says concerning them: 'They are wise to do evil, but to do good they have no knowledge.'[45] Or, he says also, that the wise are the disciples of the perishing princes of this world, who, 'While professing to be wise, have become fools.'[46] For, 'The wisdom of this

---

39 Cf. Luke 16.20, 21: 'And there was a certain poor man, named Lazarus, who lay at his gate, covered with sores.'
40 Job 3.17.
41 Cf Matt. 11.28: 'Come to me, all you who labor and are burdened, and I will give you rest.'
42 Ps. 125.6, 7.
43 2 Cor. 9.6.
44 Ps. 48.11.
45 Jer. 4.22.
46 Rom. 1.22.

world is foolishness with God.'⁴⁷ And because this wisdom makes men foolish, God says that He will destroy the wisdom of the wise and will set at naught the prudence of the prudent. Therefore, these persuasions of falsely called knowledge provide a cause of death to those who receive them. But, this death he will not see who was redeemed by Him who was well pleased to save those trusting in the foolishness of His proclamation.

(6) 'The senseless and the fool shall perish together, and they shall leave their riches to strangers; and their sepulchres shall be their houses forever. Their dwelling places to all generations; they have called their lands by their names.'⁴⁸ Above, he called the wise by one general name, whom now subdividing, he says are senseless and fools. Openly he said that they are wise, borrowing the term from their own opinion. As he calls those gods, who are not so by nature, following the practice of those who are deceived, so also he calls the senseless and foolish, wise. Therefore, it is possible to separate the senseless from the foolish in our thinking.

The senseless is, in fact, one who lacks common sense and who is not clear-sighted as regards ordinary human affairs. In the same way, custom calls those prudent who in the affairs of life discern the useful and the harmful, as it is expressed in the Gospel: 'For, the children of this world are in relation to their own generation more prudent than are the children of the light.'⁴⁹ They are not absolutely more prudent, but in respect to the manner of their present life in the flesh. They are also called the ministers of injustice because of their prudence in the management of their life. According to this meaning, the prudent are also serpents, who prepare hiding places for themselves and who in dangers avoid in every manner blows on the head.

---

47 1 Cor. 3.19.
48 Ps. 48.11, 12.
49 Luke 16.8.

A fool is said to be one who does not have the qualities characteristic of man. These are an understanding of God the Father and the acceptance of the Word, which 'was in the beginning with God';[50] also the light which comes from the Holy Spirit. And those persons have this mind who are able to say with Paul: 'But we have the mind of Christ.'[51] Nevertheless, the practice of Scripture has used these words reversely, saying that the impious man is senseless, in the following words: 'The fool hath said in his heart: "There is no God," '[52] and again, he calls that which is harmful to life, foolish, as the Apostle does in speaking about those who fall into foolish and harmful desires.[53] Thus the senseless and the fool are borne down to one common end, destruction. And one can say that he who lives as the heathens has been called senseless, but he who conducts his life as a Jew according to the bare observance of the law is a fool. For, God said to this senseless man because of the godlessness present in him: 'Thou fool, this night do they demand thy soul of thee.'[54] But Israel which followed the flesh was called a fool according to the prophet, who says: 'And Ephraim was like a foolish dove; they called upon Egypt, and they went to the Assyrians.'[55] Since these were completely destroyed by their own ignorance, we aliens become the heirs of their wealth. The commandments are ours, the prophets and patriarchs are ours, and so are the just in the world ours. They who perished in their own folly left us their wealth.

However, the houses of these, of the senseless and of the fool, are their sepulchres forever. For, the sepulchres of those whose life is filled with works which are dead from every kind of sin, are their houses forever. He who is dead through

---

50 John 1.2.
51 1 Cor. 2.16.
52 Ps. 13.1.
53 Cf. 1 Tim 6.9: 'But those who seek to become rich fall into temptation and a snare and into many useless and harmful desires.'
54 Luke 12.20.
55 Osee 7.11.

sins does not dwell in a house, but a sepulchre, since his soul is dead. Now, Jacob, guileless in manner and simple, dwelt in a house. Concerning him it has been written that he was 'A plain and good man dwelling in a house.'[56] But, the thoroughly depraved man dwells in a sepulchre, and does not even lay down a foundation of penance because of his dead works, but is 'like a whited sepulchre, which outwardly is very conspicuous, but inwardly is full of dead men's bones and of all uncleanness.'[57] Therefore, when such a one speaks, he does not open his mouth in the word of God, but he has an open sepulchre as his throat. If, then, one who believes in Christ does not make his actions consistent with his faith, he, because he has given his attention to depraved doctrines and because he has perverted the meaning of Scripture, hews out in the rock a sepulchre for himself.

(7) 'Their dwelling places to all generations,' that is to say, the sepulchres are their houses forever. Then, explaining what he means by sepulchres, in order that he might show that he was speaking about the bodies in which the souls, destroyed by their wickedness, dwell, he added these words: 'Their dwelling places to all generations'; for, human bodies are always called dwelling places.

These also have called their lands by their names. For, the name of an impious man is not written in the book of the living, nor is he counted with the Church of the first-born which is numbered in heaven; but, their names remain on earth, because they have preferred this transient and briefly enduring life to the eternal dwellings. Do you not see how those who are building markets and schools in the cities, raising walls, constructing aqueducts, have placed their names on these earthly buildings? Already some, having stamped their names upon the herds of horses, have formed plans to

---
56 Gen. 25.27.
57 Cf. Matt. 23.27: 'Because you are like whited sepulchres, which outwardly appear to men beautiful, but within are full of dead men's bones and of all uncleanness.'

stretch out their memory for a long time in life; and having displayed magnificence in their sepulchres, they have put their names on their monuments. These are they who are wise in earthly things and who think that the present glory and remembrance by men are sufficient for them for happiness. Even if you should see one of those who are exceedingly proud in their falsely named knowledge and who devote themselves to certain depraved doctrines to which they have assented, and instead of the name of Christians, have named themselves from one of the heresiarchs, Marcion, or Valentinus, or one of those fashionable at present, understand that these have called their lands by their names, devoting themselves to destructible men and, in short, to earthly things.

(8) 'And man when he was in honor did not understand; he is compared to senseless beasts, and is become like to them. This way of theirs is a stumbling block to them: and afterwards they shall delight in their mouth.'[58] 'Man is a great thing, and pitiful man is something honorable,'[59] who has his honor in his natural constitution. For, what other things on earth have been made according to the image of the Creator?[60] To which of the animals that live on the land, or in the water, or in the air, has the rule and power over all things been given?[61] He has fallen a little below the dignity of the angels because of his union with the earthly body.[62] In fact, He made man from the earth,[63] 'And his ministers a flame of fire.'[64] But still, the power of understanding and recognizing their own Creator and Maker also belongs to men. 'And he breathed into his nos-

---

[58] Ps. 48.13, 14.
[59] Prov. 20 6 (Septuagint version).
[60] Cf. Gen. 1.27: 'God created man in his image. In the image of God he created him.'
[61] Cf. Gen. 1.28: 'Fill the earth and subdue it. Have dominion over the fish of the sea, the birds of the air, the cattle and all the animals that crawl on the earth.'
[62] Cf. Ps. 8.6: 'Thou hast made him a little less than the angels.'
[63] Cf. Gen. 2.7: 'Then the Lord God formed man out of the dust of the ground.'
[64] Heb. 1.7.

trils,'[65] that is to say, He placed in man some share of His own grace, in order that he might recognize likeness through likeness. Nevertheless, being in such great honor because he was created in the image of the Creator, he is honored above the heavens, above the sun, above the choirs of stars. For, which of the heavenly bodies was said to be an image of the most high God? What sort of an image of his Creator does the sun preserve? What the moon? What the other stars? They possess only inanimate and material bodies that are clearly discernible, but in which nowhere there is a mind, no voluntary motions, no free will; on the contrary, they are servile through the necessity imposed upon them, through which they always behave precisely the same in the same circumstances.

Man, then, having been advanced above these things in honor, did not understand; and neglected to follow God and to become like his Creator, and, becoming a slave of the passions of the flesh, 'He is compared to senseless beasts, and is become like to them': now he is like an amorous horse which neighs after his neighbor's wife,[66] now like a ravenous wolf,[67] lying in wait for strangers, but at another time, because of his deceit toward his brother, he makes himself like the villainous fox.[68] Truly, there is excessive folly and beastlike lack of reason, that he, made according to the image of the Creator, neither perceives his own constitution from the beginning, nor even wishes to understand such great dispensations which were made for his sake, at least, to learn his own dignity from them, but that he is unmindful of the fact that, throwing aside the image of the heavenly, he has taken up the image of the earthly. In order that he might not remain in sin, for his

---

65 Gen. 2.7.
66 Cf. Jer. 5.8: 'They are become as amorous horses and stallions: every one neighed after his neighbor's wife.'
67 Cf. Ezech. 22.27: 'Her princes in the midst of her, are like wolves ravening the prey to shed blood.'
68 Cf. Ezech. 13.4: 'Thy prophets, O Israel, were like foxes in the deserts.' Cf. also Luke 13.32.

sake 'The Word was made flesh, and dwelt among us,'[69] and He humbled Himself to such an extent as to become 'obedient to death, even to death on a cross.'[70] If you are not mindful of your first origin, because of the price paid for you, accept at least some idea of your dignity; look at that which was given in exchange for you and realize your own worth. You were bought with the precious blood of Christ; do not become a slave of sin. Understand your own honor, in order that you may not be made like the senseless beasts.

'This way of theirs is a stumbling block to them.'[71] God, who manages our affairs, hinders us from walking through evil, placing obstacles and hindrances for us, in order that, recoiling from an irrational life, 'afterwards we may delight in our mouth,' 'with the heart believing unto justice, and with the mouth making profession of faith unto salvation.'[72] Paul persecuted the Church of Christ, he plundered it, he pressed on his course toward evil;[73] afterwards he delighted in his mouth, declaring in the synagogue 'that this is the Christ.'[74]

(9) 'They are laid in hell like sheep: death shall feed upon them.'[75] He, who carries away into captivity those who are beastlike and who are compared to senseless herds, like the sheep, which have neither the intelligence nor the ability to defend themselves, since he is an enemy, has already cast them down into his own prison and has handed them over to death to feed. For, death tended them from the time of Adam until the administration of Moses,[76] until the true Shepherd came, who laid down His own life for His sheep and who thus,

---

69 John 1.14.
70 Phil. 2 8.
71 Ps. 48.14.
72 Cf. Rom. 10.10.
73 Cf. Acts 8.3: 'But Saul was harassing the Church; entering house after house, and dragging out men and women, he committed them to prison.'
74 Acts 9.22.
75 Ps. 48.15.
76 Cf. Rom. 5 14: 'Yet death reigned from Adam until Moses.'

making them rise together and leading them out[77] from the prison of hell to the early morning of the Resurrection, handed them over to the righteous, that is to say, to His holy angels, to tend them.

'And the just shall have dominion over them in the morning.'[78] With each of the faithful there is an angel associated, who is worthy to look upon the Father in heaven. These righteous, then, shall have dominion over them when they have been freed from their most bitter slavery and 'shall have dominion over them' when they have come forth 'in the early morning,' that is to say, when they are advancing into the rising of the light. Contemplate the whole series of the written words. 'Man when he was in honor did not understand; he is compared to senseless beasts.' He who through his condition has dignity, but who does not know himself because of the sin which dwells in him, was compared to senseless beasts. Then, because he estranged himself from the word of God, having become a brute beast, the enemy carried him away, like an untended sheep, and cast him into hell, handing him over to death to tend. Therefore, having been ransomed from there and freed from the evil shepherd, he says, 'The Lord ruleth me.'[79] And no longer death, but life; no longer a fall, but a resurrection; no longer deceit, but truth.

'And their help shall decay in hell.'[80] It may be that he is speaking about death, since it had not been able with all its help to retain those who were being herded by it because of the One who destroyed him who holds the power over death;[81] for all of their help is old and weak. At that time the help of those men who were deceived in mind and who were proud because of wealth and glory and power will be proved false.

---

77 Cf. John 10.3-18.
78 Ps 48 15.
79 *Ibid.* 22 1. The Rheims-Douay version of the Bible has: 'The Lord ruleth me.' There is a note in the Bible which says: '*Ruleth me.* In Hebrew, *Is my shepherd,* viz., to feed, guide, and govern me.'
80 *Ibid.* 48.15.
81 Heb. 2.14.

'In hell it shall decay' since their weakness is proved. Or, perhaps, the help of the just who have been redeemed by the Lord will be delayed in hell. For, not yet had they received the promises, since God had something better in view for us, namely, that those who preceded 'should not be perfected without us.'[82] 'But God will redeem my soul from the hand of hell, when he shall receive me.'[83] Clearly he predicts the descent of the Lord into hell, who will redeem the soul of the prophet along with the others, so that he may not remain there.

(10) 'Be not thou afraid, when a man shall be made rich, and when the glory of his house shall be increased.'[84] 'Be not thou afraid,' he says, 'when a man shall be made rich.' This proclamation is necessary to the inhabitants of the world, both to the earthborn and to the sons of men, to the rich and also to the poor. 'Be not thou afraid, when a man shall be made rich.' When you see, he says, the unjust man becoming rich and the just man poor, do not fear for yourself; do not be dismayed in mind, as if the providence of God is nowhere looking upon human affairs, or perhaps, somewhere there is a divine watchfulness, but it does not reach to places near the earth, so as to watch over our affairs; for, if there were a providence, it would be apportioning to each man what is proper to him, so that the just, who understand how to use wealth, would be rich, but the wicked, who have wealth as the instrument of their wickedness, would be poor.

Now, since there are many in the nations and among the earthborn who have such notions and who, because of the apparent inconsistency of the distribution of the fortunes of life, assume that the world is not the work of providence, the Scripture addresses these to calm their uninstructed emotion. In the very beginning it had also invited them to hear the doctrines. And surely, it alludes particularly to only the person

---

82 *Ibid.* 11.40.
83 Ps. 48.16.
84 *Ibid.* 48.17.

of the poor when it says: 'Be not thou afraid, when a man shall be made rich.' These, especially, need consolation, so as not to cower before the more powerful. For, it says, a rich man has no advantage when he is dying, since he is not able to take his wealth with him; at any rate, he gained only as much from the enjoyment of it as for his soul to be deemed happy in this life by flatterers. But, in dying he will not take all these possessions, it says; he will take only just the garment that covers his shame, and this, if it shall seem best to those of his household who are clothing him. He must be content to obtain a little earth; and, since this is given to him through pity by those who are burying him, they provide it for him out of reverence for our common human nature, not granting a favor to him, but honoring humanity. Do not, then, be faint about present affairs, but await that blessed and everlasting life. Then you will see that poverty and contempt and the lack of luxuries befall the just man for his good. And do not be troubled now about imagined good things, as though they were unjustly divided. You will hear how it will be said to a certain rich man: 'Thou in thy lifetime hast received good things,'[85] but to the poor man that he receives evils in his life. As a consequence, therefore, the latter is consoled, but the former suffers pain.

'And he will praise thee when thou shalt do well to him.'[86] Concerning the earthly man and him who thinks that the only good things are the advantages of this life—wealth and health and power—concerning him, indeed, he says that such a man will praise God when he has fared well, but in precarious circumstances he will utter a curse. Leaving the poor man, he now addresses his words to God; in the charge against the rich man he takes up the fact that he gives thanks to God only in prosperity, but no longer remains the same when some of the circumstances are darker. Such is also the accusation

---
85 Luke 16.25.
86 Ps. 48.19.

employed in the charge of the devil against Job,[87] that Job did not reverence the Lord gratuitously, but he had a reward for his piety—wealth and the rest of his possessions. Therefore, for a proof of the virtue of the man, God stripped him of what he had in order that the gratitude of the man toward God might shine through all things.

(11) 'You shall go in to the generations of your fathers.'[88] I believe that he is saying about the sinner that he knows God as much as the practice of his fathers has handed down, but that he has acquired nothing more by his own power of thinking, nor has he added to his knowledge of the truth by himself. You, O God, he says, are as near and he has as great an idea about You as existed in the generation of his fathers. And here he displays the idle, wholly earthly and carnal spirit of a man who rolls in riches and luxury and who has his mind choked with the cares of life. Therefore, 'he shall never see light.'[89] Having entrusted their guidance to blind teachers, they have deprived themselves of the advantage of light. This saying: 'He shall go in to the generations of his fathers,' also has some such meaning. That is to say, as regards those who are overtaken in an evil life and in doctrines coming, indeed, from their fathers, but alien to piety, not only will You punish them but You will also seek out the authors of the depraved teachings. This is what is meant by: 'He shall go in to the generations of his fathers.' Not only he who has evil thoughts about God is blameworthy, but also he who has led others to this destruction. Such are they who have received this evil from their forefathers, and who, because it has been strengthened by long continued custom, have difficulty in washing it out. 'He shall never see light.' For, they are sent 'Into the darkness outside, there will be the weeping, and the gnashing of teeth.'[90] This they endure according to the just

---
87 Job 1.9.
88 Ps. 48.20. St. Basil uses the second person in place of the third.
89 *Ibid.* 48.20.
90 Matt. 8.12.

judgment of God, since in this life they hated the light because they did evil.

'Man when he was in honor did not understand: he hath been compared to senseless beasts, and made like to them.'[91] An abominable statement! Man? He who is 'a little lower than the angels,'[92] concerning whom Solomon says: 'Man is a great thing, and pitiful man is something honorable'?[93] He, because he did not perceive his own dignity but bowed down to the passions of the flesh, 'hath been compared to senseless beasts, and made like to them.'

---

91 Ps. 48.21.
92 Heb. 2.7.
93 Prov. 20.6 (Septuagint version).

# HOMILY 20

*A Psalm of David on Hope in Defeat*

(ON PSALM 59)

WHEN I COMPARED the eagerness with which you listened and the inadequacy of my ability there came to my mind a certain similitude of a young child, already rather active but not yet weaned from its mother's milk, annoying the maternal breasts which were dry from weakness. The mother, even though she perceived that the sources of her milk were dry, being pulled and torn by him, offered him her breast, not in order that she might nourish the infant, but that she might make him stop crying. Accordingly, even though our powers have been dried up by this long and varied bodily illness, nevertheless, there is set before you, not a pleasure deserving of mention, but some things which satisfy, because your extraordinary love is strong enough to appease your longing for us even by means of our voice alone. Therefore, let the Church of God be saluted and let it be taught to say what we were just saying: 'Give us help from trouble: for vain is the salvation of man.'[1] So, perhaps, the meaning of the psalm does not at all permit us to allege weakness, if indeed affliction is a patron of help and not an occasion of infirmity. To those, then, who were rejected through sin, but then received again through the kindness of God, it is appropriate to say: 'O God, thou hast cast us off, and hast destroyed

---

1 Ps. 59.13.

us: thou hast been angry, and hast had mercy on us.'² Or rather, since the homily on the meaning of the psalm has fallen within the series, let us apply ourselves within due limits to the explanation of it.

(2) The history of the present psalm, in the very same words as the title,³ has not yet, even to this time, been found anywhere in the inspired narratives. However, accounts equivalent to it will be found by those who seek diligently for it in the second book of Kings, in which it is written: 'David defeated also Adarezer the son of Rohob king of Soba, when he went to extend his dominion over the river Euphrates. And David took from him a thousand chariots and seven thousand horsemen, and twenty thousand footmen. And David destroyed all the chariots: and only reserved of them one hundred chariots.'⁴ And a little later it says: 'And David reigned over all Israel: and David did judgment and justice to all his people. And Joab the son of Sarvia was over the army.'⁵ And after a little while: 'And the children of Ammon sent and hired the Syrians of Rohob, and the Syrians of Soba, twenty thousand men; then Joab saw that the battle was prepared against him, and he chose from all the sons of Israel, and put them in array against the Syrians. And all the auxiliaries of Adarezer saw that they were overcome by Israel, and they fled to Israel and served them.'⁶

We find that the title of the psalm agrees with this fragment of the history, except that the time of this inscription is that

---

2 *Ibid.* 59.3.
3 The title of this Psalm, comprising the first two verses of the Psalm and, according to Maran, omitted in the manuscripts possessed by the Benedictines and in the early Basel edition, is found only in the Paris edition, to which it was probably added to make St. Basil's explanations clearer. The title is as follows: 'Unto the end, for them that shall be changed, for the inscription of a title, to David himself, for doctrine, when he set fire to Mesopotamia of Syria and to Sobal; and Joab returned and slew of Edom, in the vale of the saltpits, twelve thousand men.'
4 2 Kings 8.3, 4 (Septuagint version).
5 *Ibid.* 8.15, 16.
6 *Ibid.* 10. 6, 9, 19 (Septuagint version).

at which David was most magnificent and illustrious for his brave deeds in war. Therefore, it is worth investigating how he begins with lamentations and dirges, when he ought to be very happy and cheerful because of his valorous deeds. Some of the words are the words of those who are celebrating a festival; others, of those who are sad. An epinicia is a speech for a general festival, not only for the soldiers, but also for the farmers, the merchants, the artisans, and all who share in the blessings of peace. How, then, 'O God, hast thou cast us off, and hast destroyed us'?[7] Truly, He has helped the victors. But, how did He destroy those whom He enriched so much, delivering to them arms and chariots, and horses, and subjects, and tributary lands, all Arabia, Phoenicia, and Mesopotamia?

It is worthwhile to notice whether the words contain some ingratitude. For, he had first destroyed Adarezer the king of Soba, and had taken from him a thousand chariots and seven thousand horsemen and twenty thousand infantrymen, and again, had subjected to himself the king of Syria, who was giving aid to the fallen one, and he had made him a tributary, and in one instant of time had slaughtered his twenty-two thousand. When the sons of Ammon were drawn up in battle line beside the gate of the city, he had conquered them in a third victory through Joab the commander in chief, who separating the force into two parts, met some in front, and going around, overpowered those in the rear. How is it that amidst such valorous deeds he is making such gloomy and sad utterances, saying: 'O God, thou hast cast us off, and hast destroyed us. Thou hast been angry, and hast had mercy on us'?

Certainly, the time of the writing of the inscription was this period of brave accomplishments, but the force of the writings has reference to the end [of time]; moreover, he says that the end is that which will pass away at the consummation of the world. Therefore, he says that the psalm has been written for those who will be changed.

---
7 Ps. 59.3.

It is possible to understand this in general in regard to the whole race of men, because the advantage from the psalm affects all. Those who are changed and those who will be changed are they who neither preserve the same condition of body nor continue always in the same opinion, but, who, when they are changed in body through the modifications due to the time of life, change their mind in regard to the various occurrences. Some of us, in fact, are children, and others, adolescents, while others have become men; and again, we are completely changed when we have grown old. Some of us are in more cheerful states of affairs; some of the others of us have experienced the harsher conditions of the times; some are ill; and others are enjoying themselves; some are in the married state; others in the midst of sorrows. Or, since the saying was not 'to those changed,' but, 'to those who will be changed,' and the words contain an indication of prophecy, because the tense is changed to the future, it is more consistent to understand that those who will be changed are those who, having given up the foolish customs of their fathers, will regulate the conduct of their lives by the strictness of the Gospel. Accordingly, the psalm was not written to the Jews of that time, but to us who will be changed, who are exchanging polytheism for piety, the error concerning idols for the knowledge of Him who made us, who choose lawful self-control instead of lawless pleasure, who substitute a psalm and fasting and prayer for the flutes and choruses and drunkenness. If, then, someone would say that the psalm was written for us, he would not err from the truth. Therefore also, the divine oracles are ours, and in the Church of God they are read aloud at each assembly, like gifts sent by God, nourishment for the soul, as it were, furnished through the Spirit.

But, the psalm was also written for an inscription on a column; that is to say, the hearing of it should not be just casual and you should not engrave these things on your mind for the brief time of memory, then permit them to be confused and obliterated in the same way as things written on perishable wood meet with speedy destruction; but you should keep them recorded on your mind as on a column, that is, settled immovably and steadfastly in your memory for all time. And, if the Jew rejects us as strangers to what has been written, from the very writings let us shame him, revealing the absence of discrimination in the general call; the manner in which it brings together things that are separated, calls together those which are far off, and makes the many into one through faith in Christ. 'Galaad is mine,' he says, 'and Manasses is mine.'[8] He mentioned Ephraim, and he added Juda, and also counted Moab. He threatens to enter into Idumea, and he proclaims the subjection of all at the same time: 'To me the foreigners are made subject.'[9]

(3) Therefore, 'O God, thou hast cast us off.' You have cast off those who in proportion to their sins removed themselves to a distance from You. You have destroyed the accumulations of our wickedness, doing good to us because of our weakness. You were angry, since 'we were by nature children of wrath,'[10] having no hope, and being without God in the world. You had mercy on us when 'You set forth Your only-begotten Son as a propitiation for our sins,'[11] in order that in His blood we might find redemption. We would not know that we were having these kindnesses done to us, unless 'Thou hast made us drink the wine of sorrow.'[12] By wine he means the words which lead the hardened heart to conscious perception.

'Thou hast given a sign to them that fear thee: that they may flee from before the bow.'[13] Moses caused the doorposts

---

8 *Ibid.* 59.9.
9 *Ibid.* 59.10.
10 Eph. 2.3.
11 Cf. Rom. 3.25· 'in Christ Jesus, whom God has set forth as a propitiation by his blood through faith.' Cf. also 1 John 4.10.
12 Ps. 59.5.
13 *Ibid.* 59.6.

of the Israelites to be signed with the blood of a lamb;[14] but You have given us a sign, the blood itself of a Lamb without blemish, slain for the sin of the world. And Ezechiel says that a sign was given on the foreheads of the persons. For he says: 'Go ye after him and strike; do not spare, nor be ye moved with pity. Utterly destroy old and young, maidens, children, and women; but all on whom there is the sign do not approach.'[15]

'God hath spoken in his holy place: I will rejoice, and I will divide Sichem.'[16] Sichem is a special place given by Jacob to Joseph, a type of the covenant which seems to have been presented to Israel alone. Accordingly, I shall bring this special covenant and inheritance of the people for apportionment, and I shall make it common to all the rest. Therefore, after the covenant has been divided for all, and the advantage from it has been made common to all those who are having kindness done them by God, then, too, the deep valley of the tabernacles will be measured; that is to say, the whole world, as if by certain lots, will be divided by dioceses in each place. At that time also He will join together things that are far apart, He 'who makes peace whether on the earth or in the heavens,'[17] 'and he who has broken down the intervening wall of the enclosure will make both one.'[18]

(4) 'Galaad is mine, and Manasses is mine.'[19] Galaad is a grandson of Manasses; this is said in order that he may show that the succession of the patriarchs, from whom is Christ according to the flesh, comes down from God. 'And Ephraim

---

14 Cf Exod. 12.7: 'And they shall take of the blood thereof [of the lamb], and put it upon both the side posts, and on the upper doorposts of the houses, wherein they shall eat it.'
15 Ezech. 9.5, 6 (Septuagint version).
16 Ps. 59.8.
17 Col. 1.20
18 Cf. Eph. 2.14: 'For he himself is our peace, he it is who has made both one, and has broken down the intervening wall of the enclosure, the enmity, in his flesh.'
19 Ps. 59.9.

# HOMILY 20

is the support of my head. Juda is my king.'[20] He will join together by agreement the parts that are severed. 'Moab is the pot of my hope.'[21] Or 'a pot for washing,' another of the interpreters says; or 'a pot of security'; that is to say, the excommunicated man, who has been forbidden with threats to enter the Church of the Lord. For, the Moabite and the Ammonite will not enter until the third and until the tenth generation and until everlasting time.[22] Nevertheless, since baptism possesses remission for sins, and produces security for the debtors, he, showing the deliverance through baptism and the affection for God, says: 'Moab is a pot for washing,' or 'a pot of security.' Therefore, all 'foreigners are made subject,'[23] bowing down under the yoke of Christ; for this reason He will set His shoe in Edom.[24] The shoe of the divinity is the God-bearing flesh, through which He approaches men. In this hope, pronouncing blessed, the time of the coming of the Lord, the prophet says: 'Who will bring me into the fortified city.'[25] Perhaps, he means the Church, a city, indeed, because it is a community governed conformably to laws; and fortified, because of the faith encompassing it. Whence one of the interpreters gave out a very clear translation: 'Into a city fortified all around.' Who, then, will permit me to see this great spectacle, God living among men? These are the words of the Lord: 'Many prophets and just men have longed to see what you see, and they have not seen it.'[26]

(5) 'Give us help from trouble.'[27] Let us not seek help from strength, nor from a good condition of body; let us not ask to obtain succor from anyone of those among men who are con-

---

20 *Ibid.*
21 *Ibid.* 59.10.
22 Cf. 2 Esd 13.1: 'And therein it was found written, that the Ammonites and the Moabites should not come in to the church of God for ever.'
23 Ps. 59.10.
24 Cf. *Ibid.*
25 *Ibid.* 59.11.
26 Matt. 13.17.
27 Ps. 59.13.

sidered renowned. Not in the amount of money, not in the pride of power, not in the height of glory is victory gained, but the Lord freely gives His help to those who seek Him through excessive affliction. Such was Paul,[28] who made his afflictions his boast. Therefore, he was able to say: 'When I am weak, then I am strong.'[29] 'Give us, therefore, O Lord, help from trouble,' since 'tribulation works out endurance, and endurance tried virtue, and tried virtue, hope. And hope does not disappoint.'[30] Do you see where affliction leads you? To hope that does not disappoint. Are you ill? Be of good cheer, because 'whom the Lord loves, he chastises.'[31] Are you poor? Rejoice, because the blessings of Lazarus will receive you in turn.[32] Are you held in dishonor because of the name of Christ? You are blessed, because your shame will be changed into the glory of an angel. Let us persuade ourselves, brothers, in the time of temptation not to run away to human hopes, nor to seek assistance for ourselves from them, but in tears and in groanings and in assiduous prayers and in strenuous watchfulness to make our petitions. For, that man receives help from troubles who despises human help as vain and stands firmly on the hope that is founded on Him who is able to save us, in Christ Jesus our Lord, to whom be glory and power forever. Amen.

---

28 Rom. 5 3.
29 2 Cor. 12.10.
30 Rom. 5.3-5.
31 Heb. 12.6.
32 Cf. Luke 16.22: 'And it came to pass that the poor man died and was borne away by the angels into Abraham's bosom.'

## HOMILY 21

*A Psalm of David for Idithun and
a Body of Singers*

(ON PSALM 61)

WE KNOW TWO PSALMS with the title 'For Idithun,' the thirty-eighth and this one that we have at hand. And we think that the composition of the work is owed to David; that it was given to Idithun for his use that he might correct the passions of his soul, and also as a choral song to be sung in the presence of the people. Through it, also, God was glorified, and those who heard it amended their habits. Now, Idithun was a singer in the temple, as the history of the Paralipomenon testifies to us, saying: 'And after them Heman and Idithun sounded the trumpets and played on the cymbals and all kinds of musical instruments to sing praises to God.'[1] And a little later it says: 'Moreover David the king and the chief officers of the army separated for the ministry the sons of Asaph, and of Heman, and of Idithun: to prophesy with harps, and with psalteries, and with tympana.'[2]

Both psalms treat, for the most part, of patience, through which the passions of the soul are reduced to order, all arrogance is banished, and humility is acquired. For, it is impossible for anyone who has not accepted the lowest and last place with respect to all, ever to be able, when abused, to

---

1 1 Par. 16.41, 42.
2 *Ibid.* 25.1.

conquer his wrath, or when afflicted, to rise superior to his trials through patience. He who has acquired consummate humility, since he has condemned beforehand his greater vileness, will not be disturbed in soul in the midst of reproaches by words of disgrace; but, if he hears 'poor man,' he knows that he is a poor man and in want of all things, and that he has need of daily sustenance from the Lord; and, if he hears 'lowborn and obscure,' he has already accepted in his heart the fact that he was made from clay. Therefore, in regard to that he says: 'I said: I will take heed to my ways,'[3] and he explains the rebellion of the sinner and his own patience. 'When the sinner,' he says, 'stood against me, I was dumb, and was humbled, and kept silence from good things.'[4] Then he continues, saying: 'And indeed all things are vanity: every man living,'[5] then, 'He storeth up; and he knoweth not for whom he shall gather these things.'[6]

In the proposed psalm he begins in the form of a question, speaking, as it were, to his own soul, as if in consequence of the words previously spoken. In order that the soul, subjected to the pride of the flesh, may not be provoked to anger and sadness, 'Why,' he says, 'do I make my soul, which was entrusted by its Creator, God, with the rule over the body and its emotions, the slave of evil passions?' Accordingly, there is need to rule the passions and to serve God. It is impossible for it to be ruled by sin and by God; but, it must prevail over the evil and be subjected to the Lord of all things. Therefore, the prophet, threatening him who brings on the temptations and stirs up a great throng of evils in him and who has a great desire to enslave the will of the spirit and subject it to the flesh, as if refuting his idea against him as vain, says this: 'Why do you force me to serve those whom it is not right? I have a Lord. I truly know my King.'

---

[3] Ps. 38.2.
[4] Ibid. 38.2, 3.
[5] Ibid. 38.6.
[6] Ibid. 38.7.

## HOMILY 21

(2) 'Shall not my soul be subject to God? For from him is my salvation.'[7] He tells the reason for his desire for subjection—because his salvation is from God. It is characteristic of an artisan to take thought for the safety of his works of art. Or, by the words, 'from him is salvation,' since he foresees prophetically that there will be the future grace of the Incarnation of the Lord, he says that it is necessary to serve God and to love Him, who first directed such kindness toward the human race, as 'not even to spare His own Son, but to deliver Him for us all.'[8] Now, it is a custom in Scripture to call the Christ of God, salvation, as somewhere Simeon says: 'Now thou dost dismiss thy servant, O Lord, because my eyes have seen thy salvation.'[9] Therefore, let us subject ourselves to God, because from Him is salvation. He explains what salvation is. It is not some mere active force, which provides us with a certain grace for deliverance from weakness and for the good health of our body. But, what is salvation?

'For he is my God and my savior: he is my protector, I shall be moved no more.'[10] The Son, who is from God, is our God. He Himself is also Savior of the human race, who supports our weakness, who corrects the disturbance that springs up in our souls from temptations. 'I shall be moved no more.' Humanly he confesses his disturbance. 'More.' For, it is impossible that there should not be some disturbance from temptations in the soul of man. While we are committing small and few sins, we are in a way mildly disturbed, being tossed about like the leaves by a gentle breeze; but, when our vices are more and greater, in proportion to the increase of our sins the disturbance is wont to be intensified. And some are moved more; but others, to the extent of being thrown down, even the self-rooted being overturned, whenever the spirits of evil, more

---

7 *Ibid.* 61.2.
8 Cf. Rom. 8.32: 'He who has not spared even his own Son but has delivered him for us all.'
9 Luke 2.29, 30.
10 Ps. 61.3.

violently than any hurricane, sever the roots, as it were, of the soul, by which it was supported through faith in God. I, accordingly, he says, was disturbed as a man; but, I shall not be disturbed more, because I am supported by the right hand of the Savior.

(3) 'How long do you rush in upon a man? you all kill, as if you were thrusting down a leaning wall, and a tottering fence.'[11] Again the homily fights against the depraved ministers of the devil, charging a lack of moderation in the snares laid by them. Certainly, men are weak animals; but you rush on, not content with the first attack, but you bring on a second and a third, until you subdue to such an extent the soul which has fallen beside you that it is very similar to a leaning wall and a tottering fence. Now, a wall, as long as it maintains an upright position, remains steadfast; but, when it leans, since it has been weakened, it needs must fall. For, heavy bodies, if united into one, stand erect after inclining, but those which are composed of several parts no longer admit of correction when they endure pressure on one part. The homily shows, therefore, that the nature of man, which is composite, was one inaccessible to plots for a second fall. 'You are God's tillage, God's building,'[12] it is said. The enemy has shaken down this building; the Craftsman has repaired the rents made in it. Thus the fall was necessary because of sin, but the resurrection was great because of immortality.

'But they have thought to cast away my price; they ran in thirst: they blessed with their mouth, but cursed with their heart.'[13] The price of man is the blood of Christ: 'You have been bought,' it is said, 'with a price; do not become the slaves of men.'[14] The soldiers of the evil one planned, there-

---

11 *Ibid.* 61.4.
12 1 Cor. 3.9.
13 Ps. 61.5. St. Basil interprets 'édramon' in the third person plural. Both the Vulgate and the English translation consider it the first person singular.
14 1 Cor. 7.23.

fore, to render this price useless to us, leading again into slavery those who had been once freed. 'They ran in thirst.' He is speaking of the eager plots of the demons, because they run against us, thirsting for our destruction. 'They blessed with their mouth, but cursed with their heart.' There are many who approve evil deeds and say that the witty person is charming; the foulmouthed, statesmanlike; the bitter and irascible they name as one not to be despised; the niggardly and selfish they praise as thrifty; the spendthrift, as bountiful; the fornicator and lewd, as a man devoted to enjoyment and ease; and, in general, they gloss over every evil with the name of the proximate virtue. Such men bless with their mouth, but curse with their heart. For, by the auspiciousness of the words, they bring every curse upon their life, making themselves liable to action at the eternal Judgment because of those things which they approved.

Again, he speaks to his soul, urging its obedience to God. 'But, be thou, O my soul,' he says, 'subject to God: for from him is my patience.'[15] He shows the magnitude of the temptations, and he speaks the words of the Apostle, that He will not permit us to be tempted beyond what we are able to bear.[16] 'From him is my patience.'

(4) 'In God is my salvation and my glory; he is the God of my help, and my hope is in God.'[17] Blessed is he who exults in none of the lofty things of life, but regards God as his glory; who holds Christ as his boast; who is able to say, according to the Apostle: 'But as for me, God forbid that I should glory save in the cross of Christ.'[18] Many are glorified in body, who devote their time to gymnastic contests, or, on the whole, who are vigorous in the flower of their age; and many, because of their valor in the wars, who consider the murdering of those

---

15 Ps. 61.6.
16 Cf. 1 Cor. 10.13: 'God is faithful and will not permit you to be tempted beyond your strength.'
17 Ps. 61.8.
18 Gal. 6.14.

of the same race bravery. In fact, rewards in wars, and the trophies raised by a general and by cities, are according to the magnitude of the slaughter. Others are glorified because they put walls around cities; and others, because of the structures of the aqueducts and the buildings of the great gymnasia. That man who has spent his wealth in fighting wild beasts and who exults in vain words of the people, is puffed up with the praises and thinks himself something great, having his glory in his shame.[19] He even shows his sin inscribed on tablets in conspicuous places of the city. Another is extolled for his wealth; another, because he is a skillful and invincible orator, or he is acquainted with the wisdom of the world. It is proper to pity the glory of all these, and to deem happy those who make God their glory. For, if a certain one thinks he is something great because he is the servant of a king and is held in great honor by him, how much ought you to exalt yourself, because you are a servant of the great King and are called by Him to the closest intimacy, having received the Spirit of the promise, so that, sealed with His approval, you are shown to be a son of God?

Since he is conscious of the use of sincere hope in God, he invites the people to a zeal equal to his own, saying: 'Trust in him, all ye congregation of people; pour out your hearts before him.'[20] It is impossible for us to become capable of divine grace, unless we have driven out the evil passions which have preoccupied our souls. I know doctors who do not give the salutary medicines before they have drained out by means of an emetic the matter that was causing the sickness, which the intemperate had stored up in themselves through a bad diet. Even a vessel which has been filled before with some ill smelling liquid, unless it has been washed out will not admit an inpouring of perfume. Therefore, it is necessary for that

---

19 Cf. Phil. 3.19: 'their glory is in their shame, they mind the things of earth.'
20 Ps. 61.9.

which first had possession to be poured out, in order that it may be able to contain that which is being brought in.

'But vain are the sons of men.'[21] He knew that not all follow his instruction nor permit themselves to hope in God, but that they have their hope in the follies of life. Therefore, he says: 'But vain are the sons of men, the sons of men are liars.'[22] Why vain? Because they are liars. Where, especially, is their deceit proved? 'In the balances used for defrauding,'[23] he says. In what sort of balances does he mean? All men do not weigh in the balance, do they? All men are not wool sellers, or butchers, are they? Or do not handle gold or silver, or in general exert themselves about these materials which the merchants are accustomed to exchange by means of scales and weights, do they? But there is a large class of artisans, which does not need scales at all for its work; and there are many sailors, and many who are always engaged about courts of justice and the duty of ruling, among whom there is deceit, but the deceit is not practiced through scales. What is it, then, that he means? That there is a certain balance constructed in the interior of each of us by our Creator, on which it is possible to judge the nature of things. 'I have set before thee life and death, good and evil,'[24] two natures contrary to each other; balance them against each other in your own tribunal; weigh accurately which is more profitable to you: to choose a temporary pleasure and through it to receive eternal death, or, having chosen suffering in the practice of virtue, to use it to attain everlasting delights.

Men, then, are liars, since they have destroyed the tribunals of their soul, and the prophet deems them unhappy, for he says: 'Woe to you that call darkness light and light darkness;

---

21 *Ibid.* 61.10.
22 *Ibid.*
23 *Ibid.* (Septuagint version).
24 Deut. 30.15 (Septuagint version).

that call bitter sweet and sweet bitter.'[25] For me, he says, the present; who, indeed, knows the future? You weigh badly, choosing evils instead of blessings, preferring empty things to the genuine, placing the temporary before the eternal, electing passing pleasure for unending and unbroken joy. Therefore, 'the sons of men are liars in the balances used for defrauding.' They wrong, first, themselves, and then, their neighbors; for, since they are the wicked advisers to themselves in their action, they are a bad example to the others. It is not possible for you to say on the day of Judgment, 'I did not know the good.' Your own balances, which provide sufficiently the discrimination between good and bad, are presented to you. We test the weight of the body by the inclinations of the balance, but we determine the choices of our life by the free judgment of our soul. This we call the balance because it can incline equally both ways.

(5) 'Trust not in inquity, and covet not robberies.'[26] Above he said: 'Trust in him, all ye congregation of people.' He saw the hesitation in their obedience, and he declared: 'But vain are the sons of men.' Again, he bids them not to trust in iniquity. He who judges that wealth, collected unjustly, is sufficient means for him to be strong and powerful is like a sick man who alleges good health in serious illness. 'Trust not in iniquity.' This itself hinders you in every good work. 'And covet not robberies.' He exhorts us not to be covetous of other men's possessions.

'If riches flow around, set not your heart upon them.'[27] If you see anyone exceedingly rich, do not deem his life happy. If from all sides and from plenteous sources money flows around you, do not accept a superabundance of it. 'If riches flow around.' Admire the expression. The nature of riches is

---

25 Cf. Isa. 5.20: 'Woe to you that call evil good, and good evil: that put darkness for light, and light for darkness: that put bitter for sweet, and sweet for bitter.'
26 Ps. 61.11.
27 *Ibid.*

a state of flux. They run past their possessors more swiftly than the torrent; they are wont at one time to pass by one, and again, another. As a river, swept down from a height, approaches those standing on the bank, it at the same time reaches and immediately withdraws, so also the satisfaction from riches has a very swift and slippery presence, being wont to change time and again from some to others. Today the field belongs to this man, tomorrow, to another, and a little after, to still another. Look at the houses in the city, how many names they have received in succession since they were constructed, being called at one time from the name of one possessor, at another, from that of another. And gold, always flowing through the hand of him who possesses it, passes to another, and from him to still another. You are more able, when you have caught some water, to hold it in your hand, than to preserve riches lastingly for yourself. So it has been well said: 'If riches flow around, set not your heart upon them.' Do not be further affected in your soul, but accept the use of them, not as if loving exceedingly and admiring some good thing, but as if choosing its service as something practical.

Then he brings up a decision for all that was said, not now from his own words, but one which he heard from God Himself. 'God hath spoken once, these two things have I heard,'[28] he says. And let it not disturb anyone that what was said is, as it were, incredible, namely, that God spoke once and the prophet heard two things. For, it is possible for someone to speak once, but for the things spoken on the one occasion to be many. A certain man, in fact, when he met someone once, discussed many things, and he who heard his words is able to say: 'He talked with me once, but he spoke about many things.' This is what was meant on the present occasion, the manifestation of God occurred to me once, but, there are two matters of which He talked. He did not say: 'God spoke of one thing, but I heard these two'; for, thus the statement would seem to

---
28 *Ibid.* 61.12.

have some discrepancy in it. What were the two things which he heard? 'That power belongeth to God, and mercy to thee, O Lord.'[29] God is powerful, he says, in judgment, and likewise merciful. Trust not, therefore, in iniquity, do not hand yourself over to riches; do not choose vanity; do not carry around the corrupt tribunal of your soul. Knowing that our Lord is mighty, fear His strength, and do not despair of His kindness. Now, in order that we may not do wrong, fear is good; and in order that he who has once slipped into sin may not throw himself away through despair, the hope of mercy is good. For, power belongs to God, and mercy is from Him.

'For thou wilt render to every man according to his works.'[30] 'For with what measure you measure, it shall be measured back to you.'[31] Have you afflicted your brother? Expect the same. Did you snatch away the means of your inferiors, maltreat the poor, cover with disgrace by reproaches, blackmail, make false accusations, tamper with other's marriages, swear falsely, change your ancestral boundaries, attack the possessions of orphans, oppress widows, prefer the present pleasure to the blessings in the promises? Expect the reciprocal measure of these. In fact, what each one sows, such also shall he reap.[32] And yet, if you have performed any good acts, expect also manifold compensations in return for these. 'For thou wilt render to every man according to his works.' If you remember this sentence throughout all your life, you will be enabled to flee many sins, in Christ Jesus our Lord, to whom be glory and power forever. Amen.

---

29 *Ibid.* 61.13.
30 *Ibid.*
31 Matt. 7.2.
32 Cf. Gal. 6.8: 'For what a man sows, that he will also reap.'

# HOMILY 22

*A Psalm of Thanksgiving
for Deliverance from Death*

(ON PSALM 114)

HAVING ARRIVED so long in advance at these sacred precincts of the martyrs, you have persevered from midnight until this midday appeasing the God of the martyrs with hymns, while awaiting our arrival. The reward, therefore, is ready for you, who prefer honor for the martyrs and the worship of God to sleep and rest. But, if we must undertake a defense of ourselves because of our delay and, to a great extent, desertion of you, we shall tell the cause. It is, that, as we administer a church of God, equal in honor to this, which is separated by no short distance from you, we spent in it the earlier part of the day. Since the Lord has permitted me to perform the liturgy for them, while at the same time not altogether disappointing your love, return thanks with us to the Benefactor, who guides by His invisible power this visibly weak body of ours. In order that we may not be distressed at detaining you further, after discoursing briefly on that psalm which we found you singing on our arrival, and feeding your souls with the word of consolation according to the power that is ours, we shall dismiss all of you for the care of your bodies. Now, what was it that you were singing?

'I have loved,' he says, 'because the Lord will hear the voice of my prayer.'¹ It is not in the power of everyone to say: 'I have loved,' but of him who is already perfect and beyond the fear of slavery, and who has been formed in the spirit of adoption as sons. He does not add to 'I have loved,' the word 'someone,' but we supply in thought 'the God of the universe.' For, that which is properly beloved is God, since they define 'beloved' as that at which all things aim. Now, God is a good, and the first and most perfect of good things. Therefore, I have loved God Himself who is the highest of objects to be desired, and I have received with joy sufferings for His sake. What these things are, he goes through in detail a little later— the pangs of death, the dangers of hell, the affliction, the pain, all things whatsoever that are desirable to him because of the love of God—and he shows forth the hope which was stored up for those who receive sufferings for the sake of piety. For, I did not endure the contests, he says, contrary to my will, nor by force or constraint, but, I accepted the sufferings with a certain love and affection, so that I was able to say: 'Because for thy sake we are killed all the day long.'² And these words seem to have equal weight with the words of the Apostle and to be spoken by him with the same feeling, 'Who shall separate us from the love of Christ? Shall tribulation, or distress, or persecution, or hunger, or nakedness, or danger, or the sword?'³ Therefore, I have loved all these things, knowing that I endure the dangers for the sake of piety under the hands of the Lord of the universe who sees and bestows the reward. 'Because the Lord will hear the voice of my prayer.'⁴ So, each one of us is able to perform the difficult tasks enjoined by the commandments whenever he displays his conduct of life to the God of the universe as if to a spectator.

'Because he hath inclined his ear unto me.'⁵ 'He inclined,'

---

1 Ps. 114.1.
2 *Ibid.* 43.22.
3 Rom. 8.35.
4 Ps. 114.1.
5 *Ibid.* 114.2.

he said, not that you might take some corporeal notion about God having ears and inclining them to a gentle voice, as we do, putting our ear close to those who speak low, so that by the nearness we may perceive what is said, but he said, 'He inclined,' in order that he might point out to us his own weakness. Because through kindness He came down to me while I was lying on the ground, as if, when some sick man is not able to speak clearly because of his great weakness, a kind physician, bringing his ear close, should learn through the nearness what was necessary for the sick man. Therefore, 'He hath inclined his ear unto me.' The divine ear, indeed, does not need a voice for perception; it knows how to recognize in the movements of the heart what is sought. Or, do you not hear how Moses, although he said nothing, but met the Lord with his inexpressible groanings, was heard by the Lord, who said: 'Why criest thou to me?'[6] God knows how to hear even the blood of a just man,[7] to which no tongue is attached and of which no voice pierces the air. The presence of good works is a loud voice before God.

'And in my days I will call upon him.'[8] If we have prayed on one day, or if in one hour for a brief time we were saddened by our sins, we are carefree as if we had already made some compensation for our wickedness. However, the holy man says that he is disclosing his confession which is measured by the whole time of his life, for he says: 'In all my days I will call upon him.' Then, in order that you may not think that he called upon God because he was fortunate in this life and because all his affairs were successful, he describes in detail the magnitude and difficulty of the circumstances in which, when he was involved, he did not forget the name of God.

'The sorrows of death,' he says, 'have compassed me; and the

---

6 Exod. 14.15.
7 Cf. Gen. 4.10: 'The voice of your brother's blood cries to me from the ground.'
8 Ps. 114.2.

perils of hell have found me.'⁹ Properly the sorrows of death have been agreed upon as the pains of childbirth, when the womb, distended with its burden, thrusts out the fetus; then, the generative parts, being compressed and stretched around the fetus by spasms and contractions of the muscles, produce in the mothers the sharpest pains and most bitter pangs. He transferred the name of these pains to those which besiege the animal in the division of soul and body at death. He says that he has suffered nothing moderately, but that he has been tried even to the sorrows of death and has arrived at the peril of the descent into hell. Now, did he endure only these things for which he is exalted, or did he endure these things frequently and unwillingly? Nothing that is forced is praiseworthy. But, look at the nobility of nature of the athlete. When 'the sorrows of death compassed me, and the perils of hell found me,' I was so far from succumbing to these trials that I willingly proposed to myself even much greater trials than these. Trouble and sorrow, I, as it were, willingly devised for myself; I was not unwillingly seized by them.

Indeed, in the preceding words we read: 'The perils of hell have found me,' but here, 'I met with trouble and sorrow.'¹⁰ For, since I was found to be unyielding there in regard to what was brought on by the tempter, in order that I might show the abundance of my love toward God, I added trouble to trouble, and sorrow to sorrow, and I did not rise up against these sufferings by my own power, but I called upon the name of the Lord. Such is also the declaration of the Apostle, who says: 'But in all these things we overcome because of him who has loved us.'¹¹ For he conquers who does not yield to those who lead on by force, but he is more than conqueror, who voluntarily invites sorrows for a demonstration of his endurance. Let him who was in some sin to death¹² say: 'The sor-

---

9 *Ibid.* 114.3.
10 *Ibid.*
11 Rom. 8.37.
12 Cf. 1 John 5.17: 'All lawlessness is sin, and there is a sin unto death.'

rows of death have compassed me.' 'For everyone,' he says, 'who commits sin has been born of the devil.'[13] Now, when I, he says, committed sin, and was pregnant by death, then also I was found by the perils of hell. How, then, did I cure myself? Because I devised trouble and sorrow through penance. I contrived for myself a suffering of penance proportionate to the greatness of the sin, and thus I dared to call upon the name of the Lord. But, what was it that I said? 'O Lord, deliver my soul.'[14] I am held in this captivity, so You give ransom for me, and deliver my soul.

'The Lord is merciful and just.'[15] Everywhere Scripture joins justice with the mercy of God, teaching us, that neither the mercy of God is without judgment nor His judgment without mercy. Even while He pities, He measures out His mercies judiciously to the worthy; and while judging, He brings forth the judgment, having regard to our weakness, repaying us with kindness rather than with equal reciprocal measurement.

'And our God showeth mercy.'[16] Mercy is an emotion experienced toward those who have been reduced beyond their desert, and which arises in those sympathetically disposed. We pity the man who has fallen from great riches into the uttermost poverty, him who has been overthrown from the peak of vigor of body to extreme weakness, him who gloried in the beauty and grace of body and who has been destroyed by most shameful passions. Though we at one time were held in glory, living in paradise, yet, we have become inglorious and humble because of our banishment; 'our God showeth mercy,' seeing what sort of men we have become from what we were. For this reason He summoned Adam with a voice of mercy, saying: 'Adam, where are you?'[17] He who knows all things was not

---

13 Cf. 1 John 3.8: 'He who commits sin is of the devil.'
14 Ps. 114.4.
15 *Ibid.* 114 5.
16 *Ibid.*
17 Gen. 3.9.

seeking to be informed, but He wished to perceive what sort he had become from what he had been. 'Where are you?' instead of 'to what sort of a ruin have you descended from so great a height?'

'The Lord is the keeper of little ones; I was humbled, and he delivered me.'[18] According to natural reason human nature would not stand unless the little ones and those still infants were kept by the Lord. For, unless it was preserved by the custody of God, how could the fetus in the mother be nourished or moved while it was in such narrow spaces, with no room for turning, and while it lived in dark and moist places, unable to take a breath or to live the life of men, but, on the contrary, was borne around in liquids like the fish? And how would it last even for a short time after it had come out into this unaccustomed place and, lacking the warmth within the mother, had become chilled all over by the air, unless it was preserved by God? Therefore, 'the Lord is the keeper of little ones; I was humbled, and he delivered me.' Or, you may understand these words thus. When I was turned and became as a little child and received the kingdom of heaven as a child and through innocence brought myself down to the humility of children,[19] 'the Lord, the keeper of little ones,' since I was humbled, 'delivered me.'

'Turn, O my soul, into thy rest: for the Lord hath been bountiful to thee.'[20] The brave contestant applies to himself the consoling words, very much like to Paul, when he says: 'I have fought the good fight, I have finished the course, I have kept the faith. For the rest, there is laid up for me a crown of justice.'[21] These things the prophet also says to himself: Since you have fulfilled sufficiently the course of this life, turn

---

18 Ps. 114.6.
19 Cf. Matt. 18.3, 4: 'Amen I say to you, unless you turn and become like little children, you will not enter into the kingdom of heaven. Whoever, therefore, humbles himself as this little child, he is the greatest in the kingdom of heaven.'
20 Ps. 114.7.
21 2 Tim. 4.7, 8.

henceforth into thy rest, 'for the Lord has been bountiful to thee.' For, eternal rest lies before those who have struggled through the present life observant of the laws, a rest not given in payment for a debt owed for their works, but provided as a grace of the munificent God for those who have hoped in Him. Then, before he describes the good things there, telling in detail the escape from the troubles of the world, he gives thanks for them to the Liberator of souls, who has delivered him from the varied and inexorable slavery of the passions. But, what are these good things?

'For he hath delivered my soul from death: my eyes from tears, my feet from falling.'[22] He describes the future rest by a comparison with things here. Here, he says, the sorrows of death have compassed me, but there he hath delivered my soul from death. Here the eyes pour forth tears because of trouble, but there, no longer is there a tear to darken the eyes of those who are rejoicing in the contemplation of the beauty of the glory of God. 'For God has wiped away every tear from every face.'[23] Here there is much danger of a fall; wherefore, even Paul said: 'Let him who thinks he stands take heed lest he fall.'[24] But, there the steps are firm; life is immutable. No longer is there the danger of slipping into sin. For, there is neither rebellion of the flesh, nor cooperation of a woman in sin. Therefore, there is no male and female in the resurrection, but there is one certain life and it is of one kind, since those dwelling in the country of the living are pleasing to their Lord. This world itself is mortal and is the place of mortals. Since the substance of visible things is composite, and every composite thing is wont to be destroyed, we who are in the world, being part of the world, necessarily possess the nature of everything. Therefore, even before the soul is separated from the body by death, we men frequently die. And let

---

22 Ps. 114.8.
23 Isa. 25.8 (Septuagint version).
24 1 Cor. 10.12.

not the saying appear incredible to you, but consider the truth of the matter.

In twenty-one years man is wont to undergo three variations and vicissitudes of age and life, and in each week[25] its proper boundary circumscribes the past and displays a visible change. The age of infancy is limited by the loss of his teeth about the first week. The prescribed time for a child who is capable of learning is until youth. The youth, having attained to his twenty-first year, when he begins to cover his cheeks with the first growth of beard, imperceptibly disappears, since the adolescent has already changed into the man. Accordingly, when you see a man who has laid aside the progressive increase according to age, who is already advanced in his reasoning, and who bears no trace of youth, will you not think that the past has died in him? Again, the old man, transposed into another form and another disposition of soul, is evidently another man, as compared with the former. So that the life of men is wont to be fulfilled through many deaths, not only by the change in the passing from one age to another, but also by the lapses of the souls through sin.

But, where there is no alteration either of body or soul (for there is no deviation of reasoning, nor change of opinion unless some difficult circumstances take away the constancy and tranquillity of the reason), that is truly the country of the living, since they are always like themselves. In this, especially, the prophet promises that he will be pleasing to the God of the universe, since he will be interrupted by nothing from the outside in his pursuit of a true servitude and of equal honor with the angels. 'We strive,' it is said, 'whether in the body, or out of it, to be pleasing to him.'[26] That is the country of the living, in which there is no night, in which there is no sleep, the image of death, in which there is no eating, no drinking, the supports of our weakness; in

---

25 Of years; i.e., each seven years.
26 2 Cor. 5.9.

which there is no disease, no pains, no remedies, no courts of justice, no businesses, no arts, no money, the beginning of evil, the excuse for wars, the root of hatred; but a country of the living, who have not died through sin, but live the true life in Christ Jesus, to whom be glory and power forever. Amen.

# INDICES

# GENERAL INDEX

Aaron, 318
Abiathar, 166
Abimelech, 247 f.
Abraham, 175, 179, 180, 199, 216, 248, 295, 305
Absalom, 165, 166, 177
Achaab, 239
Achis, 247 f.
Achitophel, 165, 166, 240
acorns, 80
Adam, 326, 355
Adarezer, King of Soba, 334, 335
Ader, King of Syria, 239
Aegean Sea, 61
Aegon, 47
Aelian, 108 n.
Aethopian Mountains, 47 n.
almond, 78
aloes, 289 f.
amber, 80
Ambrose, Saint, viii, 74 n.
Ammon, 334, 335
Ammonite, 339
Amnon, 270
Amphiscians, 96
angel, 176, 257, 327; angels, 4, 76, 148, 153, 209, 235, 258, 268, 276, 303, 323, 327, 331, 358; dark, 263; guardianship of, 258; hosts of, 9, 29; of the Lord, 76, 176, 257
Anomoean, 150
ant, 98, 138, 140, 188, 232
antipelargosis, 126
Apostle, 11, 30, 86, 91, 166, 169, 194, 197, 211, 224, 241, 245, 250, 251, 254, 264, 268, 270, 274, 283, 294, 300, 311, 314, 319, 322, 345, 352, 354; apostles, 210, 260, 295, 312
apple tree, 80
Aquila, 282
Arabia, 335
Arabian desert, 60
Araboth, 166
Arachi, 165
Arachite, 166
Aratus, xi, 90 n.
Araxes, 46
Archangels, 9
Aristotle, x, xi, 5 n., 7 n., 10 n., 12 n., 14 n., 15 n., 16 n., 17 n., 41 n., 47 n., 48 n., 50 n., 51 n., 59 n., 61 n., 73 n., 78 n., 89 n.,

107 n., 108 n., 110 n., 112 n., 113 n., 121 n., 122 n., 123 n., 124 n., 125 n., 126 n., 127 n., 128 n., 131 n., 132 n., 136 n., 137 n., 139 n., 140 n., 144 n., 145 n., 154 n., 187 n., 201 n.
art, 23, 25, 45, 343; arts, 11 f., 45, 55, 95, 188, 359; imaginary, 92; medical, 72
Asaph, 341
Ascians, 96
Asia Minor, x
asp, 146, 207
ass, 118, 138
Assyrians, 322
astrology, 90
Athenians, 307
Athens, x
athlete, 270, 354; 83, 157; of God, 167
Atlantic Ocean, 101 n., 115
atoms, 5
Atomist philosophy, 5 n.
Augustine, Saint, 74 n., 151 n.
Augustuses, 248
autumn, 95, 96
avarice, 109, 133

Babylon, 205
Bactrus, 46
Balkh, 46 n.
balsam tree, 80
baptism, 200, 210, 263, 339
Basil, Saint, 74 n., 90 n., 151 n., 167 n., 181 n., 248 n., 249 n., 261 n., 277 n., 295 n., 304 n., 344 n.
basilisk, 146, 207

bats, 121, 129, 130, 255
bear, xiii, 139, 144; Bear, 102
beauty, 220 f., 222
bees, xii, 123 ff., 131, 188, 232, 257
beetles, 122
Beseleel, 10
Black Sea, 46 n.
blessed life, 10
British Isle, 60
Britons, 98
bull, blood of, 71
Bythinians, 60

Cades, desert of, 206
Cadiz, 59 n.
Caesarea, x
Caesars, 248
calf, 142, 204
camels, xii, xiii, 119, 144
Carmel, 202
Caspian Sea, 61
cassia, 289 f.
caterpillar, 132
cattle, 132, 140
Caucasian Mountains, 46
cedars, 74, 203 f., 208; of God, 204; of Libanus, 203, 204
Celts, 56
cetaceans, 107, 108, 111
Chaldean, 90, 91, 113
Chanaan, 292
Chanaanite, 292
charity, 10, 228, 290, 314
Chinese, 132
Choaspes, 46
Chremetes, 47
Christ, 36, 138, 148, 153, 155,

164, 168, 169, 171, 195, 197, 198, 202, 204, 205, 213, 216, 238, 241, 256, 261, 262, 263, 264, 267, 270, 271, 273, 279, 283, 284, 287, 289, 290, 291, 292, 293, 295, 299, 300, 302, 308, 312, 326, 337, 338, 339, 340, 343, 345, 352; Christ Jesus, 245, 292, 317, 359; body of, 284; bride of, 295; cross of, 283, 345; disciples of, 252, 256; kingdom of, 291; lips of, 283, 284; mind of, 322; Author of victory, 231; Bread, 260; of life, 260; true, 258; Bridegroom, 222, 291; Co-worker, 39; Farmer, true, 76; God-bearing flesh, 339; Godhead of the Only-begotten, 196; Jesus, 200, 229, 237; Lamb of God, 204; Lawmaker, 190; Light, everlasting, 304; true, 85, 86, 255; Lord, *passim*; Lord Jesus, 294; Christ Jesus our Lord, 65, 82, 103, 134, 191, 284, 340, 350; blood of our Lord Jesus Christ, 318; body of the, 284; flesh of the, 289; Man God Jesus Christ, 317; Only-begotten, 39, 44, 278, 288; Orient, 304; Peacemaker, 256; Second Person, 147; Physician of souls, 313; Ruler, 278; Savior, 180, 228, 284, 289, 291, 298, 305, 309, 343, 344; Sheep, 204; Shepherd, true, 326; Son, 148, 149, 200, 204, 231, 234, 343; only-begotten, 337; of God, 289; of Man, 308; Sun of justice, 85, 255, 304; Unicorn, 205; son of, 204; Word, 222, 234, 235, 259, 280, 281, 285, 287, 322, 326; divine, 117, 230; heavenly, 258, 284; of God, 38, 213, 284, 285; of the Lord, 231, 234, 235

Christianity, 149
Christians, xii, 95, 245, 324
Church, 14, 41, 51, 65, 76, 79, 114, 153, 214, 261, 267, 272, 273, 284, 291, 292, 294, 295, 302, 303, 304, 312, 313; of Christ, 326; of the first-born, 323; of God, 21, 313, 333, 336; of the Living God, 198; of the Lord, 339; sons of the, 295
Chusi, 165, 166
cicada, 131
Cicero, 5 n., 8 n., 40 n., 51 n.
cock, 123
Coleoptera, 121
conchs, 107
Constantinople, x
contrition of heart, 269 f.
coral, 115
Core, sons of, 275, 278, 297, 311
crabs, 106, 107, 109, 110
cranes, 122, 125
crayfish, 107
creation, 4, 10, 38, 63, 69, 71, 77, 81, 85, 103, 105, 116,

134, 136, 137, 143, 145, 148, 155, 202, 238 f., 252, 292; of the heavens and the powers in them, 235; of the heavens and earth, 3, 41; of heat, 45; of light, 33, 85; of the lights, 85, 105; of mankind, 148; of men, 147; sensible, 199

Creator, *passim*

creature, 62, 106, 119, 129, 132, 148, 197, 209, 262; creatures, xi, 10, 105, 110, 116, 120, 131, 132, 252, 255; crawling, 105, 106, 107, 117, 118, 120, 129, 132, 136; heavenly, 138, 209; inanimate, 199; irrational, xii, xiii, 84, 127; land animals, 135; living creatures, 105, 108, 117, 118, 119, 120, 132, 136, 137, 138, 300; spiritual, 9, 10; swimming, 105, 106, 118; winged, 105, 120, 121, 129, 131, 132

crocodiles, 106
crocus, 68, 70
crows, 125, 128, 131
crustaceans, 107
cuttlefish, 107
cypress, 74, 117

Danube, 46 n.
Darius the Median, 59
darkness, 26 ff., 31, 33, 35, 88, 97, 99, 242, 254, 263, 304, 330, 347
darnel, 73

David, 154, 157, 165, 166, 167, 179, 193, 215, 240, 247 f., 248, 251, 252, 277, 282, 303, 334, 335, 341
Dead Sea, 60
deceitfulness, 110
deer, 138
Democritus, 5 n.
Dermoptera, 121
deteriorations, 5
devil, 166, 179, 197, 206, 228, 292, 298, 299, 316, 330, 355; ministers of, 344; the adversary, 308, 320; demon, 84, 133, 160; demons, 152, 191, 228, 262, 298, 345; man-slaying, 84; the enemy, 54, 162, 168, 169, 178, 197, 216, 231, 243, 262, 274, 298, 317, 327, 344; of truth, 175; invisible enemies, 167, 215; evil one, 73, 231, 264, 344; prince of the world, 167, 168; ruler of death, 217; source of evil, 84; spirits of evil, 343; the tempter, 354
doctrine, 7, 47, 151, 152, 173, 180, 195, 201, 281, 283, 291, 293, 294, 307, 322, 328, 330; of judgment, 8
dog, 138, 142, 143, 185, 187, 232, 276, 301
dogfish, 107, 116
dog's-tooth grass, 68, 70
dogwood, 80
dolphins, 106, 107
Dominations, 9
Don, 46 n.

dove, 99, 207, 257, 291, 322
dragon, 146, 229

eagles, 121, 127, 137, 207, 230
East Sea, 61
Edom, 339
eels, 107, 137
Egypt, xiv, 4, 47, 58, 60, 204, 322
Egyptian Gulf, 108
Egyptian Sea, 59
Egyptians, 4
elements, 13, 17, 18, 19, 43, 44, 62, 63, 118, 201, 206, 285
elephant, xiii, 144 f., 146
Elias, 202
Elisha, 135, 239
elms, 75
Emmanuel, 305
Empedocles, 119 n.
Ephraim, 322, 337, 338
equinox, 49
Esau, 176, 295
ether, 48, 129
Ethiopia, 4, 46
Euphrates, 334
Europe, x
Eusebius, x
Eustathius of Afer, viii
Euxine Sea, 46, 61, 112
evil, 28 f., 265 f.
Ezechias, 94

fear, 238 f., 259, 262 f.; of the Lord, 262, 263
figs, 191
fig tree, 78 f., 80
firmament, 38 f., 42 ff., 47, 49, 50, 52, 85, 105, 120, 129, 132
firs, 74
fly, 93
Forces, 9
fox, 138, 139, 276, 325
frogs, 105, 106, 137

Gadeira, 59, 61
Galaad, 337, 338
garlic, 68
Gauls, 46
geese, 130
generation, 13, 24, 33, 46, 69, 137, 172, 239, 284, 303, 311; of the heavens, 19; of herbs, 82; of land and water animals, 45; of living beings, 31, 154; of the luminaries, 97; of plants, 70; of sea and air, 285; of the sun, 61, 68; of the world, 9, 10; generations, 5, 240, 295, 321, 323, 330
Gentiles, 149, 197, 198, 260, 311
Geth, 247
Gethites, 247
gnat, 93, 105, 232
goats, 72, 291; wild, 143
God, *passim*; Godhead, 149, 254; of majesty, 200, 201; Ally, 299; Artificer, 99, 102; wise Artificer, 100; Author of our present and future life, 84; Beauty, 6, 27; invisible Being, 54; Beloved, 6, 278, 279; Benefactor, 54, 84, 149, 351; first and

principal Cause, 44; Commander in chief, 306; artistic Commender, 53; Craftsman, 12, 23, 44, 55, 232, 303, 344; Master Craftsman, 19, 235; Father, 84, 148, 149, 194, 195, 196, 200, 231, 234, 235, 268, 278, 280, 293, 297, 311, 319, 322, 327; Fount of life, 6; Goodness, 6, 155, 227; Helper, 299; most High, 102, 277, 278, 303, 304, 305; Holy One, 194, 228, 319; Inventor, 5; Judge, 170, 175, 194, 233, 237, 262; just Judge, 8, 21, 172, 177, 218; true Judge, 175; King, 251, 288, 294, 342, 346; King of Glory, 239; Lawgiver, 197; spiritual Light, 6; Lord *passim;* Lord of armies, 305, 306, 308; Lord of the universe, 190, 352; voice of the Lord, 199, 200, 202, 203, 205, 206, 207, 208; Maker, 232, 324; Maker of all things, 23; Maker of hearts, 242; Master, 116, 190; Master of the universe, 52; Mighty One, 287; most mighty, 285, 287; Nature, 6, 7; Origin of things created, 6; Protector, 309; Providence, 127, 144; Provider, 84; efficient and creative Power, 44; Ruler of the universe, 45; universal Ruler, 49; Spouse and King, 292; divine and blessed Trinity, 31; inaccessible Wisdom, 6, 227; Wonder-worker, 55

Goliath, sword of, 247
Gomorrah, 241
Gospel, 166, 201, 237, 240, 251, 278, 282, 283, 287, 295, 308, 321, 336
grapes, 75, 81, 191
grapevine, 75, 80, 81
grasshoppers, 137
Greeks, 97; wise men of the, 5, 40; regions of the, 60
Gregory of Nazianzus, Saint, vii, ix
Gregory of Nyssa, Saint, vii, viii
Guadalquivir, 46 n.

halcyon, 127
haloes, 89
happiness, human, 69
hares, 143, 187
harp, 153, 213, 229
harts, 207, 208, 217
heathens, 5, 42
heavens of heavens, 40
Hebrews, 62, 97
hedge, 76
hedgehog, 140
hellebore, 71, 72
Hellespont, 61
Heman, 341
hemlock, 71, 72
Herod, 276
Herodotus, xi, 143 n., 144 n.
herring, 115

# INDEX 369

Heteroscians, 96
Hippocrates, 72 n.
hippopotamuses, 106
Hochozath, 248
holiness, 194, 218, 235, 259
honey, 258
horoscope, 92
horse, 55, 62, 97, 137, 138, 156, 243, 244, 276, 323, 325, 335
humility, 224, 270, 293, 341 f.
Hyrcanian Sea, 61

Idithun, 341
idleness, 113, 115, 140, 157
idolatry, 173, 204, 239, 292
Idumea, 337
Incarnation, 171, 213, 231, 278, 285, 289, 290, 343
Indian Ocean, 59, 108
Indians, 98
Indus River, 46
Ionian Sea, 61
Isaac, 176, 179, 180, 216, 248, 305
Israel, 50, 214, 239, 241, 243, 260, 295, 307, 309, 317, 318, 322, 334, 338
Israelites, 338
Ister, 46

jackdaws, 122
Jacob, 110, 157, 176, 180, 216, 264, 284, 295, 305, 308, 309, 323, 338
Jemini, son of, 165, 166
Jerome, Saint, viii, 275 n.
Jerusalem above, 138, 302, 304; heavenly, 252
Jew, 147, 149, 150, 173, 198, 241, 322, 336, 337
Joab, son of Sarvia, 334
Joatham, 94
Jona, 116
Joram, son of Achaab, 239
Joseph, 50, 176, 179, 248, 338; of Arimathea, 290
joy, 224, 227, 228, 289
Juda, 337, 339
Judaism, 149
Judea, 60
judgment, 232 f., 233, 234, 236, 237, 269, 355
just, the, 227, 228, 254, 267, 268, 270, 271, 273, 274, 281, 300, 302, 313, 322, 328, 329
justice, 174, 220, 228, 259, 285, 286, 287, 288, 289, 304, 314, 326, 334, 356, 359

Kerkhah, 46 n.
kingdom of God, 288, 300

lamb, 142
lammergeyer, 128
lampreys, 107, 114
laurels, 74
Lazarus, 320, 340
leopard, 139
leopard's **bane, 71**
Leucippus, 5 n.
Levites, 193
Libanus, 203, 204; calf of, 204
Libra, 92
Libya, 47 n.
lion, xiii, 137, 138, 143, 144, 146, 167, 168; lioness, 141, 143

Livy, 130 n.
locusts, 130
love, 128, 130, 142, 169, 176, 216, 227, 238, 249, 257, 278, 279, 287, 291, 313, 351, 352, 354
Lucian, 72 n.

Macedonia, 60
magicians, 102
Manasses, 337, 338
mandrake, 71, 72
Manichaeans, 27, 117, 118
Marcion, 324
Marcionites, 27
marjoram, 139
mastic, 80
Mauretanians, 108
Mediterranean Sea, 59 n.
meek, the, 252, 253, 256, 269
meekness, 252, 256, 286, 293
melody, 152, 153, 224
mercy, 211, 224, 232, f., 233, 234, 244, 245, 246, 261, 293, 334, 337, 350, 355
Mesopotamia, 335
mica, 43
mice, 137
mint, 68
mischos, 75
Moab, 337, 339
Moabite, 339
mock suns, 89
molecules, 5
Morocco, 108 n.
Moses, viii, 3, 6, 12, 13, 19, 21, 25, 26, 33, 50, 136, 179, 199, 204, 221, 244, 248, 252, 269, 279, 308, 317, 318, 326, 337, 353
mosquitoes, 105
mouse, xiii, 146
mules, 108
mullein, 139
mussels, 107
myrrh, 289 f.
myrtles, 74

Nabel the Carmelian, 276
nightingale, 129
night ravens, 129
Nile, 47
Nobe, 247
North Sea, 61, 112
Nyses, 47

oak, 117; oak forests, 77
oat stalk, 71
Ocean, 101
octopus, 110
Odollam, cave of, 249
olive tree, 69, 75, 77, 80
opium, 72
Origen, ix, 8 n.
ovipara, 106, 107
owls, 129, 130
ox, 97, 108, 118, 135, 138, 156; oxen, 98
oyster, 109, 115

pagan, 79
Palestine, 61
Palestinians, 60
palms, 78, 117; date, 80, 81

Palus Maiotis, 46
parrot-wrasse, 108
partridge, 123
Passion, 308
patience, 341 f., 345
Paul, 9, 40, 132, 141, 146, 155, 196, 214, 216, 228, 261, 282, 284, 293, 297, 322, 340, 356, 357
peace, 152, 211, 222, 228, 251, 256, 266 f., 272, 308, 309, 313, 335, 338
peacock, 123
pearl, 115
pestilence, 156, 161, 162 f., 163
Peter, 285; of Sebaste, Saint, vii
Pharaoh, 4, 179, 217, 244, 248, 307
Pharisee, 173
Phasis, 46
Philoch, 248
Phoenicia, 335
piety, 10, 157, 173, 175, 195, 261, 266, 277, 330, 336, 352
pigeons, 122, 123
Pilate, 239
Pillars, 46
pines, 74, 77, 78, 81, 139
Plato, xi, 16 n., 18 n., 23 n., 39 n., 41 n., 50 n.
Pliny, 108 n., 129 n.
Plotinus, xi, 12 n.
polyps, 107
pomegranate, 78
poplars, black, 75; white, 75
poppy juice, 71
poverty, 110, 126, 128, 185 f., 189, 255 f., 299, 301, 329, 355
Powers, 9, 301
pride, 244, 315; of the flesh, 202, 253, 257, 342
Principalities, 9, 301
prophet, 155, 170, 177, 181, 182, 214, 218, 224, 250, 264, 272, 278, 280, 281, 282, 290, 291, 294, 299, 300, 314, 315, 328, 342, 347, 349, 356, 358; prophets, 199, 305, 312, 322, 339
Propontis, 61, 112
providence, 196, 304; of God, 328
prudence, 220
psalm, 152 ff., 176, 181, 182, 193, 194, 209, 210, 213, 214, 217, 218, 234, 236, 245, 247, 270, 275, 276, 278, 283, 297, 311, 312, 315, 333, 334, 335, 336, 341, 342, **351**
psenes, 78
Ptilota, 121
puppy, 142
Pyrenees Mountains, 46

quails, 72

rain, 50, 65, 89, 95, 137
Ram, 92, 93; ram, 193, 194, 195, 207
ransom, 316, 317, 318, 319, 320
rays, 106; sting, 116
Rebecca, 248
Red Sea, xiv, 58, 59, 61, 206, 236

reed, 68, 69
remora, 115
Resurrection, 35, 170, 219, 231, 239, 290, 304, 327; doctrine of, 277; sons of, 268
Rha, 46 n.
Rhipean Mountains, 46
Rhone, 46
Rion, 46 n.
Rohob, king of Soba, 334
Rome, 130
rose bushes, 74
Rufinus of Aquileia, viii, ix, 151 n.

Sadoc, 166
Samaria, 239
Samaritan, 180
Samson, 191
sand, xiv, 58
Sardinian Sea, 61
Saul, 247
sawfish, 116
scallops, 107
scammony, 80
Schizoptera, 121
Scorpio, 92
scorpion, xiii, 146
Scripture, 21, 22, 29, 30, 31, 34, 35, 38, 39, 41, 42, 43, 44, 47, 50, 56, 61, 63, 64, 68, 73, 91, 99, 100, 101, 118, 122, 132, 135, 136, 151, 156, 162, 165, 166, 168, 169, 171, 175, 176, 177, 178, 179, 181, 193, 194, 195, 199, 200, 203, 205, 207, 208, 218, 219, 227, 236, 237, 238, 247, 249, 260, 261, 267, 271, 278, 280, 283, 286, 290, 291, 292, 295, 302, 306, 322, 323, 328, 343, 355
Scythia, 46
Scythian, 173
Sea of Asov, 46 n.
sea hare, 116
sea pens, 115
sea snails, 107
sea urchin, 113 f.
seals, 106, 107
seaweeds, 109
sedge, 68
self-control, 220
Senegal, 47 n.
Sennacherib, 244
Septuagint version, 10 n., 14 n., 21 n., 33 n., 34 n., 43 n., 45 n., 50 n., 53 n., 56 n., 70 n., 74 n., 85 n., 124 n., 162 n., 177 n., 181 n., 182 n., 184 n., 194 n., 196 n., 208 n., 221 n , 234 n., 248 n., 276 n., 281 n., 282 n., 287 n., 311 n., 317 n., 324 n., 331 n., 347 n.
Serbonian Sea, 60
serpent, 110, 139, 144, 146, 207, 208, 221, 229, 270, 308, 321
Sesostris the Egyptian, 59
sharks, 107; hammer-headed, 116
sheep, 72, 93, 108, 110, 139, 142, 193, 195, 198, 207, 291, 326, 327; wild, 143
shellfish, 115
shrimp, 115
Sichem, 338

Sicilian Sea, 61
silkworm, Indian, 132
Simeon, 343
sin, 84, 95, 147, 160, 167, 172 f., 175, 221, 225, 229, 231, 233, 237, 241, 253, 255, 257, 260, 262, 265, 268, 269, 270, 273, 274, 286, 292, 298, 299, 315, 317, 318, 319, 322, 323, 325, 326, 327, 333, 342, 344, 346, 350, 354, 355, 357, 358, 359; sins, 162, 197, 209, 210, 224, 234, 236, 265, 316, 337, 339, 343, 353
snow, 51, 95
Soba, 335
Socrates, viii
Sodom, 241
solicitude, 126, 138, 140
Solomon, 30, 161, 180, 207, 213, 331
solstices of the sun, 34, 50; summer solstice, 49, 95; winter, 46, 49
son of perdition, 166
Sons of Thunder, 201, 285
Sophonia, 311
South Sea, 61
Spain, 60
sparrows, 232
spider's web, 5; spider webs, 93
Spirit, 5, 21, 30, 31, 38, 44, 55, 103, 113, 136, 150, 151, 153, 195, 210, 225, 228, 230, 234, 235, 257, 282, 283, 290, 297, 308, 314, 336, 346; Holy Spirit, 30, 31, 152, 196, 200, 214, 224, 228, 229, 231, 234, 235, 237, 270, 280, 281, 282, 289, 293, 297, 298, 302, 312, 322; Spirit of His mouth, 234, 235; Spirit of Truth, 155, 312; common Director, 155; Paraclete, 312; great Teacher, 155
spring, 95, 140
stags, 206 f., 208
starlings, 72, 122, 130
storks, 125 f.
Strabo, 96 n.
strength, 220 f., 222
summer, 95, 96, 113
swallows, 121, 126 f.
swan, 131
swifts, 121
swine, 162
swordfish, 116
Symmachus, 282
Syria, 239, 335
Syrian, 31; Syrians, 31, 334; of Rohob, 334; of Soba, 334

tamarisk, 81
Tanais, 46
tares, 73
Tartessus, 46
Taurus, 92
terebinth, 80
testaceans, 107
Thamar, 270
Tharsis, 201
Thebes, Egyptian, 137
Theophrastus, xi, 68 n.
Thomas, 216

# INDEX

Thrones, 9
tiger, xiii, 144
tortoise, 139
truth, 4, 24, 27, 29, 37, 39, 47, 51, 54, 83, 102, 110, 147, 148, 150, 180, 197, 223, 237, 250, 253, 254, 257, 258, 259, 286, 288, 327, 330, 336, 358; word of truth, 283, 306, 308
tunneys, 108
turtledove, xiii, 127
Tyre, 292
Tyrrhenian Sea, 61

unicorns, 204, 205
universe, 5, 12, 16, 25, 42, 45, 48, 51, 83, 84, 85, 137, 177, 235, 352, 358

Valentinians, 27
Valentinus, 324
valor, 220
vengeance, 177, 204
Vergil, 73 n., 257 n.
vineyard, 76
viper, 114, 139, 146, 187, 207
vivipara, 106, 107
Volga, 46 n.

vultures, 128, 130

wasps, 121, 131
weevers, 107
West Sea, 61, 101
whales, 116
wheat, 71; black, 73
willows, 75
winter, 95, 96, 113, 127, 139, 140
wisdom, 17, 49, 64, 81, 83, 111, 114, 132, 141, 146, 147, 157, 172, 251, 287, 301, 314, 319; of the Artificer, 99, 102; of the Creator, 131, 132, 142, 232; of God, 113, 129, 314, 316; of the world, 317, 320; of the wise, 321; foolish, 136; human, 4, 283; vain, 130; worldly, 8, 83; children of, 166
wolf, 138, 141, 325; wolves, 110
wormwood, 80

Xenophon, 72 n.

Zodiac, 91, 93

# INDEX OF HOLY SCRIPTURE

(BOOKS OF THE OLD TESTAMENT)

Genesis, 3 n., 5 n., 21 n., 24 n., 26 n., 30 n., 31 n., 32 n., 33 n., 34 n., 38 n., 42 n., 47 n., 49 n., 50 n., 53 n., 56 n., 61 n., 62 n., 63 n., 67 n., 70 n., 72 n., 74 n., 75 n., 85 n., 88 n., 95 n., 97 n., 105 n., 107 n., 110 n., 115 n., 117 n., 120 n., 132 n., 136 n., 147 n., 148 n., 149 n., 156, 157 n., 176 n., 179 n., 195 n., 199 n., 234 n., 242 n., 248 n., 264 n., 295 n., 309 n., 323 n., 324 n., 325 n., 353 n., 355 n.

Exodus, 4 n., 87 n., 157 n., 170 n., 179 n., 199 n., 204 n., 217 n., 221 n., 236 n., 244 n., 248 n., 268 n., 269 n., 279 n., 284 n., 305 n., 307 n., 338 n., 353 n.

Leviticus, 119 n.

Numbers, 4 n., 275 n., 318 n.

Deuteronomy, 50 n., 181 n., 219 n., 220 n., 244 n., 347 n.

Judges, 191 n.

1 Kings, 247 n., 249 n., 276 n.

2 Kings, 165 n., 166 n., 240 n., 270 n., 334 n.

3 Kings, 202 n., 248 n.

4 Kings, 239 n., 240 n., 244 n.

1 Paralipomenon, 341 n.

2 Esdras, 339 n.

Job, 15 n., 45 n., 205 n., 215 n., 234 n., 319 n., 320 n., 330 n.

Psalms, 16 n., 34 n., 35 n., 37 n., 40 n., 42 n., 50 n., 52 n., 53 n., 76 n., 77 n., 82 n., 87 n., 97 n., 110 n., 111 n., 133 n., 138 n., 141 n., 146 n., 147 n., 151 n., 152 n., 153 n., 154 n., 156 n., 157 n., 161 n., 165 n., 166 n., 167 n., 168 n., 169 n., 170 n., 171 n., 173 n., 174 n., 175 n., 176 n., 177 n., 178 n., 179 n., 181 n., 182 n., 193 n., 194 n., 195 n.,

198 n., 199 n., 200 n., 201 n., 202 n., 203 n., 204 n., 205 n., 206 n., 207 n., 208 n., 209 n., 210 n., 211 n., 213 n., 214 n., 215 n., 216 n., 217 n., 218 n., 219 n., 220 n., 222 n., 223 n., 224 n., 225 n., 227 n., 228 n., 229 n., 230 n., 231 n., 232 n., 233 n., 234 n., 235 n., 236 n., 237 n., 238 n., 239 n., 240 n., 241 n., 242 n., 243 n., 244 n., 245 n., 246 n., 247 n., 249 n., 250 n., 251 n., 252 n., 253 n., 254 n., 255 n., 257 n., 258 n., 259 n., 261 n., 262 n., 263 n., 265 n., 266 n., 267 n., 268 n., 269 n., 270 n., 271 n., 272 n., 273 n., 274 n., 275 n., 277 n., 278 n., 280 n., 281 n., 282 n., 283 n., 284 n., 286 n., 287 n., 288 n., 289 n., 290 n., 291 n., 292 n., 293 n., 294 n., 295 n., 297 n., 298 n., 299 n., 300 n., 301 n., 302 n., 303 n., 305 n., 306 n., 307 n., 308 n., 311 n., 312 n., 314 n., 315 n., 317 n., 318 n., 319 n., 320 n., 321 n., 322 n., 324 n., 326 n., 327 n., 328 n., 329 n., 330 n., 331 n., 333 n., 334 n., 335 n., 337 n., 338 n., 339 n., 342 n., 343 n., 344 n., 345 n., 346 n., 347 n., 348 n., 349 n., 350 n., 352 n., 353 n., 354 n., 355 n., 356 n., 357 n.

Proverbs, 10 n., 30 n., 111 n., 114 n., 124 n., 162 n., 174 n., 180 n., 184 n., 185 n., 190 n., 194 n., 196 n., 208 n., 243 n., 272 n., 281 n., 324 n., 331 n.

Ecclesiastes, 58 n., 151 n., 177 n., 228 n., 271 n., 287 n.

Canticle of Canticles, 116 n., 222 n., 250 n., 287 n., 291 n.

Ecclesiasticus, 100 n., 314 n.

Isaia, 14 n., 47 n., 56 n., 69 n., 76 n., 118 n., 191 n., 199 n., 206 n., 211 n., 229 n., 233 n., 237 n., 244 n., 263 n., 269 n., 272 n., 274 n., 277 n., 281 n., 282 n., 303 n., 315 n., 318 n., 348 n., 357 n.

Jeremia, 58 n., 82 n., 167 n., 171 n., 179 n., 180 n., 181 n., 194 n., 217 n., 248 n., 251 n., 272 n., 276 n., 299 n., 320 n., 325 n.

Ezechiel, 181 n., 201 n., 273 n., 325 n., 338 n.

Daniel, 52 n., 179 n., 205 n., 206 n.

Osee, 315 n., 322 n.

Joel, 35 n., 90 n.

Amos, 35 n., 43 n., 260 n.

Michea, 211 n.

Sophonia, 311 n.

Zacharia, 304 n.

Malachia, 85 n., 196 n., 255 n., 304 n.

(BOOKS OF THE NEW TESTAMENT)

St. Matthew, 7 n., 30 n., 76 n., 89 n., 90 n., 94 n., 110 n., 157 n., 158 n., 160 n., 166 n., 167 n., 172 n., 182 n., 191 n., 195 n., 196 n., 200 n., 206 n., 208 n., 209 n., 211 n., 218 n., 220 n., 232 n., 237 n., 241 n., 242 n., 252 n., 254 n., 256 n., 257 n., 262 n., 263 n., 265 n., 268 n., 270 n., 278 n., 280 n., 281 n., 286 n., 291 n., 293 n., 295 n., 300 n., 305 n., 306 n., 307 n., 308 n., 313 n., 320 n., 323 n., 330 n., 339 n., 350 n., 356 n.

St. Mark, 74 n., 201 n., 279 n.

St. Luke, 76 n., 166 n., 167 n., 190 n., 207 n., 220 n., 224 n, 268 n., 272 n., 273 n., 276 n., 283 n., 308 n., 319 n., 320 n., 321 n., 322 n., 325 n., 329 n., 340 n., 343 n.

St. John, 26 n., 76 n., 149 n., 166 n., 168 n., 171 n., 179 n., 180 n., 198 n., 201 n., 202 n., 204 n., 231 n., 234 n., 250 n., 255 n., 257 n., 264 n., 265 n., 266 n., 270 n., 279 n., 280 n., 285 n., 289 n., 290 n., 292 n., 302 n., 308 n., 312 n., 319 n., 322 n., 326 n., 327 n.

The Acts of the Apostles, 4 n., 26 n., 84 n., 146 n., 204 n., 228 n., 254 n., 300 n., 307 n., 319 n., 326 n.

The Epistles

St. Paul to the Romans, 7 n., 11 n., 36 n., 54 n., 124 n., 135 n., 160 n., 197 n., 219 n., 223 n., 229 n., 243 n., 245 n., 249 n., 254 n., 264 n., 274 n., 283 n., 293 n., 300 n., 304 n., 309 n., 314 n., 317 n., 318 n., 320 n., 326 n., 337 n., 340 n., 343 n., 352 n., 354 n.

1 Corinthians, 4 n., 7 n., 47 n., 76 n., 91 n., 103 n., 128 n., 171 n., 175 n., 196 n., 197 n., 223 n., 229 n., 243 n., 249 n., 250 n., 254 n., 258 n., 264 n., 267 n., 270 n., 277 n., 278 n., 283 n., 289 n., 297 n., 302 n., **303 n., 311 n.**, 312 n., 318 n., 319 n., 321 n., 322 n., 344 n., 345 n., 357 n.

2 Corinthians, 40 n., 169 n., 194 n., 225 n., 237 n., 238 n., 244 n., 254 n., 256 n., 261 n., 270 n., 282 n., 284 n., 319 n., 320 n., 340 n.

Galatians, 169 n., 210 n., 228 n., 261 n., 345 n., 350 n.

Ephesians, 114 n., 141 n., 178 n., 228 n., 234 n., 238 n., 243 n., 256 n., 263 n., 264 n., 267 n., 279 n., 309 n., 337 n., 338 n.

Philippians, 86 n., 138 n., 149 n., 207 n., 211 n., 222 n., 230 n., 257 n., 266 n., 278 n.,

283 n., 284 n., 292 n., 299 n., 312 n., 326 n., 346 n.

Colossians, 9 n., 30 n., 132 n., 138 n., 149 n., 251 n., 264 n., 265 n., 267 n., 293 n., 302 n., 306 n., 338 n.

1 Thessalonians, 249 n.

1 Timothy, 202 n., 214 n., 322 n.

2 Timothy, 151 n., 174 n., 281 n., 356 n.

Titus, 155 n.

To the Hebrews, 29 n., 138 n., 148 n., 149 n., 208 n., 250 n., 284 n., 303 n., 319 n., 324 n., 327 n., 328 n., 331 n., 340 n.

1 St. Peter, 211 n., 241 n., 286 n., 316 n., 318 n.

1 St. John, 354 n., 355 n.

St. Jude, 35 n.

Apocalypse, 264 n.

BOOKS PUBLISHED BY
EX FONTIBUS COMPANY

# CONTENTS

SACRED TEXTS—SCRIPTURE, LITURGICAL TEXTS, AND PRAYER
THEOLOGY—PATRISTIC AND MEDIEVAL
THEOLOGY—MODERN AND HISTORICAL
HISTORY AND CONTROVERSIES
LITERATURE—GREAT BOOKS AND GOOD BOOKS

CATALOGUE LISTING AS OF APRIL 29, 2019

# BOOKS PUBLISHED BY
# EX FONTIBUS COMPANY

*http://www.exfontibus.com*
*contact@exfontibus.com*
*http://www.facebook.com/exfont*
*exfontibuscompany@gmail.com*

*Our books are sold on our own website, at Amazon.com, & through other retailers*

*Get the latest news on our page!*

### SACRED TEXTS—SCRIPTURE, LITURGICAL TEXTS, AND PRAYER

*Biblia Sacra—The Holy Bible in Latin and English [3 vols.]*
A beautiful parallel Latin/English edition of the Bible of the medieval Catholic Church, using the Latin of the Clementine Vulgate and the English of Douay-Rheims Challoner Revision. **Vol. 1** includes the Pentateuch (Genesis, Exodus, Leviticus, Numbers, Deuteronomy) and the Historical Books (Joshua, Judges, Ruth, Samuel/Kings, Paralipomenon/Chronicles, Ezra/Nehemiah, Tobit, Judith, Esther). **Vol. 2** contains Job, Psalms, Proverbs, Ecclesiastes, the Song of Songs, Wisdom, Ecclesiasticus (Ben-Sirah), Isaiah, Jeremiah, Lamentations, Baruch, Ezechiel, Daniel, Hosea, Joel, Amos, Obadiah, Jonah, Micah, Nahum, Habakkuk, Zephaniah, Haggai, Zechariah, Malachi, Machabees. **Vol. 3** contains the entirety of the New Testament.

*Biblia Sacra—New Testament and Psalms in Latin and English*
An elegant smaller volume containing only the New Testament and the Psalms. [This third edition enlarges the formerly-cramped font.]

*The Septuagint, with Apocrypha, in English (Second Edition)*
The Septuagint (LXX), the ancient Greek translation of Jewish sacred writings, is of great importance in the history of both Judaism and Christianity. Translated from Hebrew and other originals in the two centuries before Jesus, the Septuagint

provides important information about the history of biblical text. It captures a moment in time, illuminating for us how Greek-speaking Jews of that time read and interpreted the Hebrew Scriptures that they translated. In its time, it made the Jewish Scriptures accessible to peoples and cultures outside of Judaism through *koine* Greek, the common language of the Mediterranean world. The Septuagint was the Bible of Greek speaking Jews; it was the Bible of the first Christians. It is cited in the New Testament and by the great luminaries of early Christianity. In this edition of the famed translation by Lancelot C. Brenton, many archaisms have been removed and personal pronouns rendered consistent with modern English—yet without sacrificing any of the accuracy, power, or beauty of the original translation. [This second edition corrects several errors from the first edition.]

## *Kyriale Romanum*

Gregorian chant has long transmitted the mystery and majesty of the Catholic liturgical tradition. Newly republished, the Kyriale Romanum of 1961, preserves between its covers an invaluable patrimony of ancient and medieval chants for the Ordinary of the Mass that can be used with both the extraordinary (1962) and the ordinary (post-1970) forms of the Roman Missal. It collects from the Graduale the most frequently-used chant settings throughout the liturgical year, with eighteen mass settings, six credos, and numerous settings for feasts and holy days, including the solemn procession on the feast of Corpus Christi. This beautiful and affordably-priced volume is of great value to all who wish to encounter this venerable musical tradition of the Roman Rite.

## *The Prayerbook of Ælfwine of Hyde*

Decades before the Norman conquest of England in A.D. 1066, a Benedictine monk at Hyde Abbey named assembled a small prayer book from the tradition of early Saxon Christianity. That monk, who later became Abbot of Hyde, passed to his heavenly reward but fifteen years before the influx of Norman culture from France would reshape the prayer and liturgical tradition of English Christianity. The prayers that are preserved in his book bear witness to the zeal and vigor of early English Christianity, with a poetry that stirs the soul over ten centuries since first they were prayed.

# THEOLOGY—PATRISTIC AND MEDIEVAL*

ST. IRENÆUS OF LYONS

## Against Heresies and Other Writings

The complete text of *Against the Heresies*, with fragments of other writings. Available nowhere else as a standalone volume. Bishop St. Irenaeus of Lyons wrote his *Against Heresies* ca. A.D. 180 to preserve the Christian rule of faith against the Gnostic heresy. To vindicate the Incarnation against the Gnostics, he described and attacked their principal doctrine: the evil origin of the natural world. Affirming the unity of Old and New Testaments, the goodness of the Creator and the created world, and finally the mystery of divinization whereby human beings are elevated into the divine life, the saint produced an outstanding example of early Christian biblical theology. For the early Fathers, doctrines were taught to safeguard the confession of God's saving love revealed through His Incarnation as Jesus Christ. Of such work there is no better example than Irenaeus, disciple of Polycarp, disciple of John the Evangelist.

ORIGEN OF ALEXANDRIA

## Against Celsus (Contra Celsum)

This is Origen's great apologetical work, undertaken in answer to the attack on Christianity by the pagan philosopher Celsus. The text that Origen composed to refute Celsus's self-styled Λόγος ἀληθής (*True Discourse*) consists of eight books, and belongs to the latest years of his life. It has always been regarded as the great apologetic work of antiquity; and no one can peruse it without being struck by the multifarious reading, wonderful acuteness, and rare subtlety of mind that it displays. A great work, well-deserving the notice of the students of Apologetics and of Early Christianity in general.

ST. ATHANASIUS OF AELXANDRIA

## Essential Writings on the Incarnation [Forthcoming]

In collaboration with Christian Classics, an imprint of Ave Maria Press of Notre Dame, Indiana.

ST. AMBROSE OF MILAN

## Theological and Dogmatic Works

These works present the thought of St. Ambrose, the bishop whose preaching first renewed St. Augustine's interest in Christianity. Included in this volume are several of Ambrose's works on the chief doctrines of the faith: "The Mysteries," "The Holy Spirit," "The Sacrament of the Incarnation of Our Lord," and "The

---

* Chronological listing.

Sacraments," including his famous teaching on the transformation of bread and wine into the Body and Blood of Christ.

ST. BASIL OF CÆSAREA

*Exegetic Homilies*
Basil the Great, of Caesarea, here offers homilies on the creation of the cosmos (the Hexameron, or the Six Days), God's providential ordering of the world, and on selected Psalms. A great work of early Christian biblical exegesis and a monument of patristic theology, now available in an attractive and affordable edition.

ST. JOHN CASSIAN

*On the Incarnation of the Lord, Against Nestorius*
Near the end of his writing career, Cassian the monk was commissioned by an archdeacon—the future Pope Leo the Great—to write a reply to the Christological positions of Nestorius, who saw in Christ two subjects, that of the Word and that of the man Jesus. Cassian's foray into ecclesiastical controversy, a cannonade of arguments from the Scriptures and the early Fathers, offers a blusteringly-effective representation of the general Christological views of East and West. Unsurprisingly, for one such as Cassian who was so concerned with the heights of Christian sanctity, it places special emphasis on the distinction between Christ's divinity and the indwelling of the Word in the saints—for the full divinity of Christ is what indeed makes it possible for *Christ* to be said to dwell within those saints who tread the heights of union with God. What he lacks in the precision of an Athanasius or a Maximus the Confessor, Cassian more than makes up for in the passion of his argumentation.

ST. GREGORY THE GREAT

*Dialogues*
In the series of dialogues that he patiently holds with his deacon Peter, St. Gregory describes a vision of sacred stability in an unstable world; this stability is to be found in the saint's life, lived in the love of Christ and anchored in the power of God. Through tales of miracles and examples of charity, including a famous dialogue on heaven, hell, purgatory, and the power of the Mass, Gregory illustrates the guiding hand of providence in the life of the saint and in the divine power manifest in that saint's deeds and words. Through these stories he aims to teach his readers to offer themselves on the "altar of the heart" as a living sacrifice of love in union with the sacrifice of Christ on the Cross.

## *Moralia in Job (Morals on the Book of Job)* [3 vols.]

Pope Gregory the Great (r. 590–604) wrote his *Moralia*, or moral homilies on Job, one of his greatest works, before his accession to the See of Peter. Seeking a life of contemplation, Gregory had retired to a house on Rome's Caelian Hill, forming the monastic community of St. Andrew's. Shortly thereafter, however, he was sent obediently but unhappily to Constantinople as papal nuncio (*apocrisarius*) at the court of the Byzantine emperor. There too he gathered a small community to whom he delivered his famed homilies on Job. For Gregory, Job is a figure of Christ, who suffered innocently—not for his sins but for the increase of his merits and the salvation of others by love. These homilies span Christian doctrine, from Creation to final Judgment, from the height of angelic hierarchies to the innermost depths of the human soul. Confident that the Holy Spirit has not idly chosen the words of Scripture, Gregory finds a depth of allegory out of which he draws a brilliant picture of Christ, whose humanity must mark our own and whose Cross is our path to eternal rest. A beautiful meditation on suffering, on the path from fear to love, and on the healing and glorification of the individual soul which, as a member of Christ's body, comes to participate in the life of the holy Trinity. When Gregory was elected bishop of Rome just a few years later, he would continue to draw on and to develop the teaching herein, to guide the spiritual lives of his flock amidst the terror-filled final dissolution of the Western Empire. The teaching of the *Moralia* became a source for the doctors of the middle ages, including Hugh of St. Victor, St. Thomas Aquinas, St. Bonaventure, and many others. Western Christianity today owes an incalculable debt to the homilies that Gregory preached to his small circle of ascetics so many years ago.

## ST. JOHN OF DAMASCUS

### *Writings*

St. John Damascene, among the greatest of the Eastern fathers during the patristic age, produced his work *The Fount of Knowledge* as a summary of Christian philosophy and theology. It is one of the most important works of the Greek patristic age. Included are "The Philosophical Chapters," "On Heresies," and the justly-famous "Exact Exposition of the Orthodox Faith"—a veritable *Summa* of the doctrine of the Eastern fathers. Now available in an attractive and affordable edition.

## ST. ANSELM OF CANTERBURY

### *Complete Philosophical and Theological Treatises*

We are proud to re-print Jasper Hopkins' philosophically sensitive translations of the complete treatises of Anselm of Canterbury, the "Father of Scholasticism." The present volume contains, in English translation, all of St. Anselm's treatises, as well as his important Meditation on Human Redemption and four of his didactic letters. Collectively, these constitute his intellectual writings. Included are: *Monologion*; *Proslogion*; *Debate with Gaunilo*; *De Grammatico*; *On Truth (De Veritate)*; *Freedom of Choice (De Libertate Arbitrii)*; *The Fall of the Devil (De Casu Diaboli)*; *Two Letters concerning Roscelin*; *The Incarnation of the Word (De Incarnatione Verbi)*; *Why God Became a [God-]man (Cur Deus Homo)*; *Philosophical Fragments*; *A Meditation on Human Redemption (Meditatio)*; *The Virgin Conception and Original Sin (De Conceptu)*; *The Procession of the Holy Spirit (De Processione)*; *Letters on the Sacraments (De Sacramentis)*; *Foreknowledge, Predestination, Grace, and Free Choice (De Concordia)*. In an appendix is included a scholarly bibliography of resources on Anselm.

## *Cur Deus Homo*

Available here in an attractive paperback edition, Anselm's famous treatise *Cur Deus Homo* (Why the God-Man?) attempts to show believers that, far from being an unfitting and irrational act, God's incarnation as man was a suitable, even (contingently-speaking) a *necessary* act by which to restore balance to a cosmos afflicted by sin. Anselm's "satisfaction" theory of atonement formalized a tradition with its seeds in the patristic period and set the context for much reflection on the Cross in the Middle Ages and throughout the Reformation period.

## *Cur Deus Homo and Other Works on Christ [Forthcoming]*

This selection focuses on Anselm's treatises, meditations, and prayers that address the Incarnation, the Cross, the Resurrection, and the role of Christ in the spiritual life. Among other works are included his *Epistle on the Incarnation of the Word*, the famous *Cur Deus Homo*, his *Meditation on the Humanity of Christ*, *Meditation on the Passion of Christ*, *Meditation on Human Redemption*, his *On the Dignity and Woe of Humanity's Estate*, and others.

### HUGH OF BALMA

## *On Mystical Theology [Forthcoming]*

Translated by Jasper Hopkins.

### HUGH OF ST. VICTOR

## *On the Sacraments of the Christian Faith (De Sacramentis).*

Hugh of St. Victor (1096–1141) was a renowned medieval philosopher, theologian, and mystical writer. Because of his great familiarity with the works of St. Augustine, he is sometimes called "the Second Augustine." His work *On the Sacraments of the Christian Faith (De Sacramentis Christianae Fidei)*, composed about 1134, is his masterpiece as well as his most extensive work. It is a veritable *Summa*, a dogmatic synthesis unrivaled in Hugh's time.

By "sacrament," Hugh means not only grace-giving ceremonial signs and actions but also all "mysteries" of the Scriptures, the natural world, and the Church by which God elevates humankind into His life. Hugh's theology draws on Augustine, Gregory the Great, Anselm, and Abelard; and Hugh was also in contact with Bernard of Clairvaux. In the *De Sacramentis*, Hugh separates all of history into the "work of creation" and the "work of restoration." The work of Creation is the triune God's creative activity, the natures of created things, and the original state and destiny of humanity. Hugh's description of the Six Days of Creation is heavily influenced by Augustine's exegesis of Genesis. Divine Wisdom is the archetypal form of creation. The creation of the world in six days is a "sacrament," that is, a spiritually-illuminating mystery for man to contemplate. God's forming order from chaos to make the world is an instruction that guides human beings to rise in love from their own chaos of ignorance to become creatures of Wisdom and therefore beauty. This kind of mystical-ethical interpretation is typical for Hugh, who finds Wisdom's instruction everywhere in creation and in the Scriptures.

The work of Restoration includes the Incarnation of God the Son "with all its sacraments." Here the word "sacrament" refers to the means of salvation that flow from the Incarnation itself, including what are now called the traditional "seven sacraments." Hugh reflects on the mystery of God's freedom—why the Son came into the world even though this was not strictly necessary. Over all, Hugh's work is both an exegetical treatise and a work of spiritual instruction—an example of the inseparability of doctrinal reflection and spiritual growth as understood by this great twelfth-century theologian.

NICHOLAS OF CUSA

*Speculative Theology [Forthcoming]*
Translated by Jasper Hopkins.

*Early Sermons [Forthcoming]*
Translated by Jasper Hopkins.

*Didactic Sermons [Forthcoming]*
Translated by Jasper Hopkins.

*Last Sermons: 1457–1463 [Forthcoming]*
Translated by Jasper Hopkins.

ST. CATHERINE OF GENOA

*The Treatise on Purgatory*

St. Catherine of Genoa's treatise gives her teaching on the repentant soul's purification by the fire of God's divine love. A beautiful meditation on both the love of God and Christian perseverance.

THEOLOGY—MODERN AND HISTORICAL\*

JEAN DANIÉLOU, S.J.

*From Shadows to Reality: Studies in the Biblical Typology of the Fathers*

From the first centuries of its existence, the Church has interpreted the historical events recounted in the Old Testament as being "types" or "figures" of the events of the New Testament and of the sacraments instituted by Jesus Christ. Jean Cardinal Daniélou, one of the foremost Catholic scholars of the twentieth century, and a theologian especially concerned with the relationship between history and the Christian revelation, examines in this book the typological interpretation of the Fathers of the Church and their contemporaries during the first three centuries of the Christian era. Among examples he discusses are the crossing of the Jordan by the Israelites as a type of baptism, Rahab as a type of the Church, and the fall of Jericho as a figure of the end of the world. The complex interpretations of Adam, the flood, and the sacrifice and marriage of Isaac are also described in full and commented on. The work is divided into five books entitled "Adam in Paradise," "Noah and the Flood," "The Sacrifice of Isaac," "Moses and the Exodus," and "The Cycle of Joshua". Each book is divided into chapters discussing the various types and the interpretations of Irenaeus, Clement, Gregory of Nyssa and their contemporaries, including Philo.

ÉTIENNE GILSON

*The Philosophy of Saint Bonaventure [Forthcoming]*

ARTHUR F. KRUEGER

*Synthesis of Sacrifice According to Saint Augustine: A Study of the Sacramentality of Sacrifice*

Sacrifice is, for Augustine, simply that life of love that is both the perfect worship of God and the core of participation in His divine life. Arthur Krueger's is the only book-length study of this central theme of Augustine's theology. Krueger considers the bishop of Hippo on sacrifice and priesthood, both in the abstract

---

\* Alphabetical listing.

and in the concrete sacrifices of the Old and New Testaments. He particularly investigates these themes in their relation to Augustine's notion of sacrament, which Krueger presents as a "binding and synthesizing concept" at the heart of the great theologian's sacrificial teaching.

EMILE MERSCH, S.J.
## The Whole Christ
In the Scriptures, both the Savior in heaven, alive without suffering as victor over death, and the suffering Christians dragged to prison by Saul, are depicted as constituting together one man, who is, therefore, as Augustine called it, the "Whole Christ." In that mystic unity, Christ, the Incarnate Word, is the Head. We are the members. As for His sake the members suffer persecution He suffers in them, and on the contrary, as He is the Incarnate God they in turn are divinized through their union with Him. Through this same union they are, as co-members, most intimately united also with each other; and finally through their union with Christ as the second Person of the Triune God they are united with the Godhead, with the Most Blessed Trinity. This, Emile Mersch tells us, is the mountain peak of revealed religion, a teaching that pierces into the heavens far beyond our earthly ken. To seek understanding thereof is to ascend into fuller life with Christ. He unfolds this teaching by recourse to Scripture, to the early Church fathers, and to the great doctors of the Catholic tradition.

## The Theology of the Mystical Body
As a sequel or companion to *The Whole Christ*, this doctrinal, speculative study endeavors to investigate how and in what measure all dogmas can be seen as discoursing of the "whole Christ"—to ascertain whether dogma is always and everywhere Christ. Emile Mersch writes: "*We would see Jesus* (John 12:21). We are setting out in search of the truth which Christ has brought. Our aim is to see Christ who is the truth, to see Him in it and it in Him. For the truth is like a great panorama that shows forth what He is, depicting Him in His divinity, in all mankind, and in Himself, and nothing but Him. Is He not light and life?"

JOHN HENRY NEWMAN
## Oxford University Sermons
Newman's fifteen sermons on faith and reason, sanctity, and the development of doctrine; preached before the University of Oxford between A.D. 1826 and 1843 by John Henry Newman.

AIDAN NICHOLS, O.P.

*Epiphany: A Theological Introduction to Catholicism (Second Edition)*

Now in its second edition. Renowned Dominican theologian Aidan Nichols presents the Catholic faith as a unique source of illumination for the good, the true, and the beautiful. That faith, he argues, is destined to be, and humbly offered as, light for all peoples. It was as "light" that that the babe Jesus Christ was hailed by the aged prophet Symeon when he was presented in the Jerusalem Temple. The Church, too, has applied the term "epiphany"—shining forth—to his first, pre-verbal contact with the Gentiles, as his mother held him out to the "magi," the representatives of the non-Jewish nations. Thus the title of this book.

The book is a theological "Introduction" because one could hardly encapsulate all the illuminating richness Catholic Christianity can offer. Still, Nichols skillfully weaves into his own work a truly-catholic gathering of other great lights from the tradition.

This is a traditional theology and, as Nichols writes, "a consciously non-liberal theology, but not, I think, an illiberal one, for its subject is the generosity of God in his revealing Word and sanctifying Spirit. . . It is not a neutral work, since it aims to arouse a 'Christian maximalism' and the boldness to seek in Catholicism's theological tradition inspiration for present and future."

This second edition corrects some errors in the original.

EDWARD DENNIS O'CONNOR, C.S.C.

*The Dogma of the Immaculate Conception [Forthcoming]*

A history of the dogma of the immaculate conception, given in a series of scholarly papers published half a century after the dogma's promulgation. Long out of print but useful to the novice and the specialist alike, this volume takes the long view of Church history and tradition, showing a doctrine's development in action.

JOHN SAWARD

*The Way of the Lamb (Second Edition) [Forthcoming]*

MATTHIAS SCHEEBEN

*Mariology (complete in one volume)*

Writing in the nineteenth century, Matthias Scheeben forged a new creative synthesis of the teaching of the Fathers and of the scholastics. Scheeben's work had a decisive influence on later Catholic theologians such as Hans Urs von Balthasar. His primary theme is the nuptial union of God and the created order through the Incarnation, a marriage of heaven and earth that begins in the conception of Christ in the womb of the virgin Mary. Mary, therefore, is the temple in which God and humankind are reconciled. This and all that flows from it and preceded it by way of preparation is the subject-matter of his work Mariology. He draws together the teaching on the Incarnation, on deification, on the Marian dogmas, sacramental theology, and ecclesiology in a truly beautiful work. Originally published in two volumes, the entire work is gathered here in a single volume for the first time. It has been out of print for decades, now made available once more.

### THOMAS G. WEINANDY
## *Jesus the Christ*

Father Thomas G. Weinandy—sometime Oxford tutor and later head of the Secretariat of Doctrine for the United States Conference of Catholic Bishops—opens the fascinating world of Christian theology to all readers. In clear language, he begins in Scripture to draw out the plan of salvation, leading the reader through the development of the Church's grappling with the glorious and paradoxical conviction: That no-one less than God Himself has lived nothing less than a human life. From within the life of the Trinity,to the womb of a young woman, to the Cross upon Calvary, the empty tomb, and the ascension into heaven, Fr. Weinandy unfolds the theological consequences of the Incarnation as the central belief of Christian faith in an understandable Catholic introduction to the theological wisdom of the ages. He hopes that it may be of use to every Christian who wants to understand Jesus and His work of Salvation better.

## HISTORY AND CONTROVERSIES

### DOM JOHN CHAPMAN
## *Studies on the Early Papacy*

Dom John Chapman, fourth abbot of Downside Abbey, was a renowned scholar of early Christianity. On the question of the papacy in the early Church, he eschews selective apologetics in favor of a reasoned study of textual sources in the context of historical events. At these pivotal moments, he argues, the bishop of Rome both took and was expected to take a prominent and indeed authoritative role. This volume offers much substance to those who wish to take up the question of papal prerogatives. Chapman argues in favor of the Catholic claims, but does so with such care as a historian that his work has received high approval even from such an eminence as the famed Anglican historian Henry Chadwick who, in his own book on the history of the early Church, saw fit to recommend Chapman's work to readers interested in the question. There have been many successors to

Chapman but few, if any, have engaged precisely with the matters that he discusses with such detail and clarity. His book, therefore, remains an important voice in the modern conversation.

EMILY HICKEY

*Our Catholic Heritage in English Literature of the First Millennium*

(Originally entitled *Our Catholic Heritage in Pre-Conquest English Literature*). Ms. Hickey's reflections sweep us into a magical world of ancient epic, poetry, and allegory--by the verses of Cædmon and Bede; in stories of the Phoenix, the Cross, and King Alfred; in old runes and lost loves--in all of which one again and again discovers that Christ has been the narrative's subject all along. She writes: "This little book makes no claim to be a history of pre-Conquest British Literature. It is an attempt to increase Catholics' interest in this part of the 'inheritance of their fathers.' It is not a formal course, but a sort of talk, as it were, about beautiful things said and sung in old days: things which to have learned to love is to have incurred a great and living debt. I have tried to clothe them in the nearest approach I could find to their original speech, with the humblest acknowledgement that nothing matches that speech itself. If this little book in any way fulfils the wishes of those who have asked me for some thoughts on English Literature, I shall be glad indeed."

## LITERATURE—GREAT BOOKS AND GOOD BOOKS

Ex Fontibus Company is proud to present reprints of some difficult-to-find literary texts, such as Alexander Pope's translation of the *Iliad* and the *Odyssey*. However, our offerings are not limited to only the great books. We have also chosen to reprint some that are merely "good" books—yet not for that unworthy of our attention. Indeed, in his book *The Death of Christian Culture*, Dr. John Senior (1923–1999), founder of the once famed Integrated Humanities Program at the University of Kansas, offered a list of 1,0000 "good books" that prepare one to read the "great books." Among the "good" he includes such volumes as the Tarzan novels by Edgar Rice Burroughs:

> Taking all that was best in the Greco-Roman world into itself, Western tradition has given us the thousand good books as preparation for the great ones. . . . For us today, the [useful] cutoff point is World War I, before which cars and the electric light had not yet come to dominate our lives and the experience of nature had not been distorted by speed and the destruction of shadows....[These books are] part of the ordinary cultural matter essential for an English-speaking person to grow in.

Ex Fontibus offers the following—both good books and great—as points of entry into that heritage.

### ROBERT HUGH BENSON
*Lord of the World*

> Interesting it must be to all to whom the deepest convictions of a man's heart are of moment. And in the artistic balance and taste of Father Benson's literary power every reader will find delight.
> —*The New York Times*

> Mr. Benson sees the world, . . . generations hence, free at last from all minor quarrels, and ranged against itself in two camps, Humanitarianism for those who believe in no divinity but that of man, Catholicism for those who believe in no divinity but that of God.
> —*The London Times*

> "The book as art is beautiful, delicately balanced, deeply inspired, intelligently executed.
> —*Putnam's*

One of Pope Francis's favorite novels, Benson's 1907 apocalyptic tale of the Antichrist is one of the first modern dystopias. Humanism has eliminated world conflict but practices a subtle barbarism upon the human mind. Religion is either suppressed or ignored. The Catholic Church, confined to ghettos, occupies an increasingly perilous position in the public square. The populace turns toward euthanasia as the solution to bodily pain and spiritual crisis. Meanwhile, a mysterious figure of apparent hope, Julian Felsenburgh, rises to become the head of a single world government. The plot follows a priest, Father Percy Franklin, who finds himself caught up in the final and increasingly open struggle between Antichrist and Christ. *Completely re-typeset with Latin phrases translated in footnotes.*

ROBERT HUGH BENSON

## The Dawn of All

Benson's alternative to *Lord of the World*, this later novel vividly imagines the final peace of the world in the triumph of Christianity and the re-establishment of the Church at the center of daily life. A mysterious priest who cannot remember his own name, nor even anything of the past, must make his way as a Monsignor in a world undergoing a dramatic transformation in preparation for the return of Christ. The world itself becomes an image of the priest's soul. Benson himself writes: "In a former book, called *Lord of the World*, I attempted to sketch the kind of developments a hundred years hence which, I thought, might reasonably be expected if the present lines of what is called "modern thought" were only prolonged far enough; and I was informed repeatedly that the effect of the book was exceedingly depressing and discouraging to optimistic Christians. In the present book I am attempting — also in parable form — not in the least to withdraw anything that I said in the former, but to follow up the other lines instead, and to sketch — again in parable — the kind of developments about sixty years hence which, I think, may reasonably be expected should the opposite process begin, and ancient thought (which has stood the test of centuries, and is, in a very remarkable manner, being "rediscovered" by persons even more modern than modernists) be prolonged instead." As always, the story is rendered with suitable dramatic tension and — as is characteristic of Benson — a spiritual conflict of individual souls that matches the large-scale conflicts in the wider world. *Completely re-typeset with Latin phrases translated in footnotes.*

CHARLOTTE BRONTË

## Jane Eyre

*Jane Eyre* (originally *Jane Eyre: An Autobiography*) was published in 1847 under the pen name "Currer Bell." The novel follows the emotions and experiences of its title character, including her growth to adulthood and her love for Mr. Rochester, the byronic master of fictitious Thornfield Hall. In its internalization of the action — the focus is on the gradual unfolding of Jane's moral and spiritual sensibility and all the events are colored by a heightened intensity that was previously the domain of poetry — Jane Eyre revolutionized the art of fiction. Charlotte Brontë has been called the 'first historian of the private consciousness' and the literary ancestor of writers like Joyce and Proust. The novel both reflects and heralds the literary movements of its day, containing elements of social criticism, with a strong sense of morality at its core, an individualistic protagonist, and explorations of class, romantic attraction, religion, and the social position of women.

EDGAR RICE BURROUGHS

*The Tarzan Novels, Vol. 1 (Five Novels), Second Edition*
The Tarzan novels initiate the young person or the adult into the thrilling and sometimes terrifying world of nature, a world in which one can glimpse something of the eternal Beauty—undimmed even by the savage violence of man and beast. Welcome to the "primeval forest." This omnibus collection presents the first four complete novels of the thrilling adventures of Tarzan of the Apes, along with the collected *Jungle Tales* of Tarzan's early life. Son of an English Lord, raised by the savage apes that killed his father, found again by a civilization that he would never quite come to call his own, he was at home in the jungle in which he was reared. Swinging through the treetops, bane of lions, tamer of elephants, terror of cannibals, finder of lost cities, and beloved of the American woman Jane Porter, this knight of the forest, never trained in chivalry, was known to the outside world as John Clayton, Lord Greystoke—but to himself and the denizens of the jungle in which he grew up, he would be forever Tarzan, King of the Apes. Included in this volume: *Tarzan of the Apes*; *The Return of Tarzan*; *The Son of Tarzan*; *The Beasts of Tarzan*; *Jungle Tales of Tarzan*. A new introduction gives the history of Burroughs' novels and addresses certain points that later writers have rightfully questioned. [This second edition enlarges the previously-cramped font, for a more enjoyable reading experience.]

*The Tarzan Novels, Vol. 2 (Four Novels), Second Edition*
This omnibus collection, second in a series, presents the next four novels of Edgar Rice Burroughs' enthralling Tarzan of the Apes. In *Tarzan and the Jewels of Opar*, the ape-man engages in a battle of wits and strength with a corrupt Belgian soldier, as they struggle to lay claim to the treasures of a long-lost colony of Atlantis—a struggle made more difficult by Tarzan having lost his memory! In *Tarzan the Untamed*, World War I disrupts the peaceful life of Tarzan with his wife Jane on their East African estate. Taking up once more the way of the savage ape-man, Tarzan vows vengeance against the German soldiers that he believes to have murdered his wife. His adventures take him through and across a deadly desert, fighting enemies all the way. In *Tarzan the Terrible*, Tarzan finds himself in the

mysterious country of Paul-ul-don, an evolutionary island in the African jungle interior. Here dinosaur descendants and intelligent tailed ape-men live amidst fabulous lost cities. In *Tarzan and the Golden Lion*, our hero rebuilds his life in Africa, only to be abducted and held prisoner in the lost city of Opar, whose priestess would have him as her mate. Trekking through the legendary Valley of Diamonds, Tarzan finds himself followed by a mysterious man—who is Tarzan's own double! From his stirring descriptions of the jungle itself to his adept conjuring of scenes of action and mystery, Burroughs does not fail to deliver the thrilling narratives that have made Tarzan so very famous. [This second edition enlarges the previously-cramped font, for a more enjoyable reading experience.]

JAMES FENIMORE COOPER
*The Complete Leatherstocking Tales (2 volumes)*
Cooper's epic historical romances of frontier and Indian life in the early American days created a unique form of American literature. In two volumes five novels are collected, following the order of the stories' internal chronology (rather than historical publication order).
Volume I—*The Deerslayer*; *The Last of the Mohicans*.
Volume II—*The Pathfinder*; *The Pioneers*; *The Prairie*.

HOMER
*The Iliad, translated by Alexander Pope*
> The thing that best distinguishes this from all other translations of Homer is that it alone equals the original in its ceaseless pour of verbal music. . . . Pope worked miracles in highlighting the play of vowels through his lines. . . . Every word is weighted, with a pressure of mind behind it. This is a poem you can live your way into, over the years, since it yields more at every encounter.
> —"On Reading Pope's Homer," *The New York Times*, 6/1/1997

> Many consider [this translation] the greatest English Iliad, and one of the greatest translations of any work into English. It manages to convey not only the stateliness and grandeur of Homer's lines, but their speed and wit and vividness.
> —Daniel Mendelsohn, "Englishing the Iliad: Grading Four Rival Translations," *The New Yorker* Blog, 11/1/2011

> For Homer to take his place among our classics it must be the case that a rendering could exercise the same spell over the collective ear as English-language poets. You could not memorize Fagles, or Lattimore——or Hobbes, a few phrases apart——while Pope, even at his least Homeric, is memorable. . . . Pope is not superseded.
> ——David Ricks, Kings College, London, *Classics Ireland*, vol. 4, 1997

When Alexander Pope's majestic translation of Homer's Iliad appeared between 1715 and 1720, it was acclaimed by Samuel Johnson as "a performance which no age or nation could hope to equal." Pope himself was only 25 years old. While other translations have since claimed distinction in this or that respect, Pope's translation remains unrivaled in its melodious beauty. This is the Iliad that has formed generations of British and American culture through a beauteous poetics that lends itself to easy recollection. With a clean and crisp text illustrated by the inimitable line drawings of Flaxman, this edition finally gives to audiences a fitting rendering of this monument of English verse which captures uniquely the song of Homer himself.

## *The Odyssey, translated by Alexander Pope*

The tale of Odysseus's return from the war at Troy, seeking Ithaca his home and Penelope his wife. Along the way he encounters the murderous Cyclops, the treacherous Circe, and the nymphs, gods, and goddesses who variously assist and impede his homeward journey. Many are his travails and dramatic his final homecoming wherein he joins battle with Penelope's erstwhile suitors. As with the Iliad, Pope, who had two collaborators on this project, renders Homer into a muscular and euphonious English poetry worthy of reading aloud. This volume is likewise illustrated by Flaxman.

J.-K. HUYSMANS

## The Durtal Trilogy

Joris-Karl Huysmans's trilogy of novels charting the religious and life journey of Monsieur Durtal, who once investigated a satanic order in decadent late nineteenth century Paris (*Là-bas*, "The Depths" or "The Damned"), and now, turning toward God and becoming a Catholic, undertakes a mystical journey of sorts through a monastery (*En Route*; "On the Way"), the cathedral of Chartres (*La Cathédrale*, "The Cathedral"), and finally enters life as a Benedictine oblate (*L'Oblat*, "The Oblate"). This trilogy is intensely autobiographical, following the pattern of Huysmans's own life. Huysmans was an art critic as well as a novelist and thus the exquisitely constructed *Cathedral* has been used by generations of visitors as a guidebook to Chartres Cathedral. This edition offers the flowing translations that brought the original to an English-speaking audience, but with footnoted annotations explaining many of the erudite Huysmans's more obscure references to the artists, saints, and plant-life that populate the unfolding epic of Durtal's journey. Huysmans and his character Durtal are central to French author Michel Houellebecq's best-selling and controversial novel *Submission* (2015).

JOHN HENRY NEWMAN

## Callista: A Tale of the Third Century

Callista, a young and beautiful Greek girl, has just arrived with her brother in North African Carthage. Though she is a gifted young woman, she is unhappy with her life. Wooed by a troubled and lovesick young man named Agellius, Callista is drawn into his own struggle between a newfound Christian faith and the traditional pagan beliefs of his mother, a witch. After a terrible plague of locusts, a popular rage breaks out into persecution against the Christians and both Agellius and Callista must face for themselves the question of what indeed is the truth. Written by Newman after his reception into the Catholic Church, this novel of the early Church is surely a bright light in a flourishing nineteenth century genre that produced few classics and many mediocrities. Indeed, Charles Kingsley, whose later attacks prompted Newman's own *Apologia Pro Vita Sua*, had essayed an earlier effort at early Church fiction with the novel *Hypatia*. To Kingley's dismay, Newman's *Callista* had been received as the better work. *Callista* is rich in prose and vivid in its imagining of Christian life in the early Church.

Made in the USA
Middletown, DE
23 December 2024

66594987R00248